GROWING UP
PSYCHEDELIC

Entr'acte: Vermont, 1972

Growing Up
Psychedelic

Becoming Human
in a World of Spirit

DAVID EYES

BLTC PRESS · SANTA CRUZ

Growing Up Psychedelic
Becoming Human in a World of Spirit
by David Eyes

Published by BLTC Press

Santa Cruz CA

www.growinguppsychedelic.com

Copyright ©2023 David Eyes

All rights reserved. No portion of this book may be reproduced in any form without permission from the publisher, except as permitted by U.S. copyright law. For permissions contact: info@bltcpress.com

Cover illustratation *Breakthrough* by Timothy Eyes, from the *Gates to Soul Wisdom* oracle deck. Used by permission of Connecting New Dots LLC

Frontspiece photograph by Michele McNamee

ISBN
    paper: 978-1-60551-300-3
    ebook: 978-1-60551-301-0

R5

Dedicated to my wife,
Marije Miller

And with loving remembrance of:

Andy Reed
Steve Miles
Nancy "Nico" Condon
Jeri Thomson
David Nachman

Outside In,
Inside Out

Perpetual Change!

Acknowledgments

I first wish to thank, with deep gratitude, all of my immediate companions in my journeys through the psychedelic state. Although the account here is as close to the truth as memory and my inner fidelity will provide, I have chosen to fictionalize the names of all of the friends and fellow trippers introduced here. Some of the most beloved of these are no longer on this side of the portal of death. To all of you, I am profoundly grateful that you have shared these moments of intense being with me. I hold you all in my heart.

Many people have helped and supported me during this writing. These include my early reviewers and others who shared developmental conversations about the material and who helped greatly in, among other things, ironing out both perspectives and structural issues: John Baring, Bill Barnes, Daniel Bittleston, Scott Clements, Mia Cosco, Anthony D'Ambrosio, Julie Dolci, Jeanne Elliot, Peter Fowler, Juli Hazlewood, Scott Lawson-King, August Mohr, Aimee Phelps, Ben Sibley, David Szetela, Gretchen Ulrich. I would also like to thank my therapist, Dan Bass, who encouraged both my (almost) daily discipline, and also to simply tell my story. A nod to Daniel Kottke, whose musings about his own memoir possibilities help stimulate my own ripening thinking. Also, a special thanks to Serene Silva, a catalyst in bringing this work about. My close friends and colleagues in the anthroposophical community here in Santa Cruz have been unstintingly encouraging and interested.

A good portion of this work was written during morning hours at some of our fine Santa Cruz coffee shops. To the baristas on the West Side at The Abbey, The 11th Hour, and Cat and Cloud — thank you! The coffee no doubt helped and the smiles, interest, and friendly vibes in general helped make my morning efforts a pleasure.

During the writing, I had the opportunity to volunteer with the many good people at the Zendo peer support project at Burning Man in 2022. It was a delight to participate in the Zendo camp and engage in heart-deep conversations with a number of you. The up-close engagement with so many young people who are making their own journey in the realm of psychedelic exploration with such sincerity, enthusiasm, and questioning, along with a desire to serve, was a special dose of inspiration.

My son Timothy was my most helpful early reviewer. His insights across the spectrum of the subject matter were invaluable. The love, interest, and support of my other children — Althea, Nicholas, Mycah, and Ayla, were treasured as always. Thanks to Timothy also for cover art, and photo help from Nicholas.

Of course, the most unwavering support was from my wife and life partner, Marije Miller, who was my companion, sounding board, and thoughtful reviewer throughout the process. Her love for and understanding of who I am has made the work of self-disclosure here a process I have been able to pursue with inner confidence.

Preface

Today there is a resurgence of interest and hope around the potential therapeutic, spiritual, and celebratory applications of psychedelic drugs. In some ways, this has been made possible in part by the social amnesia that comes with time — a fading and forgetting of the intense political repression of psychedelics at the height of the sixties counter-culture. Then, too, there was a powerful enthusiasm. Although there is much in the way of renewed innovation and further penetration into the domain of the psychedelic, we are, in some ways, also at the stage of recovering and recapitulating previously lost ground. Naturally enough, for some, this recovered ground may seem entirely new.

The narrative part of this book is rooted primarily in those earlier times. It also seeks to provide fruits of reflection matured over a lifetime, of striving for a spiritual understanding.

So this book has a dual character. On the one hand, it is largely a memoir, primarily of the period in my young life when I experimented — or, with a bit more dignity, explored — psychedelics, LSD in particular, with a certain intensity. But it has another side. This side reflects my first impulse to write, which came out of a desire to attempt a more general work that examined the phenomenology of psychedelics from the perspective of the anthroposophical worldview of Rudolf Steiner.

Psychedelics present a domain of experience that our concepts and language are, by and large, inadequate to clearly articulate.

Yet a complete understanding and healthy development of psychedelic agents must be supported by a worldview that can serve as a container for their far-reaching spiritual implications. Anthroposophy provides an image of the nature of the human being and of our origins, that is expressly suited to provide an understanding of the psychedelic experience, in a way that can most fully speak to the scope of what may be encountered there spiritually.

After several false starts, I came to see the prospect of surveying the vastness of the reported literature to summarize or condense it into a representative and illustrative "canonical phenomenology" as beyond my capacity.

Consequently, I found myself choosing to limit myself to those psychedelic phenomena that I knew best — my own. In resorting to my own biography, I inevitably found myself enmeshed in the telling of a wider story, one that increasingly took on contextual details beyond the recounting of this or that acid trip. And so the character of a memoir emerged.

Having found my way into the study of anthroposophy — which process is a part of this story — it was straightforward for me to then write about my psychedelic history in a way that was informed by that perspective. Despite this personal nature, my hope is that in my reflections and attempted insights, there is sufficient material to be relevant across the generality of psychedelic phenomena.

The unfolding of my own development was such that it led me, alongside more intimate, internal soul-wrestlings and awakenings, into a parallel spiritual-intellectual path. I sought to uncover the fuller meaning of these experiences and, more importantly, find a further way toward the spiritual realities they revealed to me.

This carried me across the study, to varying degrees of depth, of many of the world's spiritual, religious, and esoteric traditions. These included, of course, the traditions and practices from the East — Buddhism, Hinduism, and Taoism — already well-embraced by some of the pioneers of the psychedelic adventure: Aldous Huxley, Timothy Leary, Alan Watts, Ram Dass, and many others. At length, however, I was drawn to the deeper elements of the Western esoteric tradition, culminating in a life-long study of Rudolf Steiner's anthroposophy. This has become the center of gravity of my spiritual life and practice, both intellectually and heart-inwardly. In the early stages of my journey, I also devoted myself to studying Gurdjieff's Fourth Way. Further, prompted by the writings of John Lilly, I also participated for a time in the Arica Institute of Gurdjieff's would-be post-psychedelic successor, Oscar Ichazo, the unintending inaugurator of what became the "enneagram of personality."

Progressing toward my eventual application of anthroposophical teachings to some of my more "far-out" experiences, my story thus encompasses a brush-up with a fair amount of literature on esotericism, consciousness studies, and so on. This telling may, at times, take the reader away from the more colorful rainbow of lived experience into the seeming monochrome of cold intellect, of the "head trip."

Clarity of thought in spiritual matters is nonetheless imperative if psychedelic culture is to mature. There is a wish expressed in some circles to have a "science-based" approach applied to validate psychedelics. Yet the limits of our current approach to science must be expanded to become once again capable of existing within a broader spiritual worldview, itself intellectually (and artistically) rigorous in its fashion. Without this development, I am anxious that the possibilities that a true renaissance implies will fail to appear.

My wish is that following the story of my pathway can carry you into a curiosity about the insights into the psychedelic experience that I see possible through the teachings of Rudolf Steiner. And that, along the way, you are motivated to digest what, at times, might feel like a slide into a somewhat more academic presentation.

Psychedelics and anthroposophy can both have a profound heart-opening effect. Both likewise can require, at stages, the earnest application of reason.

Steiner's enunciation of his anthroposophy, or spiritual science, reflects a mature, sober, and sophisticated framework of ideas suited to the spiritual challenges of the modern world. Although there is a clear history of the use of plant medicines as sacraments in earlier times, their broad resurgence in the present time challenges us to understand them in the context of a forward-looking post-industrial spirituality.

There are numerous footnotes scattered throughout the text. In that the story took place fifty years ago, I have tried to include therein details of interest — people and events — for those who did not live through these times. I have also included references to works mentioned in the text. And in trying to keep the narrative forward-moving, I also include in the notes various digressions that may, for some, yet be of interest.

David Eyes
St. John's Tide
Santa Cruz

World knowledge, self-knowledge:
From one to the other
Shuttle the questioning longings of the soul.
Often answers seem to beckon,
Consolingly resolving riddles of existence:

But wait — the next swing of the pendulum
Gives birth from the solution
Yet another new life mystery.

Rather than seeking the foundations of being
In world-knowledge,
and rather than seeking self-discovery
In man's eternal being:
In the cosmic world, seek selfhood
And in the self, the world-all -

Although the goal of knowledge is not achieved;
You yet are on the way
Into the opening life of knowledge,
soul-carrying, spirit-lifting, world-revealing.

                      Rudolf Steiner
                      Berne, Switzerland October 20th 1920[1]

Contents

	Acknowledgments	vii
	Preface	ix
	Verse	xiii
1	It's not like you see God	1
2	In Search of a Psychedelic Model	20
3	Turning the Corner	29
4	Incipit Vita Nova	53
5	Entr'acte	79
6	Mountains come out of the Sky	86
7	Summer Sunshine	108
8	Tent of Mystery	117
9	Welcome to the Metasociety	138
10	I found the Miraculous	153
11	Twenty Suns Twenty	166
12	Return to the Well	178
13	Integrating	184
14	Interweaving Destinies	205
15	Lucifer and Ahriman	216
16	That Tiny Word	225
17	Reincarnation, Living Time, and Eternity	233
18	Psychedelics and Alchemy	251
19	To Dose or not to Dose	267
20	Therapy and Celebration • Container and Intention	287
21	Closing Thoughts	299
	Notes	306

1

It's not like you see God

"David, it's not like you see God or anything!"

Thus spoke my close friend Alan. It was sometime in the late winter of 1970, shortly after I turned fifteen; we were passing outside between classes. I was again discussing the whys and why-nots of taking LSD. I was the one yet to be "experienced," and continued to probe with questions.

He and I had become friends during junior high, in eighth grade, when I returned to public school from a one-year exile at a private school (my parents thought I was underperforming). I befriended him and his neighbor Paul, to start, through the mutual interest Paul and I had in making 8mm films.

Alan was a somewhat broad-shouldered guy, his brown hair in the process of growing longer, as was mine. He had the facial hair to sport a rich pair of the then-popular sideburns (Jealous. I couldn't grow a legitimate mustache until my forties). He and Paul were neighbors and lived near the beach; often, I hitchhiked to one of their homes, and the three of us would hang out.

He was enthusiastically engaged in rock music, particularly the San Francisco scene; he was often the first to tune in on this or that new musical group. Alan had a well-developed sense of humor and seemed an endless source of jokes, including sometimes practical jokes.

He had first dosed on LSD at Woodstock[2] — the music festival considered a defining event of the counter-culture era — the previous summer. Now, along with the rest of our hanging out, pot-smoking, and poker-playing circle of guys, he had since tripped somewhat routinely (once or twice a month) across the fall semester of 10th grade. I was the last holdout in my immediate circle. That day we spoke back and forth until finally, as we were about to mount the steps to the blacktop in front of the cafeteria, he turned, looked at me, and announced this as "the final word," with a certain exasperation and mild disdain.

I don't know what I would have said previously, but it would have reflected my general anxiety that LSD was not something to be trifled with.

Well, that shut me up. The gauntlet, as it were, was down, and there was no helping it but to suck it up, stop dithering, and take the plunge. With his assurance that I would not be experiencing any heavenly encounters and the turmoil that implied, I decided I was ready. I hadn't quite strictly been concerned that I would see God. As it was to happen, that might well have been one worry to have had.

I first learned of LSD (Lysergic Acid Diethylamide, or colloquially, "acid") in 1964 or 1965—at the age of nine or ten—by reading about it in the Life Science Library volume titled *The Mind*.[3] The Life Science Library was a subscription set of books—you would receive one every month. My mother — an inquiring woman, keen for us to grow up informed and curious, had signed us up. I would study them avidly as they arrived. They were profusely illustrated on every page, in keeping with their being produced "By The Editors of Life" — *Life*[4] Magazine, that is, the weekly photo news magazine that was a primary source for the reception of glossy, full-color images of the world during the sixties—long before the internet, obviously, and also before color TV became ubiquitous. Not so coincidentally, the publishers of *Time* and *Life*, Henry and Clare Luce[5], were among the first wave of the LSD and psychedelic elite of the fifties. From their first experience in 1954, when it was completely unregulated, and on into the sixties, when it became controversial, they tended toward a favorable editorial slant.

I found the whole book fascinating as, with magazine-style illustrations, it covered the full spectrum of psychology and neurology of the time. Moreover, the topic of psychology had come to be somewhat of an interest through happenstances such as having a good friend whose father was a psychiatrist; a bit through my mother (a philosophy major in school) studying for a Master's in psychological testing; and last but not least, a twenty-five cent booklet on *Dream Interpretation* my mother purchased for me at the supermarket checkout.

The Mind included an account of the discoverer of LSD, Albert Hoffman's[6] first intentional LSD experience, wherein he is quoted as:

> I lost all control of time; space and time became more and more disorganized and I was overcome with fears that I was going crazy. The worst part of it was that I was clearly aware of my condition though I was incapable of stopping it. Occasionally I felt as being outside my body. I thought I had died. My 'ego' was suspended somewhere in space and I saw my body lying dead on the sofa. I observed and registered clearly that my 'alter ego' was moving around the room, moaning.[7]

The section continues with another two pages devoted to research, theory, set and setting, and more.

I found the "out of body" perspective fascinating and the whole description somewhat terrifying yet intriguing. I discussed my interest with my mother and shared the idea of this being something I might want to explore as an adult—rather in the way one might discuss the possibility of being an astronaut. She was not unsupportive, and I internalized a sense that she, too, found it intriguing.

This was all before LSD had become a broadly controversial question. Timothy Leary[8] was in the process of becoming the leading popularizer of the virtues of LSD; he indeed had just been fired from the psychology department at Harvard, where his increasingly undisciplined psychedelic studies ran afoul of academic protocol and politics. His first popular publication, *The Psychedelic Experience*[9], was also published in 1964. This was co-authored with Richard Alpert,[10] later to become Ram Dass, and Ralph Metzner[11] — all of whom were part of the Harvard psychedelic studies project. Leary had not yet fully emerged as the wild-eyed LSD prophet but was *en route*, step by step, to becoming, according to President Richard Nixon,[12] "the most dangerous man in America" and a fugitive from the law.

In 1964, the Beatles had just appeared on the Ed Sullivan Show, taking America by storm. Also that year, the US Congress passed the Gulf of Tonkin resolution — which set the stage for the war in Vietnam and years of misery and protest throughout the sixties.

The military draft was still far from its 1966 peak of 380,000. Military dead in 1964 was 206—the anti-war movement, a key driver of the anti-establishment counter-culture — along with LSD and the hippie movement, was not yet underway. However, the civil rights and "free speech" movements were rapidly warming up.

LSD was, in 1964, in the socially acceptable legal status of a research drug. While the article in *The Mind* registered a deep interest, at the same time, I also internalized that this is a powerful, scary, profound experience, definitely belonging in the province of mature adulthood. This essentially correct perspective remained active as I found myself growing into a high school scene that was well along into incorporating it into its general party culture.

Fast forward from age nine to my junior high and early high school years. A lot of counter-culture had flowed under the bridge; LSD had been classified as a Schedule I drug (no medical use, high abuse potential). The generational conflict was at a peak, and the baby boomer cohort was exploring itself with a vengeance and fighting like hell to avoid and protest the draft and the war in Vietnam. It was also acting out hedonistically with increasing abandon, fueled by drugs and the now widely available birth control pill. Timothy Leary was in jail by the time Alan and I were discussing LSD. Rock and roll was the vehicle of a common culture, manifested most dramatically by the Woodstock festival. A new spiritual awareness was dawning in some, catalyzed by "all of the above" and widely socialized in the 1968 trip to India by the Beatles[13]. For most of those drawn to that new awareness, the light of that pathway was seen to rise in the East. In the West Coast scene, Zen had already established itself in the milieu of the fifties beat culture of literary figures like Allen Ginsburg[14] and Jack Kerouac.[15] From there, it is a short step to Ken Kesey,[16] who was to first try LSD as a volunteer at a Veteran's Administration hospital in Menlo Park, CA. This erupted into Kesey's Merry Pranksters, a form of proto-hippies romanticized in Tom Wolfe's *The Electric Kool-aid Acid Test*.[17]

A few months before this dialog between Alan and myself, I had somewhat predictably begun smoking marijuana regularly with my friends. This seemed to happen inevitably. The arc of my initiation into the counter-culture scene, of which marijuana and psychedelics were an integral part, could be traced by the musical trends of the times we grew up in—my Junior High school years started in seventh grade listening to the more pop style of rock and roll influenced by the Beatles-inspired (musical) "British invasion" — including softer groups like the Monkees, The Loving Spoonful, the Turtles, and also some of the progressively edgier acts like the Rolling Stones, The Who, Bob Dylan, and so on. The flavor of the music scene evolved, such that by ninth grade, bit by bit, radio song by radio song, and album by album, it had morphed into the full-blown acid-rock of the Jefferson Airplane, Janis Joplin/Big Brother, Jimi Hendrix and of course, the fully psychedelicized Beatles of the *Revolver* and *Sergeant Pepper* albums. Lyrics of songs by the likes of the Beatles, Donovan, and the Jefferson Airplane were laced with LSD-influenced ideas.

This progress is typified in my life with a memory of my visit to New York City with one of my close grade school friends, at age 13 in 1968, to see the just-released film *The Monterey Pop Festival*. This documented a precursor to the Woodstock Festival in Monterey, California, that drew together many of the San Francisco acts of the acid-rock scene with bands from LA and Britain. It showcased the next generation of artists, such as Jimi Hendrix and Big Brother and the Holding Company with Janis Joplin. Emerging from the film — the scene of Hendrix setting his guitar on fire, among other things, having been a bit mind-blowing for us — we wandered south and found ourselves in the East Village. We would have walked past the just-opened Fillmore East[18] and then wandered on into Tompkins Square, bustling with full-on hippies. We were probably gaping about as tourists when a young woman with a military jacket and John Lennon-style "granny glasses" asked us if we wanted to buy some pot. We were both mildly shocked insofar as we believed and assumed we were too young to be sized up as potential customers[19].

The leading edge of the college students just ahead of us — that is, of older brothers and sisters — was already fully engaged in the counter-culture, anti-war political movement, and drug scene. By the end of our final year of Junior High School in 1969, the adjustment was being made internally amongst myself and my peers to the idea that sooner or later — probably sooner — we would start to smoke pot.

It was probably somewhere between ninth and tenth grade that I finally won the battle with my father about not having to cut my hair. It was already at a "shaggy early beatle" length, and as high school progressed, it was to grow down past my shoulders in the typical "hippie freak" style of that era.

Even though I was by the fall of that year regularly smoking pot with my male friends, the acid trips they began indulging in that fall were, at first, somewhat "on the down low" and only whispered about in my presence. But before long, it had become a commonplace event, and the question that stood before me, voiced internally and outwardly by my friends, was: when will you get with it?

My interest, having been implanted at nine years old, prompted me to learn and read much more than a bit about it since it moved across the headlines in the years since. It was nevertheless still, in many ways, quite mysterious to my young, still-forming fifteen-year-old mind. The anti-psychedelic propaganda machine had since gone into high gear, injecting fear and illegality into the equation. Art Linkletter[20] — always a benign, folksy, and avuncular figure in my life as a child through his TV show, *Kids Say the Darnedest Things* had ferociously led the public charge against LSD after the death by suicide of his LSD-using daughter. The false "scare story" was widely circulated in the press that LSD use would cause chromosome damage[21]. The milieu was culturally complex, especially if you were a 14 or 15-year-old kid. And once I had started smoking pot and, apparently, not immediately turned into a junkie, the establishment credibility, as far as providing the straight story on drugs, was gone. So it was pretty clear which side of the counter-cultural divide I would land on.

Although I adapted to the idea that LSD was now part of the high school scene, I was perplexed by the casual nature of its usage. Somehow, this powerful substance was being used *merely* recreationally, as if it were simply like smoking pot, only more so. And stories would pop up locally about bad trips — or trips with a "bad" component. In addition, with the broad experimentation with, and use of, drugs of all kinds among the local high school population, there were occasionally "death by misadventure" types of stories in the news that, one way or another, had a drug angle to them.

By the point of Alan's rebuke, my recreational drug use was otherwise in full flower — funded, I think, primarily by lunch money. Our suppliers were other kids with access to some source or other, presumably an older brother or sister or young adult hippie type. With Alan having spoken what proved to be the final word on the question, it was now just a matter of a short number of days. With my friend Ted (also a friend of Alan's and part of our immediate circle), I embarked on my first psychedelic dose, my first trip.

Ted had moved into town in ninth grade and probably first befriended Alan on the football team. Ted was good-looking, tall, and muscular. While perhaps not a particularly good student, or interested in studies, he was yet clever and intelligent and, at times, could be a deep thinker. He was the only aspiring rock and roller among us, starting to study guitar in tenth grade. The rest of us, however — with Paul and I taking the lead technically — did produce light shows together at area dances.

By the time we landed in high school in tenth grade, there were five of us, also including my friend George, who, like Ted, had also come to town as a "new kid" in ninth grade. We smoked pot together, played poker, traveled into New York City to see concerts at the Fillmore East and elsewhere, and generally palled about. This was the group I was to first explore psychedelics with.

As it happened, perhaps auspiciously, it was not LSD that just then happened to be the readiest psychedelic to be had that week, but instead, mescaline.[22] As part of my previous studied curiosity about psychedelics, I had already read (with only a dim sort of comprehension) Aldous Huxley's[23] *The Doors of Perception*[24], where he recounts his experience in the 1950s with mescaline. As I was also in general fond of Huxley from his literary works, the gentle cachet of mescaline, with the implied benediction of Huxley, made the prospect of my virgin voyage seem a bit less daunting.

Before recounting my first psychedelic journey, I want to advise the reader that the nature of street drugs being what they are, the dosage of a given hit that one might acquire, was pretty far over the lot. Based on comparisons with somewhat more carefully dosed experiences in literature, my sense is that in terms of what was in circulation at that time, a given dose of LSD, the primary psychedelic I used, might vary between 100 or 125 micrograms to upwards of over 300 micrograms. My vague sense is that the "typical" dose would be around 150 to 200 micrograms, well into the high-moderate range. Generally, we expected that splitting a dose would still yield a passable, if milder, experience. The reader will need to infer from the experiences recounted here some appreciation of the likely dosage range by gauging the intensity of the episode. My first mescaline dose was perhaps roughly the equivalent to 125 mcg or so of LSD.

With little clarity on my side about how things were going to unfold, Ted and I "dropped" right around lunchtime: if Ted can do it, I thought, so can I. We anticipated it would require about a class period (fifty minutes) to "get off"[25] and experience the onset of effects.

Staples High School, where I grew up in suburban Westport, Connecticut, was very open — both the physical campus and permissively. Students were allowed to come and go — leave school — as their class schedules permitted. The blacktop in front of the cafeteria that Alan and I had been walking toward that winter day was a giant smoking lounge where everyone would congregate between classes and for lunch or study hall. As part of the place's generally lax and permissive tenor, it was also quite easy, with a generally low consequence, to skip classes, which I did pretty often.

While I was free that period, and planned to skip class the rest of the afternoon, Ted needed to attend one more class. So while he went to class, I was parked in the cafeteria with one of our friends, Ruth.

I first met Ruth in my tenth-grade biology class. Alan and I were desk mates, and Ruth sat in the row directly in front of us. Her family had just moved from New York City to Westport, although she had summered in Westport for some years. She had reddish hair, was slender and shapely, and had a certain New York City savoir-faire while being very spirited and fun.

She and I played the card game "spit" for the hour, which required focused attentiveness and quick hands. She was more skilled at it than I was. Somewhere during that time, the mescaline began to come on; and Ruth (likewise, like Ted, already among the "experienced") coaxed me playfully through the onset — which was gentle and not completely alien in that it felt like I was first, just getting *very* high on pot. From the get-go, it was also clear that it was a different, more intense experience that was inevitably to take me farther in its own direction than pot ever would. I also knew quickly that I would enjoy it and, with a bit of help from Ted, manage well enough. Looking back, I can imagine that this onset period probably had some imprinting effect relative to Ruth; she was to figure again later as a significant player in pivotal trips. But to begin with, it started as just a "slightly *very* high" card game in the school cafeteria.

The class period ended, and it was clear that I was feeling the effects come on with increasing strength as the minutes rolled on. Ted located me in the cafeteria, and together we headed to his locker to drop off his books before we hitchhiked into town. As we walked away from the cafeteria, things began to shimmer. Being together and both starting to get off, I think we reinforced each other's experience of being high; by the time we got to the building where his locker was, we were feeling beyond giddy and about to be having a little bit of difficulty maintaining walking-in-the-halls decorum. Unsurprisingly, Ted had some slight trouble managing the unlocking of his locker and reorganizing his things, which seemed highly amusing; and at the peak of his fumbling, who should walk by but one of the Vice Principals, a rather dour, tall and, to us, quite aged grandfather type who seemed to have very little sense of humor. He appeared to eye us suspiciously, but fortunately, he didn't stop or speak with us. With a sense of having just gotten away with something, we quickly bolted the campus, suppressing fits of laughter — the susceptibility to which was a hallmark of my early trips.

It was at this point that it was clear to me that, indeed, I had entered a new realm of being and knowledge. Although it is a bald fact that the experience is essentially ineffable and indescribable and unlike anything one might have experienced, it is possible to describe approximately certain things, such as some visual effects. Most striking is the phenomenon of "trails" — where a wave of the hand yields a flutter of snapshots of the motion through space, with after images of movement appearing frozen in space and time for brief moments. Suddenly one sees a stop-motion strobe picture of the entire motion existing at once before the images collapse back into the resting hand. One can also feel ecstatic, blissful physical rushes of energy up and down one's body.

The *Through the Looking Glass* sensation was palpable — everything seemed different, alive, and humming. Although one's entire sense of things was churning, at the dosage level we were at, the intensity was such that one could still maintain an inner equilibrium if one relaxed and "went with it."

I don't recall the trip from school into town, a few miles away. Arriving, we first headed for the Pet Shop ("Fur, Fin and Feather") — something of a hangout for us; the owner was a "head" himself, who we sometimes smoked pot with.

Our friend George had become a tropical fish enthusiast and especially enjoyed the animals in the store; he had been our original connecting link with the owner. It was a pretty old, funky place, with lots of animal sights, sounds, and smells—but because of our friendship with the owner, a safe spot to ride through my acclimation to my first psychedelic peak. I'm pretty sure our friend, the owner, knew we were tripping. Staring into the fish tanks, I saw in fascination layers of detail previously unnoticed — some of which were probably not actually there.

The dose was perfect: reasonably mild but strong enough to give a first taste of the full psychedelic state. I continued to experience the sort of typical medium-dose psychedelic phenomena — visual trails, colored hallucinations overlaying the "normal" visual—dazzling geometric figures and flows of color. Enhanced sensory awareness. Bodily rushes. The mentioned susceptibility to fits of laughter at the slightest hint of humor from Ted — after all, we were both "in the know." Beyond these specific phenomena of the basic medium dose psychedelic state, there was an overriding feeling that everything was more vivid, engaging, and intrinsically valuable, that one had entered into a new realm where the streets were not paved in gold but where a new and different sense of reality and possibility pervaded.

My detailed memory of the several hours we spent in town is spotty, although I remember particular highlights as we roamed up and down the main street, in and out of the various stores, and wandering back to the pet shop. One memory is of going into the record department of one of the shops and seeing an album cover with one of the most horrific photographs of the My Lai massacre in Vietnam — unsettling but a sadly typical visual from the news[26]. Also, running into the mother of a classmate of mine who was friendly with my mother and her trying to engage me in a genial way—I was filled with anxiety that I would be unable to maintain the appropriate manner. Still, I was able to wiggle through it. I also remember walking up and down the streets of the town and repeatedly glancing at my faint reflection in the plate glass windows angling away from the doors to the showcase windows of the shops. I think I was trying to stay grounded and reinforce that the familiar "me" was still there.

Later, inside the public library — we had likely gone in to use the restrooms — we ran into a bit of a peculiar-looking couple in perhaps their forties, he markedly shorter than her, who asked us where the Town Hall was. They were getting married and bursting with excitement: it seemed an impromptu decision on their part. Bemused, we pointed them down the block; it seemed a rather strange encounter but somehow fit the crazy magic of the trip. Who knows what became of them?

The afternoon grew late, toward the time when Ted and I would each be expected to have come home from school. Ted took off, and I likewise headed home. Home for me was a short walk from town, over the bridge, and up the hill on the other side of the river.

I found that I was still very much tripping when I got home, although the peak had passed. I remember parking myself in the armchair in the living room and talking with my mother, who was trying to have, I think, a pretty typical "How was your day" type of conversation.

I quickly came to realize that I was only able to form words into sentences with great difficulty and what seemed to me long pauses in between. Apparently, I had not attempted much in the way of responsive adult conversation during my wanderings with Ted downtown, so I didn't anticipate this would be a problem. Nevertheless, it was my first real experience of this sort of "dissociative aphasia."

Dissociative phenomena like this appear in many forms in psychedelic states, and experiencing them can provide an angle of insight into the spectrum of transformations of consciousness as, ultimately, awareness of the spiritual world develops.

I'm sure that my mother sensed "something was up" with me but, perhaps wisely, didn't push the point as I could — somewhat — carry the thread, just very slowly and with a great inner effort of concentration.

And together with everything else, it also happened to be Friday night. At some point, I realized that I had made a date to see a movie with a girl from school, which I had no doubt been looking forward to all week. This required not a little scrunching up of courage to propose in the first place. I'm not sure when or to what extent I had considered the intersect of these two activities — my movie date and my first psychedelic trip, the latter being spontaneously decided on that morning. I'm sure that my mother (who would be driving the car to pick up my date) would have mentioned it as one of the conversation topics. Somehow I managed to beg off the whole interview with, I expect, a plan as to when to leave (in a few hours) and a claim to need a nap first.

In my room upstairs, I lay in my bed. I very soon was focussed internally on a world of images that rose up in me — somewhat like hypnagogic imagery, only more vivid, animated, and "lit up." The image that I particularly remember taking hold was of a brilliantly lit, colored, and fast-moving "inner world" of a solar-system-like imagination. Pictures of brightly colored planets flowed easily, like a more active dreaming/daydreaming. They seemed to occupy a "planetary space within" as if contained in an inner armillary sphere[27].

Any threshold dose of psychedelics will make you susceptible to a new sensitivity to what may be described as the *texture* of experience. Primarily visually, but with an accompanying rhythmic-breathing aspect, one can find oneself "tuning in" — as I did — on patterns, and possibly energies, flowing through one's experience that were unperceived or unnoticed before. Gazing at a grain of wood, a pattern of fabric, or simply a scattered arrangement of objects can metamorphose into a deep penetration into fractal-like shapes now seen as emerging out of the background of what was previously taken as simply the noise of a given coat of paint, a given surface of material, or a given arrangement of things. The outlines of the forms thus seen can themselves be seen to transform, to metamorphose, to highlight now this and now that, and also to detach from the items that initially revealed the patterns and continue inward as an internal visionary process.

This can fascinate and also overwhelm; it can carve new channels of feeling in your sensed body. This kind of kaleidoscope of vision and sensation — which is what psychedelic art tries to capture — is, for many people, part and parcel of the attraction of psychedelic experience: an entirely new sense of reality and, correspondingly, of self. At the same time, especially as intensified at higher doses, it is an edge wherein the accustomed moorings of the sense-world experience become increasingly disjointed, and the awareness of the inner motions begins to deconstruct (disassociate) our habitual patterning of thought.

After exploring and enjoying this state alone in my room, I eventually became restful; things were dying down. Finally came the time for the movie date. I can only think I went through the motions on autopilot, as I was still somewhat mesmerized by my internal psychedelic process. I do remember the girl; I do remember the movie (*Z*), but I am sure I was even more intensely non-present to the dating situation than your most typically awkward fifteen-year-old kid.

That was my first trip. Gentle, medium dose, fun, interesting, confidence-building in the sense of "I can do this," introducing me to the social and interpersonal awkwardness possible when presenting yourself normally while in an intensely different reality. No major catastrophes. And for now, I felt pretty well dialed in on not "seeing God" or anything too disruptive or transformational. And my checklist of "drugs I have tried" got another notch. My appetite for experimentation was reinforced.

Through the spring and into summer, I tripped close to a dozen times or a bit more—the next also being on mescaline, only a few weeks later. It was similarly enjoyable; the only fixed memory of it was lying on my friend Paul's lawn and looking up at the moon (in daylight) and knowing that a space flight was in progress. This would have been Apollo 13. It hinted at a sense of the cosmic, the beyond-earthly.

And then I was ready for acid — similar, but a little more "electric" and with a feeling of much more significant headroom being available dosage and intensity-wise. These experiences were all within the circle of my four other closest male friends (Alan, Ted, Paul, and George). Sometimes the five of us would dose together, sometime I would trip with one or two others; occasionally, another male friend would join in. The logistics of these eight-hour adventures involved the usual teenage subterfuges, sleeping over at friend's houses when their parents were away, and so on — although we all developed "sea legs" that would allow us to function (provided nothing too out of the ordinary took place and we avoided the peak time) around our parents and other adults. The duration of a trip being at least eight hours, one often had to put in an appearance at the family dinner table, do homework — whatever, trying to skate on the near side of "acting normal" while being very much not normal.

By late May of that year, I was pretty much on my way to being a committed acidhead. I was loving it.

I began to become aware of one particular thing during this time. There was a sort of unspoken rule among my friends — not emanating from me — that sought to ensure that we all stayed tethered to the here and now — at least, after a fashion. If, for example, one became too enthusiastically engaged with the fascination of, say, emerging forms and shapes suddenly morphing out of the grain or pattern of some everyday thing or an interesting weave or shimmer which suddenly quivered alive with layers and matrices of colored energy in a previously unnoticed geometry — one would be chided, mocked or ridiculed and "brought back down to earth" with some remark that would color your interest as of a "hippy dippy" nature. It was as if there was a sense of a current flowing in the background, an undertow, always ready to pull you into its overpowering domain. These pushbacks always disappointed me, as I was willing to, and wanted to, "go deeper." Nevertheless, it was somehow understood that one's experience needed to maintain a certain ratio between focus on the consensus reality and the parallel alternate track. If one allowed the psychedelic world to become predominant, one would be yanked back by the others.

I will mention that despite these socially-enforced guard rails on the experience, a more profound vision would nonetheless penetrate. I recall very clearly tripping with Ted, George, and Alan in the basement of George's house — where we often played poker together — and suddenly perceiving what I would have to describe as a clairvoyant perception of the "pranic aura" of Ted's breath. It was as if the air circulating in and out of his mouth and, more particularly, nostrils, was perceptible in shades of color, forming definite swirls and eddies of a cosmic energy in the space around him. I registered it as "I am seeing something real here," although I lacked the concepts or context to take it anywhere. And quite likely, rather than prompting a "back to earth" type admonishment, my pause to observe this was unnoticed by the others. My attention likely was soon diverted by whatever the following unrelated remark one of my friends made was.

Once, at George's house, one of Ted's friends from where he used to live on Long Island visited and joined us tripping. In the joking back and forth, suddenly, a stream of ad-libs turned into what felt like an exercise in telepathic suggestion, where off-the-wall punch lines were delivered by the friend who should have had no likelihood of providing the in-joke answer. It was startling; we would pause, register that "something" had happened, take it in, and move on.

Situations could develop around the general atmosphere of widespread and fairly indiscriminate teenage drug use. But, again, this was during the anti-war years, the post-Woodstock year, very *us* vs. *them* generationally.

LSD, in particular, certainly contributed to some serious psychiatric outcomes. A kindergarten friend I had drifted away from but still felt connected to was reported hospitalized after a "bad trip." He was to commit suicide a year or so later. In later times I came inwardly to have a sense of how his psychedelic experiences may have overwhelmed him. I do not believe he was under the influence when he killed himself. It is hard to know if his LSD use was causative, or perhaps self-medication for existing symptomology.

Before my first trip, my friend Paul in my immediate circle had had a "challenging" trip that at first, panicked Alan and George, who were tripping with him. He had become unresponsive and withdrawn while they were walking on the beach, and they rang me to help them figure out what to do (presumably because I would be straight enough to deal with it while leaving them out of it). However, by the time I got there, he had come down. He was in fact responsive and self-possessed enough (while still high) to take part in "pranking" me by at first appearing completely catatonic on my arrival, curled up in a corner. Fooled you!

Scary stuff. Feeling young and immortal, we essentially chalked all this up to bumps in the road, or "accidents" — that wouldn't happen to us.

Although generally speaking, I was enjoying psychedelic drug use "recreationally" it *could* start to wear thin in certain ways. We also all smoked pot, or as available, hashish, pretty much every day, and experimented with various other things, drugs like uppers and downers — neither of which I came to enjoy particularly.

The positives were plentiful: a definite ecstatic high that could be shared with others; a total transformation of the sense world into a variation of a living psychedelic art poster; body rushes, and a greatly enhanced sense of apparent wit that expressed itself in cleverness infused with merriment. One of our favorite typical pastimes while tripping was listening to a record album of the multi-layered storytelling of the Firesign Theater,[28] a "radio skit" ensemble, which told absurd stories laced with multi-layered cultural "in" jokes, ironies, absurdities, and comic effects — all of which could be profoundly experienced and appreciated while lying on the floor of a dark room on 150 micrograms or so of LSD. Likewise, of course, music too would be greatly enhanced in the dark. In general, your zaniness and sense of humor were significantly enhanced if you were inclined that way. The fundamental characteristic is that *any* psychological attribute can be amplified.

But then, on the other hand, there was "crashing" — the energetic depletion after eight hours of psychically arduous experience coupled with high-intensity neurological and endocrinological activity. And, in my experience, this became one of the weak points when at last, you put yourself to bed alone in the dark; all manner of apprehensions can rise up. For me, this might be a certain foreboding, perhaps accompanied by quasi-nightmarish ideation and visualization, that one would have to navigate one's mind away from. But again, for me, it never quite became too overwhelming or took the upper hand. It was generally regarded as a situation where one "took the bad with the good" — with, generally, the experience of the "good" being very favorable. Smoking a joint when coming down seemed to soften the crash.

Of course, it was around that time that any number of other age group peers were also starting to experience psychedelics for the first time, and I remember the intensity of shared enthusiasm that would express itself when you first identified with another of the "experienced" cohort. It was such a transformational new capacity — to experience life so intensively this way — and it seemed clear that it would change the world. We told each other how venerable we would be when we told our grandchildren that "we were there" when the psychedelic wave first began. Expecting, of course, that psychedelic use would become mainstream by the time we became adults and wrested control from the establishment.

Yet in 1970, although the hippie counter-culture was penetrating our world at many, many angles, there (unsurprisingly) wasn't a coherent worldview around psychedelic drugs. However, from Tim Leary on down, all manner of ideas were in circulation. But for my little crowd, it was at the start, a recreational, hedonistic, escapist *adventure* against the backdrop of a turbulent and confusing world.

This continued into my junior year; I remember tripping at home on a school night and trying to do my chemistry homework. Quite an effort!

In these first two years, across the several dozen trips I took with my friends, there were others I recall notably. The rock group *The James Gang*,[29] who were taking off, came to my high school when I was in tenth grade[30]. Ted and I had tickets to the first show; we dropped acid and found seats in the front row. Joe Walsh (later of *Eagles* fame) played awesome rock and roll, more or less in our faces. The presence of a mid-tier professional light show greatly enhanced this. Through his connection with the high school technical staff, Paul sat in to assist with it. When the first show was over, we walked onto the stage and behind the rear projection screen, gave Paul a shout, and had a peek at the gear they had set up for the light show. After our chat, we walked back into the hall the way we had come and realized that they were already letting in the audience for the general admission second show — so we cheerfully resumed our (unpaid for this time) front-row seats. It was a great trip.

I can also recall toward the end of my junior year — a pending but unspoken psychedelic hiatus already making itself felt — I tripped on what proved a relatively low dose by myself and attended a performance of *Waiting for Godot*; Alan was Estragon, and his friend Daniel — who some years later was to marry our friend Ruth — was Vladimir. On the one hand, it was a bit of a bleak and desolate experience; on the other, somehow a cathartic one.

And then, somewhere centered around the middle of my junior year, there was a very palpable tapering off of the interest among my friends in further psychedelic adventures. I experienced this as somewhat of a loss — I was still up for it but wanted companions. Although I didn't really have an idea of where it might be going, I knew that the experience was still calling me.

I attributed it to the wearing-thin effect, although from another angle, I might also characterize it as the recognition that to go further down this pathway would require a willingness to undergo some kind of challenging transformation. Simply pressing the "play" button again on these experiences was, otherwise, an exercise in some sort of psychic depletion. Or you could just say that folks were, for the moment, getting a little burnt out and giving it a rest. But it did feel like someone had pressed the "pause" button, but not in a strictly overt way. It just sort of happened. Obviously, we were all also continuing to grow up in all kinds of other ways.

2

In Search of a Psychedelic Model

Over fifty years ago, that conversation with my friend Alan was pivotal in the transformation process — across a lifetime — from a still-forming teenager to the person I find myself to be now, with age 70 in sight. And so I was thus introduced at the rather tender age of fifteen to these powerful agents, in essentially a recreational context. To say it was unreflecting on my part would be an overstatement. Still, I clearly lacked a comprehension of where this path might lead beyond the novelty, adventure, and power that the experiences provided. It felt like I had migrated into a strange new territory but only penetrated the outer edges. A vast unknown slumbered beyond.

Through my particular destiny, I came to find myself in my formative years living at the crest of the greatest expansion of the use of psychedelics. It was an environment wherein, despite having become illegal, their use was highly normalized across many peers within my age cohort. This coincided with a turbulent and transformative period in humanity's ongoing cultural and, more deeply, spiritual evolution, then acting itself out in the increasingly Americanized West.

Throughout the explorations across these years by numerous individuals and thinkers of various persuasions, there have been many works that have contributed to expanding our grasp of the domain of the psychedelic. At the same time, no comprehensive model has been found that accounts for the spectrum of possibility that these agents have revealed.

Before continuing the account of the years that followed, where my use of psychedelics became a more intentionally sought quest for higher consciousness and spiritual transformation, some words to provide a first mention of the teaching that came to be the center of my spiritual growth and striving: Rudolf Steiner's anthroposophy. Across the later years of family, career, health episodes, and love relationships, with their challenges, I have pursued the study of various spiritual teachings and found my spiritual home centered in the worldview of anthroposophy. I have striven to bring my life and practice in line with his teachings as I understand them[31].

An appreciation of the essential insights drawn from anthroposophy is fundamental, in my view, for our many-troubled world at large. In some ways, they are especially so for the burgeoning psychedelic culture if its progressive impulses are to achieve its best possible destiny as a factor in the forward-moving development of humanity.

The word anthroposophy — from the Greek *anthropos*, human being, and *sophia*, wisdom, has been given a rhetorical emphasis by Steiner as denoting "consciousness of being human." He describes it as "a path of knowledge leading the spiritual in the human being to the spiritual in the universe."

Anthroposophy provided me with a teaching that allowed me to make sense of the challenging and soul-shattering experiences that unfolded as my involvement with psychedelic drugs continued in my youth. This has deepened in the many years since. Tracing the steps of my journey, it is hoped that by looking at some of the key elements of my experience, it will be possible to shed light on some of the deep questions that come into play when one begins to experience psychedelic consciousness as the dawning of a spiritual reality. This will challenge any number of the received understandings that hold sway in our collective life and awareness.

My notion of spirit embraces something far beyond the content of things, forms, images, thoughts, patterns, and structures that we can experience with our everyday minds.

The psychedelic encounter can reveal a content that is much more variegated, lovely, terrifying, complex, beautiful, meaningful, and fulfilling than that of the everyday world of the familiar. In the right circumstance, this content beyond "the familiar" can be understood and discovered as relating to an emergent spiritual world. While it can be dramatically revealed by psychedelics, the reality of the spiritual world, of course, is that it is an eternally-existing supersensible reality beyond sense experience.

This reality is discoverable by other means; it can be approached and understood with soul powers and insights cultivated outside of the context of the psychedelic venture. The self-transformation of consciousness and being — such that the individual finds their proper relationship with, and direct experience of, this spiritual world —has been pursued across millennia by many practices and traditions of humanity.

In modern times, however, spiritual tradition has collided with the modern worldview as developed over the past 200 years.

Our thinking, our whole culture, in the present time is saturated with the underlying beliefs of scientific materialism that came to the fore in the developing West during the 19th century. Along with the many valuable blessings of this unfolding, as part and parcel with it, it came to overthrow the simple, traditionally received worldview inherited in the West from centuries of the dominant Judeo-Christian stream.

The material successes of the scientific worldview can give its pronouncements and assumptions a credibility that, for some, seems irrefutable. The Churches, traditional keepers of the spiritual worldview, resisted these changes and then failed to proactively evolve in the face of the dominance of science. Consequently, it has become difficult for some to internalize the reality of the spiritual or the possibility of the spiritual.

Spiritual, supersensible reality is taken here in this writing as a given — although not as understood by tradition alone either. The possibility of an adequate picture of the spiritual and the spiritual human being in the post-psychedelic era will require an advance in our basic conceptions. Today, science alone can only attempt to explain man as the product of forces and substances of the earthly.

IN SEARCH OF A PSYCHEDELIC MODEL

The psychedelic experience of millions has emerged into this context.

Spirit is the unborn, the undying, the eternal. It is the creative behind and beyond the aggregate of particles we imagine comprise the world we experience through our senses. It is the source of the moral and of individual freedom. The encounter with the psychedelic state can be an instrument that unlocks our inborn capacity, as spirits, to perceive the supersensible realities of the spiritual world. Whether or not this "unlocking" is salutary, heath-giving, and yields an actual reality that the individual can comprehend and integrate, will depend on myriad factors, some to be explored here.

Rudolf Steiner spoke out of his clairvoyant experience of this spiritual world, that is, his own higher cognition. He formed an independent spiritual initiative — that was realized from a perspective standing on this side of the triumph of scientific materialism as it first blossomed in the 19th century. He understood the evolution toward modern consciousness profoundly and developed a worldview, a spiritual vision, that could harmonize with modernity. Most importantly, he could also present a new articulation of the spiritual world as a world of direct experience. His teaching, which he came to refer to as *anthroposophy* (or alternatively, and less exclusively, *spiritual science*), is something I first encountered almost fifty years ago, when I was actively exploring psychedelics.

This scientific materialism would, of course, dismiss out of hand the notion of a clairvoyant consciousness that served a valid cognitive role in the discovery of reality. However, those whose psychedelic awakening is felt and understood as providing a conduit to a higher, spiritual apprehension of reality — albeit through the veil of the artifacts of individual, personal psychology that also emerge — must countenance the idea that "There are more things in heaven and earth, Horatio, than are dreamt of in your philosophy."[32] — Shakespeare's Hamlet prospectively indicating the post-Kantian, materialistic philosophy that holds that there are fixed limits to what is knowable.

Our culture has been essentially ill-equipped to meet or speak to the individual — notably, the developing and emerging individual in their youth — in a way that can address the profound questions that can arise when the psychedelic threshold is crossed.

Those exploring psychedelics in depth may find themselves navigating a reality comprising a new "outer" world and a new experience and realization of the self. Reverting to the more familiar, everyday coordinates of what the individual previously took as the "given reality," one seeks for concepts. Although the individual may recognize in some way that their experience was an intensified encounter with what they abstractly understood previously as the religious-spiritual, it can be starkly different at the same time, in content and structure, from whatever they had previously intellectually or emotionally conceived of as spiritual. This was to prove to be my experience.

Not everyone, of course, will begin with, or come to, a recognition of the spirit in their psychedelic experience — this is obvious even when looking at the start of my own story as recounted so far. There are many degrees of engagement with psychedelic agents, and recreational or therapeutic intentions may drive the greater number of individuals who experiment with them, rather than conscious spiritual aspirations. It is, however, an essential contention of my thinking here that the recreational and therapeutic categories will ultimately require a new spiritual framework. The spiritual possibilities of psychedelics need to be comprehensively grasped before a stable and fully healthy expression of the other contexts can emerge within society. I see this as a long-term process; these other areas (therapeutic and recreational) will continue their own development meanwhile. Human culture as a whole is likewise in need of a profound shift in values and the concepts that support them. It is possible that a healthy development of psychedelic culture will contribute to this.

Psychedelics, in their way, demonstrate the possibility of alternative states of knowing from the received, pedestrian "consensus reality," which has come to serve as the default basis of our knowledge of the world. In Steiner's teaching, the idea that human consciousness has changed and evolved across the millennia is a core idea. The kind of shift which this experience can and has created in millions of people should open the door to an understanding of our origin and development that can incorporate this idea of consciousness-evolution.

After progressing in stages through my psychedelic years and taking up an increasingly intentional, self-guided path of seeking, I came to find that the teachings of Rudolf Steiner's anthroposophy provided me with the clearest insight into my youthful experiences.

It provided a worldview and a path of practice that could speak to, and fulfill, the yearnings that were first awakened in those times. As I relate my experience with LSD and other psychedelics, this anthroposophic worldview will have formed the primary lens of any insights I attempt to share. Where it fits my story, I will, in places, provide comments out of Steiner's teachings as I can. It will enter the narrative somewhat nonlinearly — as part of the pieces I have puzzled together. And in the latter part of the book, having completed the account of my psychedelic years, I will expand on Steiner's teaching through themes, riddles, and questions that emerged from that lived journey. I will also discuss, where relevant, other teachings and explorations encountered during those years.

An example of this type of comment would be, for example, to mention how in looking at my dissociative aphasia while I was trying to speak with my mother during my first mescaline experience, this fell later into place somewhat while reading Steiner. I encountered his initially odd-sounding statement — speaking of the way in which the souls of the dead communicate — that they lose their ability to use *nouns*. I found that, in recalling my state, where words seemed to drift away, I could internalize a sense of what he might have been talking about. This is simply an almost trivial example, although it fits into a broader discussion to come about disassociation and shifts in consciousness.

Who was Steiner? Steiner emerged as a spiritual teacher in Germany at the beginning of the twentieth century. His own background was scientific, philosophical, and literary. But also, he had, from childhood, experienced a direct awareness of supersensible elements and beings. He was to strive inwardly his whole life to develop this capacity more consciously and to bring it into connection with the modern, outer world.

As a young man, he had worked for a number of years as the editor of the definitive edition of the scientific works of Johann Wolfgang von Goethe.[33] Goethe's influence can be profoundly felt across the development of anthroposophy.

It is a peculiar personal note, a synchronicity[34] of sorts, to recall that as a child, I first came to be aware also of Goethe (who was to be so influential on Rudolf Steiner) as a historical figure through the same book, *The Mind*,[35] that I first learned about LSD from. There is a two-page spread therein that depicts various historical figures and assigns them an imputed IQ. Goethe stands out in this presentation as having the highest IQ of all of them. I remember this distinctly because, first, the IQ was so notable, and also that my mother corrected me as to the proper pronunciation of his unfamiliar name.

Goethe's scientific work was rooted in a completely different mindset than the materialistic science of the 19th century; it was instead approached as a form of *participatory knowing*, wherein the mind of the investigator is an active participant in the unveiling of nature.

Steiner's teachings about higher stages of knowledge, of higher consciousness; the way in which he distinguishes among the different members of the human being as body, soul, and spirit; his insights into reincarnation and of the life between death and a new birth; his articulation overall of a post-Darwinian, post-Kantian spiritual world view — all can be a most helpful reference point in the quest for comprehension of psychedelics. It is his *image of the human being* as born out of a spiritual cosmos that is of the greatest importance to internalize as humanity moves forward. As psychedelic explorers, we may turn to this in seeking to establish our footing in a worldview that can embrace the content of psychedelic consciousness.

For all of its breadth and depth, Steiner's thought meanwhile seems to exist in a strange cultural limbo. His work is so diverse, unconventional, and outré, despite his thorough-going philosophic perspectives, that he is often dismissed out of hand by academics. And even among many in the area of spirituality and consciousness studies, where one might suppose there would be more familiarity with his ideas, he is often left out of the dialog.

In trying to write about the confluence of anthroposophy and the psychedelic, I am mindful of a sense of humility and inadequacy to the task. As stated in my preface, my initial impulse was to try and write something that would speak in general terms about the two frameworks. I quickly became aware that it would not be possible — for me, at least — to author a more rigorously structured and authoritative work on the general theme of "psychedelics and anthroposophy" that I might have wished to see created and which the topic ultimately deserves.

Instead, I found myself falling back on my own autobiographical psychedelic memories, which may serve to include *some* instances of the basic phenomenological raw material for discussion of the meaning of psychedelics relative to the perspective of Rudolf Steiner's anthroposophical teachings. This "anthroposophical" perspective found herein is, to be sure, uniquely mine as a particular student of anthroposophy. It should also be self-understood that my entire study of anthroposophy has, in turn, been viewed through the lens of these earlier psychedelic encounters.

I am mindful of the subtle (and not so subtle at times) streak of narcissism that seems so easily creeps into the accounts of those who try and chronicle their psychedelic encounters. It cannot be denied that any process of self or spiritual development implies self-absorption as a given, for which I must beg the reader's pardon. Or, so it has seemed to me as I have read, still with great interest, some of the notable writers of psychedelic accounts. And so the accounts of the specific "trips" herein are necessarily wrapped in a context that embraces other personal memories of the specific time and place in which the story evolved.

Psychedelics are seen by some as providing a path in itself. For others, it serves more as a stepping stone. In my life, it was a doorway into a direct beholding of all of the wonder of the spiritual world and its reflection on earth, and in turn, it became an invitation to deepen my insight, experience, and knowing along other paths.

These early steps have included not only wonder but also toil and trial. There were intermediate steps before I found myself centered in anthroposophy, and these explorations are intertwined in the story of my growth toward anthroposophy. In their place, they provided their own light in various ways.

I wish, in particular, to be able to show how Steiner's work illuminates some of the challenges that can be experienced in the stages of a spiritually-seeking psychedelic exploration. And for some, it may also point toward a further path that builds upon the views opened up, and that serves when the world of the everyday is engaged again.

Helping to enlarge the perspective of those who strive to think seriously about the meaning and proper use of these agents; helping those who have experienced psychedelics as a challenge to their received thoughts and beliefs about the world and the spirit; helping those who are contemplating the possible exploration of psychedelics as they increasingly are talked about in positive terms: these are all outcomes I might hope to achieve in sharing my story and thoughts.

I see myself as one who has been affected profoundly — in my own view, favorably so — by my own, now long-ago, intensive use of psychedelic drugs. I look at the ongoing cultural redemption of psychedelic exploration with hope and excitement and likewise care and concern that its positive possibilities at length find their proper place in the human adventure.

3

Turning the Corner

Returning to the flow of my journey through psychedelics, I found that, as it would happen, Alan's assurance that I wouldn't see God was eventually to prove pretty much incorrect. Instead, my psychedelic experience was ultimately to branch, to blossom, flower, and explode — into what, for me, was a leap into a living experience of the spiritual world; that is, the domain of discarnate spirit beings, of gods, of a new relationship to the self, of the divine, of the Void, of God, of the Cosmic All.

It was to change the course of my life inwardly and somewhat less visibly, outwardly. I have spent the fifty-odd years since pursuing the inner broadening of my insight into all that I have glimpsed, tasted, and known through these psychedelic journeys. In my experience, the encounter with deeper levels of the psychedelic state has provided material and riches to fuel a lifetime of ongoing integration. Integration work in the immediate aftermath of a psychedelic session can be best understood as the creation of a platform for continued unveiling.

I want to reiterate here at the start that although the web of words unfolding in these pages will be full of, to begin, pictures and happenings from my psychedelic experience, and further, thoughts and ideas steeped in various psychological, intellectual, or cosmic schemes, the center of gravity of it all for me is the quest for the *spiritual*.

And meanwhile, at the start of my psychedelic journeying, it would be safe to say that I was in a typical adolescent agnostic phase. But, there would have been behind this a vaguely established image of the God I was "not to see," so something about that background fits here.

As a child, I was baptized in the Episcopal church. I attended church and Sunday school with a certain regularity until my confirmation at around eleven or twelve. My relationship with the church was essentially benign; as a child, it fit l into the "my little town" picture of the world of the late fifties and early sixties. I went through a phase of reading intently in bed at night, at age eight or so, from an illustrated *Bible Story Book* that a friend of my grandmother's had given me for Christmas. I was especially interested in the Creation / Garden of Eve story and, partly because his name was my name, the story of David and Goliath, leading on to the story of Solomon. There were years in childhood when, along with Sunday school, I would sometimes say my prayers at night.

There was not a lot of the guilt, sexual repression, abuse, or fire and brimstone, which seems elsewhere to have completely turned off any number of folks to Christianity and the Church. Around the age of eleven, I found myself noticing that the church in our town was not too demanding of its believers. I began to see it more as a social game and that our church seemed to be well-represented by affluent and upwardly mobile types. This observation somewhat deflated any claim to some unique authority. I was also aware that the Catholic church, which was also well-represented by my schoolmates, seemed a bit more demanding and, in its way, burdensome to my Catholic friends. All that said, I remain kindly disposed toward the Episcopal church.

This observation of mine was around the time of my confirmation, and at this point church attendance was to be left to my choice. I tended to stay home thenceforth, except for occasions such as Christmas. Shortly after that, my mother let it out in conversation that she and my father "weren't sure if they believed in God or not." A sort of non-committal agnostic stance appropriate to the hyper-rational worldview of the post-war years. (This would have occurred quite close to the dramatic in its day *Time Magazine* "Is God Dead?" cover[36] in 1966.) I think I was somewhere between a bit shocked and feeling this was just the other shoe dropping from the Santa Claus and Easter Bunny story. At any rate, it helped create the space to put religion aside as a teenager.

Nonetheless, as part of my perhaps peculiar reading interests[37] around that time, I had started in on Dante's[38] *Inferno*, slogged through the *Purgatorio*, and skimmed through *Paradiso*. From a literary point of view, evil and damnation are a bit more interesting — Dante's "guided tour of hell" sounded like it would be a good read! While the *Paradiso* was at times a bit tedious, I did grasp it as a journey of the soul's ascent to God through the planetary spheres until the ultimate achievement of the vision of the *celestial rose* at the threshold of the vision of God.

From childhood, I was interested in the medieval; this was part of it, I was fascinated by the baroque detail of the pre-scientific worldview. My translation — John Ciardi's[39] — was extensively footnoted with medieval worldview details. I had, as a younger child, nonetheless, lapped up everything the scientific space-race worldview could offer as well, reading many books on science. I was further charmed by Greek Myths and had a passing awareness of Hinduism by the time I was nine or ten. I would also around this time have first attempted Goethe's *Faust*, part one.

When I was nine years old, I attended the New York World's Fair and (among many other things) happened to visit the pavilion of the Latter Day Saints (Mormon) Church. I recall that there was a short film about Mormonism, and it had an enactment of their belief in the pre-existence of souls before birth and showed a "soul" being beckoned into earth life by an angel. I mention this because of the connection of the idea of the soul's pre-existence with the idea of reincarnation — the Mormon concept is about as close as this comes in the West to reincarnation. At any rate, an idea was planted.

I similarly recall at perhaps ten or eleven, I answered an ad in *Popular Science* magazine by the "Rosicrucians"[40] It was a tiny ad that talked about "Cosmic Consciousness" — "A split second in eternity." I did receive a glossy mailing. It struck me at the time as a little on the hokey side and sort of like an Elks club on steroids or some such. (The connection between this Rosicrucian organization and the Rosicrucian path in the sense of anthroposophy is tenuous).

Both point to roots in the 17th-century movement that emerged in Europe, greatly influencing esoteric and mystical trends of thought.

Other streams drifted in while I was ten or eleven; my parents had received a little volume *Zen Buddhism*[41] as a gift. I enjoyed reading it a lot and felt I could "click" with Zen.

I had a couple of experiences under anesthesia with something of a visionary character. I had a tooth pulled and felt myself going under and then passing into some spiral, twisting labyrinth, at the center of which was a figure representing Christ Jesus. As soon as I reached the center, I woke up. Later when my tonsils were removed, I was induced directly with ether. I remember the fumes as they were dropped onto the mask and transitioning through a somewhat hellish, throbbing, and pulsing streaming of lights around the form of my body — rather as if my soul were being forcibly torn from my body before going under altogether.

Between my parent's having shared their ambivalence and nosed around variously on my own, by eighth or ninth grade, I was sufficiently untethered religiously to toy (briefly) with the idea of forming my own quasi-pagan religion, inspired chiefly by the example of the made-up religion of Bokononism in Kurt Vonnegut's *Cat's Cradle*. I suppose I still felt there was a hole to fill, but it was unclear what to fill it with.

It was against this all but discarded conventional religious background that, starting around age sixteen, the approach to an inkling around spiritual self-transformation began to emerge against the backdrop of my psychedelic experimentation.

The series of these experiences began to be headed in a new direction during my senior year of high school, less than two years since my first trip.

The psychedelic hiatus among my friends referred to earlier had remained effectively in force during the summer of 1971, between my junior and senior years of high school. Other things were happening. I was sixteen, recently in possession of my driver's license. The various distractions of adolescence kept me preoccupied. During the psychedelic lull, on my sixteenth birthday, I received a requested copy of Arthur Janov's *The Primal Scream*, my curiosity no doubt stimulated by the publicity given to it by John Lennon and Yoko Ono. It was likely the first "self-help" or pop psychology book that I was to read in earnest. What engaged me, I suppose, was that it seemed to invite a radical growth process and propose a new explanatory model of the psyche. At age sixteen, I naturally possessed minimal insight into myself.

An important thing that happened during my junior year, during the psychedelic pause, was that I became good friends with Milo. I often carried with me a travel-sized magnetic chess set, and while hanging out in the cafeteria, he approached me, asking to play. We at first became regular chess companions. He almost always beat me.

He was tall and broad-shouldered, with long curly dirty blonde hair and a beard, giving him a full-on freaky hippie look. He was extremely good-natured and generally smiling. He could sometimes look like he might have skipped a shower.

Our school, with 600 students in each of the three classes, naturally had various cliques and social circles. Milo and his younger brother Andy, who was in the class below, were part of a more laid-back, full-on hippie ethos crowd that spent their time drinking beer, smoking pot, and playing folk music on their guitars. Over the months, my connection with Milo tightened, and I began to flow freely between that crowd and the circle of my friends Alan and Ted.

We were later to become sensitive to each other's spiritual strivings. His brother Andy was to become interested in Meher Baba.

Milo was unusual in both circles I moved in, in that he would only "recreate" drinking alcohol (beer) — this stood out considerably among the otherwise pot-smoking crowd.

We came to spend a lot of time together and grew quite close.

Memories of the summer before my senior year contain a few highlights of note before the pause in regular psychedelic use was to conclude. First was the psychological breakdown of my friend George. He was an integral part of my circle of friends. This circle — including also Alan and Ted — had by this time grown smaller in that Paul had left with his parents for England for his father's two-year job transfer. Paul later returned just as the rest of us were graduating high school.

Meanwhile, George and I, along with Alan and Ted, smoked pot, went to parties, hung out, went skiing, played poker together — often in the basement of George's parent's home — and more. Going back to junior high school, my relationship with George started off somewhat wobbly; he was a "new kid," and I think he saw me as some kind of rival for a "seat at the table" in our circle of friends. This friction had resolved by tenth grade, and we had done acid together at least a dozen times. He has his own story, but he intersects with this one here by way of setting a kind of milestone that I had a close view of.

One night that summer, he and I were at loose ends, and after driving around in his VW van scouting something to do, we decided to head to my parent's house and swim in the pool.

When we arrived, he took off his shoes and waded in at the first step. I suppose we intended on skinny-dipping as we hadn't changed into bathing suits. After taking the first step into the pool, he stopped, sat down on the edge, his feet in the water, and hesitated. His mind seemed to oscillate between a decision to go forward, and to retreat. He seemed preoccupied with something and, after a few minutes of dithering, got up and drove himself home. It was a little odd.

Early the next day, I learned from Alan that his mother had committed him to the psychiatric ward of the area hospital that morning. He had since escaped and was "at large." I never knew what the precipitating scene at home was. He was quickly found and re-admitted; the diagnosis was "acute schizophrenia." Somewhat coincidentally — or perhaps it was somehow a triggering influence — his family was slated to move to another state very shortly; his father had accepted a new job. His hospitalization ended after a week or two, and almost right after, they were to move. A somewhat awkward farewell party was held. Although there was a "going through the motions" of a goodbye party, there was a suddenly very palpable aversion to — or at any rate, an awkwardness around getting too close to him. As I recall, no one else from our immediate circle of male friends showed up at the party. Although we all "moved on" once he was gone, it felt clear that, in part, at any rate, his susceptibility to mental instability was likely triggered by drug use overall. It is worth noting that, as far as I knew, he did not have any LSD experience among our group that presented as a net "bad trip." In hindsight, one might find in his general day-to-day behavior "personality issues," if one is looking for them, that provide a suggestion of underlying disturbance. But you might have said that of any of us.

Although I felt sympathy for my friend's trials, I did not take it as a particularly cautionary incident relative to my own psychedelic drug use. I felt basically sane and, as we all did, had the typical youthful immortality delusion. Our belief then was that what had surfaced was primarily sourced in an intrinsic psychological disposition.

It needs to be clearly and soberly stated and understood early on here that exploration with psychedelic drugs is no trifling matter. In my own experience, I would experience my own intense "soul trials" as part of my psychedelic maturation process. The range of the possible "challenging trips" goes from merely unpleasant, through frightening, to intensely disorienting, to terrifying and, in some cases, soul-shattering beyond the boundaries of the session. This is to be contrasted with traditional spiritual practices of self-development, which themselves can be very demanding in their own way, but, on a good path, follow a much more measured approach. Despite the attraction of the possibilities psychedelic experience seems to offer, it is natural and prudent to at the same time observe a certain trepidation and caution, even if one's pursuit is perhaps only out of curiosity or recreational interest.

The other highlight that summer is connected with an excursion I made with a girl I was friendly with, to visit one of her friends (with whom I was also friendly) staying at her mother's family home in upstate New York. It was an altogether delightful trip — smoking pot, drinking beer, and canoeing on the lake with two lovely teenage girls for a week. Among these activities, I spent part of the time reading Herman Hesse's *Siddhartha* in my lovely, yellow-painted, sunny guest room in their old colonial house. By this time, various counter-culture influences were ripening in me — Hesse was very popular, and *Siddhartha* was among his best-known books. It is a fairly light read. I had a general familiarity with the story of the historical Buddha — enough to know right away that this book was somewhat an "alternate history" — but it planted a seed and, in a concrete way, deepened the idea that a transformation, leading to a higher consciousness, was possible. I internalized that an individual (such as myself) could pursue this as a definite path.

Although it did not become an obvious turning point at that time, something was taken from it: a sense that I would like to have the kind of oceanic experience depicted at the end. Or, more deeply: aspire to it as a state of being.[42]

Summer was ending soon, and shortly before the beginning of school, I came across the just-published paperback edition of Fritz Perl's *Gestalt Therapy Verbatim*[43]. I read through it quickly, and it dialed me into the awareness that there was a "human potential movement" underway and of some of the transformational dynamics being explored. It also tuned me into the Esalen scene in California, which would intersect again with me a bit further on. The ins and outs of Gestalt Therapy are a whole topic in themself; at any rate, the book coming into my hands rather serendipitously was a next step in a rapidly accelerating series of works of stimulating, transformative influence.

And then the business of being an increasingly long-haired high school student resumed that fall. Our group's social interest in psychedelics suddenly picked up again, to a large extent prompted, as far as I could make out, by an interest in doing acid with like-minded girls. In the earlier years, exploring psychedelics was (mostly) something guys did with their guy friends and girls did with their girl friends. By 12th grade, the overall sexual interest was high enough that this seemed both like a fun thing to do and perhaps more navigable; we had a couple of years now of getting high, on pot and whatnot, at parties and such with a particular circle of girls.

There were then one or two occasions that fall when my friends Ted, Alan, and I would dose with Ruth and her friend Annie. They were largely riotous affairs, with some stand-out memories, but not transformational. But the pace picked up. Availability of LSD continued to be steady — some kid or other was always dealing it. I remember being dosed in school once that fall in my last-period physics class (I thought I could make it through before I got completely off) and finding myself extraordinarily interested in and able to follow the teacher's multi-stage instructional problem through a series of related propositions. I noticed the rest of the class had dropped the thread several steps earlier. I could give the hoped-for (but largely unexpected) answer. The teacher was impressed, turned to the class, and said, "Now he's using his mind!". Indeed I was, with a three-dimensional visual of the problem constructed in my mind as he went along (it did require a lot of focus, but it was fun exercising my "mental muscle" amid everything starting to pulse and wobble around me).

The distractions of adolescence being what they were, however, the temptation to leave school before the last period became too much for me, and I had all but dropped out of that last-period physics class by the second quarter. I knew there was to be a reckoning at home for this, which contributed to an accumulating shadow of ill-ease. I was keeping a growing inventory of what would have been disapproval-prompting secrets from my parents. The inner division forming between how I presented myself to my parents and other "straight" adults and who I was with my friends became more pronounced, creating inner tension[44]. Another such secret that fall was I managed to get a ticket for racing (not simply speeding,) which petrified me because if convicted, I could potentially lose my driver's license until I was twenty-one. I avoided telling my parents about it until shortly before the court date. As it happened, I was to wiggle out of it thanks to my parent's attorney painting the "he's a good kid" picture in court.

My late summer readings signaled the beginning of an accelerated study of books falling somewhere under the general heading of self-transformation and growth, initially on more or less a separate track from my social psychedelic use. In the local bookshop (where, since childhood, I would regularly browse), I stumbled upon a copy of P. D. Ouspensky's[45] *In Search of the Miraculous*. I really didn't know how to categorize it, but I was straightaway intrigued, fascinated, and mildly terrified by it. The book details Ouspensky's contact, initially in St. Petersburg, Russia, at the time of the revolution, with George Gurdjieff[46] (c. 1866-1877 - 1949) and his teachings. Gurdjieff's influence was very catalyzing and will be variously referenced going forward. Ouspensky eventually broke with Gurdjieff and taught what he referred to as "The System" independently[47].

Although there are any number of followers of Gurdjieff active today, in the late sixties and early seventies, his works were particularly in vogue among a fairly broad class of people exploring a new spirituality or worldview. Among others, LSD advocate

Timothy Leary absorbed elements of his work and worldview (in his rough and ready way). One can trace elements of Gurdjieff (somewhat randomly) in various Leary ideas. A wave of books came into print, authored by the various followers of his teachings in the early half of the 20th century.

I felt intuitively that there were significant truths in what Ouspensky wrote about in *In Search of the Miraculous*. The work and ideas of Gurdjieff were to become and remain a focus of my study and a guiding light (and challenge) as I continued through my psychedelic years and beyond. As the years progressed, I became more discerning in sorting through its various assertions and teachings. Nevertheless, it remains a significant body of work that is worth acquaintance with.

Its impact on my thinking and experience requires a bit of digression for the reader who is otherwise unfamiliar with it.

The *Miraculous* that Ouspesnky was seeking was an experience of higher states of consciousness, sometimes characterized by him as awareness of higher dimensions (e.g., "The Fourth Dimension") and a sense of eternity. Although I didn't connect the dots at the time, I sensed some connection between what Gurdjieff and Ouspensky were on about and the still vaguely understood possibilities I had experienced with LSD.

The specific content of Ouspensky's *In Search of the Miraculous* notwithstanding, what it fostered was the idea of an existing, cosmic spiritual order that could be — in some ways, anyway — rationally understood and that was at the same time, interconnected with the inner, psychological life of the human being; that there was an elemental interchange to be discovered. And, somehow, there was a thread to be explored flowing between time and eternity.

For Ouspensky, this sense of eternity, in particular, revolved around his concept of *eternal recurrence*, an idea he derived from Friedrich Nietzsche[48]. In a nutshell, it is the idea that we repeat our single lives endlessly. Significantly, this was not integral to what Gurdjieff himself taught, nor strictly in line with Nietzsche's actual views. Ouspensky, regardless read into a few stray comments of Gurdjieff a writ to incorporate this idea as a primary theoretical extension of the "system" which he taught.

This idea would come to influence me for a time and required me to think through and past it to develop, as I penetrated Steiner's thought, a deeper understanding of the idea of repeated lives in the sense of reincarnation and their relationship to the ideas of time and eternity.

Gurdjieff, as Ouspensky recounts in *In Search of the Miraculous*, characterized his path of transformation as "The Fourth Way" as opposed to the ways of the Fakir, The Monk, and the Yogi — that is, spiritual aspirants who worked with the body, the emotions, or the mind. Gurdjieff proposed to work on all three in the midst of daily life as opposed to the retreat to the monastery or the ashram, thereby accelerating the development of the desired higher states of being or consciousness and "harmonious development" of the individual human being. He referred to his method — perhaps wryly— as "haida" yoga, using a Russian word with a sense of "quick." This idea of "working on one's self" amid the world parallels, in some ways, Steiner's concept of the Rosicrucian path, the path of pursuing spiritual development while at the same time being fully engaged with the world.

Gurdjieff's essential assertion was that humanity is "asleep". Individuals are seen as wholly identified with non-essential parts of their being and, consequently, without meaningful freedom and functioning essentially as machines. His characterization was presented in harsh contours, and he was generally dismissive of the aspirations of the everyday specimen of humanity. In the context of Ouspensky's work, Gurdjieff appears to speak magisterially as one in possession of hidden truth. Steiner characterizes the phases of sleep, waking, and non-ordinary consciousness with more carefully graded distinctions; he describes the human being of today as asleep in their *willing* but awake in their *thinking* and essentially dreaming in the *feeling* life.

I struggled against this idea — no one wants to think of themselves as "asleep" and functioning robotically — even as I tried to grasp Gurdjieff's sense of awakening.

An essential part of Gurdjieff's method consisted of self-observation and self-remembering. Through self-observation, one was to learn to see one's habitual, unconscious mechanical behavior, as reflected in what Gurdjieff described as the multiple

I's that one identified with, providing an illusory sense of self, but were, in fact, usurpers of the moment who could come into being temporarily in response to some suggestion or stimulus. However, they would just as readily recede whence they came, leaving the containing self — or the latest situationally conditioned transitory occupant — to deal with the consequences.

Self-remembering is, first of all, the effort to be present in one's experience without losing one's self in identification with it.[49]

Gurdjieff saw the human as threefold, with three "centers" — thinking, emotional, and moving (aligning very well with Steiner's threefold human of thinking, feeling, and willing). One is to observe how a given "I" can be associated with a given thought, feeling, posture, or movement. Observing this, one sees how the operation of one function can trigger an automatic and unconscious response from another function.

Self-remembering can be understood in part as the practice of non-identification with the "transitory," usurping I's. To begin with, one cultivates the neutral "witness" who observes and records the behavior with detachment. This development of the witness is a generally recognized essential spiritual practice.

These practices can be seen as a conscious cultivation of a particular type of dissociative state; Gurdjieff himself advised that no one can practice it continuously without it driving them crazy. And indeed, I certainly found that it could induce a definite kind of anxiety. Much later, I would realize how this mirrors, from the other side as it were, Steiner's description of how these functions (thinking, feeling, and willing) spontaneously disassociate as one moves into higher cognitive states.

Ouspensky and Gurdjieff also discussed drugs — principally opiates, hashish, and cocaine — as potentially having a secondary role in the path of self-development. However, their times were essentially pre-psychedelic as far as the Eurocentric universe was concerned. Nevertheless, it seemed the path and methods they were discussing somehow aligned with the domain of psychedelic possibilities. Their "taking notice" of drugs as potentially useful tools appeared to validate the correlation of the LSD experience with a path aligned along Gurdjieff's lines.

Gurdjieff's cosmological scheme was vast, breathtaking, and challenging. It is perhaps comparable in scope and complexity to some of the abstruse schemes in the Kaballah[50]. Gurdjieff explained that underlying everything was the action of what he called "the law of the octave."[51]

This both captivated and puzzled me from the start. My intuition told me *there is something in all this*, but it was only years later that I came to see the ways in which one could see in it an "operationally correct" description of things. Gurdjieff's explication of his teaching is, in my view, somewhat misleading, but it was again part of his method to make his students unearth his true meanings. Although it is, in one sense, a non-musical abstraction, an understanding of the primal phenomenon of musical experience is in the end a prerequisite for a deeper understanding of these ideas. I was at the point I encountered these ideas more or less untutored in musical theory, having failed repeatedly at piano, violin, and guitar as a child.

It is essentially a model for understanding the possible alignment or coherence of the individual with the cosmic harmony of the spiritual world.

Gurdjieff would weave the operation of this "law" into his cosmological ideas, depicting the whole of creation as a scale, with correspondences from planetary to galactic objects representing individual notes. This, of course, is similar to the idea of the "divine monochord" of, for example, the mystic Robert Fludd;[52] and can be seen as having points of contact with the "Word" of St. John's Gospel and the "Om" seed-syllable of Hinduism.

Without going further into all this, the most directly relevant takeaway is how he derives from his system a scale of *energies* of different degrees which as it were, "fuel" higher psychological functions — that is, higher states of consciousness.

I would shortly find that elements of this scheme were employed by psychedelic explorer John Lilly,[53] who was soon to become a significant influence and who, in turn, had adopted them through his contact with Oscar Ichazo[54].

Related to his teaching of cosmoses and energies was the "food diagram,"[55] which presented schematically an image of the energetic interaction of the three kinds of "food" as Gurdjieff told it: the regular food we eat; secondly, air, and as a third kind of food, "sense impressions." These ideas, too, became profound riddles to me, which I carried over into my study of anthroposophy much later. These ideas later would shed light on certain more obscure threads in Steiner's thought.

Although we have the commonplace saying that something is "food for thought," it was to me a superficially *very* odd (and intriguing) teaching that sense impressions could be considered "food" for the human organism. Or, more specifically, an energetic substance that can create the "fuel" needed for higher states of consciousness.

As someone already consuming a pill (by mouth, a kind of "food") and experiencing an intensive modification of consciousness, this idea was particularly interesting. In connection with this, I remember a conversation with a girl on the blacktop in front of the cafeteria at school, where she rather weightily commented, "LSD made me realize what food is." That is, something powerfully energetic that we transform into *ourselves*, our own being, our own consciousness.

Gurdjieff's system also incorporated a scheme of "reciprocal maintenance" — the idea of a "Chain of Being" which functions together to maintain existence in a kind of "cosmic ecology." This idea was later found in Steiner, again expressed rather differently.

Ouspensky's version of Gurdjieff's "system" also includes a theory of "eternal recurrence," which is the idea that everything in the universe, most significantly, our own lives, repeats endlessly, exactly, again and again. Think of the film *Groundhog Day*[56], but without memory of the previous iteration. Ouspensky characterizes this as a form of doom that can only be escaped if one can achieve a certain consciousness "outside of time." Only in this way can fatefully bad decisions be avoided and destiny altered. Ouspensky understands recurrence as the idea that at death, "something" in our being is transferred back in time to the moment of our birth, at which point we exist exactly as before. Alternatively, across trillions of years, the entire universe eventually exhausts all possible material combinations, returns to its initial (material) starting point, and repeats the cycle identically. In all this, Ouspensky has the belief that with the right kind of inner work, it is possible to change from one recurrence to the next.

The eternal existence of things occurring in time is, meanwhile, and from a quite different perspective, essential to understanding what will be found when we start to look at Steiner's understanding. Many aspects of his worldview emerge from a clairvoyant consciousness characterized as being able to "read" in the *Akashic*[57] chronicle. Eternal recurrence is, for me, an awkward attempt to picture things of time from an eternal (timeless) perspective — or, conversely, to picture eternity from the perspective of time.

The *Akasha* refers to the finest, spiritualized etheric substance from which the universe is ultimately formed. The universe is essentially created and organized within the consciousness of spiritual beings. The Akashic chronicle is essentially a record of conscious experience — existing timelessly.

Another reading in the fall of my senior year included Carlos Castaneda's[58] *The Teachings of Don Juan*.[59] I think this was making the circuit of "drug books" and was read first rather in the manner of Hunter Thompson's *Fear and Loathing in Las Vegas*[60] — a wild book about drugs. Castaneda's book clearly indicated that there were realms to be explored, however, that were a bit "farther out" than what our garden variety "teenage kid" tripping was like. The early series of Castaneda books were to captivate me over the next few years — until the realization that a fair amount of charlatanry was involved and that Don Juan was a pious fraud at best.

Around this time, my friend Ruth — with whom I had tripped, along with others, for the first time that fall — commented to me, having read Castaneda herself, that likely "we couldn't have trips like that, you need to be an Indian or something." I contradicted this thought as illogical and affirmed that we could (or perhaps should) seek such states far from our ordinary psychedelic trips for ourselves if we wanted to. This conversation presaged what was to be an ongoing back-and-forth with her along the theme of "what is possible" as my psychedelic experience expanded.

That fall, discovered in my mother's library, was a copy of Alan Watts'[61] *The Book: on the Taboo Against Knowing Who You Are*[62]. Alan Watts is a whole topic in himself. Still, the leavening takeaway from this first book of his I read was my discovering the idea that, gosh, I myself may be God (just as everyone else was, of course) — just particularized into the form of my present self — and, after the manner of the Hindu God Krishna, absorbed in the divine *Lila* or play which, as Watts described, was essentially a game of hide-and-seek. I was to read several of Watts' other books, including his *The Joyous Cosmology*[63] (subtitled, *Adventures in the Chemistry of Consciousness*) — which was to be a significant influence a few years later, as will be described subsequently. He was a leading figure in the West Coast Zen - Beatnik - Psychedelic - Esalen[64] scene.

At some deep level, I bought into this idea — at any rate, abstractly — that yes, of course, I (and we) are God. Non-dualistically. So much so that sometimes, this thought inhibits me from relating to the divine whole-heartedly solely as a creature, which is a wish that I can sometimes feel a longing for. Meanwhile, however, as I exist and know myself, it would seem I am not a bundle of purely sacred attributes. This extreme of non-dualism also plays into the Buddhist idea that the only reality is the original Buddha mind and that, therefore, the only valid goal of spiritual striving is *nirvana* (or Hindu *moksha*). This attitude tends to motivate a world-denying spirit that I find myself disinclined to; or rather; I aspire to a world-affirming, evolutionary interpretation of our cosmic situation.

Somewhere that fall along with all this, my mother finally was to confront me about my marijuana use. Although everyone in town knew there was a huge teenage drug scene, very few parents wanted to probe too deeply into the question of the possibility of their own child's drug use. In my mother's case, whatever suspicions she must have had were confirmed when she found a package of rolling papers in my denim jacket, which she was (thoughtfully) going to launder for me. I gave her a more or less unvarnished picture of the scope of my drug use (but I'm sure minimizing the frequency). This included telling her about my LSD use, and I remember being somewhat disappointed that she did not want to ask me about what it was like for me. I suppose expressing intellectual curiosity would have interfered with her role as keeper of the straight and narrow. My drug use being outed, this naturally led to their use being "forbidden," which, as a thing to be taken seriously, lasted for me, I think, two or three weeks. My friend Ted's parents also had recently caught wise around this time, this, along with his report card resulted in his being transferred out of school, held back a year, and sent to a private boarding school a few towns away. Where ironically, the bored and unsupervised kids tend to do a lot of drugs.

As all of these events, studies, and readings were developing throughout the fall, the final weeks of 1971 loomed, and two key things happened further.

First, Ted and I dosed on some hits of windowpane acid. There is nothing particularly unique about "windowpane" other than the medium: it is a tiny sliver of a transparent gelatin sheet impregnated with LSD. A couple of factors, however, led to this being, on the whole, a mostly unpleasant experience for me: to begin, it was a more potent dose than the "usual" (whatever that meant, exactly) one that we had perhaps expected. Greatly complicating the situation, I hadn't coordinated the timing of things such that I had come up with a suitably convincing cover story with my parents that would allow me to stay out all night. We spent the early part of the evening at a teen dance at a church downtown, which would have ended around eleven or so — that is, absent some alternative plan, the time when my parents expected me to be home. The problem was we were still peaking. For a reason I can't recall, Ted needed to borrow my car — that is, my parent's car — and pick someone up or some other errand, so he dropped me off at home and then left, promising to return the car later. Before dropping me off, we drove around a bit and observed with incredulity how our arms were "magically" steering the car as, due to the trails we would see whenever we moved the steering wheel, we couldn't distinguish the "actual" position of our hands at any particular moment. Relax and enjoy it.

Although driving like this under the influence of LSD is a rather terribly irresponsible thing to do, on the order of drinking and driving, my sense — for what it is worth as a phenomenon, not as a justification — was that despite the disassociation involved, one really could "relax" and trust the body and its reflexes to know what to do, at least in an unchallenging driving situation. It is an example of the kind of disassociated independent functioning that can occur in certain psychedelic states. Later, however, it will be seen how unexpected challenges can completely upset the psychic applecart.

Before the start of my senior year, my older brother had married and moved out of the house. I moved into his downstairs bedroom, which had its own back-door entryway. That night I snuck in, kept the lights off, and climbed into bed, signaling perhaps with a shout to my parents that I was home.

I lay in bed, fully tripping, with a strong undertone of anxiety. I was afraid lest my parents would come in and want to speak to me, which I was concerned that I couldn't manage without the likelihood of triggering their suspicions. Fighting against the trend of the psychedelic stream is a painful struggle. It simply amplifies the sense of threat that provoked one to try and suppress things in the first place.

I began to imagine all sorts of things based on various noises — unmuffled cars roaring in the street blocks away; the noise of the engines seemed demonic; the sound of (so I would think) my older sister coming home from her date and my father, for some reason, upbraiding her for coming home late — likely a projection of my own fear of being confronted by my father; the sound later of Ted dropping the car off — with my hypersensitive listening, I felt sure he would be attracting my parent's attention.

I imagined catastrophic scenarios from each of these — experienced as if they were actually occurring: that Ted lost control of the car in the driveway and plowed through a flowerbed, that my father had some angry blowup with my sister. All the while, I was trying to be quiet and still as a mouse, although I was pulsing inside. Although these pictures seemed real and triggered by actual sounds, another part of me had to consider they were perhaps fabrications of my tripping mind.

Somewhere in all this, arising from the deep anxiety I felt in my chest, the then-current on the airwaves song by the Temptations[65], *Ball of Confusion*,[66] materialized in my head like an earbug, complete with a psychedelic visualization of the whole earth globe boiling over with war, with rioting, with inter-generational, racial, military, and cultural strife and, in general, a pre-apocalyptic conflict. Of course, there was plenty of actual social and geopolitical turmoil in play and in the news at the time to inspire both the song and the apocalyptic scenario. This was all a symptom of the developing tensions and conflicts in the outer world alongside my teenage soul with its "secret life."

At length, perhaps hours, I shut this all out and was able to get to sleep.

When I awoke the next day, everything was apparently no worse for the wear. The car was parked in the driveway with the keys under the mat, and the flowerbed was intact. My father and sister behaved normally. But not a fun trip overall.

The *Imagination* of the *Ball of Confusion* I experienced is an example of how psychedelics can animate a vivid internal dreaming-perceiving which can be a picture of some reality — in this case, both of the world and my own inner state. As William Blake said: "Fear and Hope are — Vision!"[67].

The other notable event that fall was pivotal. Some weeks after the windowpane trip, my mother (the drug prohibition having faded into the category of things not talked about) brought to my attention, sitting together at our kitchen table, an interview in *Psychology Today*[68]. The subject was John Lilly, as interviewed by Sam Keene; Lilly was soon to become well-known as a psychedelic explorer, as established by the publication of his forthcoming book, *The Center of the Cyclone*.[69]

My mother had subscribed to *Psychology Today* for years, and I often read it with interest. But, curiously, what had intrigued her the most was Lilly's description of experiencing what we nowadays, in new-age speak, describe as "Spirit Guides" — higher beings from another realm, experienced in altered states of consciousness, and, particularly as Lilly recounted, conditions of extreme distress — including psychedelic states. The article also went into his experience with Dolphin communication, isolation tanks, LSD research, and finally, his participation in the early days of the Arica Institute[70]. I don't recall her saying anything one way or the other about the LSD part of the story, although it was a central element.

Well, the whole article captured my interest, and his new book was on my list of gifts asked for and received at Christmas — along with Gurdjieff's *Beelzebub's Tales to his Grandson*[71], Arthur Avalon's (aka Sir John Woodroffe 1865 - 1936) *The Serpent Power*, the classic reference on Kundalini yoga, and also Castaneda's second book, *A Separate Reality*. I can't say whether the gift of a book about psychedelic drugs to their sixteen-year-old son was an act of naïveté, parental indulgence, or — wisdom.

The whole flavor of Lilly's book was both "far-out" and, at the same time, presented a cooly rational facade. This latter was appealing, no doubt, to my parents — as well as to the "boy scientist" in me. I had absorbed science with the enthusiasm of a child of the sputnik[72] era and was still baselining my "how does the universe work" paradigm largely on it, despite the shifting sands of my latest thoughts. The jacket flap proclaimed the book "offers a rational and scientific explanation of how the mind operates in the LSD states and other special states of consciousness, however achieved."

The gift's effective wisdom, or lucky blessing, was to become all but instantly apparent within a week. I consumed the book in the three days after Christmas and made headway on the other books. It spoke to many possibilities of "higher" consciousness through LSD and also to an intersect with the Esalen scene, where Lilly wound up for a time. He recounts several very far-out, any way you look at it, LSD explorations, many of them pursued in the isolation tank he developed — floating in body-temperature saline in the dark, for hours at a time, while on pure, high-dose Sandoz[73] LSD. Lilly's isolation tank eventually evolved into the "floatation tank," which persists today as a sort of meditative "spa treatment" in centers sprinkled here and there.

He also devotes a whole chapter to what he titles, perhaps with overtones of Dante, "A Guided Tour of Hell." The "bad trip" or simply "bummer" was already a well-known possibility in psychedelic culture and was assiduously avoided to the extent possible — certainly in our little cabal. In Lilly's case, he was given over to an experience where he came face to face with the soul-crushing spiritual implications of some of his deep-seated core beliefs arising from his training as a scientist.

This is consistent with the general amplifying nature of the psychedelic experience: it can amplify and extend in a psychologically intense "real-feeling imagination" your own deep-seated psychology in terms of beliefs, assumptions, fears, and so on — whatever underlies your approach to living your life. The psychedelic explorer needs to be prepared to confront these beliefs and fears as if in some magic mirror.

Lilly, an M. D. who did extensive research in neurophysiology, had developed a model of the human mind as a kind of "biocomputer,"[74] and he had come to describe psychedelic drugs as "metaprogramming" agents — tools to allow the "self-metaprogrammer" within the biocomputer to rewrite the software of their mind. The essence of his "guided tour of hell" experience was that he began to see himself as quite literally "nothing but" a "program" within a much larger "cosmic computer" that was the underlying reality of existence.

Connected with this was the most timely takeaway in my reading — his assessment after his negative trip of how important it was to be and remain present and conscious for the negative experience, no matter what happened, to have an active observer at least "recording" the episode.

> At no point during an either negative or a positive experience of a high energy level, can one afford to shut off one's consciousness," he states. "If one is going through a pure negative experience, the extreme negative emotion should be allowed to be imprinted on this negative space so that one's self-metaprogammer does not return there.[75]

I observed, somewhat paradoxically, that despite his trip's hellishness, he retains the "self-metaprogrammer" and "biocomputer" models. From a certain angle, this model can be empowering in the sense that we have the agency to change the beliefs that determine our experience of reality, but it seemed at the same time to reinforce his hellish vision of the cosmic computer.

A passing memory of that week was of hanging out with Ruth and Annie at Annie's house, listening to records. Ruth suggested that I check out the music of the group. Yes, whose *The Yes Album* was starting to get traction. Their music became an inspiring companion, especially during my psychedelic years.

When New Year's Eve came a few days after finishing the book, I would again be, in my typical teenage fashion, in pursuit of appropriate holiday revelry. I was somewhat at loose ends; Alan and that set of friends, my likely first choice, had made some plans without me. I was to instead hang out with another group, that of my friend Milo's. As I mentioned, this set was a bit more inclined to a genuine "hippie" worldview, as opposed to the somewhat more socially prevalent "let's party" mentality, which was that of my immediate circle of Alan and Ted. Anyway, I was up for action and had some acid. It wasn't the windowpane but something I had picked up recently — I would acquire hits of acid simply as available to maintain the option of tripping when desired. I was feeling enthused by the expansive parts of Lilly's book. I persuaded one of Milo's friends, Raymond, to drop with me. We had never tripped together before, and he was reluctant, but I coaxed him, and for the moment, prevailed. We crushed it up and snorted it (an experiment in faster absorption that had worked well before, the tablet itself was likely milk sugar), but after ten minutes, he changed his mind and managed to blow it all out of his nose — interestingly, something you can't easily do (change your mind) if you (as typically) swallow the pill.

I had no experience with this acid, and there was a vague suspicion that it was on the low-potency side.

Raymond's abandonment of our planned psychedelic adventure had cooled my excitement, and we soon wound up going to a party we had heard about. There were around fifty or so kids there, no parents, lots of drugs and alcohol. People just hanging out. At first, it seemed to me that I was not getting off, aligning with my vague suspicion of the low potency of the drug. My memory of the party is primarily one of sitting with two or three other guys, drinking a half gallon of white wine between us, and smoking more than a few joints, chatting and laughing — it seemed fun and jolly. This must have gone on for hours until, eventually, midnight rolled around. There was champagne, and a hash pipe was passed around. I had to pee, so I went outside, the bathroom being in high demand. Naturally, it was cold — wintertime in New England — and I think this gave me a bit of a shock as I had stepped out without my coat. Standing outside, I realized, "gee, I guess the acid did kick in," but I was so otherwise drunk and stoned that it was just another part of the toxic brew I had concocted. This level of binging was a bit extreme even for me and was carelessly engaged in, with the justifying thought that, after all, it was New Year's Eve.

Finally, somewhere between midnight and one, my friends all started to leave, heading back to Milo's house. There was a toast to the new year, another hit on the hash pipe. I grabbed another one of my friends who needed a ride, and together we drove back.

The party had been on the far side of town. I was driving my parent's car, and I realized that I was entirely out of it as soon as I started going. I now fully realize, yes, I'm tripping! The car seemed to be driving itself, and we had no idea where we were — each fork in the road seemed the same; there appeared to be almost no connection between my brain, the steering wheel, and the road. The route was mostly along back roads, so we didn't have to deal with other cars. Somehow at length, primarily directed turn by turn by my passenger, Max (who certainly would have been less intoxicated than I was), we managed to arrive safely, somewhat surprised, relieved, and impressed with ourselves. It helped that Milo lived near Max's house, so his homing instinct was at work.

I remember going inside to warm myself for a bit, then going out to join a circle of friends who were gathered there smoking a joint. Milo's parents were at home; they were on the "cool" side (but not so cool we could smoke pot in the house); that is, they were tolerant and of the "we'd rather they were here safe than out wherever doing who knows what" persuasion.

Six or seven of my friends formed a circle, standing in the snow, about twenty feet from the house. I strode forward eagerly: and then, about eight feet away from them, I suddenly found myself lunging to the ground, vomiting forcefully at their feet.

I continued vomiting and was brought into the house into the bathroom. Milo's younger brother Andy very compassionately held and comforted me as I continued puking into the toilet.

It was now an unbelievably miserable situation. I couldn't stop vomiting. It's not a fun thing at all to be doing while you are at the same time tripping. I simultaneously wanted to be taken to the hospital and given morphine or whatever so I could pass out, and I was terrified that that would happen. By now, all the hallmarks of the psychedelic were present in the sense of hyper-awareness — the drug was breaking through the alcohol stupor, and my mind was racing around in panic.

At the same time, *something* in me was hanging on. Having just read Lilly's *The Center of the Cyclone*, and its "Guided Tour of Hell," I clung to the necessity to not black out during extreme negative states: to remain conscious so that one can learn and imprint the lessons of the hellish experiences.

And so I hung on, clinging to the toilet until the vomiting had exhausted itself. Milo's parents put me to bed in his sister's room; and also, very kindly, made an excuse to my parents the next morning with the story that I had just "mixed beer with liquor" that night. I went home to my room, and during the next three days, I was sleeping and semi-delirious. In a way, it was like a modern-day re-enactment (or perhaps, a caricature) of a three-day "temple sleep" initiation. Apparently, on the third day, I rose. I recall various surreal dreams and visions that felt inspired by, among other things, the Castaneda book I had been reading.

The whole thing was really, really awful, but something in me had been steeled to be able to remain present while in the state of being all but utterly out of control under the influence of LSD. Apparently, my sense of having this inner resource was to prove a critically valuable prerequisite.

4

Incipit Vita Nova

Being young and all, I was pretty much back on my feet after my three days. I was aware of having survived an ordeal.

Through January and February of the new year, I don't recall dropping acid after the New Year's episode, although it is entirely possible that I did, again recreationally. However, I do know that within a couple of weeks, I was back to feeling, give or take a little, my usual self — looking into the calendar of rock performances at my high school, I can recall being fully "present and accounted for" at a J. Geils[76] rock concert at our high school around the third week of January.

Other things were happening. I had basically given up on my physics class, after a valiant last-minute cram for the midterm, which pulled me somehow back up to a B for the semester, despite having been absent the second quarter.

And then, somewhere in February, I happened into an all too short relationship with Erin. Although I had been quite interested in girls since I was around eleven and had various dating, hand-holding, and the odd kissing occasions, nothing had blossomed into anything resembling a serious boyfriend/girlfriend relationship. Erin was a lovely connection that serendipitously happened and quickly became, while not full-on sexual, intimate, and playful at the get-go. The way it unraveled following my next psychedelic episode was the loss of a connection dear and sweet, which I look back on both fondly and with regret.

After really little more than a couple of weeks of this budding romance, two things happened.

One was that I went away for a self-guided weekend "consciousness exploration" (or some such) retreat with my then-friend Ash, who I think I had induced to read Lilly's book by then.

Ash and his family had moved into town around the same time that George left. We developed a connection that included an interest in psychedelics and its farther-out possibilities. We were to trip together a number of times and, of course, spend a fair amount of time smoking pot and generally hanging out. He was in the class below me and intersected with several social groups.

We planned to hole up in the charming carriage house that my older brother and his wife were now living in, in New Jersey, where they had a spare room. Interestingly, it was a finished room accessed by walking from their apartment through an unfinished attic, which gave it a sort of a *Magician's Nephew*[77] vibe. We didn't have a clear program in mind. We didn't have any psychedelics, although quite probably some pot. However, we did bring a boxful of books that we were somehow going to study and cram over the weekend as part of a quest, if not for enlightenment, at least for "higher consciousness."

The carton-load of books we brought along was indicative of how quickly I was hoovering up all manner of mystic and psychedelic texts, the contents of which rapidly filtered into my internal frame of reference.

Since the beginning of my senior year — starting with *Siddhartha*, *Gestalt Therapy Verbatim*, *The Book*, *In Search of the Miraculous*, and *The Center of the Cyclone*, as I have mentioned already, I had been on a tear reading all — as my lights attracted me to — that I could find about spiritual and self-development matters.

Although the number of books we dragged along outweighed any capacity to actually read them during a weekend, I did, however, read two things that made a big impression: Jung's[78] introduction to the *Tibetan Book of the Dead* (found in my parent's copy of *Psyche and Symbol*[79], a Jung anthology), and *The Joyous Cosmology* by

Alan Watts, his idealized psychedelic journey. These were both preparatory catalysts for what was soon to come.

We may also have done some awkwardly-informed breathing exercises or some such — likely, some meditations cribbed from Lilly's book or else from Ram Dass' *Be Here Now*[80].

In Jung's *Commentary on the Tibetan Book of the Dead*, I read with fascination his comments on the *Chonyid Bardo*[81] which he quotes as follows below:

> Then the Lord of Death will place round thy neck a rope and drag thee along; he will cut off thy head. tear out thy heart, pull out thy intestines, lick up thy brain, drink thy blood, eat thy flesh, and gnaw thy bones: but thou will be incapable of dying. Even when thy body is hacked to pieces, it will revive again.
>
> The repeated hacking will cause intense pain and torture.

Jung's text goes on to describe this as the "disintegration of the wholeness of the Bardo body, which is a kind of subtle body constituting the visible envelope of the psychic self in the after-death state."[82] While I didn't quite know what to do with this image, it presaged in a certain way the psychological deconstruction that was to come.

Watts *Joyous Cosmology* is a charming account of an idealized psychedelic voyage. I think it helped me to organize inwardly certain trends forming in my psychedelic thoughts and aspirations. It blends experiences and characterizations I could recognize as "typically psychedelic" with elements of the spiritual perspectives I found in his book *The Taboo Against Knowing Who You Are*. It ends with a cosmic vision more or less analogous to Dante's epiphany of the *Celestial Rose*[83] at the culmination of the *Paradiso*. It had a certain completeness that I internalized whispering to myself, "Yes, I would like to have a trip like that."

The only other particularly distinct memory of that weekend is recalling the fascination that overcame me while gazing at pewter candlestick holders my brother and his wife had in their living room. When I later read about Jacob Boehme[84] being inwardly transformed by the glance of sunlight on a pewter dish, I thought of this. My "slightly rewired" sense perceptions from my dozens of acid trips had heightened my sensitivity to subtle lighting effects in my environment.

With everything I had been reading, I was, it would seem, prepping for some new, transformational psychedelic journey. Although I didn't have any clear notion of how I might precipitate such an event — how I might transition my psychedelic use from recreational "thrill seeking" into real *seeking* — I did have a conviction that states of consciousness like those of Lilly, Castaneda, and Watts were possible *for me*.

That was the first thing; the second was that I think either immediately before or after the weekend cloistered at my brother's, Erin came down with a bad cold or flu, and I didn't see her for most of the following week, as she didn't come to school (I did have a very brief visit with here at home that was ended abruptly when her mom found us making out in her bedroom). By the end of the week, she had almost recovered, and we had made a plan to go to the last performance of the school play (the psychodrama *David and Lisa*). I was very much looking forward to seeing her again that Saturday night.

As Saturday rolled around, things developed rather differently.

Without Erin to meet with (who incidentally was younger than my friends and me), I naturally reverted to hanging out with my usual group of classmates. Meanwhile, the high school troupe of players always had a traditional cast party after the last show, and somehow it had been organized that the party was to be held at my friend Alan's house — while his parents were out of town, as they very often were. The house was a classy, very architecturally modern made-to-be-a-party-house. Alan, Ash, and several other of my friends had roles in the play. With his parents away, the word was already out that it was to be a much bigger and wilder party than the more staid and chaperoned usual cast party.

By late morning, as Alan's parents were known to be away, his house had already become the hang-out magnet for my immediate circle of friends. Along with Alan and Ted, our friends Ruth and Annie were already there when I showed up.

Sometime in the early afternoon, someone had the not terribly unusual idea amongst our group that we all drop acid at the party that night. Someone knew a kid who had just come into hundreds of tabs of orange sunshine that he was dealing. I remember we scraped together some money and drove to where he was, down the beach road a mile or so. I remember him counting out the twenty or so hits we bought from his baggie chock full of orange "barrels" of sunshine. At least a dozen of us would wind up dropping acid by the time the party really started after the play was over. I was immediately caught up in the buzz.

Some fairly short time after we got back, Ruth and Annie wanted to drop right away — they were just hanging out and weren't going to the show that night. They were ready to start the party. It seemed like a reasonable idea, and since it was still (somewhat) early, I figured I could get it together to pick up Erin later. I also probably didn't want to be "missing out" while hanging out all afternoon while Ruth and Annie were tripping. At this point, my default assumption was that I would be functional on acid, although I suppose I also didn't really think appropriately hard about it but rather just went with the moment's impulse.

What I hadn't quite reckoned on was, first, that I had, for some time now, been half-consciously prepping myself for an acid trip at "the next level" and more particularly, the *very* much higher-than-average dosage that these hits contained. My guess is that it was quite likely the genuine "Brotherhood of Eternal Love"[85] orange sunshine, which clocked in between 300 and 350 micrograms — quite a dose. But I *didn't* have the "mystical journey" intention formed consciously; just a fun trip at a party, along with a welcome date with my girlfriend (who I'm sure would have been a bit surprised had I shown up "merely" very high and tripping to pick her up — I don't think we had so much as smoked a joint together, and doubt she had a notion I was such a psychedelic enthusiast).

Again, as none of us had done this new "flavor" of acid before, we didn't know what to expect. Ruth and Annie had likely done half a tab each, but I (by default, really) did a whole. Most doses of acid I had taken were more likely in the 150 to 200 microgram range —

powerful, but with experience, manageable. Although looking at the series of events, my two previous trips (the windowpane and the New Year's Eve party) hadn't been entirely "manageable".

I remember next going to watch TV by myself while I was waiting to get off. A Marx Brothers movie was on, and I lay on the couch in the little TV area adjacent to the kitchen downstairs, watching it. After what seemed like only fifteen or twenty minutes, I began to feel the typical wave of mild nausea and vague unease, coupled with the onset of visual effects — colors, "hallucinations," visual trails. The black and white Marx Brothers video became overlayed with transparent pastel colors and became a bit hard to follow.

There are any number of visual and sensory phenomena associated with the psychedelic state at the lower-middle dosage range and/or as part of the "neophyte" range of sensations, and I was already very familiar with them; the overload of this type of sensory phantasmagoria was a big part of the ostensible feeling we were pursuing.

The observing mind can, to begin, readily categorize this realm of the psychedelic simply as mere "hallucinations" or "disturbances" of the normal sensory apparatus — somewhat in the manner, for example, of the way we can provoke the display of geometric colored forms by closing our eyes and rubbing them. Psychedelic visual effects are, however, much more intense, continuous, and "overlaid" on top of our "normal" sense of reality than the phosphenes seen when rubbing our eyes. And we can categorize strange bodily sensations — the typical "acid rush" — as "nothing but" happenings in the body. Even amplified feelings of euphoria or anxiety can be localized as somehow "of the body" or simply "a feeling" in the same way we associate our day-to-day awareness with being closely associated and identified with our bodily form. And about this, we may have any number of opinions or beliefs as to the degree of dependency of our psychic being upon our bodily nature. Likewise, if we feel ourselves "psychically energized" — our thoughts being driven into new angles, rhythms, and perspectives — we can still consider these thoughts as our private affair, taking place entirely walled off from the happenings of the outer world.

In general, although such experiences could grow very intense, our collective approach, as mentioned earlier, was to keep the more absorbing phenomena relegated to the background. We would avoid allowing attention to them to persistently become the foreground of consciousness. There was a general subtext that "this way madness lies," packaged in a veneer of "we're too cool for all of that 'far-out' stuff."

This begs the question: what were we all really looking for in pursuing these states? Certainly, we sought a "high" and exhilaration; escape from the bounds of the "normal" — but definitely within a structure that maintained (or tried to maintain) some sort of safety net against the drug getting the upper hand.

Although I wasn't clearly aware of how my own inner shifts relative to all this would affect the way my psychedelic use would unfold, I was soon to find out.

While I was watching the Marx Brothers, Ruth and Annie had gone upstairs to lie down in the dark and listen to music while they got off. As I was now definitely starting to get off myself, I went upstairs to see how they were doing. It was a short walk up the stairs and down the hall, but it transpired that the onset of the drug accelerated rapidly and continued to intensify, it seemed, with *each step*. I was no longer "starting to get off." I was rocketing off the launch pad.

As I approached the doorway to the bedroom at the end of the upstairs hallway, a moment came when I began to very rapidly go through a complete transformation of my sense of embodiment. As I walked down the hall, looking and thinking ahead to my destination, I began to feel and know that my thoughts were quite literally swimming out of my head, out of my body, I began sensing my reality in an entirely new and different way. All of my previous psychedelic trips, insofar as they comprised visual or perceptual changes, were overlaid upon the "everyday" sense-world, or else were "close your eyes and go inside" affairs, where the "inside" was distinctly bound by one's skull. It had seemed, these earlier modifications in the sense of reality were self-generated. That is, it seemed that one would most likely try to explain it as reflecting "nothing but" a (profound) shift in our brain processes.

Thoughts familiarly known and seen as "inside" now became forcefully detached from my inner space; and seemed to swim, as elemental living beings, with their own form and impulse of activity, propelled by a wave of force pushing up my spine and bubbling out of my head. I felt as if I were one step away from floating out of the body, and that the tight association between one ordered thought and the next, as managed by my "reasoning self" had given way to a dismembered thought structure, and that I had "spilled over" into a broader reality. In my new reality, thought was of an entirely different quality. Everything outside of me became part of a new world permeated by a livingness of a nature similar to my, by now, much more vital inner "thought" experience. It was a complete rupture from the shell of consciousness I had known and identified with *my whole life* to this point.

To begin to experience thought in this way is to gain a sense of what Rudolf Steiner means when he describes our everyday thoughts as "corpses" of the living thought that is the underlying spiritual reality.

There was a brief period of transition as I beheld the process first, entirely from "within," and then as the thoughts tumbled out of me, so did my sense of being enclosed within the surface of my skin. My "presence" was enlarged such that my sense of connection to my body — which I naturally identified as "my self" — was somehow loosened.

I now understand that this process was an extension, or variation, of the same dissociative trend observed in a much less intense form during my first trip. At that time, while talking with my mother, I struggled with a mild aphasia — due to my limited ability to draw thoughts into connection. Now the "disassociation" was from the adhesion of my thoughts to the "bag of skin"[86] I hitherto believed I was inside of.

This was a completely novel state, unlike anything that had happened to me in my previous dozens of LSD trips, yet it seemed immediately valid — something was happening to my deepest inner soul-spiritual structure.

What came into focus was a world where the sense-perceptible was still present, but there was a new dimension to it that was more than simply overlaid colors and patterns, and could be described as a saturated background of vividness, of livingness, of soul-quality. Something of my soul having spilled out, everything was possessed of soul to a degree; everything was alive in its degree;

and moreover, was embedded within a sense of space that was again, as a background, all-pervading and alive and permeated by living elemental thought. Not merely painted in pretty colors but *alive* as a living thought organism.

At the same time, my self, or now, my "formerly inner self," was also an object or entity within this new context and radiated its own quality upon the scene — as if I were simultaneously dreaming the entire time, and my dreams were projected or overlaid onto the now-enlivened domain I had entered. My "self who dreams" was awakened and overlaid on the scene.

This analysis or decomposition into layers of experience as I am describing now was, of course, not recognized as neatly or cogently as I am attempting here; it was, as I said, turbulent and confusing. I was greatly disoriented as I tried to navigate and focus within this space. But, at the same time, it was not entirely unfamiliar; it was somehow obvious that I was living into an enlarged and expanded sense of my own very self, in contrast to the previously understood more narrow type of affair. In a way, this sense that "after all" it was still just an unfolding of *my own* psychic content provided some sense of much-needed ballast.

There must also have been an inner embrace — coupled with trepidation — with the now clear, rapidly accelerating knowledge that the transformational threshold I had been reading about and seeking was now forming itself.

After this initial "transition," I could still perceive my surroundings from one perspective, as before: the room, my body, Ruth lying on one of the twin beds — with the usual "trimmings" of the psychedelic state — I also was at the same time aware that I had passed through the Looking-Glass[87], Alice style; and that my mind needed to adapt (quickly) to a different order of things. There was a part of me that could relate to these changes in, so to speak, the same way the mind adapts itself to the occurrences of the dream state as 'normal'. There was also a background sense that one was in a different phase of reality and that it was perhaps only the next step or level in a series of further phases, yet to be known, discovered, or to unfold upon me.

I wandered over to the other empty bed. Annie must have been in the next room at this point.

Before continuing with the increasingly non-ordinary experience that was to develop, a comment, comparing my state with a description by Rudolf Steiner of the process of going through the first stages of initiation. These of course are described as if occurring in deliberate, disciplined steps and unfolding in a classical, archetypical manner; and as such — as with any description of the spiritual world — are translated into a form that can employ words derived from the world of the senses to paint a picture of a reality that is fundamentally of a different nature.

However, they are useful in clarifying the apparently chaotic dynamics of the psychedelic process — which, as in my case, can quite likely occur without the preparation that Steiner both enjoins and assumes in making his descriptions.

In his work, *Knowledge of the Higher Worlds*[88], he devotes a chapter to the phenomenon of "The Splitting of the Human Personality During Spiritual Training."

He states:

> Still, at the beginning of our spiritual development we perceive things belonging to another world without being able to connect them with our everyday material surroundings.
>
> ... nothing about the way we think, feel or will is arbitrary. Every idea that becomes conscious is connected by natural laws to a particular feeling or act of will. For instance, when we enter a stuffy room we open the window, or when we hear our name called, we answer the call.
>
> ... these seemingly simple connections between thinking, feeling, and willing are the foundations ... upon which our whole life is built.
>
> ... this connection in the finer organism of the soul is reflected in the coarser physical body ... In the course of higher development, however, the

threads connecting these three basic powers are interrupted, severed

Steiner describes this disassociation as taking place as the result of disciplined practice and meditation. Still, the characteristic quality is the same in that the soul feels itself as disjoint, with the connections between thought, feeling and action no longer prompted unconsciously, and with the sense of "self" inherent in these connections completely transformed. Understood correctly, this corresponds largely with Gurdjieff's ideas that in the "awakened" human being, the thinking, feeling, and moving functions operate under *conscious* direction, not functioning by an automatic chain of suggestion and association between them.

And then, as I lay on the bed, I sensed the presence of what seemed to be a dream, alongside my perception of the darkened room; it could be somewhat described as feeling awake while sleeping or of a second being dreaming beside me. I felt the vague presence of otherworldly beings who seemed to be shifting through the images of a futuristic, science-fiction dream, hovering, approaching my earth-existence from somewhere "out there" in the outer-space heavens surrounding the earth.

My eyes closed, but I could "see" in the space above me on the bed. It seemed a group of beings was huddling around me, looking at me, consulting each other — I was aware that they seemed to be conferring with each other. I had the distinct impression that I was being examined by a team of doctors trying to figure out how to "fix" me. I'm unsure what the defect was — that my soul had suddenly spilled out of my body, or some deeper wound or defect? It was also a familiar feeling for me, insofar as I had been injured badly or sick several times as a child, requiring hospitalization and medical attention, with the attendant hovering above of caregivers. This otherworldly visitation was not entirely abnormal-seeming in that I had been socialized to the idea of communion with "higher beings" in psychedelic states through the accounts in Lilly's *The Center of the Cyclone*. In the chapter titled "Guided Tour of Hell," he likewise experienced beings who were trying to "repair" him. And indeed, it seemed I was in more or less the self-same situation, absent that chapter's "cosmic computer" framework.

Then I started to dream inwardly — or more properly, flow into an Imagination — shutting everything out and turning within. Pictures lit up inside of me.

It seemed that my body was like a tree. Its branches were dense and leafy and glowing with light. It further seemed as if the branches of the tree must have been a spiritual picture or imagination of my brain (that thing inside me, now expanding and spilling out above me), the tree trunk my spinal column. My awareness rippled upward across my "head," that is, to the ends of the branches of the tree, like a wind creating a wave through the branches or like a squirrel running and hopping to the ends of the tree limbs. Beyond the edges of the tree was a swelling oceanic ether of light and darkness. Its "space" however, was coincident and overlapping with the space of the physical room I was in and still aware of existing in with my physical body.

In my reverie, I was thus also aware of Ruth lying in the other bed a few feet away from me — as I had come into the room, we must have exchanged a few words. I assumed she was moving through her own onset phase of the acid as she lay in the darkness in the other bed.

Suddenly, my dreamy awareness of her became like a wave rolling through the ocean-ether of the space between us *toward* me: all at once, her image was before me, as a luminous, soul-spirit form, with her essential features delineated in the ripples of light. It was as if she had — in some completely real sense, flowed out of herself, just as I had, and popped into my head — only now of course, my "head" was spilling out of me — as a being composed of light, composed of the radiance of our now freely-floating forms. Somehow her thoughts communicated themselves within me as if they were her spoken word, and she "said" (that is, thought) words to the effect "isn't this cool!" — a likely enough comment — smiling and glowing, a rush of enthusiasm bursting out of her visage of light — the "this" being the shared consciousness-of-light, the dawning expansion. I can call it dream-like to describe its flavor, but it seemed absolutely real; as completely real, though utterly different, as anything known through my senses, but dawning out of an experience of our — as I, at any rate, knew it — body-free selves. There was a palpable sense of contact, like the beating of a wave upon the shore.

From my latter-day anthroposophical understanding, it was like a revelation echoing what Steiner describes as the passage of the soul into the spiritual world every night, where among our other tasks, we meet with those we are connected with in our earthly sphere of existence — although we normally do not retain consciousness of this upon awakening. This quality of having a double existence and a twofold consciousness is one of the great riddles of spiritual knowledge.

I dropped out of this. I stood up. I was suddenly aware of multiple, disconnected planes of my being, levels of myself, domains of energy: one part of which was the pimply hormone-laced teenager, on drugs in a dark room next to a cute teenage girl (and scared to death to contemplate that); part of me was a godly spirit who had just realized what seemed like a timeless, light-filled soul touching — that could easily have been said to have been only a dream. And part of me was just a confused and ill-prepared bystander, trying to make sense of it all.

I spoke her name. I wanted to test my reality and see if she had shared the same state, if I had actually been "touched" by her.

She answered saying simply, "What?"

I felt her presence. What did I want? What did she want? Did we share something, or was that only me? Was there a way to share that moment of connection while relating to the world of outer things?

"Nothing ... " I said, trailing off.

I felt that I couldn't have articulated what had just happened without sounding crazy to her.

This idea of another being speaking "inside" of one's self — and conversely, of speaking to another being "inside" of them — is described repeatedly by Steiner and is a key aspect of the highest stage of spiritual cognition — what he calls Intuition.

There was something very palpable in the scene that echoed the Imagination story of the Garden of Eden before the fall — a man, a woman, and a tree. Suffused with light.

From a more "real-world" perspective, one might describe this all as a projection of the feminine other or, in Jungian terms, the unconscious Anima. Or just a stage in my own expanded soul-awakening process.

For all of that, it was lived as having the touchstone of reality, even within the psychedelic realm where many appearances are recognized as "unreal".

I stood up and began to wander back into the hallway. I can't put what follows into any exact sequence. I don't know how long the gaps of time were; I know it was light outside when I first dropped, and although Alan's room was dark initially, I think the shades were drawn, but it was still light outside. From the moment of walking in the door, however, I was on a roller coaster that I wasn't going to get off of for many hours. I must have had some back-of-mind sense that I was expected by Erin later, but as of that moment, I was struggling to keep my grip on three-dimensional earth reality while completely new soul-spiritual states unfolded. I continued peaking, the dose coming on stronger and stronger.

After some time I went back downstairs to the kitchen; I saw Annie. She smiled appreciatively at my stoned and dazed appearance. The disassociation effects were intensifying, and suddenly, I felt as if my body would no longer cohere, that I was composed of unconnected particles that at any moment would simply fall into a pile of dust. It seemed like an invisible container that held my body together had become unzipped, up and down the front of my body, and my inner contents could fall out. The fact that I still appeared to cohere at all was simply, as it now appeared, merely a habit — one that was rapidly running out of gas.

Transitioning into a knowledge of the spiritual world involves letting go of our point-wise geometry, where everything is believed to be composed of "solid" three-dimensional particles that cohere by physical forces such as gravity. As we habitually identify ourselves with our physical body, the realization that our psychic and physical coherence are not identical — can be distressing! The forces (understood in the sense of Steiner as "etheric" forces) that bind the soul to the body have become "looser" in their adherence to the shape and form of the physical; the "etheric" body, which normally maintains the architecture of the human body, has begun to expand in a manner similar to the way it expands after death when it completely relinquishes its hold on the physical body.

My understanding of Steiner's concept of the etheric is something I only came to in stages. Aside from representing the forces of growth, the etheric forces are also understood as the forces "of the cosmic periphery" — which can be thought of as forces that are polar opposites of the gravity-laden, pointwise image of atomic particles that we usually think of the world as aggregated out of. If gravity makes the apple fall, the forces of the periphery raise the apple above the earth in the first place. Steiner sometimes characterizes etheric forces as a kind of *suction* as opposed to gravity.

A key element to grasping Steiner's concept of the ether and etheric body is found in his use of the ideas of projective geometry[89], a form of non-euclidean geometry also referred to as the geometry of "counter space". It elucidates Steiner's notion of how etheric forces flow from the cosmic periphery, the infinitely distant. When one "gets high," one might start to feel "spaced out" — that "spacey" feeling is one of the hallmarks of what is meant here as the *loosening* of the etheric body.

"What's keeping me together?" I asked Annie. It was an anxious question. Puzzled but amused, she smiled and gestured with her flattened hand, cutting the air in front of me like a knife and tracing a line from the top of my head down to my feet, right along my vertical axis. Her perception of my coherence seemed full of confidence and grounding will forces, so I accepted that I probably wasn't about to fall apart.

"You're — you!" she said emphatically and with mild amusement and laughter. She then led me through the sliding glass doors onto the large lawn at the back of the house. It was dark outside; night had come.

Her eyes sparkled. Everything was throbbing with energy. Although it was now dark outside, everything had a subtle, electric glow. It seemed somehow implied in the situation that both she and Ruth were possessed of greater knowledge of this expanded state that I was in now, so full of bewilderment. I assumed that they had a deep knowledge of the realm I was now awakening to already "under their belts." As they consumed only half a tab each, they were flying a bit lower than I was, which would have accounted for their relative apparent calm. I believed and hoped that they would guide me through what was turning into a journey of initiation.

The lawn was littered with golf balls — Alan's father would practice back there. Annie picked one up and threw it in the air. It created intense and powerful trails and seemed to impart an echo of that energy to each of the balls I could see lying on the lawn, small glints of light in the dark backyard. It seemed there were dozens and dozens of them, replicating all across the lawn, and they were all possessed of some elemental energy. It seemed as if I were surrounded by psychedelic, gnomic, chirping crickets in the form of golf balls. Or golf balls in the form of crickets.

I wandered back inside. I was seriously unsettled and deranged. I felt myself coming to pieces; I could no longer cohere internally. Psychedelics can cause the etheric energies that, as it were, maintain the puppet strings of our wonted self and its habits of feeling, action, and perception, to start to fly apart, thereby upsetting our internal balance, our sense of grounded selfhood. The higher the dosage, the more rapidly and forcefully this will tend to occur.

I walked back upstairs toward Alan's room. The record player was playing "Bitch" from the Rolling Stone's *Sticky Fingers*. It is a very raunchy song if ever there was one: pounding and dripping with sex. It was a current favorite of Ruth's, and she was digging on it. The side[90] was to repeat again several times.

Others had started arriving for the party. Alan and the ones who were in the performance would come later. There was a steady flow of arrivals throughout the evening.

As I again walked down the upstairs hall, it seemed that I heard noises from Denise's room (she was Alan's younger sister). It was the last door on the right before Alan's bedroom door at the end of the hall. Somehow, I began to imagine that an orgy had begun in Denise's room — an orgy of such energy that I could feel it outside the hall. I could feel the sexual-psychic energy of my friends emanating from the room; I could feel it intersecting, interacting, copulating, interpenetrating. With everything loosened inside of me, among other things, my teenage sexual energies were boiling within and projecting outside of me.

I felt excluded; I felt afraid; I felt drawn to it. I opened the door — nothing, only some of the other people hanging out in there.

This specific "imagined orgy," including the sense of exclusion, is a not untypical psychedelic phase, at least as reflected in Timothy Leary and Ralph Metzner's *The Psychedelic Experience*. It also relates to the bardo phase of being drawn to images of copulating couples that are said to draw one back into incarnation.

I began to wander between Denise's room and Alan's, which was still dark. I seemed to take into my soul the whole "Bitch" side of Sticky Fingers album — take it on, identify with it, but profoundly unsure what it meant. "Dreaming" intensely the words and mood of the song formed my soundtrack. I especially felt the song "Dead Flowers" was about me, about me dying — I began to feel that I must be dying.

And you can send me dead flowers every morning

Send me dead flowers by the mail

Send me dead flowers to my wedding

And I won't forget to put roses on your grave

And "Sister Morphine" — I got myself all tangled into some kind of story of self-destructive opiate use, as if were a user. And I felt I was descending deeper and deeper into an unknown reality, where things were, so clearly, not what they had seemed.

Well it just goes to show

Things are not what they seem

Please, Sister Morphine,

Turn my nightmares into dreams

Oh, can't you see I'm fading fast?

And that this shot will be my last

I would hear the words "... the scream of the ambulance" and think it referred to me, that an ambulance was coming for me. Although whatever the calamity or incident that required the ambulance to come was yet to happen, I would think I heard one coming, I sensed it as though my mortal destiny was becoming increasingly critical as the "sound" of the ambulance traversed the space approaching me. I felt that there was a fatality being sorted through the world of possibility. However, I found I had the "magical" power to push away, repel its approach, "no, not now" — possibly, diverting the fatality elsewhere — was it the Irish death coach, the *Cóiste Bodhar*[91], which, once dispatched, cannot return empty?

Shadowed by mortality, I moved into a feeling a sense of deep loss in my connection to my mother if I were to die — that it would make my mother very sad. I didn't want to do that, and this feeling, I think, helped somewhat anchor my grip on outer reality. Many years later, when my mother passed away at a reasonably goodly age, I looked back to those thoughts and feelings as representing in a certain way part of my inner "cutting of the cord" with the mother element, although again, it was at the time felt as grounding.

The Stone's album side kept playing over and over — I would wander in and out, lost, confused, and inwardly distraught.

At one point, having parked myself on the carpeted floor in Denise's s room, Ruth and Annie sat next to each other on the bed and started talking in a very excited, gibberish way — at least, it seemed like gibberish to me, but at the same time, it seemed that they were speaking a language that encoded deep levels of meaning; and as they spoke and gestured, energy would flow back and forth between them and inside them, traversing multiple levels of their being and touching each level with a communication payload before circuiting back. It seemed they were engaged in a deep and very enjoyable communication, referencing realities on multiple dimensions — expressing different semi-autonomous parts of their being, as coordinated by an over-arching self. This scene reinforced my belief that they were on a higher plane of knowing than I was and that they were stable and fully confident interacting on what seemed like multiple levels.

The radical difference in my reality had gone far beyond the initial *Through the Looking Glass* adaptation/adjustment. The perceptions and apparent revelations were accumulating with the net effect of leaving me psychically stunned and barely able to maintain any degree of self-composure. I had a series of Imaginations that haunted me: dream-like pictures, freighted with feeling and reality, representing some underlying soul-spiritual truth. I felt like I could look back on my life as something that had been propelled, like a rocket ship, out of the spiritual world, out of the void, out of the source of creation — propelled to a certain intended destination, with a set amount of fuel — soul fuel of thoughts, feelings, love, desire, wishes, impulses — and that the rocket had now veered horribly off course, and the fuel was almost spent: in other words, there was no more "juice" to fuel my existence in this incarnation — this, *my* life. A science-fiction metaphor for a profoundly distressing sense of self.

Alternatively, this sense could also be interpreted as a "failure to launch" not into the course of my life in earth-existence; but into the psychedelically fueled "higher consciousness" that was possible to me through this state, but falling instead into the gravity field of my lower, unevolved and disorganized, "lower astral body."

This sense of having "spent all my fuel" resonates with the anthroposophical idea that we do indeed come into incarnation with a specific soul-spiritual bundle of forces in our etheric body, forces that we have gathered from the spiritual breadths of the universe, gathered from the cosmic periphery into our individual life-body (etheric body) which, in life, works to build up the human form out of earthly substances. It is viewed as having, in a certain sense, a very definite sum of spiritual forces which are intended to unfold as we live into our earthly destiny and which, in fact, impel us forward to find precisely the life and life situations that we are seeking in our present incarnation. Steiner describes how in the case of a life cut short by accident, for example, the "surplus" of forces can be "used up" and "consumed" very quickly — as if one were to inwardly fast forward through the "planned and provided for" life-existence in the instant of death; or, outwardly, the unconsumed etheric forces "live into" the environment, lending themselves to the broader purposes unfolding in the world. Although we each come into life with an image of the archetypal human being embedded within our formative being, we also have specific karmic, or destined, predispositions. The astrological idea of a birth chart can be understood as a way to conceptualize this individual imprint.

Upon consideration years later of this sense of "spent rocket fuel," I can also understand it as reflecting instead that I was in the process of losing my given, conventional guidance and motivation in life and that the forward motion in pursuit of my destiny would hereafter have to be inwardly self-directed. *Incipit Vita Nova.*[92]

In anthroposophy, the etheric body is also understood as a "time body" — that is, the spiritually formed element that not only directs the growth of our life in the world ("growth" being a time phenomenon) but is also, as time body, forms the mechanism of connection between our eternal (and hence, timeless) selves which dwell, in actuality, in the spiritual world, and the series of "present moments" that constitute our life in time. The sense of having "been propelled" to that present moment of time can be seen as a dawning awareness of the whole continuum of the etheric body existing backward in time to the earliest beginnings of earthly self-consciousness. Behind this "dawn of self" lies the vista of our pre-earthly spiritual being.

This "time body" is what is seen and known when, near death, life "flashes before one's eyes" in a complete tableau image. The feeling I had looking back at my life toward the source of my "soul energy" was a species of this kind of vision.

Feeling thus, I thought I would need to be reborn — and the thought of living through the perceived *effort* of another infancy and childhood filled me with a certain dread, as the dread of an onerous task. I had waited so long to get to the age I was (17) — I didn't want to have to give up and start over — wait another thousand years, even! I had a glancing thought I would, somehow, become a tree "again" — that my consciousness would sleep (like a tree) for a thousand years (between incarnations) existing, growing unconsciously, before I had another chance to be reborn, while humanity on earth continued to evolve. Somewhere in all this, at different moments, the words and sounds of the song *Eskimo Blue Day*[93] — "... the human dream, doesn't mean shit to a tree".

And somewhere across all of this, there was a feeling of oppressive suffocation.

Having "crossed the threshold," I was existing as if "outside of time" — and although things were happening, there were outward events, the feeling was that this state — of hellish anxiety, confusion, and deprivation (of my previous sense of self) would last forever. The simultaneity of sensing one's self "out of time" — which is interpreted as being forever — and the current flow-of-time imprint is projected as if into "eternal time" — yielding the sense of being "eternally damned" in the present state. It was an existential "No Exit" scene.

Eternity, I was to begin to discover, can be sliced in many different ways by our time-limited minds.

It had grown later; others were continuing to wander in for the party. Annie's older brother and some of his friends (they were all in a band together) breezed in for a bit; they saw me, wasted on the floor, (at this point, I was, I would not quite say, "catatonic" but more than a bit wide-eyed and staring, and all but immobile). They then started smiling and laughing — it was friendly, in some way, compassionate, and seemingly knowing. I thought to myself, "These older guys are more knowledgeable about acid than me; they've been through this!" I suppose it gave me some hope, but at the same time, I questioned if they could truly know what I was going through. This feeling of others being more "in the know" and attuned with this other state was, really, part of the state itself. The feeling was: everything you thought you knew about reality is wrong. There are levels upon levels of reality happening in, around, and through everyone and everything. They all *apparently* exhibited coherent and orchestrated behavior against the background of this completely new reality arising within and all around me; ergo, they must be seeing/knowing it and capable of at the same time remaining their "normal" functional selves.

Ted's younger brother Scott and his friend Jay wandered in and sat on the bed. I had stood up again, although still uncomprehending the total picture. To my expanded, clairvoyantly soul-seeing sight, they seemed like nothing other than two minor Luciferic imps or diabolical *putti*. I could see raw, sulfuric horny teenage sexual energy oozing out of them, amping them up for mischief. They actually seemed to have little horns. They casually began to start messing with my head. They must have somehow sensed that they were acting out scenes from my unconscious and played along with them. It's hard to say whether I should call it good-natured and playful or little-boy spiteful. I don't recall what they said exactly, but there was an undercurrent that was a bit threatening and seemed to allude indirectly to the mounting existential dread and anxiety that I was feeling. At the same time, there was actually nothing overt other than, I suppose, behaving as if they were "in" on a secret that they were not going to tell me, laughing inwardly as each glance or gesture of theirs provoked a puzzled or mildly panicked response from me.

I lay again on the floor, immobile and listless. People came and went in Denise's room. Some of her friends, several years younger, began chatting back and forth. It seemed they were discussing the various boys who were at the party. In their girlish back and forth, I overwhelmingly sensed, it was all about finding "the one." This idea of finding "the one" suddenly appeared to me as an overpowering cosmic drive in the hearts and souls of these young girls.

And then, I was as if alone and still. There was a large sliding glass door behind me, to a balcony. It was now very dark outside: and the darkness out the window assumed cosmic proportions — I was gazing into some infinite, black void of existence, hovering beyond — a soul space wherein all souls were contained, wherein the "within" of everyone merged into a vast unitary expanse of darkness. One could see across the voidness into the souls of others: one could feel that there was a spiritual connection between all souls in this darkness; we all, in some way, were connected through some kind of cosmic backplane[94]. I sensed that within each of us, there is a depth at the bottom of which we are all connected, although normally, our eyes are directed away from it.

And then, from the far distance within that space, I felt the approach of some infinitely distant, higher being — a being whose survey embraced the interior of all souls on earth below, through the darkness. I felt its gaze approaching my soul, as if it were scanning the souls of millions and millions of beings, piercing its knowing into the soul-depths of each, coming closer. In some way, by my attending to it, I was myself beckoning, attracting it toward me, directing it in thought; yet at the same time, it terrified me: I felt (I knew) that I would be obliterated if it should pierce me directly with its seeing, if it came closer, transforming my reality with its presence. And I would be judged: less for deeds than for feebleness of being. And so I bid it turn away; or rather, I turned away from it, pushed it away — in somewhat the same magical manner I had caused the imagined approach of the ambulance to recede. When I began to sense it coming closer, I could sense also that there was a host of partially differentiated beings surrounding the all-seeing core. These other, surrounding beings were a spirit surface that was most closely penetrated by the core, that adhered to the core, as we on earth adhered to our physical selves; the depth of their penetration by the core illumined the darkness of the infinite abyss.

It seemed to me that this was God.

Rudolf Steiner speaks volumes about the higher spiritual beings, or hierarchies as he refers to them, or alternatively and collectively as simply "The Gods" or "The Good Gods." About the Godhead itself, he is somewhat more reticent as to its actual nature, although one can find specific references here and there as well as more generally a reference to, to begin with, "The Father God."[95] It is generally within the context of the Christian Trinity or "Three Persons of the Logos" that he discusses the being of God, although he might also speak for example of Brahma[96] or Ahura Mazdao[97].

He also remarks how what many people think of as "God" or even, more directly, pray to and immerse themselves in, is really simply their own angel — the singular hierarchical being that is associated with an individual human and which can also be understood as representing the "higher self". My read of these remarks is that he is, in part, pointing to the narrowness and quasi-narcissistic way many of us think of God, how small and narrow our conception is, and finally, how distant our comprehension of the true immeasurably vast nature of the Godhead is.

Having turned away or shut out the presence sensed "out there" in the void — across an abyss of darkness, I re-focussed on the physical room. In the corner of the room, there was a hanging chair. It was formed of wicker, as a basket; it was egg-shaped and was suspended from the ceiling by a spring. I had comfortably sat in it many times in the past; when sitting, it provided a sense of being in a womb-like nest.

In turning away from the higher being, I came to behold that the chair — suspended there in the room like a large egg — had somehow become the *embodiment* of the soul-penetrating, soul-annihilating force that I feared looking across the void to God; and rather than approaching or penetrating me inwardly, — that it was now standing before me, penetrating into and embodied in my earthly, sensory world — and, vaguely menacing me, rebuking me. At the same time, I felt one with it: something flowed between us: it tore open the three-dimensional space of the room and leaked into the void, the space, my soul — the same backplane of existence that was behind the souls of all beings.

It must be somehow visualized that the soul and being nature that was a moment previous "out there" yet within, and continuous with the inward essence of all beings arrayed beneath and around it, had now "leaked in" to my outward physical space, overflowing the objects. The "egg chair" had become ensouled.

I was both fascinated by it and turned away. I can still see it, piercing, gazing, examining, and somehow exhorting me.

I now interpret this phase of the overall state, and specifically, the way that I related to the "egg chair," quite clearly as a species of what Rudolf Steiner refers to as the "Guardian of the Threshold" or the "Double" (*doppelgänger*).

Discovering the nature of the Guardian and learning to approach, recognize, listen to, and learn from it, is one of the core concepts of the anthroposophic pathway into spiritual development, often characterized as the development of a clairvoyant perception of the spiritual world.

Steiner's characterization of the nature of the Guardian can be conceptualized through his material as a being having very definite contours; it is sometimes characterized as being an actual "Double" in appearance — implying that it has a form that mirrors the (physical) appearance of the individual. While I have no doubt it may appear to visionary sight as having the uncanny appearance of a physical Double, in my view, one of the key principles to grasping its nature is to start with the thought that it is both a part of one's self and, in transitioning the threshold, an externalization of those parts of the self that are "untransformed" — unable to consciously reflect the purity and goodness that is the nature of the spiritual world. In this sense, it resembles Jung's concept of the Shadow, although Jung's concept is limited through being tied to his theory of the Collective Unconscious rather than a recognition of the spiritual world. Being able to abide its concrete presence in one's expanded field of consciousness is key to being able to perceive spiritual reality, and not one's own "stuff," in the expanded state of spiritual or psychedelic perception.

Eventually, I was able to stand up again. I began to speak somewhat more coherently — the acid was beginning to wear off a bit, although I would be up all night. The party was now going in full swing all around the house. A bunch of other people dropped acid that night — although I have no clear idea what any of them went through. I probably smoked some pot, hung out, and listened to some music as the evening continued through the night.

And so, we were all up all night; by morning, I felt cleansed and renewed, but still mostly confused, and of course, crashing. There can be a palpable physical "brain cleanse" feeling after a psychedelic trip that can come along with the exhaustion and depletion.

I made some kind of stumbling attempt to communicate something of what I had seen and been through, which went more or less nowhere. There were no shared, articulated concepts.

When morning came around, a few of us — including Ruth — gathered in Alan's older brother's room and tried to summarize or review ... *something*. It seemed that others were sensing that a certain *something* had transpired for everyone overnight. I tried to say something about finding a way to acknowledge we all had a soul connection. I remember Ruth saying that "Maybe David's right" — about what, I'm not sure; she might have been referring to my earlier argument about our ability to have the "far out" kind of trip read about in Castaneda. Or, something else.

The aftermath in the days and weeks was a struggle to try and make sense and re-integrate into my day-to-day world. When I realized I had stood Erin up on our date I was mortified and filled with shame — such that I was unable to even try to reconnect and explain. I couldn't begin to. It felt clear to me that I had seen a completely different side of existence, one that is totally unseen and unacknowledged by everyone. I had the definite idea that I had somehow seen or been in the (distant) presence of God.

Back in school, I shared this with one of the High School guidance counselors in the week that followed. At my always-progressive high school, we had a program — intended to bridge the "generation gap" — that took the form of a full-bore encounter group[98] (very much the fad of the times) type of session, weekly, between groups of parents, teachers, and students. They were facilitated by various guidance counselors. I had a connection with the facilitator of my group. I tried to confide in him. On hearing that I thought I had seen God (while on acid — I apparently felt safe disclosing that) he backed quickly away, almost in terror it seemed, and told me "You're strictly on your own with that." Possibly the wise and appropriate thing for him to say. I was somehow under the baffling impression that there was a more general knowledge of "these things" and that I was just starting to be let in on the secret, and that there were those (adults) who knew, or ought know, the secrets.

After about three weeks or so later I was "back to normal" enough that I could seek out Erin and try and offer regrets. She generously acknowledged the sweetness of our brief connection, but in the time since, and, unsurprisingly, she had taken up with another guy. Pondering the karmic unfolding of this loss of what seemed full of promise, I years later had occasion to think for a moment of Odin sacrificing his eye to gain his magical knowledge.[99]

5

Entr'acte

After the cast party — my first "over the threshold" trip — I know that, after I had re-grounded myself in the immediate weeks that followed, I took acid at least three or four more times in the spring semester of my senior year, which would have been at least once a month, if not more frequently.

After such a shattering night, one might suppose that I would undertake a different posture relative to psychedelics; but such is this resilience of youth and delusion of physical immortality that my sense of being well-grounded in myself and of being capable of resuming the exploration — and enjoyment — of psychedelics asserted itself. And in many ways, I was to begin to feel more solidly grounded in myself than ever, and to feel my sense of insight into the world of spiritual ideas and concepts growing.

Either by design or happenstance, I was not to dose again with the same "full hit" of the orange sunshine as I had at the cast party — that is, until just before the end of the school year.

Throughout the spring I continued my reading. I had latched on to Steve Gaskin's[100] *Monday Night Class*[101] — Gaskin was an eclectic "psychedelic teacher" straight out of the Haight-Ashbury[102] in San Francisco. He brought under one roof a variety of spiritual teachings and applied them to the psychedelic journey. Many things started to make sense reading him. He fluidly borrowed and blended ideas from Zen, Hinduism, Astrology, Christianity, and so on into an enthusiastically spirit-embracing culture. Pot smoking and the use of natural psychedelics became an integral part of the lifestyle he promoted and lived, along with natural childbirth, vegetarianism, and all the other trimmings of the hard-core hippie ethos. He founded a communal farm in Tennessee along with hundreds of his followers. At times, the idea of going to live there seemed attractive.

Somewhere along the line, I borrowed my sister's copy of Ram Dass' *Be Here Now* which soon migrated to my shortlist. My sister seeking along her own path, and several of her readings cycled their way down to me.[103] It was dawning in me that there was a spiritual, cosmic reality of vast proportion and a moral foundation (karma) which, however, I had yet to fully square myself with. Nor had I fully grasped the extent of the interconnectedness of various traditions and teachings that I was, bit by bit, exposing myself to. But it did seem as if I was transforming and maturing a bit. I think to the extent that I was trending toward a certain mold, I probably was starting to identify along the lines of Steve Gaskin's San Francisco "hippie-beatnik" posture. Dig, man.

The Gurdjieff work continued to hold my interest and also inspire a certain kind of rigor even as I explored the "far-out." That spring, I discovered that the mother of a friend of mine, Lauren, had in their library at home (where I would sometimes visit) several volumes from the Gurdjieff work (her mother participated in the Gurdjieff Foundation[104] in New York). This included the first volume of Maurice Nicoll[105]'s *Psychological Commentaries on the Teachings of Gurdjieff and Ouspensky*[106], which I was lent. I wound up borrowing several over time books, one of which included the volume *Rama/Krishna*, an extract from Édouard Schuré's[107] *The Great Initiates*[108]. Schuré was a contemporary and admirer of, and sometime collaborator with, Rudolf Steiner. I believe this was my first real brush with a book in Steiner's "spiritual neighborhood."

Sometime subsequently that spring, I asked my father to try and pick me up a copy of *Psychological Commentaries* if he could find them at a bookshop in New York, where he commuted during the week. I was expecting to be lucky if he found *Volume One* that I had returned to Lauren's mother. To my surprise, he very magnanimously came home with the complete set of five volumes. My father maintained a curiosity about his children's spiritual explorations but seemed at the same time to maintain a "safe distance" and a reserved judgment about them.

Another title from the Gurdjieff work (or more correctly from Ouspensky's circle) that I was loaned Lauren's mother was Rodney Collins[109]' *The Theory of Celestial Influence*. On one level, it is an impressive effort. He attempts to blend ideas derived from his understanding of Ouspenky's "System" with explanations found in conventional scientific, cosmological, and biological perspectives into a comprehensive picture in which cosmic influences are shown playing into human life. It is an attempt at a scientific rationalization of astrological thinking from the point of view of the "System."

In some ways it is a *tour de force* tying together correspondences and relationships that reinforce an image of self-similarity or "as above, so below," between man and the universe. In the end, along with some of his other works, it comes across to me as attempting to build up a "reality" of spirit from what are essentially earthly forces and ideas about the nature of things as derived from sense observation. It does play into some of Ouspensky's notions of time and in particular, includes a striking picture of what he describes as "the long body of the solar system," which he provides an illustration of.

A "long body" is simply the picture of anything in the world as it exists in the so-called "fourth dimension" of time. If you were to picture the long body of a human being, it would appear as a millipede traversing the environment, leaving behind a trace of itself at every instant as it moved, in time, across the world, from birth to death. Correspondingly, the long body of the solar system appears as a brilliant long extension through space surrounded by the spiraling forms of the planets. There is somewhat of a correspondence between Collin's long body — conceived as a physical body existing in time, and the "time body" previously mentioned in reference to the etheric body. The *etheric* time body, however, is entirely non-physical.

I will mention that this idea of the long body is also dealt with in Maurice Nicoll's *Living Time*[110], which I also read from the library in Lauren's home. He discusses extensively Ouspensky's notion of "eternal recurrence," which concept was forming itself in my mind. This image of the "long body" was to appear in thousandfold greater grandeur subsequently.

Spiritual influences and interests were seeping in here, there, and everywhere, at least among some of my peers. The crowd of friends around Milo were particularly attuned to the teachings of Meher Baba[111], instigated primarily through the influence of Pete Townsend of the rock group *The Who*.[112] I read a bit of Baba, and some bits of it stuck with me. It had a certain vibe, and at another level, was yet another system that needed to be sorted with all the other systems pouring into me. Milo's younger brother Andy — the one who had cared for me during my New Year's Eve plight — was in particular very keen on Baba.

I was very aware that internally, I was continuing to change rapidly heading toward the end of the final semester of high school. Although, as I said, I had recovered my stability (such that it was) and sense of self, the cast party hovered in memory above the background of my day-to-day life like a giant mural or tableau.

During those weeks and months following the cast party, I tried here and there, against the background of our social life as part of the same crowd, to communicate to Ruth *something* of what was changing in me, continuing the dialog begun when we discussed if it was possible to have the "truly far out" — meaning, increasingly to me, spiritual-cosmic — experiences with psychedelics rather than the "merely recreational" kinds of trips we had had.

I wasn't particularly successful at this; it felt like there was some curiosity alive inside of her that was intrigued, but couldn't find a way to square it with what had already formed as her given view of the world. The fact that I also thought that she was attractive — if a little out of my league or that I was "not her type" — and was thus radiating male teenager vibes at times, doubtlessly didn't help the effort.

Lilly's *Center of the Cyclone* was read and re-read. The latter third of the book is devoted to a scheme of "levels" of consciousness, identified with number labels (3, 6, 12, 24, 48) which are meant to correspond with the vibrational levels in the scheme of creation in Gurdjieff[113]. He maps the various psychedelic states he described to the 12, 6, and 3 levels. There are also "negative" mirror states. There is a certain rationality and resonance to the scheme, but in the end, it is, to me, only a partial view of things. Lilly describes states realized during his study with Oscar Ichazo in Arica, Chile, along with dozens of folks there from the Esalen Institute, as if they were the result solely of spiritual practice uninfluenced by outer agents. As it was later to unfold, these gloriously described states were all LSD induced.

And yes, springtime continued to be peppered with acid journeys. I recall with appreciation a really lovely, modestly dosed trip when Alan and I visited Annie's parent's cottage in Vermont during spring break. Ruth and our friend Julie were also visiting there. It was warm springtime, but there were still cool clumps of snow on the ground as Julie and I enjoyed a mild dose of acid together. The five of us — the others, not having dosed — climbed through the woods of a nearby park. My really big memory of that day was seeing for the first time a full-on beaver dam and also sitting in the sun with Julie on a large rock across which a mountain stream cascaded. I had my portable eight-track player with me too and was listening with great delight to my increasingly favored music, that of Yes and their new album *Fragile*, echoing through the woods.

On the way home, Alan and I stopped in Boston, where I interviewed for admission to Emerson College, my application there being a rather last-minute move. I had been fairly ambivalent about applying for college. As it happened, I was shortly accepted, and expected to study theater there. Largely under the influence of Alan, I had taken a bit of interest in acting and had a small role in the fall production of *Romeo and Juliet* — but by the time Spring's *Lisa and David* came, my interest was meanwhile vacillating, and I didn't participate (other than of course, by way of the cast party).

I also tripped a couple of more times with Ash. He had read Lilly's book, and we would discuss/philosophize about ideas in it. We tripped once in the woods north of town, winding up at Lauren's in the late afternoon. If I recall correctly, it would have been that evening that, alone in my room, I found myself navigating into a deep "inner contemplative state," feeling very centered in inner communion with my deep self and wondering if I could ever communicate or share that depth with another. It had an echo of the inner state that first arose at the cast party while lying in bed in the dark, only this time, in solitude.

My friendship with Lauren took root during that springtime. I first got to know her as Alan's girlfriend during the fall of our senior year; she was part of the incoming 10th-grade class. She and Alan, I think, only lasted a couple of months, but we had become friendly during this time. By the end of the year, I would visit her somewhat regularly; and through the connection of her mother's involvement in the Gurdjieff work, I felt a certain link and safety with her as I explored my own path. And meanwhile, we began to enjoy each other's company. She was my date to the senior prom, and we doubled with Ted and Ruth. In times to come, we would stay involved with each other's lives on and off through the years.

The Arica Institute, as described by Lilly in *The Center of the Cyclone*, was starting to launch its missionary initiative and make itself known in New York City. There was some talk or promotional event scheduled that Ash, along with our friend Peter, wanted to attend. There had also been a small notice in the *Village Voice*[114] announcing a talk, that same evening, as we thought at least, by the all but invisible Carlos Castaneda. I borrowed my parent's station wagon and we put a tab or two of LSD into a half gallon of wine (even though the drinking age was 21 at that time in Connecticut, it was usually easy to buy alcohol at a local liquor store without serious challenge, as long as there was no one else in the store).

We drove into the city and tried to find the first (Arica), then the second (Castandeda) location, both without luck. Being high on acid probably didn't help our navigation of the city. I remember the three of us wandering into a restaurant to use the toilet, sufficiently upscale that it had a washroom attendant; we were brandishing the wine bottle as we sauntered in. We offered a swig to the attendant by way of a tip; he shook his head knowingly, sensing that we were more than a "little" high from the effects of the bottle and that if he took a sip, he would get more than the usual bargain. We eventually gave up and drove home from what proved to be a wild goose chase.

Another night, Ash and I along with another friend, Jason, were at a party where we had the sudden inspiration to drop acid that night and, ostensibly, devise (how this would occur was unclear) a new "revolutionary educational curriculum" for high school/college that would be better suited for the transformational consciousness that was evolving. Or something like that. My parents were away, and we had the house to ourselves. That was the good news: the bad news was that Jason had brought along Frank Zappa's *200 Motels* (the soundtrack to the film), and he and Ash decided that what they really wanted to do was to devote themselves to listening to it once the acid kicked in. I have more than a little fondness for some of Frank Zappa's work and respect overall, but *200 Motels* is not a great soundtrack for acid. My primary recollection then is that of moping around the house, high on acid, and annoyed.

I was able to rescue a nice memory of the otherwise, to me, mostly dreary evening when many years later Jason would recall to me how at dawn we all climbed onto the roof of the house to greet the sunrise.

Back to Gaskin. Among the various phenomenon of the psychedelic process that he weaves into his talks, the phenomenon he describes as *ego death* features as a central theme in Gaskin.

I was sure what he referred to was like what I went through at the cast party — Gaskin's "ego death." What exactly this is and what "ego" means will concern us further.

The school year was rapidly coming to a close, and with it, my high school years. My several psychedelic ventures since the earth-shattering cast party night seemed to bounce between mild immersion in nature, to somewhat wildly chaotic urban adventures, to pretty ho-hum. This was about to change.

6

Mountains come out of the Sky

Blossoms of spring were readying to make way for summer. On a Sunday night, three days before the end of the school year, I was hanging out with my friend Milo. High school graduation was around the corner.

My friendship with Milo — whose brother Andy had rescued me amid my horrible New Year's Eve nightmare — had progressed since our first game of chess in the cafeteria during our junior year; we had become serious pals. He was well-liked and had his own crowd, which overlapped with that of his younger brother. I mixed with them fairly often, and like most of the other kids at school, they were all — with the exception of Milo — potheads, and would also drink recreationally. He had only begun dabbling with marijuana late into our senior year. He was also a special friend of Derek, who had graduated the year before. Derek was a dyed-in-the-wool suburban hippie type — long, long red hair, purple fringed leather jacket, the whole look. Derek, meanwhile, had himself done plenty of dope and acid. I knew him somewhat tangentially, but he and Milo had become tight, and so sometimes, the three of us would hang out together. Milo and Derek were both readers of the eastern spirituality of the Meher Baba, Paramahansa Yogananda[115] ilk. So there was a definite intersect there.

That Sunday night, we wound up at Derek's house, and somehow, it evolved that the three of us would do acid together the next day — this would be Milo's first trip. And though I can't recall if I still had some of the orange sunshine left over from the cast party or re-acquired some more, I had three such hits at home at that time. I didn't think to myself, *hey! — remember, this is the strong stuff.* I had after all, a few "normal" trips under my belt since. I just thought: "This is good acid." Indeed, I only somewhat dimly grasped the relationship between dosage and intensity, in that there seemed to be a broad "middle range," which seemed to encompass most of what showed up on the street. While dosage is key, any number of other factors influence the net trip.

Milo, driving his family's VW Bus, was going to get Derek first — his side of town — and then pick me up "to take me to school" — which would have been typical enough in itself, cover-story-wise.

My developing mindset being what it was, I did spend a few early morning minutes in the playroom of my parent's home, experimenting with some of the hatha yoga exercises found in *Be Here Now* — which I had been reading in fits and starts. The gesture was significant, having never attempted to transform or prepare myself for a trip by means of anything approximating ritual practice. Neither had I taken acid with anything approaching this level of intentionality. However, the surface agenda was simply to spend the day together in the woods surrounding one of the several area reservoirs with which Derek was familiar.

Derek and Milo sat in the front. I climbed in and sat directly behind them, halfway between the two front seats. Excitement similar to going to a concert or ballgame enlivened our greetings. We departed, but about half a mile away from my parent's house, as we pulled up the road headed for the reservoir, deeper into the "country" of suburban Connecticut, we dropped — a whole tab each of orange sunshine.

Our ride was to the north. It would take less than twenty minutes to get to the reservoir. We were keen on getting off soon. As we came within a mile or two of the place, we turned down the road heading westward, over a railroad bridge, and past the nearby village center. Once past the town, we forked south, and a half-mile down the road, turned right down "Old Huckleberry Road."[116]

The road was rutted and narrow, almost one lane, and crowded by the plants and bushes overhanging upon either side. We traveled down a hill, past the driveways of two or three homes set back from the road. At the bottom, the road broadened, smoothed a bit, and veered left onto a causeway that crossed a large pond — almost a lake. This was the "lower reservoir." We crossed in a minute and then turned left along the far bank, then hugged to the right as the road climbed along what proved to be the front side of the "upper reservoir." The road was rutted again and dipped up and down through what was now a dense wood. We looked for a place to park close to the upper reservoir. Milo quickly pulled in to the right, into an apparently well-worn unofficial parking spot well in from the road. There was the odd "No Trespassing" sign here and there, posted by the Water District, which we casually ignored.

We weren't off yet. But we were thrilled. We were free and knew we would be traveling into a world unlike that to which our day-to-day youthful lives were accustomed. Derek and I were excited on behalf of Milo, who would be having his virgin voyage. Inwardly I had a different feeling about dosing with Derek and Milo, a sense that we were somehow "dharma brothers."

We headed into the thick of the wood; Derek had brought his frisbee with him, which we began to toss as we headed in. The wood was at first too thick to see the water of the upper reservoir from where we stood, but a few frisbee tosses in, climbing somewhat as we went, we came by the water's edge.

The upper reservoir, smaller, oblong, but broader at one end, where it spills down to the lower, was little more than a mile in circumference. Its banks were varied; near where we stood, a small wooded shelf of land jutted into the water, dimpling the reservoir with a slight elbow. To our right, the banks were hilly, with rocks protruding where the weather had washed the land away. Across from where we stood, the face of a tall, stony cliff stood fifty feet or more above the water. These rocky traces of New England's glacial, ice-age past dotted the landscape. All around were trees and forest, and though there were homes within the mile from where we stood, for all the eye could see, it was as if the native wilderness.

Our plan was simple: we would circle the water along its edge. We tossed the frisbee along, as the way narrowed and widened again as we sought or avoided the small rocky ledges.

Playfulness — unremarkable in its way as that of any youths on their last day of hooky before school's end — soon mingled with the wine of the giddy first effects of the drug. A household dog had tracked us and joined our game of catch. We chattered, our words sliding toward the intermixture with gibberish. We gave our new canine friend a gibberish name. But our companionship with him was short; he was to wander off.

I was drawn to the water's edge, climbing onto a small shelf upon which had grown a tree, now shorn of leaves and branches but solid and leaning toward the open space over the water. Its trunk formed a Y, which drew the focus of the eye down the length of the reservoir into the sunlight, framing a view of the landscape of trees and water beyond.

I was definitely getting stoned. My head was humming, my gaze transfixed. Suddenly, with an inward breath, I seemed to breathe in from the sky — or, the cosmos? — a draught of fluid, soul-energizing light, laden throughout with an electric spark, pressing next within as if to escape again through my pores after blending first with all the passions that lay hidden, simmering deep within me. Although the earlier cast party was a pathway "over the threshold" (of the spiritual world), this influx of felt and seen cosmic energy was experienced with pure mutual welcoming, unlike the dread and confusion that overshadowed most of the earlier trip (although the initial episode of the cast party, when I lay on the bed, was purely positive as well).

"Hydrogen 12," I instantly remarked to myself, cross-referencing this according to what I understood of Gurdjieff's teaching regarding the "higher psychic elements" within man's nature. "Hydrogen 12" is the "element" that feeds the soul in higher states of consciousness, corresponding to what John Lilly described as "satori 12, the blissful sharing body" in *The Center of the Cyclone*. I thought no more on this but felt that I was venturing into territory that I had the "maps" of Lilly and Gurdjieff for, and thus, a bit more confidence as I encountered the otherworldly. I became momentarily enraptured as the play of soul and world energies stabilized (somewhat!), within and without me — then turned to join my companions as we continued round the lake.

In short order our steps next brought us to the far end of the reservoir. A small creek flowed into the reservoir there and across our path. We could have forded it in one or two steps, but a tree trunk had fallen to conveniently form a bridge across. Although we were fairly stoned by now, we were not unable to focus. By centering ourselves and trusting our feet and legs to do the work, we all crossed the bridge without a misstep. This "trusting the body to do the right thing" was familiar to me from driving a car while tripping — the centering and effort at self-command merged with the delight in accomplishment. From there, I led the way up the broad wooded hill on the other side. The acid was in full rush now, and, breathing in the country air, I began to dream myself as being "at one" with the world of nature all around me. Each step, each glance, each breath seemed in harmony and perfect synchronization with nature around me. Thoughts of the "Tao[117]," as I rather superficially understood it, sprang up — in a narcissistic "Look at me — so this is the Tao, baby!" sort of way.

But at the same time, I knew something wasn't quite right — "little I" was still present, willfully deeming itself to be the source and center of the ripples of flowing harmony. I could feel the pressure of my inflating self filling up my soul — threatening from somewhere in the background to disharmonize the whole with its ludicrous misproportion. Deep within, a second man was welling up inside of me, soon to burst my outer shell.

But the distraction of the climb's effort deflated me somewhat, and as I neared the top, I was no longer quite so "puffed up" with myself. The broad hill, leading us away from the water, narrowed to a pathway through the trees heading to the crown of the rocky ridge we had seen rising above the lake from the other side, which had been our climb's target. I hurried, anxious to turn back toward the water and regain the view of the reservoir from the heights. A branch blocked the final step; I pushed the bough aside and strode to the peak, thirty or forty feet above the lake.

I lunged forward, half-stumbled, and was stunned altogether as my view suddenly expanded from the narrow dark of the wood to the ethereal freedom of the sky. A luminous part of me escaped and continued forward as I stopped — spreading out over the lake, over the trees below, into the cloudy bright and blue sunlit sky, out beyond the earth, into the space beyond, till it touched against the end of the world and bounced and rippled back again to me. The ripples loosened every thing of the world from the stern grip of the earthly, and made their finer parts free to breathe the now heaven-drenched air.

I existed for moments in pure, absolute wonder.

And suddenly, my soul seemed to stand forth within my expanded sphere of self, withdrawn like a sword from the scabbard.

Steiner often uses this characterization of the sword from the scabbard in describing the awakening of the "second man." It seems to wholly and aptly describe the way this unfolded within.

Something had catapulted itself outside myself — an impulse similar to the swarming out of thoughts when I was first getting off at the cast party, but this time, I came more fully, freely loose, and touched the whole sky-blue world, whose pure and simple holy beauty permeated my mind. I sensed the second man, roused from sleep, from the dream world of his usual dwelling, young — but older than my birth, and native to a land beyond this earth, a world I now sensed. Sensed, seen, felt, yet at first, unrecognized, as might be a childhood friend, long separated, met again in older age. And thus, though partly hidden in shadows of confusion and unknowing, he spread a canopy of unearthly, cosmic thought before my brain. And now my eyes resettled on the scene below the rocky ledge, my comrades having come alongside me.

What first had pierced my shell-of-self earlier on the water's other shore down below, as intoxicating force, now here high above, riddled my brain as thought. Thought cosmic, stern, majestic, all-penetrating yet all-profound, unfathomed, and riddling. And though now suddenly possessed by powers of mind of subtlety of tens by tens-fold normal, I was just as suddenly possessed by the demand that I solve the now-remembered riddle of my *self*. Though glimpsed, my second self submerged again within the depths of obscure thought, beyond which dimly dwelt a newly sensed parent source of all.

Within my expanding sense of self, whose aura was brimming with eddies of deepest thought and obscure intimations, I felt the presence of something hovering within — with partly a similarity to the God of the deep void and partly the presence that had inserted itself into the hanging chair. It was not fearful, rather bestirring to penetrate the riddles of self-knowledge.

My "normal" self-on-acid teetered before me as within the surge of my thought rocked from side to side. With a few words, I stayed loosely engaged with the activity of my friends — each of us in our own state of stoned amazement before the view below. The first question was, how did I get here?

I had been here, in this state, once before — the earlier cast party trip a few months ago. That had been my first step over the threshold into a wonder and a terror — and a knowledge — accepted but still largely uncomprehended in the intervening months, wherein I had resumed my "recreational" tripping behavior. Yet the intervening time had also been deepened somewhat by a more comprehending reading of the various works I was more and more pursuing on spiritual topics.

I realized that "someone" — and it must have been *me* — had conspired to trick "me" into signing up for this state — by dosing. Things were now rapidly becoming much more intense than consciously anticipated, yet with a strange, conspiratorial orchestration somehow sensed as having been acting itself out to bring me to the present state. The intentionality differed from wanting to go to the movies and finding yourself there an hour later. That makes sense. I had wanted to get high in the woods (well, really high), and now was "looking at my brains," spread out "all across the table," trying to figure out how the pieces went back together. Part of me had led my steps to this point — and part of me had played along as the sucker. I was experiencing myself as composed of different "actors" with distinct perspectives on how my story was to unfold. This is all part of the disassociation of the composed "daily self" when the "larger self" emerges as the dominion of sense perception loosens its grip. Part of that is realizing that different phases of consciousness can be active and disjoint and unknown between each other.

Well, there was nothing to be done! I was still half-materialized in the here and now — I might as well keep moving along. Although our conversation struggled to articulate our situation, we knew we were mostly either dumbstruck or babbling. So we moved on around the lake, heading down from our high vantage. As I turned, looking forward along the lake again, I sensed the bright sun and pictured behind its brilliance something that was the "shining void" of Buddhism. Like pilgrims climbing stony peaks such as this, the seekers of the world (all of humanity) struggle, climbing toward it — toward nirvana, toward moksha, liberation, release — through numberless lifetimes. Did this life find me closer, or farther, from the goal? My forward steps seemed, perhaps, to veer my path minutely toward it.

From the perch above the cliff, the hilltop broadened as it ran below, and we were led into a thicket of short, bushy trees. The frisbee still seemed to be with us and could snake its way tossed along the ground ahead as we plowed through the branches, which whipped as we let them loose again. In seeking the path of least resistance along the way, we traveled as if through an invisible maze formed by the thick and thin of the branches. I took the lead, our playfulness returned, and an animated, luminous picture world, where each sight of earthly form was painted with a living world of pictures daily unseen, hovered about each of us, and everything we rested our thoughtful gaze upon. The little wood sloped down, then ended as the hill grew steeper. And so we climbed a short way down, finding ourselves again on the water's edge before another small shelf of land that jutted into the reservoir. We had traveled more than halfway around from our entry point: we were on the other shore.

The pines above formed a tent; fallen needles textured the ground below in earthen browns, while the branches painted the edge of the sky above in green. The trunks served to communicate the heavenly above to the earthly below. Derek and I sat and talked; our thoughts, words, and conversation flowed between the seen, and, gesturing, pointed gropingly at the world of unseen thought overflowing our brains. There was a sense of interlock similar in a way to the gibberish conversation pictured at the cast party between Ruth and Annie. Here our tone was sober, weighty, wondrous, and joyful.

As we sat there, marveling at the scope of thought and consciousness that had arisen within and between us, I looked back again to the threshold-crossing I underwent at the cast party — by the way, at first, of a general mood and a realization that I was again in that reality and, for the moment, in a much more centered state.

Anyway, remembering how I had felt a different soul connection with others at the party — as I was now similarly experiencing with Derek and Milo — I thought again of Ruth and of my essentially unsuccessful attempts to describe and share with her in the straight state, what I was feeling as the unlimited possibilities of wonder, of spiritual growth and awareness and perception, of being, that was even now stage by stage unfolding before me. I had tried, in various conversations, to articulate what I was experiencing through the acid, and what I was beginning to find my way into with a newly opened spiritual orientation.

Sitting there, stoned on acid, my soul being stripped naked before the universe, I felt, in thinking of her, I could see into her and sense her being; comprehendingly, as a being of the same nature I was discovering myself to be. Not aloof, but somehow as if in dialog.

A recent phone conversation with her came to mind, and I realized that she had, not in so many words, but at a soul level, told me that she was not to voyage alongside me through the door I was seeking to pass: that was not to be part of her path. I comprehended and accepted this with, on the one hand, serenity and, on the other, a certain sense of loss, but also a clearly-felt sense that her story would continue well, in its own timeline and its own way. It was clear to me by then that my perspective was shifting across the barriers of a single lifetime, a single incarnation. With school ending, it was to prove that she and I would never have occasion to do LSD together again, although we have maintained a lifelong friendship.

And it was a strange reversal, in its way, insofar as during the cast party, my belief had been that she, Annie, and more or less everyone else to some degree or other, was already through the door and acting out of the consciousness that was just dawning for me. It now seemed that I was the one navigating the new world, and others remained, as it were, behind in the realm of the known. I wanted to bring others into this space.

But as far as the arc of the particular journey on that day, this centered state was just a phase — into a shuffle of interpersonal boundaries and different realities that was about to unfold on a new level.

During all this, Milo had taken his clothes off without our taking particular notice; we turned and saw that he was skinny-dipping in the reservoir. We saw him splashing around by the shore and contemplated joining him. Still, our mood was physically indolent, and we were absorbed in a shared reality detached from attraction to the activity of swimming.

Milo paddled farther from shore without our noticing. He was a strong swimmer. Suddenly he called to us, "Bring my clothes across. I'm swimming to the other side."

How long this took to register, I can't say. In the numb instant before it did, Milo had dived ahead and, with a few powerful strokes, was already swimming intently and was past the point of recall. When the shock had dissipated and the reality came into focus, my panic was instantaneous, as it seemed was Derek's. Maybe Milo's buffer of psychedelic naivete had prevented the effects from penetrating to the core depth that it had for Derek and I. In our stoned interlock, our anxiety and panic fed into each other. We were so hight that neither Derek nor I would have trusted ourselves in our state to swim the maybe one hundred yards of the reservoir, and we feared for Milo.

I felt I would need to save him should he become distressed — as I imagined he would. But I, weak swimmer that I was, was sure I would drown myself in trying! And suddenly, every childhood fear of drowning pulsed within me, carrying me back to my earliest infancy and past, as if reaching back to the watery womb itself. The same force of the thought wave that I had projected across the water and into the skies at the peak overlooking the reservoir now traveled across time across my life, as if to the instant of birth, and rippled back again. This was the first stage, as it were, of shuttling my consciousness across my etheric time-body, the existence of my life in eternity.

Gathering Milo's things, we ran forward to the stony water's edge — the shortest path around. With each step, fear, shame (at my lack of courage should I need to rescue Milo), and confusion scrambled my inner world. My adrenaline pumped. We looked up anxiously from time to time, now glimpsing Milo, now losing sight, but running onward. A pre-vision bored itself within me: Milo drowning, sinking to the bottom — his body being brought out by divers. Tomorrow's newspaper: "Youth drowns at reservoir while on LSD." Out of the headline news and into my life.

Two-thirds of the way around, we looked up again to the far shore ahead and saw Milo had emerged onto the land. He had climbed upon a boulder on the water's edge and sat there, smiling, his face beaming at us like the sun. Relief came, stilling the original forces of agitation but leaving a secondary turmoil active, rattling around inside, and ready to stir things up again.

What follows now cannot be placed into the proper time sequence. Instead, a series of vignettes remain in memory, with only an approximate order linking them.

I must have been first to finish the journey round the edge when, the immediate cause of panic having vanished, my adrenaline-charged brain refocused on the spot across the lake we had just left behind us.

Milo was breathing hard when we caught up with him. He was still undressed, and as he panted, now lying on the grassy bank near the spillway to the lower reservoir, one could see soul forces pulsing in and out of him, streaming through his body as it gasped its fill of oxygen. He seemed full of vital, pulsing, sexual, youthful potency.

Charged perhaps by Milo's naked vitality, there then seemed to stand, looking back across the lake, my left-behind last thoughts of Ruth. Only now, what had been a spiritual contemplation of her extra-earthly spirit, was now tinctured with an amorous longing for the feminine, for the entire world of woman. The world of the other shore, now left behind, was seen a separate, heavenly-feminine world. I pictured the souls of the other young women in my life dwelling there as in a soul-world drenched in all the beauty and pleasure of an all-permeating feminine nature. It was a soul world now seen as lost by having incarnated as a man. The attainment of a desired reunion seemed, however, almost unreachably distant — and which to attain would be as fraught with peril as swimming to the farther shore.

My blood pulsed with each step; out of the rhythm, I heard music calling: a song I had heard a thousand times before — now echoing through the depths of memory and desire: "Let's spend the night together/Now I need you more than ever/Let's spend the night together now..." All of the Rolling Stones raunch dripped through me, and tugging at my guts and heartstrings like tiny razors shredding me within, amplifying the already biting rush of adrenaline. The distant shore, the heavenly erotic ideal. The ocean between: death.

After Milo dressed and caught his breath, we lay together in the sun on the grass. Derek commented something about being on planet earth — men traveled to the moon in those times. He may have read something in the paper about some recent astronomical event and been remarking it, or just talking in wonder. Again, something within me pulsed into the far reaches — the farthest sphere, wherein worlds thrilled and echoed in harmonious communication, the perspective where earth is truly one of numberless cosmic worlds — and then traveled to earth again, into the ground, causing it to quiver with world-life. I looked around at the vibrating world, at the trees standing before me. They too quivered with particles of life. I felt them and conceived them as composed in some way of the atoms of physics as conventionally understood, but revealed now as a dance of light.

Staring at a tree, I locked my eyes on the smallest atoms of life within. The surface of the tree opened like a series of gates, each sliding open like an elevator's doors, providing step-by-step a window to the next level within. Another gate opened within, top to bottom; another, side to side, within that, each revealing finer and finer tissues of the tree's body. Within each step, I peered deeper into the microscopic structure inside of the tree until, after a few moments, the last gate opened, revealing two or three particles, as small as the atom, seen closer than close, but made of pure, pulsating white light, shimmering, dancing, and oscillating beside each other. Entranced one minute, I lost a grip on myself the next and shook off the picture, dropping to my knees, anxious lest the fabric of the whole world would collapse before me into a million million specks of light — a replay of my feeling of incoherence, of my bodily particles not staying together, that I felt at the cast party. This time, rather than feeling that I would collapse into dust, it seemed the world itself might.

At this point, I had lost all but the last shred of a consensus-reality "reality principle" and wandered puppet-like through promptings of my own fantastic inner states and the outer gestures of my two friends. The reservoir was alive with churning life, desire, soul, wherein one's self could drown. It was laden with overtones of birth, of death, of rebirth, and sexuality. It seemed to swarm as a multitude of beings — whose weaving together was at the same time a tearing to pieces of the boundaries of self, of my self.

And then I sensed I was silently urged by Milo and Derek to cross. One of them probably said something, kiddingly, like, "Your turn next!" I could *feel* their thoughts coming toward me. My turn was next to suffer the hero initiation Milo had won. Yet as before, I did not trust at all in my strength to bear me across. If I wandered into the water, I would surely drown myself in the first depths!

The sense of urging persisted. Go, they seemed to say. You will be reborn. But first you must die. Suddenly lost, forlorn, I felt again that my soul had broken its winding spring: the contents of my life were overflowing, spilling into the world around me, floating away, drowning in the greater life. I must reemerge from the world ocean, the world womb. I would be driven out, across, by the parent-god. This god would rebind the world into a properly enclosed seed of a reborn human being — would pierce the world with a formative poke of the finger into the shattered sands of my world, a push into my spine, my head, of enfolded human life, to ripen in the ocean-womb of the lake before emerging again. The god must penetrate into the womb; I become the seed again. Unlike the sense of loss of the results of the effort of having grown from childhood to teenage maturity that I feared at the cast party, this was a challenge to *actively* seek rebirth, a new seed — by crossing the "ocean."

This push into incarnation that I was seeing I later came to see reflected in the image in a sketch inspired by Steiner, which showed the forms of human beings in the process of descending to incarnation, impelled by a downward-thrusting hand, pointing downward to the earth[118].

The "ocean" of the lake seemed to be filled with a churning life: with interweaving and intertwining soul-beings, whose spirit-countenances would emerge visibly as if upon the waves of the ocean, only to re-blend with the pool of souls — or was it simply, "soul-stuff?" It had a seductive attraction, but I knew that my "reality" of having a separate existence would end if I entered the waters of the lake; not only was I liable to physically drown, but the churning vortex of interconnected beings would shred, and splinter the "self" I was only just aborning as a teenage earthly creature.

Panic was intense. I would not submit to the pull. I resisted. I faced the water and looked back across my life to a now-remembered birth seventeen years ago and across beyond that into a world of soul and spirit, a world of divine origin: left behind but still present. Though glimpsed, this world I was still parted from; even as suddenly, deeply, longingly, I again felt the world of the feminine, of woman, now parted, across a gulf, which suddenly had divided the world into two chambers. On my shore was the dry and sterile world of men. Opposite stood, shrouded and drenched in glowing warmth and comfort, the world of woman. Images of all my woman (they were girls then) friends, their souls and spirits — seeming now as all the beauty in the world — looked out across, as through a window, at us, at me, and my soul recoiled in anguish thinking never these two worlds were to unite; never would I penetrate to the bliss and warmth on the other side.

Having evaded — and thus, failed — this challenge, this test, now my human value, my worth, was diminishing, was felt as having grown less and less. As if I was no longer fit to be reborn, only to die. Laughing, Milo and Derek pointed to a horse turd we suddenly came upon as we resumed our circuit around the lake. It was rich and steaming with life in the sunlight, yet rank and low. It was I, fit now only for cosmic manure. Selected, I felt, for death because the space I was taking up with my life burdened the world of existence more than the value it received through anything I gave back through my living.

On we moved, somehow fording a spillway that passed from the upper reservoir to the lower. Somewhere there was a hint that in the lower reservoir there was a similar soul pool to what I saw when I looked across the upper lake, only this was somehow experienced as being wholly in another, pre-earthly domain, where souls "slept" before awakening — to earth life, to spiritual awareness, or to, perhaps, awaiting some "last trumpet" at the end of time, or — all of the preceding.

I contemplated and sensed with foreboding the prospect of exiting this world. I felt myself detaching, disassociating from my increasingly less "tightly-wrapped" connection with my body. Suddenly each little life, each soul — Derek, Milo, my family, others — such too as my life, seemed to be surrounded by a shell, each a complete world of its own, an egg: wherein, all-interpenetrating, our various lives were shared but yet enclosed in a solitude in the face of the spiritual world. To leave the life of those others — my family, mother, friends, those with whom I was inter-grown — I would outfold myself from each of their dreaming lives, turning my world inside out. I would withdraw the part of myself I had inserted into each of their worlds. I could *see* this. It was as if a copy of myself — truly, part of myself — existed within each of their distinct, individual worlds. Their world would continue, minus my presence. Mine would spread out over all, beyond, into the periphery of theirs. It was as if the beginning of the inversion process, turning oneself inside-out, that Steiner describes as taking place in our soul life after death. Each copy of myself would exit as through a door, from the container of each life I inhabited.

We were nearing our starting point, yet there were many paths in the woods between where we stood and there. Before entering the woods, we lay on the grass again and surrendered ourselves to the sunlight. Derek melted into the sun. Its piercing, illuminating rays were all-seeing, all-penetrating into my soul, into the darkness of all my deeds of weakness and greed and selfishness.

Among my adolescent misdeeds, I had indulged in petty pilferage rather routinely from my place of work (somewhat ironically, a drug store) — cartons of cigarettes, quarters left before store opening for newspapers pulled from the dropped-off bunch, and of course, the odd prescription (amphetamine or barbiturate) tablet lifted from a delivery. This was all rationalized by me under the "fuck the establishment" ethos that was reflected in parts of the counter-culture. Derek, though, would have nothing of it and had chastised me previously, warning me I was creating bad karma for myself. At some level, I knew he was right, and that sense of guilt, along with the soul-infirmity my turmoil reflected, immediately fueled my reluctance to surrender to the divine sunlight, which he meanwhile basked in.

I turned from it, inviting the clouds to interpose. In gentle compassion, the light would withdraw, leaving us to the cooler shadows of the clouds. The inner soul gesture was similar to the "turning away" of the ambulance, and also the approaching divinity, as I had willed at the cast party; only now, it was the clouds I moved as I tried to hide in my fear of the light.

We walked further on into the wood. It broadened; the way was somewhat hilly; the tress hung overhead. I was not coherent. I needed minding. Derek resumed his companionable role as we wandered: Milo explored further ahead.

The trees were alive with spirits. We were in a gap between worlds. Beings from higher worlds of light and color would peer at us between the stark lower branches of the pines, and we would peek back at them as through a hundred windows. Was there a vehicle, a rocket ship, an elevator upwards; was there a cosmic guide, a way, to take us wholly to these far yet seeming familiar worlds? And I felt chained to the earth, to myself.

We had arrived at a fork in the woodland path. I sat dismayed, not knowing which way to go. Derek was unconcerned with whichever path we took, he felt in harmony with his feet and the steps before him; felt grounded in his own value and merit. I was in despair. I thought I was returning to a decision I had faced again and again, always returning to it. I looked at Derek and at the scene. I saw myself as if from without. Derek commented something casually, as I understood him, about reincarnation: "... I guess we just keep coming back until we get it right ... ". Suddenly, behind us both stood selves of earlier lives, dozens, as layered, interpenetrating shadows behind our figures, the texture of each skinned with glints of light and color that seemed they could form into windows on the experiences of past lives, perceived now from some viewpoint in eternity. These lives had driven us (again) to this crossroads. It seemed that standing at the crossroads was a curse, was doom, and that incarnation itself was doom.

This feeling of "here I am again" was, in my immediate retrospective view of this episode, to insinuate itself as being an instance indicating the reality of Ouspensky's idea of "eternal recurrence." Ouspensky had made it part of his "system," whence I had absorbed it through my readings that spring. This perspective shifted as I grew to understand Steiner's views on reincarnation.

Milo returned. He could be seen strolling peacefully through the woods, as if acting at the shepherd boy, playing on his wooden recorder. He was quietly radiant and calm. Then, turning to us he smiled and said: "Everything's dying," and indeed, even as the lush green of springtime was ripening into summer around us, Milo had perceived the autumn death of the world.

Together, we turned toward the lake. A rocky ledge, a small hilltop, weather eroded pathways between, we found on the banks two or three younger high-school kids, long-haired and likely stoned. Our state was instantly transparent to them. Stoned again. Theirs was simple boredom tinged with despair for and of their generation, lost without a map. Teenage wasteland.[119]

Each time we approached the water, my self-reproach and the silent urges of what seemed a higher, illumined part of my friends prompted me to the brink of certain self-slaughter in the reservoir. Looking down at the waterside again, the pathway down seemed a reverse birth canal into the womb of the lake.

Somewhere, from some upper perch, I had glimpsed the roadway around the reservoir and thought I saw heavy, yellow-painted earth-moving equipment — with powerful hydraulic "arms" and "legs" (as on a backhoe), with the strength to tear at the flesh of the earth. I now thought I heard the snorting and grinding of such machinery just down at the water. In my vision, a gate was formed of such hydraulic, crushing limbs — a gate that formed a maw of death, at the top of the birth canal, before the womb of the lake: the *Vagina dentata*[120] of the terrible mother, whose head-crushing power I was commanded to pass through.

I was at the ultimate extreme; it was do or die, my steps faltered downward. I took stock of myself, as the pull of death deepened, and questioned, all in a flash, but suddenly rational: *is this body mine to destroy, unworthy though its bearer (my self) may be? Did I create it? Was I not about to fall into the greatest sin of all?* My youthful readings of Dante, the damnation of self-slaughter, Sunday-school thoughts: was my human form but a creature of higher beings, a created thing? Then, dimly on high, for my mind was almost blackened with clouds of doubt, despair, self cursing, it glimmered through: your life is *not* yours to destroy; higher forces created it to serve a higher purpose. In that moment, I willed that even should life's savor be lost to me, as, indeed, I felt it was, I would suffer my body to serve its destined task in the world.

I stood now at the zero point. I was empty of impulse. Still the clouds of darkness and unknowing filled my head. I was waiting for a new impulse. The world within and without was ready to respond for good or bad, as I would bid it.

Could I but see, the source of darkness and light lay within myself.

In and around the lake

Mountains come out of the sky, and they stand there

These words are from the then-current song *Roundabout*,[121] and they suddenly bubbled up and sang out in my head: here before me was the lake, and the mountains were hanging out of the sky before me, earth's foundation having vanished.

The real-world rock band who sang this song on the radio called themselves *Yes,* and like a river of light, there suddenly poured into me, through my head, the positive energy that I would wield to rebuild my inner and outer world upon this affirmation. The thought sounded and re-sounded within me: *Yes!*

I could sense the presence, close yet from afar, of what I suddenly imagined to be a group of musicians who, likewise, had perceived this truth and were now reflecting its inspiration in their music.[122]

I saw and captured as my own truth, the recognition that *I* must be responsible for the positive or negative, good or bad, yes or no, of my world — my experience and relationship to the entire cosmic order. *My* affirmation would give value to the world, and to myself. It was as if I found a switch deep inside of myself that would turn everything either off or ON.

For me, this "yes" is effectively identical to the inner choice to recognize the world as the revelation of the spiritual. I also see this as the start of my turning toward the "mystic vow" I would learn of later in Steiner — itself, not a moment's promise, but an ever-deepening soul-intention.

All was not done. I felt that forces immense and powerful struggled still without me, struggling for my soul, for my destruction, but now also in the whole world without and not within me. No longer liable to death through earthly self-destruction, visible raging above me in the spiritual was the world-all battle itself. Terrible forces rent and twisted at the web of creation above; like clouds, streams of forces, and ranks of opposing beings tangled in strife. All ensnared, swirling within the storm I could see others, my friends; they were seen in spirit, drunken, dancing to the tune of thousands of toning beings, now seen in strife and disharmony. I could "see" my friend Alan, twisting in the midst, inanely chanting, repeating to himself "It all goes 'round in your consciousness, your unconsciousness," but this glimpse of him was simply a vignette in the storm above, as if a small gargoyle detailing an ornate gothic vault.

In this scope of intense seeing, rising from within above the battle scene, I beheld a revelation wherein all of our lives, the lives of all humanity, were as if tunes inscribed on a cosmic music machine — the songs engrooved (as if on a vinyl record platter), spinning our lives to the recorded tune[123], but musically wafting heavenward as a sacrificial god-intoxicating smoke or air, each being dancing either to the inscribed score or to the higher, freer tune that danced in the air above the music-machine, rippled into the air by the gestures, the downward glance, as of a smiling, prancing, flute-playing Krishna. *Lila.*

Each vision was glimpsed, each as if through a crack in the worlds; and then another. The yellow paint, seen (or imagined) upon as the earth-moving equipment earlier was now, on second glance, that of a yellow school bus, with the sound of school children boarding it. This was the vehicle to school! The cosmic school of higher life, the school of wisdom, which now I was free to board, which I had boarded in pre-earthly life! Gratefully, I saw in this that I was being taught — accepted or enrolled into a cosmic school.

Looking out again over the long, round, womb-world of the lake, my awareness was sprayed, shattered, across the sky. Colored bits and pieces of my world welled like walls of ocean waves, covering the sky with thousands of shards of light and color. My body was now (in a dream) a giant human skeleton, its spine laid down, bridging the length of the water as if the keel of a huge ship under construction. Like gunnels, my ribs were formed above, embracing the sky. The creation of a new human form awaited the crossing of the lake, the crossing the will-of-gods, up the length of my spine, weaving the out-spread forms and forces of the surrounding sky into earthly, shrunken human form.

Still, I wandered the woods surrounding the lake, and still my grip on my earthly, bodily self was slight and feeble. Upwards away from the water, my friends guided me, up a path. As I mounted, I felt my life dropping away from me. Not violently, only left behind, as I ascended, dizzily, into new heights. My journey through to the new existence would lead me through my head, through my forehead. The dark clouds were gone, and a bright light shone in my forehead, illuminating my forebrain — as if a vast unused organ of higher thought, higher consciousness — as if I had brought my head above water, and through my forebrain, I was viewing a new reality. It seemed a tight band that previously had bound my head, constricting it to narrow thought, was loosed or broken, and light poured in as my presence massed before and within my head, standing again before my second self. My life, and each of my steps today had been guided here, by this self. The promptings of my friends, their thoughts, their lives — they now foregathered there in this head, no longer "inside," in unison, as one multi-fold being, one higher *I* to bid me, it seemed, godspeed. Their voices spoke within me, my voice within them. The solitude of the separate life shells gave way to unity as each of our spirits deeply interpenetrated the other. I thought that 'I' was dying, but now not by terror and destruction, but by slipping away, passing into the unity within me, together in communion with my friends, whose souls were present within me as close as my own thoughts. It was as if they had been living inside my head *all my life*, only now, at what seemed as though it might be my final hour, I could transparently see them within me.[124]

Yet I turned from there before the final step. The battle still waged without. Doubt still could chill my heart, and within were dark and turbulent forces welling. I lay down, weakened, supplicant, worn down? My will was struggling forward. I lay down with head in hands, and buried my face in the earth, suffering myself to bury in the earth the darkness that now, again, overwhelmed me, blotting out my sight, yet I persisted somehow in my will to bear it all. With a roar and in deafening waves I was submerged, descending, as if to be swallowed by the earth and the underworld and its dark forces, descending from darkness to darkness.

And then, in a sideways, upwards glance, I all at once beheld the majesty that stood beyond it all. Beyond the earth, beyond the stars, standing in infinite splendor and infinite might, stood the pure white column of the pillar of the universe. The world tree from which all worlds were hung like boughs; or, as I would later learn of in Hindu sacred stories, the "lingam of light." Spiraling round it, in sacred service, watching over the world of worlds, were mighty beings forged of the same light. It was the spine, the axis, round which all revolved, through time immeasurable. The progress of the worlds was measured here.

Reflecting on the description of the "long body of the solar system" found in Collins' *The Theory of Celestial Influence*, as previously read about that spring, it is as if Collins' picture was a shadow or caricature of this all-glorious vision.

Though I was laying on the ground in surrender, it seems I could not retain this sight for a moment before it slipped away. Even so, just a glimpse was to see, again, as through a chink in a wall, the seeming all of eternal time and space in a moment — or rather, the perch from which is seen the all that is evolving and growing in eternity.

And soon I was being led away by Derek and Milo. Turning back across the lake, I saw again where I had left behind, peacefully, my thoughts about Ruth. The sense of separation from the world of the feminine was gone.

Restored to my seat in the back of the bus, we departed. I was shattered. Gravity was being restored, and the pieces of my daily self were slowly sorting into place. The radio played a rock anthem as we left: *Hold Your Head Up*[125] — a song about a woman extolled to be proud rather than shamed — but here received as an exhortation for me to go forth again into the world.

Driven home, I was falling away from the realm of kaleidoscoping awareness, though spirit poured and echoed through the world, reforming itself again into the landscape I had dwelt within so seemingly comfortably that morning. As we retraced our path, the road led into town and nearer and nearer again to my family's home, where I somehow feared I was to be deposited, still incoherent, on the front lawn, my clandestine drug use revealed to my disapproving parents. However, we just scraped by my neighborhood in passing, driving quickly by the familiar barn-red liquor store with the "Corner Spirit Shoppe" sign — which seemed now to betoken a new sense.

We drove on instead to the beach. The hazy skies found there seemed to both mask, and dimly reveal in masking, the glimpsed wondrous cosmic worlds that lay beyond ours. The frisbee now spun through the sky as if cosmically powered, pure energy, carrying our souls into the cosmic energy traces as we tracked its pathways going high into the air.

The grains of sand on the beach, which I embraced, sifted, shoved, and poured through my hands, were now the primal mother stuff, the cosmic prakriti[126], of the world. I began to feel my contact with the silica-laden tiny pieces of mother earth as grounding.

And then after a time, at last, there was nothing to do but to head home, exhausted, on edge, but finally passable as a self-possessed human.

Returning home, I lay for a time on the living room couch. I greeted my father on the lawn when he came home from his job in New York City around six thirty or seven. It was a lovely summer evening.

Sleep would not come until the echoes of the drug began to quiet, fourteen hours since we had started.

7

Summer Sunshine

Although this last trip was more profound and soul-churning than the cast party in many ways, it was significantly different in that I was already deeply preoccupied with the possibilities of transformation. Its content, while plumbing an abyss of soul shadows, was overall a strongly affirming, rewarding, and in many ways illuminating contact with the spiritual. I felt I had been through the soul-wringer and come out the other side "more or less" cleansed and renewed. Something was progressing. The impact of that day has remained with me throughout the rest of my life.

Once I had come down and recovered myself, there was a more integral sense of completion; and dealing with the aftermath was more a question of continuing the process of stitching the experience into my evolving worldview and inner attitude.

In the first weeks of summer, life became a bit tense for Ted, Alan, and me. Alan and I were still working at the pharmacy; Ted, who had worked there before going off to boarding school, occasionally substituted for us. Somewhat dramatically, it fell out that the pilfering of drugs that each of us had indulged in was discovered, and the three of us were — quite appropriately — thrown out in a house cleaning sweep. We managed to avoid getting into serious trouble with a combination of frantic hand-waving cover stories and repentant trips to the woodshed (lecturing) with the owner before we were all fired. Years later, I was able to make some direct karmic recompense to him. Between this event and the chastising elements of the cast party and the lake, I lost any appetite for the "fuck the establishment" ethos.

I had two further significant trips that summer. Milo and I dosed again within the next three or four weeks. The connection with nature at the lake had been highly positive, and we initially planned to camp out overnight in a field at the far side of town — we parked nearby and carried our sleeping bags in before twilight. We were trying to recreate the favorable influence of the natural setting at the reservoir. But as twilight fell, the insects that started swarming around the field proved intolerable, and we decided to pack it in and head for Milo's house shortly after we had begun to get off. I recall that before we left, I watched the evening stars come out, and I felt a sense of warmth and communion with them, gazing up into the darkening blue evening sky.

In thinking back to the intensity of that trip, I'm tempted to suppose that we possibly split a dose, as its overall energy level was not as powerful as the cast party or the lake. However, it is also possible that either the recovery time after the last trip (this would have been perhaps less than a month later) was not sufficient to reset my drug tolerance or that I had "pushed through" a certain milestone. I was able to maintain my psychedelic poise more stably while bringing in new domains of awareness.

At any rate, we went back to Milo's house. His room was over the garage — it was an attic, really, and separated by a little porch from the rest of the house, so we pursued the night there undisturbed by his family. After a while, some friends stopped by. My primary recollection was that Milo and I were able to converse "philosophically" from a newly informed and deeply shared perspective. I should comment that I hadn't per se been able to relay the details to Milo of my experience — nor he of is — but for all that, there was a "sense of things" that had evolved and fed into our everyday pondering of spiritual matters which had increasingly come to preoccupy us.

Somewhere in this conversation, we came to a shared vision of the flow and interchange of life forces between birth and death in the earth world as a unitary world process, prompting Milo to ask me, "If it all gets recycled into the system, what's the point of being a vegetarian?" I had already encountered this question in reading Steve Gaskin, replying with his answer, which was, "You can't vibe very high with animals if you want to eat them."

We talked and pondered while at the same time taking in our surroundings as they were psychedelically shape-shifting. Perhaps the biggest learning that I took from this next trip was a clear realization that when in the altered state of LSD, one can be operating at multiple semantic levels and planes of reality. One needs to pay attention to what order of reality was claiming the forefront — one can't apply the same mechanisms of integration to the expanded range of inputs that one applies habitually in everyday life. One must pay attention and learn to observe that because, for example, people *appeared* to be acting out a scene from your personal psychic mythology, it doesn't mean they *actually* are doing that — at least, not in their foreground reality. Similarly, if you become aware of how your *consciousness* is suddenly "extremely light and free of gravity," it doesn't mean your *physical* body can fly. Not that that was a risk for me, but I came to understand how some people did think they could fly and injure themselves while on acid. And most importantly, the impulse towards spiritual rebirth is not to be confused with the destruction of the body.

As the disassociation connected with the etheric loosening that can occur in psychedelic situations becomes active, the discerning semantic deconstruction of the layers of one's psychic reality becomes critical. This can be seen as one reads across the details, for example, of my lake experience. One's imaginative reading of the outer world can be overlaid with material from one's own inner process, emerging into awareness in the expanded state. One's own dynamics can interact with those of others and with the inspired influx of cosmic realities, which possess their own transformative force and their own characteristic supersensible physiognomy.

There is a counterpoise between experiencing the gestures and behavior of others as their independent conscious action instead of their "falling into" or inserting themselves into what is really one's own "semi-delusional but personally relevant" story. Because we are deeply spiritually connected to one another, one may be communicating one's soul needs, story-wise, in a way that others "play into[127]." The realization of the presence of the Double in consciousness, that is, the vital presence seen and accepted of one's own shadow, is the ballast that allows one to maintain the equipoise of discernment.

Other vignettes from that evening with Milo include a warm soul picture welling inside me that night, which I would characterize as a sense of having emerged (or, perhaps as still emerging) from a common "soul pool" along with my circle of friends. It was as if a somewhat dimly sensed memory, that we had — prior to this life — dwelt together in a "nest" or womb of soul-growth together — drawing nourishment from a shared spiritual source and having a feeling of interpenetration amongst ourselves within the "brooding" state. Although the vision had an "embryonic" quality, I would be at a loss to assert whether I felt I was living into an actual pre-birth state or, alternatively, a spiritual awareness of how we were — as teenagers — just in the process of being "born" out of our soul-astral tribal identity into a more individualized stage.

Predictably, we listened to music. I was deeply affected by a Randy Newman[128] album and the song "Mama told me not to Come[129]." I saw it as a kind of recollection of what would have been a pre-birth exhortation by the Great Mother to side-step this world of earthly incarnation. It was a mood of nostalgia for a past that was before the confusion of earth life — seen as "that ain't no way to have fun."

We were still tripping when morning came, veering toward a gentle crash. We went for a walk through a nearby schoolyard very shortly after dawn. The grass was covered in dew. It was sensed as an all-renewing gift from the heavens as the sun rose and the dewdrops sparkled. At the same time, my inner sense of depletion, as usual at the end of a trip, felt like a cleansing, as if my brain had been inwardly brushed and cleansed. And we were, of course, more or less exhausted.

I think this second trip with Milo must have been his last; by next autumn, he was thoroughly caught up in the movement that had touched what seemed like half the kids in my age group: the devotion to the thirteen-year-old "perfect master" Maharaj Ji[130] (Prem Rabat), here from India and dispensing what he called knowledge. I, however, was having none of this trip, although I know it must have represented a meaningful stage for many people. Here, there, and everywhere, so many of us were reaching out through the chaos of the spiritual sterility of the fifties post-war era and the chaos of the sixties counter-culture. Milo believed that Maharaj Ji was the successor, among other things, to Meher Baba, who had "dropped his body" in 1969.

Ever since the lake, and into this second trip with Milo, things continued to shift inside of me. The influences of the variety of writings I was sponging up and, more importantly, the humbling moral shift in how I saw myself within this hugely expanded perspective were beginning to solidify into, at any rate, the kernel of some new inner nucleus. Day to day, I was mostly just another teenage pothead with any number of issues, hangups, foibles, and what have you. But with a decided spiritual *interest*. And I also found that I was beginning to gain a new centeredness in a completely different reality when I traveled over the high-dose LSD threshold.

In late July, I took LSD again, this time with Ash; we hung out with my friend Paul, his girlfriend, and another girl visiting from the UK — Paul had just returned from two years living in London. Only Ash and I were tripping. I would say that on this trip, I first felt myself possessing a sense of full and responsible agency in terms of shifting focus between the outer context — psychedelically decorated, but nevertheless fully self-possessed — and the inner spiritually saturated context, which I experienced as powerfully rich in thought, insight, imagination, and connection with a deeper level of spiritual reality that was lighting up for me and that I felt I was being given increasingly fluid access to.

Paul's home was near the beach, and the five of us walked there after dark. On the way to the beach, I felt a delightful "looseness" from the sense of being enclosed within my skin, coupled with a rising up of energy from within my body that seemed to bubble forth in consciousness in a stable and harmonizing way. At the same time, I was a bit more detached from the "inflated" type of "apparent feeling of harmony" that had puffed me up at the lake. My "second man" within no longer felt entirely like a riddle, more like a friend.

Arriving at the beach, we began wandering up and down the sands. At one point, Paul began molding the sand into a pair of larger-than-life human figures. In his sculptural actions, molding the "electric sand" twinkling in the dark, I saw him acting out (or recreating) the creation story of humanity by higher beings. He was playful and spouting some story that accompanied his actions; I wasn't quite focused on what he was saying, but it somehow seemed to synchronize with the creation fantasy I was flowing with. After a bit, he chimed in with some comment as if a judgment of the (moral) imperfection of the creation and erased the sand sculpture. It felt magically biblical while, at the same time, playful.

Walking on, wandering the beach, something triggered a thought about my friend George mentioned earlier, who had suffered a psychological breakdown. Floating in my mind was a sense that he, I, and my immediate circle of friends formed some kind of soul collective that, through our having been born and living in the same time and space together, we were also in part co-creating and forming each other's soul structures. This somewhat echoed the feeling of the soul-nest of my recent trip with Milo. Within this sensed collective soul, it came to me that there had been some fault in the way we had upheld (for want of a better word) George.

It was not the case actually that there had been any particular outer misdeeds of ours in this regard. He was outwardly generally as well-liked as the next of us. But there was a palpable, visible sense that there was a collective involvement in his failure to find the right footing — a special need of his that I suppose had not been met in terms of being somehow "upheld in thought." Perhaps it was just a kind of cosmic survivor guilt.

Wandering on and looking out into the sky over the waters of the Long Island Sound, I transparently perceived that the firmament was pulsing and weaving with the creative thought and world-creative will activity of innumerable souls whose creative influence was forming the outer periphery of my soul-space; as if my soul-aura had expanded to touch and "see" this creative weaving amongst the stars. This intertwining of souls was strangely parallel to the living churning of the lake, which I had feared would consume me; here, it was all-welcoming and all-expanding.

I correlated this with the mystic consciousness John Lilly relates in *The Center of the Cyclone*, that of the so-called "+3" state described there as "The Essence as One of the Creators." This was, however, realized more from the still-grounded-on-earth perspective looking up, as if I were outside, rather than from the full immersion inside of the creative interpenetration that he describes.

This was a defining and liberating moment for me; I felt I was at a point of balance and top-to-bottom alignment with the spiritual cosmos whilst living out an earthly existence.

I will describe later how this came to connect with a specific indication from Steiner on the path of knowledge.

As we continued to amble further down the beach, Paul, Ash, and the visiting friend headed back toward Paul's house. Somehow I found myself left behind with Paul's girlfriend, Nancy. The three of us had spent some time together earlier that summer (she was likewise transitioning back from the UK, where she had met Paul, to her family home in Pennsylvania). As Paul would later recount to me, she had developed a certain sort of fondness for me, although I don't want to overstate this. She was lovely, and I certainly enjoyed her company, although I hadn't supposed there was anything by way of an energetic connection.

And then we sat together atop one of the white wooden lifeguard chairs that dotted the beach. I suppose one of us climbed up there first, and the other followed — to "take the view," staring out into the darkness above the water. I imagine that it was when we were already parked up there together that the others decided to start heading back home.

I don't remember how long we were there or what we talked about, but the context must have started as gentle banter. And then something extraordinary developed. It had grown cold (or seemed to me that way anyway), and I must have remarked it. Turning to my right toward her, I felt what can only be described as mystical soul-warmth suddenly and completely warming my body. She spoke something I took in as inviting, and I could feel something of her soul-essence approaching me as if she was bringing her essential self closer to me across the void of a distant soul space within her. To me, it felt there was something of a sexual-romantic nature tinging the warmth, her words, her smile. Or, the more intensely I felt what I took to be her soul-essence, the more her feminine quality was amplified, charging my response.

I retreated from this — partially due to my general insecurity with the female sex, but much more so because, as Paul's friend, the thought seemed simply illicit. As I turned away to my left, the nighttime cold was suddenly felt in my bones, and as I turned toward her again, I could feel the warmth pouring back into me, filling me from head to toe.

I have to stress that there is nothing metaphorical about all this; it was an absolutely tangible warmth experience. The warmth was not only (deeply) felt but also seemed visibly to rise and fall as part of her inner aura.

And then the moment faded; there was no real-world consequence, and we headed back to the house together, where the five of us continued our late-night chitchat. We engaged in silly conversations, interrupted for me by occasionally fading in and out a bit into far-out, internal spaces. I recall being seized momentarily with a sense of perceiving the intertwining structures of creation as the activity of "the universal mind."

It was two in the morning when Ash and I headed back to my home. It being summertime, I routinely stayed out late, although usually not that late. So I was shocked and startled to come home and find my father sitting and waiting at the kitchen table in his underwear, reading the paper, and furious that we had been out so late. It was, strangely, the only time I could think of when my father waited up for me like this. Usually, it was my mother who slept like a brooding hen with one eye half open, waiting to hear me come home — the two of us had it down to a science in terms of subtle signaling.

Having your father angry with you is not super fun when high on acid; at the same time, knowing him, I felt safe and could maintain my balance. After a minute, he stormed off — I'm sure at some point earlier that evening, he had noticed we were pretty late and began to wait up, worrying. The fact that I had Ash with me probably restrained his ire.

We headed into my bedroom, which was adjacent to the kitchen. The display of paternal anger understandably shook Ash. In a flash, I went through a sudden shift out of the father/son entanglement and saw instead that who he was as an eternal individuality and who he was in the role of my father were two distinct things. From the point of view of his father role, his behavior was completely understandable. Since I loved my father, I felt, in fact, generally grateful for his taking on the Father role with me, even if it meant doling out the occasional reprimand.

We were still pretty high, although not peaking anymore. I began to be conscious as if I were aware of how another part of my being existed purely in the spiritual world. I was creating/observing / managing the "David in incarnation" scene below[131] — while at the same time, my consciousness was permeated by the three-dimensional here and now.

As mentioned earlier, I now felt a considerable measure of "control" in adjusting my focus between the outer and deeply inner. During the earlier part of the evening, we had been with the others (who were not tripping), and Ash and I were each more or less in our own spaces, psychedelically speaking. I remember having the impulse to share some of what I was experiencing with Ash, and I focussed my attention on him and tried, gently, to permeate his soul reality with mine. I had a similar sense of merging consciousness as during the lake trip and trying to communicate something of my spiritual state. Looking back, I can't say I have any clear idea of his side of it. I was trying to bring his attention to certain qualities — higher perceptions — in our expanded field of consciousness. I vaguely remember him acknowledging to a certain extent — that he had seen something previously unseen under my direct influence. But it was momentary.

That ends the story, as best as I can recall, of my psychedelic ventures in the summer before I went to college in Boston. Excepting Ted, my first partner in these journeys, I was not to trip again with any of the high school friends I had first ventured with.

8

Tent of Mystery

My freshman semester at school in Boston, at Emerson College, is a notable chapter in itself. I had originally been interested in Emerson because I thought Alan would also attend; as it was to turn out, that didn't happen.

I was seventeen and living away from home for the first time. My dorm was in an old row house at the beginning of Commonwealth Avenue, a principal boulevard in central Boston. It was actually three houses linked together on the ground floor; you would enter through the middle house. The middle and left buildings were the girl's dorms; if you turned right, you were in the boy's dorm.

Each floor had two large rooms, front and back, with a central staircase — except the first floor, where I was assigned, where the front room was the entry parlor, furnished with a few chairs and tables.

Each large room was assigned to four students, and so I found that I had three roommates. The room also had its own bath and kitchen. This arrangement proved interesting after I met Edie, who became my girlfriend and dropped out of high school, and moved in with me, off and on, for a couple of months.

I right away discovered that two of my roommates likewise were acidheads, the third more of a "stoner jock." I was also pleasantly surprised that one of them, Hank, was an enthusiast of Steve Gaskin, whose books *Monday Night Class* and *Caravan* I had been reading avidly since the past spring. Hank was, like me, a typically long-haired guy with glasses — trending toward a bit of a "hippie nerd" look.

In the six months since my 'cast party' experience, I had managed to get a fair amount of further psychedelic experience — at a variety of dosages — under my belt. I likewise did a fair amount of wrestling with them and continued to expand my reading to provide some of the "raw material of thought" to navigate the new landscape. And while at one level, I remained a hedonistically oriented dope-smoking punk kid, I was increasingly identified with and comfortable with the idea that I was, very definitely, on some kind of spiritual path.

The college environment was a bit mixed for me in terms of drug use generally. Having come from a high school environment where at least half — or so it seemed, at any rate — of the student population were experimenting with a fairly broad spectrum of drugs (and naturally, including alcohol) in a fairly permissive atmosphere, I was both a little jaded in a "been there, done that" sense — at least as far as non-stop indiscriminate drug use was concerned. Some of the kids were just "busting loose" for the first time. The majority of the guys I would wind up hanging out with were relating to their freshman year of college as if a continuation of their High School behaviors with the "plus" of the latitude a lack of parental oversight provided. And while that was, in a way, likewise true for me, I was very definitely pursuing a journey into a deepening of the psychedelic experience, specifically, and looking for others to share that kind of journey with.

I thus arrived at a school in Boston stoked for doing more acid and exploring the new realms of being that were opening up for me.

It was at once obvious to me that the dorm arrangement would not provide a lot of privacy. Losing my virginity at college, the sooner, the better, was a goal for me; this lack of privacy seemed an issue. In the first week, I trekked to the hardware store on Arlington Avenue and purchased some hook eyes, clothesline, and somewhere dug up a hippie-style Indian print sheet, augmented by a large swath of muslin, and created a sort of personal tent

TENT OF MYSTERY

within the bigger space. So I had my own semi-private — with an emphasis on semi—space. This would prove instrumental.

I disassembled the bed and stashed it somewhere, leaving the mattress on the floor hippie-style. I had a crate of vinyl LPs right next to the mattress, with a small stereo player on top. And I had typical hippie accouterments — incense, oils, and of course, drugs — stashed here and there. And, shelved on the dresser against part of the wall of the tent, a number of books that grew as the semester progressed.

My roommates Hank and I immediately connected through our common interest in Steve Gaskin. He was also — curiously to me at the start — an enthusiast for James Joyce's[132] *Finnegan's Wake* [133]; Joseph Campbell's[134] *A Skeleton Key to Finnegan's Wake*[135] was his constant companion. I absorbed enough of Hank's descriptions to, among other things, begin to be acquainted indirectly with Giambattista Vico[136], the eighteenth-century thinker whose ideas concerning the cyclic nature of history were not only influential on Joyce but, in their way, likely served to sensitize me to the idea of the evolution of consciousness across history, as I was to eventually find it in Steiner.

I mixed with the other guys in my dorm building readily, and there was an open flow from room to room in the dorm overall and an open circulation of drugs — mostly pot, shared or sold — bongs everywhere — but also acid. I know early on, I did a couple of trips with Hank; one that involved hanging out in the dorm with some of the other guys, and another in Cambridge attending a double feature showing of the thirties film "Reefer Madness"[137] and the recently released Firesign Theater's *Martian Space Party*.[138]

I can only recall of the former experience being in an upstairs dorm with a bunch of guys, smoking pot and laughing and such. Not sure who else was on acid, but I do recall one moment where, in the middle of the conversation, I "anticipated" what one of the guys was about to say and spoke it. I had been tracking his thinking very closely and also felt a strong intuitive attunement. Whatever I said, he felt I had read his mind, and he said so with a certain astonishment. Sync.

The movie experience was, content-wise, zany and experienced by Hank and me as such. The Firesign Theater I was already fond of and knew through their records. These were complex and required multiple listenings to grab all the levels of nuance; the film was a bit too much to take in one dose.

I do recall standing with Hank, after the movie, out on Massachusetts Avenue, and having the onset of a sudden sense of the sweep of history as a soul-spiritual motion, although I can't recall the specific triggering thought — we were discussing something or other philosophically. I recalled that instant many years later reading about Steve Jobs saying that his LSD usage inspired him to want to 'move the world' or some such. The expansiveness of thought can broaden one's feeling for historical time as a living thing. Perhaps Hank had just been sharing some idea from Vico as related to his passion for *Finnegan's Wake*.

My friend Paul went to school an hour away, at Clark University in Worcester, and I would occasionally hitchhike there for a weekend visit. I dosed there once by myself. I recall having a rather extended series of inner visions picturing the ancient Hindu period and the division of humanity into castes.

I was at a psychedelic, spiritually attuned level formulating in an Imagination what I thought I knew about the ancient Hindu caste system in primary Vedic times. I found myself in vision, falling into something like a replay of what I understood of this earlier structuring of human society. It developed inwardly in the form, as it were, of a kind of mandala drawing painted in my inner seeing. This kind of separation into classes is obviously inappropriate in the modern world, where the freedom of the individual is paramount, but I was seeing it in my highly activated imaginative eye as reflecting rather an emergence of different human "types" out of some kind of primal archetypes. At the back of the picture, there seemed to be something I can I think only describe as "serpent wisdom." In the background also was the sense of how individual human souls develop through life experiences across multiple incarnations.

This was, I'm sure, influenced by my recent reading of the *Bhagavad Gita* — which I would have acquired gratis from an orange-robed, top-knotted Hare Krishna on the streets of Boston. Although it was abstract imagery, it was another example for me of how the historical past can be felt as living inside of you.

TENT OF MYSTERY

Although it was decidedly not a precision reading of what Steiner would describe as the Akashic record, it enhanced my sense of the eternal presence of past times, existing accessibly to the right state of consciousness.

Boston and Cambridge were alive with all the many trappings of the youth counter-culture scene: bookshops, restaurants, kids in the streets. I became a denizen of the many bookshops in Boston and Cambridge, searching the streams of spiritual books then finding their way into the world. I spent a lot of time at an occult/new age bookstore a few blocks down, I think on Dartmouth, in a basement shop. I have a vague memory that I may have glanced over my first book by Steiner there. Purchases there included a book by Rajneesh (aka Osho[139]) and *The Gospel of Thomas* from the Nag Hammadi Library,[140] one of the earliest publications from that find.

One of the delightful perks of dorm life turned out to be that the boyfriend of our "house mother" — our resident "grownup in charge" — happened to work for the big concert promoter in town (Don Law), and we were recruited via a sign-up in the dorm to serve as ushers at weekly concerts. I managed to see (and get paid for it) Yes — my favorite band — Elton John, David Bowie, and others, huge name acts of that time.

Probably around the end of the first month at school — September — I was to meet the girlfriend of a newly found friend, John. This was Edie. She was still in high school in Long Island, where they had grown up together. I had been making an effort to interest John, with some success, in the spiritual element of my psychedelic wanderings.

John had apparently created an interest in her in meeting me. I can still picture her bursting upon me with a charming smile and a wave while I was on the phone with someone. This was our first meeting.

And meanwhile, at some point during her first weekend visit, we went off for a walk together and found ourselves "speaking the same language" — or at least, so it seemed — regarding our psychedelic experiences. We seemed to connect and click, more or less from the get-go, on a "psychedelic soul wavelength."

And then she visited again in the next week or two, and — facilitated by the privacy my tent provided — more or less spontaneously, we fell into a sexual situation and became intimate. Naturally, this betrayal put a brake on the friendship that had been developing with John. Handling sexual relationships with integrity proved to me to be something taking years to develop.

In the next weeks, I visited her at her parent's home in Long Island. We would write. (No internet, email, or cell phones!) I got the sense she was finding the social scene at her school difficult (she was then a high school senior). I was nonetheless quite surprised when she dropped out of school, left home, and arrived in Boston to live with me — in my little tent in my dorm room, with three other guys on the other side of the curtains.

Looking back, there was a lot of turbulent stuff going on here. She was very different from me in countless ways — clearly a big part of the attraction, but at that quite tender age, I was more than a little ill-equipped to successfully surf that particular edge for too long.

Edie was a lovely soul with a wild spirit. Only later did it become clear that she was on her way to a lifelong struggle with mental illness, which was to announce itself definitively a few years after we first met. She came from a privileged, affluent family. I knew that her mother had been a lifelong recovering alcoholic with a fairly bumpy recovery. I picture this contributed to her inner turmoil, although there must have been more.

The world was to lose Edie too soon. She sadly passed away some years ago in an ambiguous cloud of drugs and alcohol.

These, however, seemed more innocent times or, more accurately, naive. Before any overt psychological issues of hers had materialized, we experienced several significant acid trips during our time together. Hank would often pal along with us, including on these trips.

Throughout my later study and reading of Steiner's work, I often find that as I piece together his descriptions of spiritual/clairvoyant perception and experience, I suddenly find that a memory-picture of a psychedelic scene arises that, in a flash, is seen as corresponding to something that Steiner wished to convey.

Almost invariably, they are descriptions of things that, taken at face value from Steiner, tend to be confounding from the point of view of our everyday understanding.

An example of this can be found in his *The World of the Senses and the World of the Spirit*, where he says (Lecture 5): "We can therefore say: Substance that can be perceived through Intuition, spiritual substance, constantly streams forth from the human being in the same measure as his physical nervous system disintegrates."

Intuition, as used above, is a technical term in Steiner (along with *Imagination* and *Inspiration)* that can be understood variously depending on context. Generally speaking, *Intuition* refers to a cognitive state of direct experience of the spiritual world through a kind of merging with the beings therein; or, conversely, as above, as a kind of "consciousness-substance" corresponding to that state and reflecting the inner nature of a spiritual being.

This connects me directly with a memory of a mescaline session with Edie and Hank. We spent a good part of the day wandering around the Boston Museum of Fine Art — in particular, enjoying the splendors of the Asian artwork collection. As I recall, I would say that we were managing to function on the edge of a moderately intense ecstatic consciousness. There were moments of disorientation here and there, but we were sailing through. The imagery at the museum was rich and alive.

I very specifically recall leaving the museum and walking about near Huntington Avenue and gazing across at Edie, who was a few steps behind me. In my psychedelically structured perception, I could visually sense and perceive how, what, for lack of a better term, there was a beam of cosmic light-energy that seemed to penetrate into her head, her brain, angling down upon her from the far reaches of the sky, the heavens, above her — bestowing ecstasy, somewhat similarly to the flash of "+12" experienced at the start of my trip at the lake. In my sensing, it felt as though it were drawing her out of her body with a bliss-bestowing power; she was smiling joyfully, and it was all part of the shared mood of delight, energy, and bliss that we were going through together. I was feeling-sensing differentiated layers of what I took to be her experience, and included in the entire perceptual gestalt was the (unsettling at the time) experience that this ecstatic state was intensively depleting something in the very substance of her physical brain. It was as if a fine substance was dripping out of her head.

It is a commonplace that the psychedelic experience will result in what is felt and experienced as a depleted nervous system, and I was already familiar with the idea that, indeed, specific neurotransmitter substances were "consumed." This coupled itself with the anxiety that this depletion was, to a certain extent, to be guarded against and that we were in a state of excess, of dissolution.

Much later, I was to find that it is part of Steiner's thought that the body is organized along two poles: the will-metabolism-limb system pole, and the nerve-sense-thinking pole, with the rhythmic-feeling system of heart and lungs mediating between them. Intrinsic to this concept is the very precise idea that the state of wide-awake consciousness that we experience every day is wrested from our body, through the nervous system, by opposing the processes of life, which of themselves tend to absorb the soul in an unconscious state, like that of the growing plant. And in so doing, it promotes destructive ("anti-growth") death processes in the nervous system that are only restored by sleep.

This idea may seem outlandish in the first encounter. Something of this idea is indicated if we consider the nature of the nerve cell tissue itself — nerve tissue is demonstrably the least vital, in the sense of least regenerative, tissue in the body.

The notion that we have of the nervous system (or brain) development when we think of learning, for example, seems to contradict this in that we suppose that the brain "grows" more organized through experience and memory. If we consider, however, that consciousness is purchased at the price of the destruction of nerve "life," it can then follow that sleep, that is, reversion to the purely living, growing (relative) unconsciousness as of the plant, is a restoration process. The restoration process of sleep rebuilds the structures which support specific newly learned cognitive processes, which are then available to be applied the next day.

This experience near the museum was snapshotted and filed away, and we continued home down Huntington Avenue.

Hank, Edie, and I tripped together at least one other time, wandering first through the Public Gardens, the large park in downtown Boston near our Commonwealth Avenue dorm. Getting off, we lay on the grass, and I became conscious of a warm channel of soul-spiritual energy rising up inside me, from deep within, up my spine, again enlivening my head consciousness. The energy seemed, in some way, to have a feminine quality. From there, the three of us were off into a new experience of the environs of central Boston. We traveled off as evening fell, traipsing through the Beacon Hill streets among the old brick fashionable homes. I recall at one corner, standing by the window of a private home, an elderly, stern, and quite straight-laced and disapproving woman glared out her window, staring reproachfully as we momentarily peered inside while we caroused a bit at the corner. I think she had been observing us before we noticed her; she at once pulled her blinds shut. One could sense the banishment from her perceptual consciousness that she was effecting; the closing of the blinds severed some kind of psychic connection formed through our momentary sharing of a gaze. As she did this, Edie commented to the effect, "Ah! I will dream of this tonight." It felt like she was speaking out of some deep insight into how our dream stories are created and formed out of the habitually unperceived aspect of our waking experience. She had felt the dream content being absorbed into her soul.

Anthroposophy indicates that, during sleep, the soul is effectively "outside the body" and living in another domain of consciousness. (More precisely, in anthroposophical terms, the I and astral body separate from the etheric and physical bodies.) During this time, we review the events of the day in reverse — most recently experienced first, then previously, and so on. We then perceive our deeds, our behavior — the impact of our existence in the world — as if inside-out, and thus sense it then as it affects other beings. This inside-out perception is thus a moral awakening. We do not retain consciousness of this on awakening, but the experience is reflected in a disordered way in our dreams. Steiner holds that there also is a spiritual, *Intuitive* content of our experience that escapes our daytime consciousness but that is "hoarded up" to be reviewed as part of this process while in our body-free state.

I would, from time to time, get glimpses, intriguing but in many ways foreign to my more rational approach, of Edie's inner world in little pictures or mutterings she made. Sometimes as she drifted to sleep at night, I would hear her whisper, "Ah, Morpheus ..." as she greeted her dream world. We would spend many nights talking together in the narrow bed, exchanging our deepest soul stories. It would seem at times that we both penetrated the other's soul deeply. This was all surrounded meanwhile by the day-to-day turbulence and relationship issues, no doubt fairly typical of teenage romances and, of course, exaggerated by the living arrangement.

Back to that night together on Beacon Hill, we strolled away and wound up on the other side of the Boston Commons, and for some reason, in and out of the subway line (the "T"), riding the escalators (we didn't get on a train — possibly we just wanted to cross under the street). As I rode down the escalator, I thought of Gurdjieff's saying in *In Search of the Miraculous:* "If you want to ride the sleigh down, you must also climb up the hill." This was tied in, in my thinking at the moment, with his whole idea of the maleficent role of the Moon in his cosmic scheme. I projected myself into the glimpsed mechanism and gears of the escalator and felt it as somehow part of a soul-crushing "recycling" mechanism of the cosmos. It was not terrifying but was a kind of meditation on the ultimate implications of Gurdjieff's characterization of the "mechanicalness" of the everyday human — being chewed up by the machine.

From there, as we rounded the Commons, we encountered a street corner preacher, a large, bible-thumping man, exhorting all to harken to the need to be saved by Jesus. He had the usual vehement fire and brimstone type of energy pouring out of him. It was not a pleasant aura to be near, and we moved to avoid him. I'm sure Edie made some comment about his bad-vibes type energy; she was always reacting sensitively (and unfiltered) to the energies of people around her.

During those autumn months, Edie was to come and go several times, returning home and then leaving again to return to stay with me.

Once after dropping her off for a trip home (sadly for both of us) at the bus station, I was wandering back to my dorm room and was startled to find my friend Ted walking — quite unexpectedly — down the sidewalk toward me, grinning.

It seems he had just dropped out and run away from the boarding school his parents had sent him to last year. He had been held back and was repeating his senior year. Apparently, my dorm was a magnet for runaways. He spent several days with me. I had lately acquired a supply of dried peyote buttons; Ted and I did these together at least once during that stay. It was not highly transformative, but I found myself navigating many of the thoughts I had been absorbing and talking with Ted more philosophically than we previously had. The topic of Jesus came up, and he (jokingly) pressed his finger firmly against my foot (I was lying on one of my roommate's beds) as if nailing me to the cross. I felt a sudden sense of identification with Jesus on the cross; the whole energy of the crucifixion welled up, assuming a sudden reality, and I jumped and pulled away — I wasn't keen to be crucified. It was a micro-stigmata moment.

In the between times (and classes, which I attended somewhat randomly), I continued to read, acquiring a miscellany of books on the topic of psychedelics and other spiritual development topics. I read further the books of Gurdjieff, Ouspensky, and other "Fourth Way" writers, especially Maurice Nicoll. I was affected by my readings of Nicoll's books on the gospels: *The New Man*[141] and *The Mark*[142] — contextualizing the parables of Jesus relative to the Gurdjieff work, the principal writings of which I was already deeply immersed. This helped bring my relationship to Christianity — or, more clearly, the Christ being — into a place where it could begin to harmonize with my experience of the spiritual-psychedelic cosmos. I already mentioned reading the *Bhagavad Gita*, gifted by the Hare Krishnas dotting the streets of Boston looking for converts. I also read voraciously many other works as well: Buber[143], Teilhard de Chardin[144], Reich[145], *The Sacred Mushrooms and the Cross*,[146] *The Day of St. Anthony's Fire*[147], *Soma: Divine Mushroom of Immortality*[148], Tim Leary's *Jail Notes*[149], On *The Psychology of Meditation*[150], to name some. Psychedelic esoterica.

Edie and I, often with Hank, would travel on weekends into Cambridge, a short subway ride away, and hang around Harvard Square, spending a fair amount of time in the bookshop at the Harvard Coop. I made my first encounter there with the co-founder of the Theosophical Society H.P. Blavatsky's[151] *The Secret Doctrine*,[152] which I found on the bookshelf and perused a bit. I was intrigued by the steampunk feel of the 19th-century reprint but wary of the "table rapping" type associations it had accumulated for me rather third hand. I had picked up from the Gurdjieff literature the idea that this was all something to be looked down one's nose at. I was nonetheless vaguely intrigued by it but generally felt given all the preceding, I didn't have the mental space to try and integrate yet another complex system. Blavatsky's writing is dense, chaotic, and difficult to penetrate.

I did, however, lift the epigrammatic words "Chaos — Theos — Kosmos" from one of the chapter titles and scrawled it with a marker across the white muslin curtain of one side of my tent back in my dorm room as a decorative element. Other spiritual ornaments I can recall included a poster over the narrow bed Edie and I shared in the florid style of the ISKCON[153] artists (Hare Krishnas), depicting Krishna and Lakshmi as eternal lovers.

Although I wasn't at all drawn to the Hare Krishna sect, they were present in abundance in their orange robes along the streets of downtown Boston, begging, proselytizing, and handing out books. Their presence and the readings would resonate with the idea from Alan Watt's *The Book on the Taboo Against Knowing Who You Are* I had read a year earlier with the message that you are all really God playing hide and seek or, otherwise (as per the Gita), phases of the divine *Lila* (play). (It should be noted that as a *bhakti yoga*[154] sect, the Hare Krishnas perceived their relationship to Krishna dualistically.) This image of Krishna at play contrasted another picture developing within me of the Christ being, of the godly incarnating as human to participate in humanity's self-transformation, and thus to have compassion on our creatureliness and suffering, our being subject to death and acting as a bridge to the divine and not simply remaining transcendentally aloof in the cosmic play. On one occasion, in my psychedelic state, I could contemplate these existing as realities simultaneously, as shades of the sacred spectrum, that could be seen as offering different textures of the godly — as if to suit the spiritual needs of the individual. One could feel one's way into this side of things or that. I was later to feel an echo of this same "holding together" in Steiner's *Bhagavad Gita and the Epistles of Paul* lecture cycle, where he describes Krishna as the "luminosity" of Christ.

In addition to the comings and goings of Edie and Ted, I sometimes found myself alone at school. I was able to keep up a little bit of connection with other friends, although, back in the day, the only way to communicate with folks at a distance other than by telephone was by mail. My friend Ruth had gone to live in Spain for the fall season, and we exchanged letters a few times. I was still somewhat awkwardly and, by this point, rather vainly, trying to communicate to her: there's something *big* and *cosmic* and *spiritual* behind all this tripping stuff we've been doing. Although I think she had a certain interest in attempting to fathom me, in the end — as I had realized back at the lake — I was to remain essentially unsuccessful in forming a real bridge idea-wise.

A bit of correspondence I still keep and treasure from that time was from Milo, who at that time would either have been following the Maharaj Ji road show, sort of "deadhead" style, from city to city or else had already relocated to California. The main burden of his letter was his urging to "get this knowledge." By way of update, he mentioned two things concerning other classmates: first, about a girl we both knew who had been recently killed in a car accident, prompting Milo to say, prophetically: "We don't have these bodies forever." And secondly and quite surprising to me, he described bumping into, of all people, George at a Maharaj Ji festival in Florida. George apparently had likewise — for the moment, at any rate — embraced Maharaj Ji.

There are a handful of scenes from when I used either LSD or peyote, but which don't coalesce into specific complete episodes in memory but rather as vignettes across incompletely recalled contexts. This whole autumn 1972 period was probably the "busiest" for me regarding the frequency (if not intensity) of psychedelic journeying.

I have two distinct memories of quite non-ordinary events while tripping solo in the dorm room — possibly, the same session. The first was something as follows: I am sitting on Hank's bed, and the only other person there is one of my other roommates, asleep in his bed. Suddenly, he sat bolt upright, woke up, looked around, and looked at me as if to say, "Why did you wake me?". And the way I experienced it, I had, through some kind of interlock, invaded his dreaming psyche powerfully to wake him up — without making a peep. It felt clear I had done something, but it was unclear (to both of us) what that was.

I can similarly recall being in the dorm, I think completely alone, with my thoughts turned to higher beings "out there" somewhere. Soon I began to feel the approach of a reality that was, layer by layer, prying apart layers and domains of intervening "reality" betwixt their world and mine. I was in some way in interlock with the "control mechanism" of its approach — I was attracting it, to begin with, and "something" was piercing through to my realm of being. Along with sensing this approach, I inwardly could hear a high-pitch pulse, and the whole scene evolved rapidly to seem as if you might imagine a flying saucer landing. However, it was clearly not a physical vehicle approaching but rather a spiritual container for a higher consciousness penetrating through depths of earthly formative energies. I was aware simultaneously of the "UFO-like" quality of the approach and that, at the same time, it was certainly *not* a material spaceship traversing mere intergalactic space. The penetration of the layers had a similar quality, but reversed, to the way in which my gaze had penetrated with the tree at the lake, peeling away down into the atomic level. This was rather the experience in reverse: a higher level of being was penetrating into my world.

The intensity of the visitation, as it approached, began to frighten me. As with my experience of "God" "out there" at the cast party, and the "drilling down" into the atomic space at the lake, of the approach of the ambulance, of the sun piercing the clouds: I could *will* the approaching vehicle to recede.

I also had one or two "high dreams" — where I suddenly came to some kind of intense, exalted, blissful, and prayerful awareness in the middle of sleep. The traversal of the psychedelic states with the frequency of those times created an overall mood and background of expanded awareness, although vague and dreamlike at times.

All the way into the January intersession, Edie was living at the dorm, although the situation had grown increasingly untenable, first simply as a practical matter. Among other things, I was on the meal plan; she would eat whatever I could bring home from the cafeteria or what we could buy for her elsewhere with my meager allowance funds. And she was at loose ends while I was in class. She had tried, without much luck, to find work. Further, the dorm lodgings themselves weren't continuously available due to breaks in the term. So she would sometimes stay with me when

I returned to my family, as at Christmas. Separate bedrooms at home. Frustrated finding work, she would one day announce she would become a Bahai (my sister's influence) or, on another, move to a commune in Tennessee that John's sister was living at (which is what she ultimately did) — or both — and so on.

Then one weekend around the middle of January, I hitchhiked home — a three-hour drive that could take as little as that to hitch, or all day, depending on one's luck. I made this trip by myself in order to visit Ruth, who had just returned home to her parents. We discussed *Be Here Now*, which her father had commented on to her somewhat derisively about the image of the "Big Ice Cream Cone" in the sky, or whatever, more or less reinforcing the sense that the hoped-for connection around spiritual possibilities was not going to be on. I was to be home the whole weekend, but after the visit, I grew restless and hitched home on Saturday — dosing myself first on some of the peyote buttons I still had. It was still midwinter; hitching was cold. In those days, hitchhiking was, however, fairly reliable transportation. I must have dosed to amuse myself on what I figured was to be a four or five-hour journey. As it was peyote buttons, I could readily count out a moderate dose.

When I arrived back at the dorm, I discovered to my surprise (and horror), that Edie was about to leave on a date with an older guy who sold the local alternative newspaper (either the *Real Paper* or the *Phoenix*) around the corner by the Public Gardens. I knew she had befriended him, but this was unexpected. Needless to say, this raised a bit of a situation, but despite my protest, she left as she had planned. I stayed home reading a volume just acquired that weekend: *William Blake and the Tree of Life*[155], which was my first real introduction to William Blake and the Kabbalah. Although I was miserable, having been turned out as I had, I spent the evening tripping mildly, trying not to think about what was happening with Edie. I became quite absorbed in Blake's thought (and this writer's Kabbalistic exegesis thereof). I was receptive to and comprehending of these spiritual ideas in my mild psychedelic state. Altogether the night was, in the end, tolerable, and I added two new significant starting nodes in my ongoing search for comprehension: Blake and Kabbalah. It was the beginning of a lifetime relationship with Blake and an ongoing interest in Kabbalah.

Although Edie subsequently absented herself from my tent, she had sufficiently ingratiated herself with my other roommates, Hank in particular, such that she (and her pet dog, which she had recently acquired) continued to crash there for another week or so. Awkward.

The last acid trip I had before I left school in Boston two weeks later was with Lorraine. We had been friends since meeting at the very beginning of the semester. She had something of a warm maternal vibe and was always super friendly to me.

Edie had, by this point, moved out of my dorm room; it was now the very end of the January semester. I was going to be dropping out.

Lorraine had never done LSD before and was ready to try. We dropped and experienced the onset in my dorm room. Although I believe I was present and "in touch" with and for Lorraine and recall specific interactions, it was also the occasion of quite a bit of inward processing of my own.

As noted, that whole semester, I had done quite a bit of eclectic reading in the domain of spirituality and some of the psychedelic writings of the time. These were very active in me, and the occasion was an opportunity to psychedelically try on some of the ideas floating through me.

One of the overriding imaginations that were present rather throughout the experience was the idea that God, in the form of Krishna — as conceived and pictured by me through, among other things, exposure through the Hare Krishnas and their illustrated *Bhagavad Gita "As It Is"* — was experiencing himself through me; or expressed differently, was co-present with my own "I," my own soul, in my heart. This awareness did not in itself confer a "divine consciousness" on me, other than I was able to witness the manifestation of Krishna, who was "having his own experience" alongside me. My life was part of his *Lila*. Colorful, dynamic traces of spiritual energy weaved in and through me, and also through him. He exuded a regal playfulness as he wandered spiritually through the environment of my life.

Although I was largely focused on my own experience of all this, it came part and parcel with the experience that the Krishna being was similarly present in others. In this regard, there was a sense that they were all in subtle communion with each other. Krishna was infinitely replicated inside of each of us — rather than without, as in the story of Krishna and the Gopis (milkmaids), who each danced with their own embodiment of Krishna.

The aura around him was perceived to be composed of an entourage of elemental thought beings who danced within and around him, composing a sentient wave rippling around and bordering him and me. I experienced this principally visually and subtly and low-key as an energetic, empathetic feeling. Other than the communal existence we were sharing, there was no direct sense of dialog. He was doing his thing; I was doing mine.

At some point, this led me to take seriously the notion (going back to my reading Alan Watts) that I perhaps really was, in my reality, God. God not simply as Krishna, who I understood then as an embodiment or aspect of God, but also the God of the Bible; and also as a "god" or godling, such as a Greek god of a pantheon or race of gods. And considering myself as such, I had to reckon with the many layers of *mortality* surrounding me and the sense also of being in some way "imprisoned." I recall leaning on the newel post of the stairway, with one foot on the first step, and having the deeply accepting feeling that "If I am god, *and* this incarnate being, then I (God) must have willed it so, and all is as it should be. This line of thought somewhat echoed what I had read in Ram Dass' *Be Here Now* about the possibility of having the "faith that moves mountains" and then realizing: you're the one who put the mountain there, to begin with, so why move them?

In addition to the influence of the Boston Hare Krishnas, I was recently engaged with Ralph Metzner's Maps of Consciousness, which reflected quite well the intersection of an essential set of spiritual, and primarily oracular, systems and the post-psychedelic mind. Ralph Metzner was part of the Harvard team with Timothy Leary and Ram Dass (Richard Alpert, as was) and, as such, was a principal author of *The Psychedelic Experience. The Maps of Consciousness* assumes in the reader an all but implicit background of the psychedelic experience and applies Jungian notions of synchronicity and the Hermetic law of correspondence ("as above, so below") to the traditions of astrology, the I Ching, Tarot, Alchemy, and the then-contemporary teaching known as

Actualism. Actualism reinforced the notion of "the God within" as the higher self very emphatically.

I was occupied in thought with one element from my readings in *Maps of Consciousness;* the idea of the left/right duality, the *ida* and *pingala*[156] of the psychic channels in Kundalini yoga. Sitting in the hallway outside my dorm room during the trip with Lorraine, near the stairway — it was more of a parlor with seating — I conjured up a very active and distinct awareness of two channels running up my spine and into my brain/head; each was an illuminated current which in some sense allowed a flow of elemental beings or energies to become active in my awareness. This provided, as I experienced it then, an underlayment to my inner process and thinking. I became aware how, simply by shifting my attention, I could "activate" one channel or the other, in which case a fountain of the respective elemental-thought beings of one or the other would bubble up inside me. And with each shift, it seemed as though my "inner structure," imaginatively perceived, danced either to the left or right accordingly, bringing an associated set of soul functions into the foreground and causing the other set to recede. Although there was a certain "coloration" to each set of visualized soul elements, the shift in dominance did not seem to otherwise change my net experience. It was both playful and, at the time, illuminating, as it definitely indicated *something* was up with this left/right thing. I was also already familiar in a general way (largely from the *Psychology of Meditation*, which I had read that fall) with the left brain / right brain observations.

Sitting in the hallway, I came to sense an expanded field of awareness in my forebrain. All of these experiences were taking place within what I saw and felt as my aura — in a supersensible domain populated (apparently) with a variety of elemental and spiritual beings who came in and out of my awareness variously. The forebrain "activation" — as my attention centered there — created a sense of communion with what I thought of then as some kind of "deva beings" — intermediate-level spiritual entities who were, as I sensed, somehow involved directly with the earth, with humans, and with their mutual spiritual evolution. I felt a sense of communion and communication with them, although not in any articulated dialog. There was a sense of their being a host or a multiplicity but resolving into a pair of beings, or a single "double being," in rhythmic sympathy with my own left/right channels.

With this sense of an "expanded aura," I was very aware that all of the material forms and structures around me were "just" materializations of some underlying energetic matrix whose fundamental reality was within my mind. I looked at an open door — the building was from the 19th century, and the door was big, heavy, and decorated with molding. I could "fix" it in my awareness, and it would appear to render itself clearly as "nothing but" a matrix of mind stuff. I had the sense that if I concentrated a *little* more, I could psychokinetically affect it, but I didn't push it and didn't think that was necessarily a wise or appropriate thing to do or attempt.

At some point, back in my room, either before or after the above, I found myself concentrating on the base of my spine, that is, my root chakra. I was familiar with the ideas of Kundalini yoga and of the "serpent power" being coiled therein. I became aware of an "electric stream of white light energy" flowing in my spine, and at the base of this vertical psychic energy current, I experienced as appearing to my vision the head of a "snake" animated at the root of the current, biting down at the root as if to anchor itself. I could direct the flow somewhat, and I found that if I "leaned in" in a certain way, it would move the energy current in a way that would tend to activate me sexually. However, sensing this (my thought motion), the head of the snake turned upward and gnashed and vibrated at me, and a shocking electrical ripple was felt. The implication: don't move your energy in that way — at least, not right now, not in this state.

I'm pretty sure that this all came about through some feeling for, or at least recognition, of the sexual charge potential or possibility with Lorraine and me. We started out, however, in, I think, a clean place on that. And there was a lot of other stuff going on internally for each of us, distracting us from that. However, this awareness of the sexual possibility suddenly came up, less as an impulse to act out but more as a flash of awareness between us of the magical power of conception we shared as man and woman, and although nothing was said, it seemed Lorraine was suddenly very aware of her womanly womb-nature and its power to engender life, and looked down at her belly and then looked up smiling in amazement. As she looked down, I also perceived a flow of cosmic energy pouring into her — almost as if a "shower of golden rain" as in the myth of Danaë and the birth of Perseus.

After a while, we decided to move ourselves down six or seven city blocks, toward Kenmore Square, to her dorm room. As we made this shift, we must have been plateauing a bit downwards, and the outer reality of walking from A to B down the city streets moved more into the foreground. I don't recall anything specific about hanging in her dorm room (I had been there before), but I do recall meeting some classmates that she knew on the street in front of her dorm and chatting with them before we went inside. I'm sure we radiated more than a little bit of psychedelic jollity and "untetheredness," which, being in a group of college kids, I sensed caused the subconscious sexual energy to flow a tiny bit more than usual.

There was a tall black guy in the group. I didn't really know him, but maybe was aware of from a large survey class or something that we might have shared. I felt, first of all, a general sort of male aggression — or assertiveness or possessiveness that could have been felt in any social posing for alpha dominance. But, because of the race thing — all of us being white except him — I could immediately sense a boatload of story bubbling in each of us, which left me feeling at first a little threatened, but I quickly shifted into the awareness — prompted again by Metzner's book, this time, the section on Actualism, that all of the pictures and images and stories that we have about the "other" are really just that and that they hide and mask the true self in each of us. The psychedelic state can give you an expanded awareness of the invisible forces, natural, psychological, and spiritual, that construct our reality, and I felt the overall feeling shift to neutral/friendly as he was introduced to us and I was, among other things able to see more clearly his challenge (1972) of being one of the few black kids in school.

Somewhere in all this, while we were still outside, the contemplated image of the angel piercing the heart of St. Theresa of Avila (as in the sculpture *The Ecstasy of St. Theresa*) appeared before me, or rather, the image of a sword piercing my heart. Although in this picture, I didn't experience as such the entry of holy love, I *did* sense feel something like "cosmic energy" and how such an entry of love *could* penetrate the soul's inner heart. It was a current of energy similar in a way to the flow of energy I saw earlier pouring into Lorraine.

I don't distinctly recall if I stayed up the night with Lorraine in her dorm room or wandered home late that night. I felt sure she was grateful that I had introduced her to the experience. In turn, I was grateful she had chosen me as her companion.

Within a short time, the term ended; I hitched home to get my parents' station wagon to collect my belongings — before heading back home, I visited Julie, who was at school in New Hampshire — she and I, along with a couple of other friends from back home, went skiing over the weekend.

I returned home to my parents, and that was the end of my first college experience.

9

Welcome to the Metasociety

The next phase sees me moving away for a time from my psychedelic explorations in pursuit of the possibility of experiencing the kind of consciousness found with LSD through other means. In a certain way, my primary phase of free-wheeling, self-guided exploration was over, but I would eventually bridge back to psychedelic exploration again.

Various things had conspired together to lead me to the decision to drop out of school after the January intersession. One was the demise of my relationship with Edie; another was something of a disaffection with the academic program at Emerson College — they were experimenting with their underclass program with a team-teaching approach; it had been attractive to me, but in terms of its execution it left me academically unchallenged — which was probably just as well, as I was very much preoccupied with my personal curriculum.

Although I was now just turned eighteen and was theoretically draftable, the draft and the Vietnam War were winding down. Although I was soon registered with the Selective Service and carried a draft card, I was not anxious that I needed to maintain a college deferment.

Most directly influencing my decision to quit school was my desire to participate in the Arica Institute, whose program was described by John Lilly in *The Center of the Cyclone* and which began as a formal program in New York. It was now opening a satellite center in Boston. That January, I attended an introductory session in a Cambridge hotel ballroom. This solidified my resolve to drop out of school, live with my parents, work through the spring season, and enroll in the 40 day training planned for Boston in the coming summer. I was optimistic that this would lead to the types of states reported by John Lilly, under the misapprehension (which he had engendered) that these were *not* the result of dosing with LSD but the transformative effect of the Arica "work."

Looking back, I have to wonder if I would have pursued Arica at all had I been aware of Lilly's pretense.

Due, among other things, to the use of the same "frequencies" or "hydrogens" as per Gurdjieff and Ouspensky to characterize different "levels" of consciousness — now correlated by Lilly with specific LSD states — plus the use of the enneagram (or "enneagon[157]" as Ichazo preferred at times), I was definitively under the impression — as were a lot of people — that Ichazo and "The School" (he talked about "The School" and "The Work" in a way that to me, appeared very much intended to imply Gurdjieffian overtones) were inheritors of the Gurdjieff lineage. That is, Ichazo was a "Master" that had been sent by the same esoteric stream (or "Source" as Ouspensky would say) that was ostensibly behind Gurdjieff. Although in later times Ichazo was at pains to distinguish himself (and his ideas) from Gurdjieff, his early back story played up his contact with a circle of "seekers of the truth" in South America that, among other things, had a background in the Gurdjieff work.

This was important to me, in that I had taken on a lot of Ouspensky's conviction that there were existent deeply hidden esoteric "schools," almost certainly from the East or Middle East, that represented the true source of help and teaching for humanity to escape its prison of Gurdjieffian "mechanicalness" and evolve to a higher level. From a broader perspective looking back, I see this slant as reflecting Ouspensky's absorption of the earlier Theosophical notion of "the Masters" coupled with his, to me anyway, somewhat Calvinistic, hair-shirt internalization of Gurdjieff's "we cannot do" teaching. The irony here, of course, is that, essentially through my psychedelic use, I knew that I was exploring realities and states of consciousness that were very clearly *not* part of Ouspensky's own world — but nevertheless, trying to apply his maps and teachings as derived from Gurdjieff. Curious.

To save the money needed to enroll in the Arica program that summer, during the spring months, I worked as a short-order cook back in Westport. Alan and Ted were not attending college and so were around town, and I assume (although my memory here is not distinct) I would have taken to hanging out and smoking pot and such as usual with them. However, with perhaps one small exception, I didn't do any psychedelics. Aside from the fact that psychedelics were no longer part of my scene in town — my friends were all now working some sort of regular job, as I was. Milo and Derek were getting organized for an extended VW Bus adventure to California and were both committed to the Maharaj Ji movement, which meant no drugs. This psychedelic hiatus was partly a function of outer circumstances, and also reflective of my decision to pursue the Arica program and the possibility of growing into "higher states of consciousness" *without* psychedelics in the precise way I then believed Lilly had. The one exception is I have a memory of sharing a bottle of wine with some friends that had been mildly spiked with LSD.

If I try to recall mood elements from that time, two things come up. One is I was still smarting from the end of my relationship with Edie: I had become pretty entangled and attached, in a naive "first love" sort of way. But the fact she was more or less out of my world mostly took care of that. I was also in the process of still generally piecing myself together from the trips of the last year and integrating multiple new worldviews I was exposing myself to. So while I am basically sure that I presented and functioned as a stable "young adult" during that time, there was a lot of time spent in fairly far-away contemplation and internal integration of some of the spaces I had gone through, along with the ongoing digestion of the many works I was reading.

Around April, I went to a weekend workshop with John Lilly and his wife, Toni at the Wainwright House[158] in Rye, New York. They were making a talking tour of the country from his home in California, traveling in their RV. His talk the first evening was quite interesting and largely couched in the context of his recent contact with Franklin Merrill-Wolff,[159] whose story of awakening resonated deeply with Lilly, and also of findings from quantum physics and speculations about astrophysics and black holes inspired by John Wheeler.[160] He was by this time retreating a bit from the enthusiasm for Arica he expressed in his *The Center of the Cyclone*. He had dropped out as a participant in the "missionary" phase of Arica that was just getting underway. But he still made use of the "Levels" that he described and attributed to Ichazo.

I notably remember learning, for the first time, about the Heisenberg uncertainty principle[161] and the associated Planck constant. This was itself an important step in the unshackling, as it were, of elements of my received and not fully thought-through belief system. I took for granted the primacy of Newtonian physics, the law of thermodynamics, and the attendant assumptions about matter and the world[162].

I felt a connection between this idea of indeterminacy and the shimmering "atoms" of light I saw at the Lake.

I similarly recalled his explanation of Gödel's theorem as disproving the possibility of a deterministic model of the universe. I understood his explanation to be that, in order to deterministically model the universe, the (physical) representation of the model would itself have to be included as part of the model and that this recursive feature alone would leave any deterministic model eternally incomplete. This is a rough and ready application of what is, more correctly, a theory about mathematical incompleteness.

During the workshop the next day, he and Toni conducted some exercises partly derived from Arica ("trespaso," a kind of eye-gazing with a partner) and others as described in *The Center of the Cyclone* from his earlier explorations. I remember one where they very effectively demonstrated a technique[163] that could induce a very direct synesthesia type of experience, where one would "see" sounds as they moved around the room. A little taste of drug-free trippiness.

I spoke directly with him during a break, asking him about his understanding of Ouspenky's concept of recurrence — which was how I was trying to explain my "crossroads" impasse at the reservoir. He, unsatisfyingly to me at the moment, simply told me that "Yes, you can experience a state of consciousness where that seems to be happening." In my naïveté, I was expecting him to *know*. I see now that this was a wise and appropriate response.

Backtracking now with what I have since learned about him, the timing of the talk closely aligns with his so-called "year of samadhi," where he was dosing himself repeatedly with Ketamine to maintain fairly continuous access to the psychedelic state. During the weekend, however, he came off with sophisticated aplomb as the scientifically astute explorer of higher states of consciousness and one who had "been there." I curiously wonder whether he may have been mildly dosing with ketamine during the weekend.

During that Spring, I also attended a weekend workshop at Arica in New York at their center on 57th Street. Aside from the excitement of participation, the only activity I distinctly remember was an exercise of "karma cleaning" — reviewing with detachment, in a group circle, past highly-charged events around "sex, money, and power." As it turned out, these groups unsurprisingly wound up focussing primarily on the sexual ones. I remember feeling, at age 18, that I perhaps lacked the depth of personal history of the generally older other participants and consequently did not have the quantity of material to fully engage in the exercise. This youthful "lack of karma" came up again as an issue briefly during my 40 day training. I was frustrated, feeling, "Can't we just jump over this karma stuff and get to the higher consciousness?"

Also during that time, I also participated in evening "outreach" circles that Arica would host more locally at a church in nearby Greenwich; there were "indications" for various basic exercises such as breathing and visualization exercises. It was a small circle of those interested.

Somewhere during the previous year, I acquired one of the works of Karlfried Graf von Dürckheim[164], published under the title *Daily Life as Spiritual Practice*. Among other things, I took away from that work was an introduction to the Japanese concept of *hara*, that is, of belly-centered consciousness, poised from the center of gravity, more or less the "pit of one's stomach," also, in Taoism, the T'an Tien, the body's inner alchemical cauldron. This turned out to be a big part of the Arica system — to be "centered" in what they called the *Kath* center. (*Oth* was the heart center, and *Path was* the head center. The provenance of these terms was never explained.) These, in turn, were correlated with the (as they referred to them at the time) syntony, relationship, and conservation instincts; the lack of "balance" between them resulted in the formation of the various nine ego-fixations corresponding to the points of the enneagram. These centers could be readily correlated with what in the Fourth Way/Gurdjieff system was described as the Thinking, Emotional, and instinctive-moving "centers."

Arica was very much *au courant* that year; its founder, Oscar Ichazo, was the subject of interviews in *Psychology Today* and stories in *New York Magazine*. Shortly before I began the training, Sam Keene was interviewing Oscar Ichazo[165] in *Psychology Today* (a follow-up to his early interview with John Lilly) and characterized Arica as a "university for higher states of consciousness." It was seen as a natural next step in the counter-culture slash spiritual revolution that was going on. It had been formed from a nucleus of a large number of people (dozens) from the Esalen Institute (itself on the cutting edge of the human potential movement) — workshop leaders and, I suppose, various Esalen hangers-on. This group had studied with Oscar Ichazo in Chile and was now poised to be the "next big thing" transformationally. More to the point, it was practically tailor-made to align with my own predispositions. Psychedelics were clearly in the background, apparently even in the case of Oscar, who claimed initiation into indigenous psychedelic use by a South American shaman during his youth. His resume looked like it ticked all the right boxes.

I moved back to Boston in mid-summer to participate in the training — having lived there previously during school, it felt well-known and comfortable. I sub-leased a room in an apartment that a couple of friends of mine from back home had rented during the previous school year. So I was familiar with it from visiting them when I was still in school. I had even hung out there with Edie back when I was in school, the day of the acid trip at the nearby Museum of Fine Arts. That arrangement worked well for me, although the neighborhood was a little sketchy; I did come home to the apartment once just as an armed robber was leaving — empty-handed.

I soaked up the doctrine as presented during the 40 day training. As the name suggests, it was a continuous day and evening training. Around a dozen of us were in the group — all young and enthusiastic, although I continued to be the youngest by years. The whole idea of a "40 day intensive" training was that it was an accelerated pathway to satori, to enlightenment — comparable in its way to Gurdjieff's "haida yoga" characterization. The work itself comprised learning various yoga-styled physical exercises, meditative techniques, psychological "clearing" techniques, chanting, bodywork, tai chi movements, and so on. It was a smorgasbord of what was happening in the hippie / new age / spiritual awakening / potential human scene. Although it was stressed by Oscar on down that, this was not merely "a cocktail" of this and that, but an extract of wisdom teaching arranged in a very definite "scientific" way to produce definite results. In deconstructing Arica, I am reminded of a saying of my art director younger brother: "Creativity is the art of hiding your sources."

Arica positioned itself as *the* critical "next step" in the transformation to a "new age" that many believed was in process[166]. In one of the first sessions, the instructions were at pains to communicate that Arica was not there to "get you high" but to prepare humanity for an "evolutionary jump" into what was called "the metasociety" — a utopian vision of awakened humanity[167].

The critical problem Arica set itself to address with its method was the minimization of what they called "the ego" — as opposed to "essence" — in human psychology. These concepts align directly with the Fourth Way ideas of "false personality" and "essence."

My own surmise, for what it's worth here, is that the Arica teachings and trainings, as delivered in America, were, to start with, something of an amalgam of Oscar's own more or less original thinking along with paper-overings providing a veneer of elements from Gurdjieff's theory, as well as some direct borrowings from it. Add in other exercises derived from the folks at Esalen, including various traditional yogic and Eastern practices — all wrapped up in a quasi-coherent story. And a dose of psychedelics as a background frame of reference for the many teachers and students who had that in their history.

Looking at Arica vis a vis the Gurdjieff work, I see three principal points - we can call them "borrowings" or "extensions" — related to Gurdjieff's doctrine, as reflected in *In Search of the Miraculous*.

The first is his teaching around "levels." In *The Center of the Cyclone*, Lilly summarizes and somewhat recasts what he took from Ichazo as a teaching of different "levels" of consciousness. He delineates a correspondence between these levels and traditional samadhi and other mystical states, as well as relating them to the various states he recounted from his LSD research before his exposure to Arica. These different "levels," as mentioned earlier, are given numeric labels (3, 6, 12, 24, and 48[168]), which correlate more or less precisely with what in the Gurdjieff work are called the "psychic hydrogens." Absent such an implied connection, their assigned values would be arbitrary and improbably coincidental. Although in the Arica work I was exposed to, there was no explication of why these "levels" are assigned precisely these number values; it is a straight shot to extrapolate a connection from a study of Gurdjieff as in Ouspensky's *In Search of the Miraculous*.

I will comment that "level" became associated within Arica with one's general state of being and attainment, of consciousness with a capital "C." This usage was generalized, implying that there was a spectrum of gradations of level, so it was possible to suggest that so-and-so A was at a higher level than so-and-so B, if only by a slight degree. This idea of one's level became something of an obsession and, as it were, a sought for hallmark of status. Oscar, for example, would purportedly designate the "levels" of various (non-Arican) gurus and spiritual teachers in slide-show commentary to Arica insiders.

The second aspect was the adoption of the enneagram, culminating in the "fixations" (or "ego-fixations"), which later was to leak out of Oscar's circle and morph over time into the popular "enneagram of personality" promoted by Naranjo, Palmer, and many others. It is patently obvious that this was more or less lifted from Ichazo and re-packaged and popularized, absent most of the context of Ichazo's theory and teaching. In the Arica system, the discovery and work with one's fixation were called *protoanalysis*[169].

It may well be my own shortcoming, but the "war against the ego" that permeated the vibe at Arica sometimes led to something seeming to me like the tar-baby story: getting stuck or trapped, in a sticky, gooey way, by that which you are fighting against. The tar baby itself, of course, is nothing but a doll without reality.

Despite the heavy use of the Gurdjieff enneagram in explaining the ego-fixations and other elements, there is no direct connection (that I am aware of) between Arica's use of the enneagram and its use of the levels — which in Gurdjieff are "inextricably intertwined" by the underlying "law of the octave" and the "law of three." In later years, Ichazo was to downplay the connection of his ideas with those of Gurdjieff.

The third borrowing, related to the second, is the adoption of a polarity of "ego" and "essence," more or less entirely analogous to the notions of "false personality" and "essence" in the Gurdjieff work and related to the enneagram. An important distinction to observe, however, is for Gurdjieff, one's idiosyncratic "false personality" revolved around a "chief feature," invisible to the individual, that colors one's self-delusion. In Ichazo, the "ego" is a fixation nucleated around one of the nine points of his enneagram of fixations.

In Gurdjieff, discerning this idiosyncratic "chief feature" was the function of the teacher and not a matter of analysis as with the enneagram.

The fixation on one of nine possible types was occasioned by what Ichazo characterizes as "imbalances" in how the basic "instincts" operate within the developing individual (that is, from infancy) and how compensating complexes or fixations obscure the pure, spiritual essence, allowing the self-seeking and always dissatisfied "ego" to emerge and dominate behavior and the view of the world and self.

In my own case, I was identified as being primarily imbalanced in the realm of *syntony* (a term incidentally no longer used in the modern Arica) — which provides the intuitive ability to "be in tune" with the environment, with others and, by extension, with the universe at large. I found this characterization provided some focus for self-inspection and self-observation. While I find the mechanics of all systems that try to explain the human psyche fascinating, labeling individuals as being "all this or all that" tends to leave me cold.

I will note here that the "ego" being set up in Arica as "the bad guy" (as opposed to "false personality" in Gurdjieff) did require some mental gymnastics on my part in correlating the teachings, in that in Gurdjieff, the goal was to achieve "real I," that is, ego, which was more or less equated with his notion of essence, although "essence" was (in Gurdjieff) sometimes characterized as a naive, child-like thing distinct from a "conscious I."

I picked up in Arica - which incorporated a set of concepts from Zen, Taoism, and Buddhism not found in Fourth Way — a frequent mention of *wu wei* — effortless effort. This contrasted — superficially, at least — with Gurdjieff's insistence on "super efforts" being needed. Of course, these can be reconciled with the right perspective, but it upset my expectation of "strict continuity" with Gurdjieff's teachings.

I think there is something to be argued for both Ichazo's and Gurdjieff's perspectives on the nucleus of the "conditioned inauthentic." Surely, our particular complex of foibles is going to be highly individualistic, and to see through them will require something of artistry on the part of the teacher/helper/therapist as well as one's self. At the same time, Ichazo provides a model for a dynamic underlying the psychological tendency to archetypical sets of limiting beliefs, perceptions, patterns, and behaviors. The lens through which one views the self and the world will influence what one sees there. If your lens is the enneagram, people will naturally be seen as falling into one type of the other.

The 40 day training work in Boston culminated in a training in what was called "Ouroboros[170]" or "psychoalchemy" (Oscar was fond of deriving Greek coinages for various components of his teaching — the better, I think, to trademark them, as well as show off his apparent erudition.) This is essentially the technique of circular breathing as described in, among other things, *The Secret of the Golden Flower*[171] as first translated (into German) by Richard Wilhelm (1873-1930) and extensively commentated on by Carl Jung. I had been familiar with *The Secret of the Golden Flower* but had not practiced it. Once introduced to the method through Arica, I also quickly came to read *Taoist Yoga*[172] and traditionalist Titus Burkhardt's[173] *Alchemy*[174], which helped me begin to connect with the deeper side of Western spiritual history.

Regarding the practice itself, I found it useful in several regards: the controlled breathing and the channeling of the so-called *chi* energy was, to a large extent, felt as stabilizing and "sorting out" of what revealed itself through this work as a bit of a tangled and knotted pattern of subjective energy flows in my system. Some were likely representative of incompletely resolved internal shifts occasioned by some of my own psychedelic turbulence. I see it as having established a more stable baseline of breath and awareness.

It can bring about or induce an *awareness* of soul-spiritual light or illumination inwardly. Where having this awareness sits relative to the individual's overall spiritual sensitivity and cognition is difficult for me to specifically assess or gauge.

This was an introduction to a very specific form of practice that has remained useful but did not directly serve as the focus of the kind of results and practice I was ultimately seeking. It was very clear that the path of *insight* was critical for me.[175] To a large extent, the type of inquiry that pursued this was dismissed by the Arica groupthink as merely so much *chicherero*, or chattering of the ego-mind (monkey mind). In Steiner, I was later to find a path forward where the absorption of material (teachings) derived from the articulate conscious spiritual knowledge of others is seen as an important stage in the development of higher organs of perception.

After the summer training ended, I returned to my parent's house. I was at loose ends, and my parents nudged me toward the idea of going back to school. It was already August, but I could quickly enroll in the fall semester at Drew University, largely through the help of an admissions officer with whom my Drew alumni older brother had a connection.

That entire school year was a bit of a wash for me. I didn't find my way in socially very well. It felt to me this was due in part to the fact that by that time, I had more or less stopped using drugs. In my age group, they were still the primary social glue. This abstinence was under the general idea that I was instead on a committed spiritual path to seek "higher consciousness" without them. Ironically, there was a notable amount of psychedelic and other drug use going on within Arica. As best as I can recall, I had largely abstained from smoking pot and so on during the training.

After I went back to school, I maintained contact with the Boston group I had done the 40 day training with; a number of them decided to rent a house in Boston together, which I visited a few times in the fall.

My intended major back at school was going to be psychology. It felt like it might be a fit. However, I found little connection with the introductory course, which was a team-taught requirement for not only psychology but also anthropology and sociology majors. One felt the breath of behaviorism looming over it all. Later in my second semester, I signed up for the (required) statistics class and dropped it, too, after being handed the thick, formula-laden text on the first day. This left me without a track toward a psychology major.[176]

In the first semester, I enrolled in the computer science 101 class, primarily wanting to "meet" John Lilly on his plane of thought regarding the "human biocomputer." Unfortunately, the assigned instructor, who was only in class for a few days, was entering the terminal phase of some cancer. The manager of the university data center replaced him. Homework was done by writing programs on the punch card machine and submitting them overnight as a batch job. If you had any errors, the job would fail. I quickly decided this wasn't the high-tech future I was expecting, so I dropped that class too. Ultimately and ironically, I would eventually pursue a career in computer technology.

That fall, it was announced there would be a "teacher training" at the New York Arica Center. Somehow I persuaded my parents to let me sign up and skip school for two weeks. With one exception, I could make arrangements with my instructors to make up the missed classwork. In a sudden fit of conformity with the "perceived fashion" of others in the Arica training, I went from my long, hippie-style blonde locks to a crew cut. I regretted this and felt awkward in myself until it started to grow back, which seemed to take forever.

For the two weeks of the training, I lived in Manhattan with a dozen or so other Aricans, sharing rooms in a large five-bedroom apartment on Central Park West, sleeping two to three a room. We were essentially camping out with no furniture. It was an interesting communal living situation with people who were young, seeking, and sincere. Most had some past history in various alternative spiritual movements or human potential settings. But, again, at 18, I was by far the youngest.

The Arica Center on 57th Street in Manhattan was done up in a glitzy, new-age, futuristic style — lots of carpet, mirrors, and vivid color contrasts. In one of the large halls, the Aces from the Tarot were painted on the wall, after the Ryder deck, along with what looked like a variation of the "food diagram" from Ouspensky's *In*

Search of the Miraculous. I'm sure there was also an enneagram on one of the walls as well.

We all received a pack of Rider[177] Tarot cards, and their study (as a book of initiation) was a significant part of the training, although it was re-interpreted with the Arica jargon and philosophy. Also, part of the training was around the Kabbalah, although in a simple outline. At this time, it became communicated to us that Oscar was being divinely guided by the high angelic being known in the Kabbalah as *Metatron*. However, this was not made a big deal of and embraced by some, ignored by others. We were assigned our fixations, reportedly by Oscar reading our faces from pictures taken on the first or second day. During the second week, Oscar spoke each night.

It was during that time that one of the more genial senior Aricans, Patrick Watson[178], clued me, over dinner one night with a couple of other Aricans also in the training, that in fact, all of Lilly's "higher consciousness" states as he reported as taking place during his training in Arica, Chile were merely further LSD trips (in *The Center of the Cyclone*). Lilly himself was to acknowledge this much later[179]. As one might imagine, this was more than a bit disillusioning. I suppose I felt I had made a small step toward the (still-distant) "inner circle" with this confidence; meanwhile, I was already deep in, buying into the promise of *some* form of higher consciousness — if only I could get rid of ego.

Later that year, I took part twice a week, commuting from school in New Jersey to New York, about an hour each way, in the next training offering, called *The Opening of the Rainbow Eye*. I also volunteered at their downtown center a few times, sometimes working the reception desk. I also taught an introductory class with my new teaching credential. The *Rainbow Eye* training included at least fifty or so New York area Aricans in various stages of their journey, although all would have taken one or the other of the "teacher trainings" previously offered. Details of the training aren't relevant here: it elaborated on some of the already familiar ideas and some additional borrowings here and there. It included more advanced breathing exercises and cultivated what Ichazo called "The 14 Pillars of Perfect Recognition.[180]"

After a time, it felt more and more that this wasn't really working for me. At eighteen, when I first did the 40 day training, I was always the very youngest everywhere I went within Arica, and after a while, the social integration challenge wore thin. Most people were in their twenties or early thirties; there was a fair amount of sexual interest and activity (although at various times in the training, celibacy was enjoined for most of the week), and I wasn't quite able to fit into the swing there.

But mostly, there was something going on that felt like there was a fair amount of "level" posturing between groups working at different paces, while at the same time, no apparent breakthroughs into sustained "satori." Instead, there was always the next training, which accelerated in cost over time. And, although the breadth of the more or less traditional esoteric teachings was educational, I increasingly sensed a lack of an underlying integral[181] system that related to what I wrestled with as genuinely riddling questions about the nature of reality.

The people initially attracted to Arica were largely sincere, striving, open, and one way or another, part of the personal development ethos that came with (among other things) the widespread psychedelic exploration of those times. However, at the time of my disaffection — which was not a complete rejection, more a drifting away — the rapid public ascendency of Arica as "the next thing" was already in decline. It looked like its fifteen minutes of fame were about to be over.

I had come to Arica thinking it would provide a rapid pathway to states of consciousness, as described in Lilly's *The Center of the Cyclone*. Failing to accomplish that — in hindsight, an unrealistic and falsely excited expectation — it had nowhere to go but down in the end.

It is fair to say and worth noting that in the spiritual supermarket of the times, it felt like everyone and their brother was offering more or less instant results if only their path was chosen.

There may have been more in terms of practice I might have benefitted from, but it was increasingly clear to me that the system of thought underlying it would not ultimately provide me with the kind of knowledge I longed for.

Ichazo died in 2020 with, I think, a mixed legacy. Although Arica remains as an organization providing ongoing training, it, at best, has lost the relevancy it once had. He was to continually over-promise and under-deliver while unabashedly viewing himself as a foundational figure in the future spiritual direction of humanity. In his published work, it is not difficult to see what looks more and more like only a veneer of philosophical depth. That said, I do think Oscar's insights into the psychological dynamic behind what became the "enneagram of personality" — which, ironically, essentially distorted his intentions — contain some legitimate, worthwhile insights.

While questions of Arica's relationship to the Gurdjieff work (which in its own right remained animating to me), the nature of self and essence, paths to higher states, and all of that continued to absorb me, my enthusiasm for active participation had begun to lose steam.

10

I found the Miraculous

Among all of my readings, from Alan Watts to John Lilly, with many points in between, as of my eighteenth year, the body of thought that most influenced my thinking was found in Ouspensky's *In Search of the Miraculous*. Ouspensky's life was characterized by his longing for some definitive incursion of the miraculous, which he felt he received only hints of through his "experimental mysticism" and employment of certain "methods" to shift consciousness — presumably nitrous oxide and possibly hashish. But his life became tinged with a poignancy of failure to break through into the truly miraculous world he believed existed, perhaps, in "the fourth dimension."

For my part, it was pretty clear that I *had* found the miraculous; or perhaps better, it had found me — most particularly in the form of my "cast party" and "lake" psychedelic experiences. For me, the problem was more about having found it, what to do with it, and what does it *mean*. Ouspensky, Gurdjieff, Lilly, and Ichazo seemed to have an idea, but something was still missing for me.

After my first full year back in college, most notably consumed with Arica trainings going on in parallel to my half-hearted studies, I again dropped out and again moved home to live with my parents.

I was unclear about where I was headed; I wasn't at all engaged academically, and my standing reflected this. I had been fairly devoted to the "next level" of the Arica Training ("The Opening of the Rainbow Eye"), performing its practices — rituals, meditations, visualizations, and fingernail clipping — without feeling any particular sense of acceleration of my inner process toward some kind of breakthrough satori or enlightenment. I had begun to notice that there was a traffic developing of Aricans "moving on" to other spiritual/human potential movements, such as EST (and likewise, of course, similar traffic flowing from EST into Arica). Popping the bubble on Lilly's "higher consciousness" experience — described so enthusiastically in *The Center of the Cyclone* — also took a fair amount of air out of the tires. I was still, however, somewhat of the view that Arica was the inheritor of the Gurdjieff tradition, although, in terms of actual practice, it was becoming clear that elements "borrowed" (some might say "lifted") from Gurdjieff were just as freely mixed and matched with other traditions.

I was still relentlessly and restlessly seeking after spiritual truth, with a capital T — driven by the need to understand my shattering and revealing psychedelic experiences.

But neither Arica, nor Lilly, nor Gurdjieff was the only game in town. For the period since (at least) the advent of the hippie movement in the sixties, there was a flowering of interest within the youth counter-culture in all manner of spiritual teachings and practices, with the majority of them being in one way or the other derived from eastern traditions. There were gurus and cults aplenty and thousands of young people driven to seek new answers and new states of consciousness. Very largely through the widespread use of psychedelic drugs like LSD, the possibility of experiencing intense non-ordinary spiritual consciousness was suddenly very real and palpable and being pursued from many angles.

Throughout these past few years, for example, I would "drop in" on meditations, events, and so on by various spiritual teachers, mostly of an eastern ilk. Going back to high school, I would hang out with friends at the charming little "Love and Serve" Indian restaurant (cafe, really) in town, across from the train station. It was managed by devotees of Sri Chinmoy[182]; once or twice I attended a meditation with him. Later, with different Arica folks, I visited Hare Krishna temple meals and also did meditations with Yogi Bajan[183], and also with Sufi Pir Vilayat Inayat Khan[184], and others. I was very eclectic in my interests.

Most typically, however, as a "book person," I would habitually frequent the spirituality sections of bookstores, looking for new sources of wisdom and guidance and new points of view.

One day soon after I had moved back to my parent's house, I was at the large department store downtown. They had a large bookcase devoted to spiritual and "new age" topics. I pored over it regularly, looking for something new — almost for a new "fix" of stimulation in my ongoing strivings to make sense of it all, to find the right path to follow or the next piece of the jigsaw puzzle. On that particular day, I at first didn't see anything new or that I hadn't considered before and rejected. Although there were, I'm sure, over a hundred or so titles available in this section, it felt picked over relative to my standards and interests. At length, my eyes fell upon the title *Ancient Myths, Their Meaning in Connection with Evolution*, by Rudolf Steiner. I had only the vaguest notion of Rudolf Steiner. (My recollection of my youthful encounter with the storefront of the old 211 Madison Avenue center didn't emerge until much later.) Without any particular foundation, I placed Steiner in the category of an Edgar Cayce[185] type of "clairvoyantism." Not to disparage Edgar Cayce, but my image of Cayce was more or less formed by the somewhat sensationally packaged mass-market paperbacks I had seen on the drugstore racks, side by side with detective novels and such. Steiner was filed together along with Cayce adjacent to the category of table-rapping, mediumistic sensation-mongers. Gurdjieff, it seemed, looked down his nose at the self-proclaimed "clairvoyants" and such like. I felt, therefore, so should I.

But my basically uninformed impression was neutral enough that I allowed my interest in the topic of myths, which I had loved since childhood, to overrule any reservations I had about Steiner. So I bought the book.

On taking it home, I first of all discovered that the volume was, in fact, a transcript of seven lectures. I was also quickly aware that the story was "already in progress," as he was clearly speaking to an audience possessing a familiarity with any number of abstruse and esoteric details which he took for granted. The content — which, indeed, did talk about ancient Greek myths, was speaking about myths as the expression of an earlier *mode of consciousness* that differed fundamentally from that of today. It also spoke of real existing discarnate higher beings, more or less matter of factly.

Most particularly, it felt that in his words and form of expression and content that here was someone who had *direct knowledge* of what he talked about through his own experience of wide-awake alternate states of consciousness and knowing, and not out of some shadowy or mediumistic "second sight."

In other words, he came across as speaking from his own knowledge of states not dissimilar to some of the psychedelic states I had traversed; and moreover, he was able to encompass it all rationally and with the ability to peel away depth after depth. The material itself was presented matter-of-factly (as being experience based); there was nothing dogmatic about any of his assertions, it was all presented with a more or less take-it-or-leave-it attitude.

This is perhaps one of the primary learnings of psychedelic experience in the modern era: that spiritual experience and spiritual knowledge can be had — with effort — in what can be understood as a highly *awake* state of consciousness. Spiritual communications from trance, mediumistic, or "channeled" sources (for example, automatic writing) will seem less trustworthy than those communicated by one who attains the knowledge in an *awake* state; and, furthermore, one in which the individual has maintained a connection with their own essential *I*. It is part of the nature of the spiritual world that beings can interpenetrate each other. One must be mindful of who one is host to.

Although there was much to comprehend, and much more uncomprehended — in part because of some of the background assumptions made, in part because of the novelty of the content — I felt almost immediately drawn into the process of reading and *trying* to comprehend what was being communicated, and feeling (as Owen Barfield[186] once remarked) generally *wiser* for having read his material.

So began a process of absorption of the huge body of Steiner's work, a process which continues to this day for me. For me, it was really a recognition, while I felt completely free to accept or believe his statements, or not — he had no requirements or axe to grind with his listeners.

Within fairly short order, I set about acquiring all of the half-dozen volumes by Steiner available around town, which in those days was blessed with several excellent bookstores, including a metaphysical bookstore. What I felt I had recognized was, here was someone whose work could "meet and exceed" in his grasp of the domains of consciousness I traversed in my psychedelic experimentation.

Steiner's teachings, absorbed from reading a dozen or so "lecture cycles," began to occupy a significant amount of space in my thinking. Although I was still somewhat connected with Arica, I had at some point during this period discontinued keeping pace with their ongoing roll-out of new programs, partly because of the continuing rise in the expense of participation and the developing sense that I might find what I was seeking elsewhere.

It became clearer and clearer that Steiner, taken at his word, was navigating in depth what someone like Lilly, floating in his isolation tank on 200 mcg of LSD, would call "far-out spaces," but through his *own* gift of clairvoyance and encountering there realities and beings that registered with me as of the same order (at least) as Lilly described and which I felt I had glimpsed while on acid — both benign and malign. For me, it was the content of these explorations of Steiner's that was at least as important as the raw experience of the brighter state of consciousness in which they were received.

Within a short period of months, I came to absorb a clear notion of his cosmology; his membering of the human being and its supersensible spiritual elements; his vision of the development of human consciousness from an earlier state of a dream-like consciousness of living in the world of the Gods, to an "awakening" to the physical world and corresponding soul-darkening obscuration of the spirit; and to his idea of the way in which repeated lives on earth — reincarnation — was part and parcel of the soul's development.

Steiner's image of the human being resonated deeply. Having been exposed to both the Gurdjieff and Arica teachings about the "I," I came to understand Steiner's teaching as the most compelling and satisfying.

Among Steiner's foundational teachings is his delineation of four basic members of the human being. His most simple everyday categorization started with, obviously enough, the *physical body*, that which is common to all the creatures and substances of the earth. In his scheme, consciousness pervades everything, and the physical world is understood as possessing what to us would be a deep trance consciousness.

The first supersensible member he describes is the etheric body or body of formative forces. These are the forces that drive growth and maintain the structure of all living forms, starting with plants. Steiner describes plants as having a consciousness corresponding to what we understand as deep sleep. The individual human etheric body is a highly complicated spiritual structure that incorporates, in a sense, an image of the entire universe and into which is woven the imprint of our individual destiny in a manner perhaps comparable to the idea of an individual's astrological birth chart — indeed, the birth chart can be seen as an attempt to create an image of the pattern laid in to the etheric body.

The etheric or elemental world itself is essentially a thought world of the higher hierarchies of beings. The forces of the etheric world flow from the periphery of the universe and are diametrically opposite the pointwise forces which underly our everyday concept of the atomistic material world, wherein the smallest entities possess the qualities of mass and gravity. When living forms are growing, the etheric body is active, and consciousness is correspondingly suppressed.

Next is the "body" — or organization — of consciousness and sensation, desires, feelings, and impulses. It is the highest member of animals, who have a dream-like consciousness. This is the astral body and can be understood as the body of the soul.

Finally, there is the *Ego or I* — The eternal spiritual part of man that persists between earthly lives. Our ordinary everyday I is just a shadow or reflection of it, and this "little ego" does not transcend the single earth life. From life to life, we rebuild our *I*-reflecting soul structures out of the elements of our destiny, formed out of our life in the spiritual world between death and a new birth.

Characterizing the *I* or Ego is a many-sided question. Steiner's use is distinctly referring to the spiritual "I am" consciousness. The psychic structure — really, a soul artifact — that we typically identify ourselves with is not this eternal *I*, but it is by virtue of having this as the primal reality of our true being that allows us to experience ourselves as "I beings" through its reflection in our earthly consciousness.

The ultimate spiritual development of the human spirit is a process over many lifetimes. Steiner emphatically affirms the teaching of reincarnation as a progressive evolution of the soul-spirit nature.

This fourfold scheme is useful for understanding many of Steiner's ideas. Behind this fourfold division are more nuanced sevenfold and ninefold structures, relevant primarily in understanding humanity's future development. Through the activity of the I, the lower members are transformed into higher spiritual members.

In our life between birth and death, our astral body and Ego detach from the physical and etheric body during sleep; the destructive influence of the astral body — that is, of our experience of consciousness — is repaired through the unconscious activity of the etheric body.

This clarified for me the experience earlier of perceiving Edie's "brain dissolving" while tripping on Huntington Avenue in Boston.

Death is the complete separation of the etheric from the physical body, which disintegrates without the living influence of the etheric. Each part of the physical body has a corresponding organization in the etheric body. The etheric body — or also its different parts — can be "attached" more or less loosely to the physical body depending on, among other things, the state of consciousness. This idea is important in the anthroposophical understanding of the psychedelic state as is discussed here.

The development of our higher nature in Steiner is understood as a transformative process wherein the spiritual I successively transforms and purifies the existing lower members: first, the *astral* body is transformed into what he describes as *spirit self,* or *Manas*; then the *etheric* body into *life spirit,* or *Buddhi*; and finally the physical body into the *spirit human being,* or *Atman*. This is a process of ages of earth time and repeated incarnations.

These members correspond in a general way with elements from Hindu tradition (Manas, Buddha, Atman) and also with Theosophical Society teaching.

Contrasting these ideas with those of Gurdjieff, as I came to see it, Gurdjieff had wanted to work with those disaffected from the Theosophical Society and dismissed as dreams and wishes the Theosophical teaching as to the existence of higher members. He instead asserted that these higher members — that is, elements capable of existence after death — had to be "grown" (or "coated" in a process by analogy with electroplating). In Steiner, these higher members are seen as latently present in the lower bodies but require transformation by the *I* for their actualization.

I suspect Gurdjieff's view was that Theosophical teaching tended to give its followers airs and pretensions in ascribing to themselves spiritual natures while, in fact, being in a position of spiritual servitude to their disorganized, mechanical, and unconscious natures.

Steiner's teaching about the components of the human being dovetails with his cosmological teaching as to the origin or birth of the lower members (and the present earth world) through a process of descent out of the spirit through a series of cosmic phases that preceded the coming into being of the present earth existence.

Higher experience, or higher consciousness, was, for Steiner, first a process of the development of *organs of perception* that can support higher cognition. The whole question of higher cognition is crucial in Steiner, as his teaching itself is presented as being derived from (or, where it aligns with tradition, validated out of) his own higher cognition. His teaching includes guidance in developing into the stages which he describes as *Imagination, Inspiration,* and *Intuition.* Each of these is a technical term outside of their everyday meaning.

My psychedelic experience to date had given me the irrefutable sense that there are higher states of spiritual perception available under the special circumstances of the psychedelic state. They must therefore be an inherent capacity of the present state of spiritual evolution of the contemporary human being.

Through the psychedelic experience — and, of course, through a certain effort of psychological introspection — it can become clear that the "lower" "ego-organization" is simply a construct, and liable to fall away and cannot be "made immortal" in the spiritual world, by any process. It is only through that of which we are "most ignorant of what we are most assured" that this can be realized and perceived. Or, as the alchemists would have it, "One must have gold to make gold."

All of this notwithstanding, I was struck yet again by what appeared at first like extreme disjunctions from the Arica teaching. The *I* — or Ego — was again restored to dignity (rightly understood). In Steiner, a new (to me) kind of distinction was being made between one's best or higher self and one's undesirable karmically conditioned elements: this was the being of the "Double" (*doppelgänger*) or, as also designated, the *Guardian* or *Dweller* of the Threshold.

I have already made reference to the Double in the experience of the cast party. In Steiner, the Double is regarded as if it were an *actual being*, spiritually, although it dwells within the self; it comes to serve a critical role in the development of one's spiritual experience and perception.

From one point of view, as a "being," it is the bearer of all of one's *unredeemed karma* — that is, deeds that are, one way or another, in opposition to the spirit and which cling to one's self. They work their way into one's destiny, weaving life scenarios out of the apparent chance factors of existence and unfolding in such a manner that one can ultimately balance or recompense harm done to self, others, and the world. In Steiner's teaching of reincarnation, one's choice of how and when to incarnate is ultimately influenced directly by one's own higher-self perspective on the path to redemption of one's accumulated karmic debt — ideally, in alignment with the broader progress of human evolution.

From the perspective of our earthly self, however, becoming aware *in the spiritual world* of this Double can, depending, fill one with fear, shame, and remorse — if we are unprepared to experience a spiritually objective picture of the nature of the being, replete with flaws, that we have become through the process of our incarnation. It is, however, according to Steiner, something that the individual will encounter "sooner or later" upon crossing, by whatever means, into the perception of the spiritual world. Although we may, through conscious intention or fate, variously find ourselves drawn to experience any number of realities in the spiritual world, the Double is always actually present as a "companion being" to our self, and we will invariably encounter it as part of our general spiritual environment. It is called the Guardian because, in its terrifying aspect, our soul's tendency will be to *retreat* from the threshold of the spiritual world, thus removing it (and the spiritual world with it) from our sphere of consciousness if we are otherwise unprepared to deal with all of the implications of the Double. With this retreat, or "warding away," I was familiar.

As Steiner explains in his *Knowledge of Higher Worlds and its Attainment*, the Double is to be accepted as one's own, and its debts acknowledged as one's own, and the resolve formed to work in life, to transform its present character as a distorted reflection of our spiritual selves, whatever this requires — and at our current stage of evolution, this is to be understood as a matter of future lifetimes. He refers to the formation of this resolve as the "mystic vow."

Given this resolve and acceptance, the Double assumes a second character — that of teacher and, very importantly, as the container, in a certain manner, of all tendencies to filter one's perception in the spiritual world with one's own distortions and "acting out" — in the field of our own perception as well as in deeds — our own karmic stories brewing within. With the ability to see, with equanimity, the presence of the Double and its aggregation of misdeeds and malformations of our being, we can better see what is otherwise to be revealed from the spiritual world and its *other* beings, our tendency to distort being tempered by the recognition of the guardian.

This characterization of the Double as the "Dweller of the Threshold" is met with in the novel *Zanoni* by the 19th Century author Edward Bulwer-Lytton,[187] which is referenced by Steiner in *Knowledge of Higher Worlds*. The protagonist is undergoing a process of initiation by a spiritual adept; however, the process goes wrong. The adept reveals to him the spiritual world and, thereby, the Double or Guardian. The Guardian appears as a demonic, terrifying spectral form; the would-be initiate shrinks from the vision and is thereafter haunted by the memory of the Double and pursues drink and dissolution in an attempt to rid his mind of the experience of the Double.

The concept of the Double is in some ways analogous to Carl Jung's *shadow*, only here understood as a *spiritual* element or being, not simply a complex operating in the subconscious mind. In Jung, the shadow is seen as influencing our waking everyday sensory life (as indeed the Double does); but in Steiner, the Double really comes into play within the context of one's existence as a spiritual being.

This understanding of the nature of this Double applies, in my experience absolutely, to the dynamics of the psychedelic experience to the extent that through the psychedelic state, the experience of the threshold is approached. One may, as it were, breeze across the threshold into a positive, joyful experience — and if the threshold is pursued, one will eventually stumble into the need for a recognition of the existence of this double. Depending on one's readiness, this will be encountered somewhere on the spectrum between deeply challenging to deeply affirming.

Although I very quickly found myself "at home" with everything connected with Rudolf Steiner's teachings, I was in awe of the vastness of its content and was somewhat mystified as to how I would possibly absorb it in anything approximating completeness. The momentum of earlier interests, which included Gurdjieff/Ouspensky, Arica/Lilly, and psychedelic drugs — although the last had receded for the moment into the background — continued to occupy my soul as well.

After returning home at the end of the spring semester of school as an allegedly "adult" 19-year-old, the relationship with my parents was occasionally fraught. I began working as a shoe salesman over the summer — which at least put some change in my pocket. And which, along with other things, bought books.

Thus that summer, my little bookshelf of works by Rudolf Steiner continued to expand. With little work or study responsibility, I was free to delve deeply into my study of Steiner, and I remember fondly the sense of freshness (and familiarity as well) in all the material I was absorbing. I could read for hours on end.

By the fall, as tensions with my parents increased around typical dependence and independence issues, they, in their wisdom, suggested that I might try living on my own, easing and motivating the process by offering me the use of their rental property, a cottage near the shore. The summer rental season was over, and it would be a couple of months until my grandparents would move in, as they did every year for wintering. I could have the place rent-free until then.

I invited Alan to move in with me. Although I don't recall specifics, I am sure I was back to the old habit of smoking pot more or less regularly; I do recall that the night before I was to move in, I was with Alan as he dropped the "moving out to live with David" bomb on his parents. His father was quite upset, and they had a bit of a row. I distinctly remember that Alan and I had done a line of coke prior (one of the small handful of times I indulged in coke), adding to the drama of the scene. Between using pot and coke, there is implied the latitude as well to resume exploration with psychedelics, although that was yet to come.

Right around when I was moving into the cottage, there was a Crosby Stills, Nash & Young, Joni Mitchell, Beach Boys festival concert at Roosevelt Raceway[188], which my younger brother and I went to. It was an all-day affair, and as it happened, we wound up sitting together on the field with a couple of cute young girls from somewhere on Long Island, one of whom was tripping fairly strongly. She had some period of mild distress, and if I recall correctly, I was able to be reasonably comforting and supportive and engaging. I don't remember many of the details. Inasmuch as I hadn't hung out with someone who was tripping for a while, I can speculate that it likely, in some way, contributed to reviving my appetite for the psychedelic experience.

After two months at the cottage, I had to make room for my grandparents and moved into a carriage house rental with an acquaintance I was friendly with. He was a year or two younger and had grown up in my neighborhood. We knew each primarily through mutual acquaintances but became quite friendly. Our landlord was a 30-something divorcee who was quite sympathetic.

Somewhere that fall, I had also switched jobs; despite having left my previous drugstore job on less than favorable terms, I secured one at another of the several pharmacies in town. After a while, working alongside other older co-workers for whom this was a career, I was starting to come around to the wisdom of completing my college degree.

As usual, I asked for books for Christmas, which this year would now consist of requests for books by Steiner.

I was officially on "leave of absence" from school, so upon deciding I would give school another try, registering for the January intersession was easy.

11

Twenty Suns Twenty

And so I resumed my matriculation and made plans to return to school for their January intersession — earning credit for a semester's class in one month, with extended morning and afternoon class periods each day.

I was excited to find that there was an anthropology class titled "Altered States of Consciousness," which was — largely through the influence and popularity of Carlos Castaneda's works — apparently now a legitimate focus under the broad umbrella of anthropological studies, even at the undergraduate level.

I had my own car, a hand-me-down from my sister-in-law. I was also just introduced through a mutual friend I worked with at the drugstore to a fellow student at Drew, a second-semester Freshman, Michael. Our first meeting was to drive down to school, a two-hour drive. And, as it happened, I found he was likewise enrolled in the "Altered States" class.

There were 20 students or so enrolled; our principal assignment for the class was for each one of us to make a study of some aspect of the subject of "Alternate States." This ranged broadly from a study of specific writers like Lilly or Castaneda to shamanic traditions, hypnosis, Wolf's *The Electric Kool Aid Acid Test*, Camus on Absurdity, Rozak's *Where the Wasteland Ends*, Voodoo, Glossolalia, Possession, William Burroughs. It was all fascinating, if a little loosey-goosey academically speaking. I surveyed Stephen Gaskin as a social/anthropological phenomenon with a socially-integrated approach to alternate realities.

Unsurprisingly, I made several friends in the class who I would later trip with: Michael, Andre, and Charli. It happened that my birthday fell in the middle of the month, and on that day, I tripped with Michael and a friend of his (I don't recall him as being in the class with us). It was my 20th birthday and the first time I had seriously tripped in almost two years (since the trip with Lorraine). The dose definitely put me (solidly) into a psychedelic space, but it was not overpowering. What remains in my memory from that acid trip, walking around the lovely campus and hanging out in a dorm room listening to records, is, first, I had a definite sensation that, while I liked who I was on LSD, I noticed that I also liked who I was, or was becoming, in my "straight" head. Something about the mood I was in as I acclimated to being on acid after a definite pause provided an ability to weigh or compare the two states of myself side by side. It is not that I hadn't liked myself, but I realized that I had become (somewhat more) "comfortable in my skin." I would attribute this largely to maturation in general as well as (possibly) that I had done some amount of inner work on myself — both psychedelically and "in real life." Alongside that, there was a greater feeling of inner stability, inner ballast. The handful of trips I took in my remaining school years had this underlying quality of stability and, at the same time, a comfort and ease with exploring any number of thoughts and imaginations of cosmic proportion while remaining rooted and present in the here and now. It could also be that the dose was simply "just right."

And so, there were also imaginations of more cosmic measure. The first of these was that, as I contemplated the fact of my twentieth birthday, I inwardly had a very palpable sense of having traversed twenty passages around the sun; it was as if I could observe the dial on the odometer turning over. There was a certain wholeness to the number twenty. This, in turn, gave a kind of "soul-echo" of rippling back (and forth) in time to my birth — that is, through the gateway out of the spiritual world, the sense of which loomed beyond, and also a sense of connection with the being of the sun as a constant, radiant source of spiritual force in my progress through the years. Somewhere there was a knowledge that behind the world of earthly appearance stood the column of light that I had glimpsed at the lake.

Then, while we were in one of the dorm rooms, listening to music, I had imaginations triggered by whatever we would listen to. I recall a reverie listening to the Kinks' *Celluloid Heroes* — a melancholic and nostalgic song about the lives of classic silver screen stars. I transposed the meaning of "celluloid" from the celluloid of motion picture film to "celluloid" — that, biologically composed of cells, that is, of flesh — and felt the song as dripping with pathos for the human condition of mortality. From there, I moved into a deeper inner world that lingers in me still: as I recall, we were listening to something "trippy and far out" by the Moody Blues — although to this day, I can't identify what it might have been (possibly *Days of Future Passed*) — I found myself drifting into an extremely vivid psychic journey into the story of the end of the world and the "Twilight of the Gods." I recognized this as paralleling what I knew of Norse mythology, although it seemed to "drive by itself" alongside the music. It was, on the one hand, dreamlike, on the other, intensely vivid and real as a vision of the far distant future. It touched me at the deepest level. The world — including the world-tree (*Yggdrasil*, an image of the enormous world-tree revelation I had almost three years earlier at the lake) — was consumed in a brilliant fire and then re-formed out of the void and ashes as a new heavenly creation, with a new primal couple, a new Adam and Eve, to repopulate mankind, emerging from the re-blossoming tree.

As I said, it appeared that I was being guided into this by the music, although it is possible the whole inner sequence was triggered by a single phrase. Scouring my memory, my most definite recollection of learning anything of Norse Mythology was, first, from *Tales of Asgard* in the *Journey Into Mystery* Marvel comic I would have read at nine or ten, and secondly, from Rudolf Steiner's *The Mission of the Folk Souls*, where a discussion of the Norse mythology takes place in the last few lectures. This lecture cycle of Steiner's I would have read fairly recently; at this point, I would have read maybe a dozen or so volumes of Steiner's lecture cycles. Although at the time I did not correlate this imagination with the reading of a few months earlier, it is of definite interest that this was also my first LSD trip after my contact with Steiner's teachings.

As I look back at what were to be the final two years of psychedelic experimentation before I essentially laid it aside, I find myself reflecting that this experience, with its foreseeing of the rebirth of the world, was perhaps the most significant during that period. I felt inwardly vouchsafed a glimpse into the far-distant future of humanity. At the time, it was taken in stride as just another phase of the complex of thoughts, feelings, and states that transpired within the many hours of a psychedelic session. I did not particularly dwell upon it until reflecting much later. Rather, I tasted it gratefully as if in passing.

As the spring semester advanced, friendships developed in the "Alternate Realities" classes continued to deepen. One classmate was an eighteen-year-old woman named Charli, who was married and living on campus with her slightly older husband, who worked in Manhattan. She was a charming woman with a certain wildness and corresponding elastic sense of sexual boundaries. She had a pixie haircut and a sparkling diamond piercing in her nose, which in 1975 was quite novel. Her spirit reminded me of Edie. We acted out a brief flirtation which advanced to the brink before dialing itself back down with a clarified resolve as to our boundaries. Nonetheless, we remained connected and retained a certain intimacy.

We did LSD together at least once - It was a fine spring day, we wandered about and enjoyed the charms of the wooded campus. The only content of conversation I recall was her chatting about some infatuation she had with a man in one of her spring classes and feeling a bit wistful hearing about it. I recall the two of us sitting under some trees near my dorm, perhaps fifty or sixty feet or so away from it. My room was in one of the larger, older yellow brick 19th-century buildings and was quite charming, as was the whole scene from under the tree. I recall experiencing the blossoming trees as conducting a flow of spiritual life forces between the skies and heavens, and the earth, welding them magically into connection and circulation.

We sat together under the trees for a while; and then we saw a mutual friend of ours stride purposively from the parking lot to our right, and down the pavement leading to the side door of the dorm. She appeared quite intent on some mission. After a few minutes, we saw her re-emerge from the same doorway, marking off in the direction she came. Charli and I looked at each other, deeply curious as to what would explain her actions. The whole skit was striking and very quizzical to us.

The next day we would learn that she had, in fact, been looking for me. My room was on the first floor, but to the far left end of the building (she had entered from the right, which we were sitting closer to), and the time between entering and leaving was the time to walk from one end of the hall to the other and back, having found no response to her knock. Had she looked up, she would have seen us. She had apparently been wanting to borrow my car, which would have been a bit unusual, although I'm sure I would have lent it to her. It was one of those peculiar synchronicities that seem to occur on psychedelics, although, in this instance, without apparent or fathomable meaning. Meanwhile, she apparently had been so focused as to render us invisible, although we were looking at her.

Later during that trip, we went to Charli's apartment. Although I can't remember the proximate trigger, I found myself shifting into a contemplation inspired by my readings of Steiner and his images of the spiritual cosmos — and found myself transported in thought and vision into a felt and seen shift toward an angelic, solar cosmic plane, while at the same time being fully aware of being present in Charli's apartment. I also sensed the spiritual presence within this scene of what I characterized to myself as, if not the seven Rishis of the Veda, some *human* sages in deeper contact with the solar spiritual plane. Perhaps they were in some way guiding my spiritual gaze.

At the same time, I was riddled with a certain sense of doubt. It could be explained as feeling as though I was trying to integrate multiple attunements to multiple cosmic realities and, from there, follow the arising of a *true* imaginative perception. But there were still alternative inner paths to integrate. Indeed, this is one of the pitfalls I believe for psychedelic research or cognition in the spiritual world: the possibility of doubt — which, from the viewpoint of Steiner, is a hallmark of the influence of *Lucifer,* who, on the one hand, can bring us inspirations from the world of spiritual light, as in this case from psychedelics. While we are still in incarnation, the gifts of Lucifer can also inject the element of doubt.

Clearly, my ongoing psychedelic explorations were beginning to be influenced by my readings of anthroposophy.

Another friend from the "Altered States" class was Andre. We became lifetime friends. Our social circles soon overlapped at school. He was a philosophy major, and we shared acid several times. I recall one trip — wandering again in springtime into the beautiful forest preserve adjacent to the campus. Not unsurprisingly, we found ourselves in a discussion of various philosophers. The element of doubt again permeated the conversation — a fairly predictable outcome if you include philosopher David Hume[189] (1711 - 1776) as an element of your conversation! I struggled to keep my inner "spiritual axis" aligned in the sea of thought, with currents blowing this way and that as Andre (who was naturally better informed as to the details of these philosophers) and I discussed, I suppose, epistemological[190] questions and their existential implications. Underneath it, I had something along the lines of an urge to tell Andre, "Don't fuck up your head thinking about all that bullshit!" but I managed to bite my tongue. In a somewhat different mood, of course, the study of philosophy can be quite deepening, but we found ourselves mining a bit of a pessimistic seam.

Other distractions occurred as we wandered the forest. At one point, we encountered Andre's roommate, and through some offhand remarks about the weather, I suddenly felt as if directly attuned to the elemental spirit being behind the formation of clouds and weather; and I seemed to be directly influencing the appearance or disappearance of cloud cover as if I were — very momentarily — possessed with the consciousness of "the Thunder God." This was a distinct sense of oneness with the weather than that at the lake, when I "hid" from the sunlight "under the clouds." I now was spiritually part of the changing skies that gather and rain to make the plants to grow and the seasons to turn. It was a brief but magical state. I wasn't avoiding the elements; I was playing with them.

Another time that spring, I tripped with a freshman I had become friendly with, Nick. I don't have a detailed memory of it and was, in fact, a bit surprised to be reminded many years later that it was his first trip. He had interesting "dialed-in" experiences that included being in the campus dining hall and experiencing that all the vegetarians were seen in color and meat-eaters in black and white. He became a lifetime vegetarian fairly shortly after that. I had already become a vegetarian myself for a time.

I probably tripped one or two more times with Andre. These and really, all of my trips in my twentieth year, were enjoyable and expansive experiences, while at the same time, somewhere in the back of my mind I was beginning to sense that this phase of exploration was winding down.

Amidst all this, I was connecting with the academic scene in a new way. I had settled on becoming an English Major — I had realized that this would provide me the widest latitude in what I was to study, and I found myself enjoying the required curriculum. I was, in general, starting to "get the hang" of the academic game while still providing plenty of time for my social, spiritual, psychedelic, and other interests. While wandering through the stacks at the library (Drew had begun as a Methodist Seminary, so there were all manner of interesting things in their library), I discovered Owen Barfield's (1898 - 1997) *Romanticism Comes of Age*[191], a collection of essays which, as the title suggests, characterizes anthroposophy as the mature expression of what was "in the air" in the time of the English Romantic poets such a Samuel Taylor Coleridge (1772 - 1834), Percy Bysshe Shelley (1792 - 1822), and William Blake. This line of thought was understandably influential in leading me to focus my English Literature studies on the romantic poets.

As it would happen, I came shortly to learn that Barfield — who I took to immediately as a brilliant writer about Steiner's ideas — had, in fact, been a visiting professor at Drew and, further, was friendly with one of my religious studies teachers. As a matter of continued coincidence, I found myself soon befriending the librarian[192] at the Anthroposophical Society's center in New York at 211 Madison Avenue (now long since gone) — the same place I had wandered past at age 13 — and learning that he had likewise studied at Drew. Neither of these connections was consequential relative to my enrollment at Drew other than subtly reinforcing the sense that I was following a karmic thread on my pathway into anthroposophy.

Once when I made a visit to the library at 211 — while I was still in school and still using LSD on occasion — the librarian showed me a purple-inked mimeographed newsletter from someone in

Manhattan who had dropped it off for the library. Apparently, The author was very actively blending anthroposophy with what read like wild LSD screeds about visiting other planets, the archangel Michael (a pivotal figure in the anthroposophical hierarchies of spiritual beings), and more. The writing was in a style that you could encounter across the hippie-spiritual spectrum that was decidedly far out and read like the original label of Dr. Bronner's[193] soap, only more so.

I left it aside — it didn't feel like it came from a place of particularly enlightened integration. It instead struck me as a bit untethered. But there it was.

Close to the very end of that school year, I became involved with Maddy. Her family lived a half hour from school, and some of her high school friends would visit, or, likewise, we would go back to her hometown to hang out with them. We had only been involved for a few weeks when, with the school year ending, there was a weekend "picnic" festival with music[194], and I'm sure at least half the campus population milling about on the athletic fields. Some of her friends from her hometown came to visit and join the party. Not too far after their arrival, Maddy told me that, along with her friends, she had just dropped acid — for her, this would be the first time. I was a little annoyed that I hadn't been part of the decision, but because I wanted to share her first trip with her, I joined in.

The only concrete memory I have of that trip, which must have gone smoothly in the daytime, was of later that night alone in her dorm room. Unsurprisingly, we began making love, experiencing at first the amplification of our youthful, new-love energy connection.

In the middle of this, I felt myself going inward. I won't say that I lost connection with her, but I had a parallel track of inner meditation: as if I were viewing a network or web of forces floating above and within and connecting with row after row of souls as if above the earth, knit into a pattern. It was, in a way, a kind of slice of the "cosmic backplane" I perceived at the cast party.

I began to consider my possible future destiny with Maddy. Although her soul as such wasn't an active part of this inward soul-state, I knew that through this web, a "door" to her soul existed. And then, following a certain psychedelic logic, my thinking came upon the idea: *I should marry her.* And so, in fact, I wound up proposing that night; and she said yes.

In the morning, still high on acid, we shared the "good news" with people we met — some who congratulated us, some who looked askance. We were still high.

Fairly soon, although we continued as a couple into the fall of the next year, the feeling that this (marriage) was "a really good idea" faded into the background, and we focussed on the relationship where it really was: just starting. An object lesson cautioning against operating heavy machinery and so on while "under the influence."

Maddy and I did, however, trip two or three more times. Once, she and Andre came to visit me during the summer at my parent's house in Connecticut, and we dropped acid and went sailing on the Long Island Sound — it was a beautiful, sunny day, and far out in the middle of the sound, we followed the wind and enjoyed the relatively low-dose acid, sailing along. The only real detail I can recall, aside from the fun of it, was that as the afternoon faded and we headed back into the harbor, I was momentarily panicked as I looked to the harbor and saw what looked like hundreds of other sailboats converging there. I thought I wouldn't be able to summon the focus to navigate into and among them. However, as we sailed closer, we fell into the queue of ships as naturally as an elephant grabbing the tail of the elephant in front of it. It was a procedure I was familiar with, having grown up sailing. Again, it is often possible to trust the delegation to habit.

Back in school the next fall, Maddy, Andre, my friend Nick, and I all dosed one night. Nick was to have been my roommate in the fall semester but dropped out a week or so prior to the start of school after his own deeply revelatory acid journey, where he came to the realization that school wasn't going to teach him anything he needed to know. He lived near the school and so would still hang out with us on campus.

That night, the four of us wandered out in the nighttime to the athletic field and lay in the middle of the soccer pitch, looking up to the stars. I knew and sensed myself as breathing together with the stars, which I now beheld inwardly as a host of divine spiritual beings or intelligences — not merely as burning suns millions of miles away. I felt connected with the spiritual cosmos as its shape, structure, and pattern were now forming in me through my study of Rudolf Steiner.

It had been over a year now that I had been reading Steiner, and his body of thought was rooting itself in my thinking. At times I was overwhelmed by the vastness and richness of panoramas of spiritual activity that he described; at the same time, ideas I had absorbed in reading began to fall into place bit by bit. Although my acid adventures during that time were not engaged in with a specific intention to deepen or realize aspects of his teaching, I found in various ways it influenced them. I will comment here that despite this rapid on-boarding, these ideas were still competing for mental real estate with the Fourth Way, Arica, and other notions I had already packed into my head — some of which were never quite "discarded" but instead reconciled with the anthroposophical worldview.

Later that same night, Maddy and I retired to my room. We made love, but I was detached in a way from the physicality of the act. The mechanics of the procedure worked unremarkably as per usual, but despite a certain interest, I found myself detached, although not in the sense one would use in describing a relationship lacking in connection, but as a real inner disconnection from myself as a physical, sexual being, while at the same time, my "inner cosmic reality" was permeated with a charge of erotic energy. I can't recall any specifically distracting psychological preoccupation, just being on another plane energetically. Interpersonally, we were relating harmoniously, albeit we were both tripping.

This would be, if I recall correctly, my penultimate trip on acid. Maddy and I spent the last few months of the fall semester processing what was developing to be our pending breakup. Although I see myself as largely at fault for precipitating this, the end of the romance proved quite upsetting to me.

In the spring semester, I ventured to embark on an independent study project with the instructor who had taught the survey course on English Romantic Poets — Wordsworth, Blake, Keats, and Shelley. I had been attuned to the resonance between these poets, and the romantic movement in general, with the soul-mood of anthroposophy through reading Barfield's *Romanticism Comes of*

Age. My study attempted, not necessarily successfully, to create an anthroposophical exegesis of Shelley's *Prometheus Unbound*. But it was an indication of the degree to which anthroposophical ideas were taking hold in me.

Sometime that spring, I palled along with a friend Zig and his girlfriend to a Jackson Browne concert somewhere not too far from campus and dosed by myself. The concert was OK, the acid so-so, and my state of mind, gloomy. And thus, my youthful psychedelic career went out not with a bang, but with a whimper. As such, it was an odd inflection point.

Looking back on that year and a half of my second period at Drew, I recall those times fondly. I made good friends and moved through dear and now distant love relationships, turned a couple of people on to acid, deepened my reading of Steiner, and began my contact with the Anthroposophical Society[195]. Initially, I didn't suppose that the Anthroposophical Society still existed when I first started reading Steiner; he had been dead for almost fifty years. My continued psychedelic explorations were almost entirely benign and enjoyable. To the extent that they were part of my spiritual process, it was primarily through inner deepening and contemplation rather than "thunderbolts of transformation" as the experiences I had when I was seventeen. I continued to see them as part of a general context of spiritual seeking and discovery from what was, to me, by this stage, a well-grounded place. The overall tenor was recreational and social, although now not merely pleasure-seeking but rather *spiritually festive*.

Toward the end of Spring, I found myself making plans to attend New York University for the Fall semester as a visiting student. Among other things, my breakup with Maddy still smarted, and I wanted a clean break. Although I wasn't really thinking about what I would do after I graduated, I had become intrigued by the idea of getting some kind of office job in New York (My friend Lauren had done this the summer before and it triggered something in me). Things started coming together when, through a connection of my father's, I was able to get a summer internship in the editorial department of a major book publisher. I moved to the West Village, subletting a funky basement apartment. Once I had moved to the city, I decided I wanted to stay and transferred to NYU and finished out my senior year there.

I was to work in book publishing for five years. Near the end of that period, I became fascinated by the advent of the personal computer. I took a few courses in computer programming and got myself an Apple II. My first wife, who I had lived with for several years, and I got married, shortly before taking my first job in the computer software world.

After a few years in the very young and exciting personal computer industry, I got a job at Apple, and moved with my young family to California.

12

Return to the Well

My life continued from that last LSD trip for forty-odd years without any further psychedelic exploration. I became more and more deeply involved in the study of anthroposophy. I developed a careeer, raised a family. By the time my first child was born, I had discontinued both drinking alcohol and smoking pot. This was largely a process of just fading away.

There is a bit more to these years relating to the unfolding of my journey that will be shared here, but let me complete the series of my psychedelic experiences first.

Around five or six years ago, I began to notice in the news (such as the *New York Times* and National Public Radio) and my Facebook feed that there was a definite shift regarding how psychedelics were being reported. By this time I was starting to slide my way into retirement, although I kept a hand in for a while with odd consulting gigs.

I had been, of course, aware all along that young people still experimented with psychedelics in college, that there was an underground of some sort and an ongoing intellectual dialog in the likes of the late Terrance McKenna[196], Daniel Pinchbeck[197] (who refers to Rudolf Steiner in some of his writings) and others. There was the whole Burning Man phenomenon — I had been a few times — which I knew was peppered with mushrooms and molly (MDMA), and so on, but suddenly — and this seemed somewhat to coincide with the legalization of recreational marijuana in California and elsewhere — it appeared that psychedelics were undergoing a cultural rehabilitation of epic proportions, and that *quite possibly*, they were at the start of a track similar to that of marijuana, from approved "medical use" to recreational and/or sacramental use after some period of years to come.

I reacted to this in a couple of ways. First, with a slightly petulant amusement at articles published as if it were "news" that psychedelic drugs might have therapeutic uses. Yes, there are already reams and reams of studies and so forth on LSD in psychotherapy published in the fifties and sixties — all buried in the "War on Drugs" and the classification of LSD as a Schedule I drug. With this, there was also the dawning realization that I was a creature of a different era. Not only was, as the Moody Blues song[198] goes, Timothy Leary dead, but so also were Richard Nixon, J. Edgar Hoover[199], and even Ted Kennedy[200], who all played roles in the clampdown on LSD.

I had already found myself shockingly aware of the distance from those times (and my advancing age) when, maybe 15 years ago, I was at lunch with an assortment of enterprise-software company colleagues who, like me, had flown in for an internal conference, and we began chatting. The question "Read any good books lately?" came up, and I mentioned I had just picked up what looked like a good biography of Timothy Leary. "Who's Timothy Leary?" asked one of my mid-late thirties colleagues, who (until that moment) I took to be not only quite intelligent but very up-to-date and informed. How *could* he not know? There was quite a fading of what used to be common cultural knowledge regarding psychedelics.

As these stories developed, I noticed myself experiencing a certain dissatisfaction with the enthusiastic popularizing of Michael Pollan. It was curious that someone my age, who seemed a bit of a johnny-come-lately to the scene and, thus, someone catching up a bit with layers of the deeper import, should emerge as a 21st-century psychedelic prophet. But — better late than never, and he is undoubtedly upgrading the cultural cachet of psychedelics, applying his journalistic and promotional skill adroitly in service of greater knowledge of psychedelics.

My other response was a concern about the apparent "medicalization" component of the cultural rehabilitation of psychedelics. This concern is felt not only for reasons of general concern regarding the medicalization of psychiatry and psychotherapy — which, from one aspect, can be seen as "the study of the soul without the soul." It is, more broadly, in light of the fact that contemporary medicine has inherently baked into it the worldview of scientific materialism. As such, a pathway to legalization through the medical model would leave little room for the spiritual element as a factor in psychedelic use. On the other hand, some might object that there are forms of therapy involved with psychedelic research that are comfortable dealing with "the needs of the soul" in a purely operational and "spiritualistic hypothesis-free" manner. For example, Carl Jung said that modern man needed a belief in the soul (or God) — whether true or not. It is, of course, a knotty problem regarding the possible societal regulation of drugs: who gets to "control" their use and distribution in a possible future world where they are legitimized — medical doctors?

These thoughts and trends were already brewing in me when a massage therapist that I had begun working with regularly let drop, somewhat casually during our small talk, that she had been sitting in an ayahuasca ceremony over the weekend[201]. Over the weeks and months of our working together, psychedelics became a conversation topic of increasingly deep interest. She was enthusiastically involved. While in the opening space of bodywork, I found my youthful interest and excitement revived. Our conversation also included a discussion of my study of anthroposophy, which she took an interest in. My impression was that her explorations were provoking, as a work in progress, a realignment of own her relationship with the spiritual.

After a few months, these conversations evolved to the point where the idea formed that my wife and I (my first wife and I had separated sometime before, and I had since remarried) would try a modest dose of mushrooms together.

Having had my attention drawn to it, I became aware that in my neck of the woods — that is, Santa Cruz in California — psilocybin mushrooms were readily available through any one of various acquaintances. Although the once-vast underground supply of LSD had long ago been suppressed (although still operating at some scale), cultivating psilocybin mushrooms had become a relatively readily acquired and practiced skill for some.

I was keen to share the experience with my wife, who had never explored psychedelics beyond MDMA. I was likewise somewhat excited and curious to discover what, after so many years, I might find in the psychedelic domain again.

I wanted this exploration to occur in the container of a private, isolated setting, away from the day-to-day intrusions. Moreover, as a so-called "responsible adult," I wanted to avoid any random encounter where I needed to present myself with strict sobriety. So we arranged to rent an Airbnb nearby; it was a charmingly converted pump house on a still active small-scale family farm. It seemed it would offer us enough privacy.

The dose was modest, less than two grams. Within the hour — we dosed well before noon — we began to move into the onset phase, which went very smoothly. We spent the first several hours in the (tiny!) upper room of the converted pump house, sharing, in stages, primarily an enlivened inner landscape and a general high. Trees and such outside the window seemed alive with nature spirits. The space was, for me, entirely familiar. The dose was of a full psychedelic threshold level but, at the same time, very mild and grounded. The variety of deeper spaces hovered nearby me without the push to move into them, although I would go inside and feel the edge.

Within it, I flowed into a definite feeling of blessedness and affirmation, as if confirming, for all of my life's ups and downs in the many years since my psychedelic youth, my path had been spiritually forward. I also found myself, during an inward reverie, wandering into a connection with a kind of cosmic soul-temple woven of light and experiencing a kind of "prayerful wishing" while thinking of my old friend George. I had not seen him in over forty years, but I understood third-hand that he was still burdened by mental illness. Deep in my heart, I wished that, in some future time, he might find a thread linking him more firmly with his true spiritual possibility. In a later review, I saw this as the progressed echo of my long-ago psychedelic musing about him at the beach with Ash, thinking then that, somehow, on a group level, his soul moorings needed to have been better upheld by his friends.

Unfortunately, I later learned that he had passed away between then and this writing.

After several hours, we were drawn to walk outside, feeling grounded enough to navigate a chance encounter with the owners, who we could see were attending to this and that. And indeed, we had a lovely chat with the owner, driving by in his pickup truck — I was to enjoy the conversation a great deal and was only slightly concerned that I was perhaps just a wee bit too voluble and chatty. People are great.

On the edge of the property, beyond a fence, there was a gentle creek surrounded by all manner of dense foliage. We walked along the path by the stream and stopped to gaze at the flowing and babbling water. The sun was shining, and the whole scene was full of life and vibrancy; I felt the same thrill and blessedness in the cosmic-spiritual glory of the earth and the earth life as I had enjoyed at the lake — with just a certain milder quality, although equally deep and rich. I knew and sensed that behind all this sun-drenched natural glory lay a source spiritual world of infinitely greater brilliance.

Wandering further through the property, feeling the echoes of the creekside splendor reverberating, I also felt the depths of my years of study of anthroposophy as a spiritual life treasure welling up inside. I greeted and recognized my psychedelic roots, like the feeling of meeting a long-ago lover and finding the love once shared, no longer felt as rooted in passion, mellowed like a fine wine, as something eternal. I felt all I had grown into with anthroposophy was fructifying my psychedelic state in a timeless way.

It was a mood that struck me as strangely akin to the musings of Alice's older sister at the end of *Alice's Adventures in Wonderland*:

> ... she pictured to herself how this same little sister of hers would, in the after-time, be herself a grown woman; and how she would keep, through all her riper years, the simple and loving heart of her childhood: and how she would gather about her other little children, and make *their* eyes bright and eager with many a strange tale, perhaps even with the dream of Wonderland of long ago: and how she

would feel with all their simple sorrows, and find a pleasure in all their simple joys, remembering her own child-life, and the happy summer days.

This richness through the anthroposophical element then was felt as something I profoundly wished I could share — especially with others who had made some kind of spiritual awakening through psychedelics.

I knew, of course, that to try and share this possibility of knowledge of the spirit as revealed through anthroposophy with those whose path included the psychedelic experience would be a great challenge for so many reasons, not least of all perhaps being my own limitations.

13

Integrating

But what of all those years in between this more recent experience and my last LSD trip at age twenty-one? There are any number of details from that span of forty years, some of which will be recalled further on in this narrative. Most importantly — after completing my youthful psychedelic explorations after a period of six years, what followed? What came is that my spiritual explorations were to continue more and more in the direction of anthroposophy.

In my earlier description of my first encounter with Steiner's work, I described the feeling of instant recognition, of having found someone who could speak to the scope and dimension of the states I had experienced. I will try and characterize it more fully. It was as if the entire catalog of my psychedelic experience, with all their many-layered imaginations, vignettes of spiritual panoramas, and deep soul stirrings, were laid out as if on a kind of three-dimensional game board, replete with players and pieces moving across previously undreamt realities, had been placed into a new context. Piece by piece, this puzzle began to be holistically stitched and woven into an intelligible and profoundly satisfying complex that was both inspirational vision and motivational roadmap — across my life and beyond. I felt I was being met in this new worldview in the totality of my experience as if what had lived in my psychedelic years was being absorbed and digested as part of an all-embracing totality. Anthroposophy, on the one hand, is a worldview; but more than that, it is a force of life that one takes into one's being. In my case, this force of life was to meet all the elements of my previous psychedelic experiences.

I also found that many of the spiritual teachings I had first met when my psychedelic explorations began their turn toward the more intentionally spiritual — in particular, the work of Gurdjieff and Ouspensky — bit by bit became reconciled with Steiner's viewpoints. For the most part, with one significant exception[202], rather than being effaced or obscured, they were — sometimes after a bit of inner wrestling with apparent contradictions — not only realized as being in alignment, but I also found these earlier ideas could, at length, shed their own light on Steiner's thought.

One thing that should be quite obvious by now is that I had pursued my psychedelic pathway without any specific method or approach. Clearly, I did navigate myself *half*-consciously from a purely recreational orientation — or from a "thirst for experience" — toward something more clearly defined as a spiritual intention. Once that threshold was crossed, I found myself in an ever-expanding, boundary-less world that was, to me, all but uncharted. As I began to investigate the different models and maps of these new spaces, I surveyed a wealth of possible directions. I then had to navigate these on the basis of my own rather seat-of-the-pants approach, rooted, however, in some "inner knowing" sense of what was right for me in accordance with my own sense for truth.

My readings and practices, my enthusiasms for this or that spiritual direction, had inevitably interacted during all this time with my ongoing psychedelic use, the one informing and shaping the other.

I thus came to enter my study of anthroposophy spring-loaded, with a boatload of content, riddles, and questions emerging from the experiences told here, mixed together with the readings and practices I had earlier encountered. I sought a path forward toward a greater conscious coherence with what I knew was a dynamic, spiritual cosmos behind the pedestrian day-to-day "reality." And I sought a self-knowledge that would guide me deeper toward it.

In hindsight, I see these phases as steps toward a lifelong process of embracing the earth-life coupled with, at the same time, an intense desire to learn more about and to grow into the spiritual world as it can be known on earth. Anthroposophy provided me with a worldview and practice that fostered this process.

In my early reading of *Siddhartha,* I found a story that was a variation of a more or less Eastern concept of the spiritual path, culminating in a kind of oceanic unity with life and the spirit. Through my study of anthroposophy, I came rather to understand the spiritual path as a journey of the soul that passes intentionally across repeated incarnations, many phases of being, many times, and cultures. I also saw that the best destiny of the individual is to work to integrate one's own striving with whatever one can come to see as the advancing trend of humanity as a whole through this earth stage. Self-transformation is ultimately world transformation. This is quite distinct from what I had internalized conceptually as the goal of Eastern teachings of *moksha* and *nirvana.*

Reading Steiner, who attempts to describe the spiritual world as he knows it through his own clairvoyant experience, one immediately confronts a world populated by hosts of discarnate beings — beings in different respective phases of their own spiritual evolution. In my own psychedelic experience, I would, at times, encounter what I took to be discarnate spiritual beings — up to and including variations on the image of God, down to nature spirits. In sorting this idea, Steiner primarily uses the hierarchical terminology originating in the quasi-historical *Dionysius the Aereopagite*[203], from *angeloi* to *seraphim*, although his characterizations are in many ways unique to his vision and are not specifically derived from tradition. In Steiner's view, the earth itself is seen as having emerged in stages out of the being of the hierarchies; indeed, fundamentally, all existence, including our own very being, is rooted in the eternal, creative contemplation of the world of existence by the "Good Gods." These formative stages were as if worlds onto themselves, from which the present earth world as we know it today was, step by step, woven out of and precipitated within the universal mind.

Since the time of Darwin, the mass of humanity living under the sway of European culture has lost connection with a spiritual "origin story" through the ideological supremacy of the 19th-century materialistic scientific worldview. In my view, it is a need of modern souls — and certainly, was a need of *this* modern soul — to have a connection with an origin story that, at the same time, could harmonize with the advances in our scientific understanding of the world. A progressive framework for understanding the psychedelic experience as a catalyst for spiritual realization needs to find a way to bridge the gap between a spiritual origin and modern knowledge and move forward from there. I found that anthroposophy could lead to such insight without resorting to the sleight-of-hand of the so-called "creationist" worldview while deflating the cock-sureness of the "nothing but" big bang/reductionist view.

Across my adult years, anthroposophy began to overlay and organize the experiences, ideas, and concepts that had accumulated during my years of psychedelic exploration. Each of us, as William Blake has said, "must create a system, or be enslaved by another man's. I will not reason and compare: my business is to create." Steiner's "system" — anthroposophy — is highly organic, multi-faceted, and permeated by Steiner's own impeccable respect for the spiritual freedom of the individual. In this way, I felt completely free to follow my already well-laden store of individual interests and ideas. I often found myself employing ideas from one stream — for example, teachings from Gurdjieff — to illuminate concepts that may have initially seemed contradictory or at right angles to Steiner's words. Such a process is one that Steiner repeatedly urged: to see things from as many different angles as possible, particularly the realities of the spiritual world, which in their nature are more changeable, multi-valent, and largely at odds with our concepts derived from the physical world.

This study of spiritual-scientific ideas, such as represented by anthroposophy, is itself affirmed by Steiner as a highly beneficial spiritual practice in itself: one absorbs elements of the spiritual world through applying one's best, most active, and most fluid thinking to spiritual ideas. As someone with a rich content of psychedelic material within, this process was, for me, a most beneficial form of ongoing psychedelic integration. This process of study and absorption of anthroposophical material has, for me, led to a recognition of the most fundamental "clairvoyant" reality: the knowledge and recognition of one's self and world as being transparently woven out of a world of spiritual beings and realities, down to our own most mundane qualities. From this fundamental note, it becomes possible to cultivate the Imaginative perception of the spirit behind and revealed through sense perception; the world comes increasingly to be seen as a physiognomy of the spirit.

It is not possible nor a goal here to try and encompass more than a thimbleful of Steiner's ideas, but there are key concepts to highlight in trying to detail my own integration of what was lived through as soul-shattering, mind-expanding, perplexing, and inspiring. The further reflections here focus on themes and riddles that had emerged during my psychedelic experiences. Themes under the headers of reincarnation, alchymy, and others will occupy their own subsequent chapters. I will try to indicate there how some of the riddles of my psychedelic years were addressed through anthroposophical ideas.

After these years of active psychedelic exploration, I continued to retain an intellectual interest in the topic of psychedelics itself.

Even so, I bypassed a lot of what continued to simmer as a "psychedelic movement." I came to think of such a movement as having been driven all but completely underground relative to the culture at large, relegated chiefly to the domain of a dwindling subset of college students. At the same time, I was predictably becoming more and more preoccupied with the pursuit of a somewhat more conventional adulthood.

Folks like Terrance McKenna, who emerged as a next-generation psychedelic torch-carrier, kind of left me cold for a variety of reasons; I didn't see in his ideas anything really useful or new, and a lot that felt mostly wrong. I would also, from time to time, pick up the latest Stanislav Grof work, although these seemed, for all their material, of truly far-out states and massive scholarship from many sources, in many ways too closely wedded to earthbound psychology. His "Basic Perinatal Matrices" model has a certain value, but for me didn't fully address the spiritual realities underlying the possibilities of the psychedelic.

Certain things from my early readings and interest more or less fell by the boards. I concluded somewhere in there that the whole Carlos Castaneda thing, such a popular stream in psychedelic interest, was mostly a fraud. I watched, from perhaps Shirley MacLaine's 1983 *Out on a Limb* onward, a certain flavor of "new-age" interest emerge. It somehow seemed to be generally lightweight and at times trending more enthusiastic than thoughtful. There are

INTEGRATING

many paths. I stockpiled works of Jung, although I have distinctly mixed feelings about him, and throughout kept my eye on John Lilly, at length posting a deep appreciation somewhere or other online when he passed away in 2001.

My mixed feelings about Jung are due to his manner in treating of the spiritual as either a hypothesis or else "nothing but" a need of the psyche, irrespective of its actuality. For me, the whole phenomenology of the so-called "Collective Unconscious[204]" is better understood as relating to an actually existing spiritual world as such. This pattern of apparently delving into the depths of the psyche and uncovering wisdom and other treasures, but at the same time adhering to some posture of "scientific credibility" or skepticism — which, in the end, fails to affirm the reality of spirit *without qualification* — is in my view, a grave conflict in Jung, Lilly, Grof, and others. This seems to be an example of "sitting between two stools," which, in the end, compromises these works as either science or mysticism. Some readers may object that they find this unqualified assent to the spirit in these individuals; for me, this sense of always taking their scientific credentials into account seems to hover in the background.

Jung must decidedly be credited for, among other things, finessing strict scientific determinism with his idea of synchronicity as "an acausal connecting principle" and also his eager exploration of implications of quantum physics. This bore noteworthy fruit in the thought and writings of second-generation Jungian Arnold Mindell's[205] more-than-metaphorical application of patterns and phenomena of quantum physics to the psychological domain.

At the end of the day, it must be recognized as self-understood that one cannot experience the spirit in actuality if one cannot affirm and will it from one's own being. Contemporary science still clings to the "limits of knowledge," as asserted centuries ago by Immanuel Kant[206]. The advent of psychedelic experience must challenge this limitation of knowledge, as did Steiner in asserting his clairvoyant perception of the spiritual world. Steiner's theory of knowledge, as expressed in his own purely philosophical works such as *The Philosophy of Spiritual Activity*[207] (*Die Philosophie Der Freiheit*), is of huge value here.

Steiner's epistemology — theory of knowledge — is the tool that can break the spell and prison of Kant's "limits of knowledge" that has undergird most establishment thinking about reality over the past centuries. If a psychedelically-informed worldview is to emerge, it must have a valid understanding of "how we know what we know" that can embrace the cognitional landscape of psychedelic experience in a manner that can validate it as a possible instrument of knowledge and not simply "hallucinations" and fantasy or purely subjective psychic processing in the manner of dreams.

Psychedelic drugs are an innovation in the life of humanity which extends the collective experience of a substantial population across the precise domain that anthroposophy seeks to illuminate: the supersensible-spiritual as an experienced, phenomenal world.

The kind of experience that psychedelic drugs may induce, and which any number of explorers are seeking with varying degrees of awareness, can confront the consciousness starkly with the soul-challenging question as to the reality of the spirit, that is, of the eternal.

The parameters of the relationships between the members of the human being, as anthroposophically understood (physical, etheric, astral), undergo profound alteration with psychedelics. It cannot, however, be asserted, as some do, that the spirit, as expressed in the *I*, is magically and necessarily absconded during these experiences. Whatever is revealed through such means — which can, of course, vary per individual enormously — will tend to become deeply embedded, one way or another, in the knowledge and moral structure of the individual, at least as much as any other intensive life experience. This implies, of course, that one has managed to be fully present to the psychedelic state.

The psychedelic process can turn one's reality, one's consciousness, and one's sense of self upside-down and sideways. The beginning of both comprehension and integration of the depths of such experience will, in the end, stem from the realization of our spiritual nature in our inmost souls. From that experienced, willed, and known foundational point, it follows that in light of the manifold depths of psychedelic use, the understanding of both world-reality and soul-spirit reality will require a re-thinking of almost everything we think we know about things.

INTEGRATING

Across my own biography, I have transformed my understanding of the fundamental nature of things away from the *one-sided* acceptance of the scientific materialist view, leading to the conviction that such a transformation is a necessity for humanity at large. There are enormous benefits derived from scientific study in terms of how we understand and manage the resources of the world, which are not at all to be rejected. At the same time, it is necessary to keep in view the larger spiritual reality which contains the things of the world, and to be aware and vigilant as to how easily material assumptions, which can be spirit-denying or spirit-obscuring, play into virtually all our discourse in day to day society. The integral conception of the world that anthroposophy can provide can make this possible.

From within our own souls, we must awaken to the truth that the universe is built out of a spiritual, not a physical, reality. And it is only within such a spiritual reality that we can thus be present as *moral* beings. One may conceive of a physical reality that determines all behavior. Or alternatively, conceive of a spiritual reality as one in which everything is determined out of a divine providence. A *moral* reality is one where we see ourselves as the possessors of, to a greater or lesser degree, *freedom* and thus agency, wherein we may be accountable for our deeds and actions. All of our deeds (including thoughts and feelings) are, in their own large or small way, inevitably decisive in the overall life of the universe. Out of our own deepest spirit (not some God of judgment "out there"), we will, as we pursue our eternal journey, again and again, come to inwardly review and assess our actions in the context of our effect on the weal or woe of our fellow creatures and of our cosmic home — the earth.

Steiner taught that this process is experienced in the life between death and a new birth, where, free from the body, we experience an inversion, a turning inside-out, of consciousness. We come to a consciousness of ourselves *as others see us* and, at the same time, recognize our own eternal highest nature.

In my psychedelic exploration, I have experienced states into which this kind of inversion, this sense of one's self as others see one, emerges out of the transformation of interpersonal boundaries that can occur.

Steiner teaches that deeds that, in whatever way, impede the forward flow of the universe of beings toward our ultimate best destiny, as seen now before us in spirit, are experienced in such states as having lessened or damaged something within one's own essential self. From this dawning awareness, the wish arises to correspondingly compensate, to repair this — both the harm to our true self, along with harm to the world and others. Out of that intensive inner process, which comprises a significant phase of the life between death and new birth, these redemptive wishes provide the forces and material out of which we find our next-life destiny is formed and woven. This weaving is in concert spiritually with others, both higher beings and the cohort of individuals with which we have experienced our previous existence.

In Steiner's picture of human life, this same self-review can also be understood as occurring reflexively in our souls every night when we *timelessly* detach from the close bonding to our physical-etheric earthly vehicle and replay the events of the day. It is part of our unfolding awareness of the backward-flowing stream of time that we come to link the "every night" review with the "continuously experienced" life review, or *kamaloka* when it is understood as occurring "after" death. Awakening to this mirror of our daytime existence is experienced as the "informing driver" of the first half of our life between death and new birth — our bardo existence, as Buddhism would phrase it. Although this process of metamorphosis is explained as if it were linear, we need to appreciate that the experience of what is known as "time" in our earthly life undergoes a radical alteration as we modulate our self-experience free from the body. The life between death and a new birth is a sojourn in, or through, eternity.

Anthroposophy is sometimes dismissed as being too "heady." And in a certain way, this is true: it does try and approach the individual human being through the world of spiritually-aligned thoughts and, more importantly, *images*. These images, however, we must learn to re-form through our own activity in the world of ideas. It is at the same time true that the reality of spirit completely transcends any particular articulation, (including, of course, that of anthroposophy), of the details of its workings that any particular persuasion or system might reflect.

To the extent that one may feel one's way into its worldview, anthroposophy, through its teachings, offers insights into the journey of humanity through this present earth realm. It can yield an awareness of the spiritual-evolutionary steps that have come before our present historical moment. In my understanding, it articulates a worldview that is also competent to encompass all that we currently know about the physical world through today's outer means of knowledge.

Rather than place our world in the context of a random big bang "creation," Steiner revives the possibility of understanding creation from a spiritual source in a way that is at the same time grounded in the possibility of an understanding of the present natural world that is consistent with the findings and discoveries of natural science. At the same time, it extends these findings congruently into the spiritual realm.

It points to a future wherein the spirit of the most profound, most ancient mysteries of all of humanity can blossom into a renewed spiritual life, one that amplifies the inner dignity and best destiny of humanity. In my own experience, having felt the fabric of time and space as it were ripped open during my most intense psychedelic experience, this knowledge, which developed through my study, was profoundly satisfying and enriching as I grew into my earthly course of life.

As a young child, I had deeply internalized in a part of my being the concepts of modern science. I remember reading my first description of the "big bang" (complete with a picture) and having the seeming satisfaction of "that explains it!". I recall reading the drama about the "Scopes Monkey Trial" — *Inherit the Wind*[208], and seeing in it a triumph of rationality against the backwardness of the State of Tennessee's 1925 Butler Act, which had made it illegal for teachers to teach Darwinian evolution in any state-funded school.

When I came to experience the soul-spiritual livingness of the world around me at the lake and gazed into the heart of things when my vision penetrated inside of a tree to the level of vibrating, dancing, light-particles, only to "drop" the vision out of a sudden awe-struck instability, I came to know that I had to overcome the materialistic understanding of the world and of myself, through a knowing that could at the same time reconcile itself to the findings of science within its proper scope of validity[209]

After many years of study of anthroposophy, I felt that I moved, step by step, onward into a body of knowledge still deeper and more rich in content than that encompassed by details experienced during the active phase of my psychedelic explorations. The psychedelic panorama, as infinitely broad as it can be, needs to be understood as an *instance* of the vision of the spiritual world, which is in itself, more expansive than the totality of what one can know through any given lens, such as psychedelics — or likewise, the lens of anthroposophy.

For me, the draw of psychedelics was always to connect with the spiritual through the sense of the cosmic — the extra-earthly existence that provides the source and ordering of the outer, sensory earth-world we appear to inhabit. Visionary moments felt and seen as permeated with a harmony with an extra-earthly cosmos of origin were full of reward and fulfillment. Through anthroposophy, I found myself able to grow more and more completely in tune with the nature of the earth-existence as well, and with its true reason for being as it unfolds within that higher spiritual cosmic ordering.

To encapsulate Steiner's vision of this true reason for being, he characterizes the mission of the earth is to be transformed from a "cosmos of wisdom" — born, as referenced earlier, out of the creative activity of the cosmic, spiritual hierarchies — into a "cosmos of love." And for Steiner, love can only truly come into being out of the condition of spiritual *freedom*.

It was a matter of many years before I clearly understood that the intensity and high-voltage nature of the psychedelic experience is not necessarily in itself the goal of spiritual striving in this life. Transformation of being is a lifetime, day-by-day process, and the growth and internalization of genuine spiritual perception and understanding of the macrocosmic reality of the spiritual world is a subtle process. Steiner often points out that, as we practice, we have many spiritual impressions that simply escape our notice due to their subtlety alongside our inattention and lack of recognition.

In my own reading of Steiner's work, I dove in somewhat into the "deep end" by having first — as if by chance — read a lecture cycle that was originally intended for members of the anthroposophical society of his day — that is, to listeners who were, in general, familiar with the outlines of Steiner's teachings. Having started with the subject matter of *Ancient Myths*, I hopped from title to title, largely conditioned, also a bit randomly, by the availability of books in the various bookshops where I would find them. My discovery process was, therefore, a somewhat non-linear process — which turned out to work well for me. There is something very "holographic" in Steiner's expositions — within a specific theme, you can find ideas, seemingly inserted as asides, that resonate with or reinforce elements scattered elsewhere.

This holographic aspect — of unity within an apparent manifoldness — in his presentation mirrors, in a way, the nature of the world process Steiner describes. Macrocosm and microcosm reflect each other, and the process of incarnation in human form (and of excarnation at death) is a process of metamorphosis — analogous in its way to the *Metamorphosis of Plants*[210] as Goethe, who was to be one of Steiner's guiding lights, proffered. In the life between death and a new birth, our souls are, as it were, turned "inside out," and our different discrete soul elements distributed — returned to — their cosmic sources, creating a state of "Dionysian Dismemberment" wherein nevertheless it is possible for the soul to maintain their *I* consciousness, albeit differently from the manner in which our sense of possession of a physical body reinforces our earthly *I* consciousness. This holographic unity of all things is maintained along the path of soul metamorphosis.

There are, of course, linear presentations of the basic elements of Steiner's teachings: *Knowledge of Higher Worlds and its Attainment*, *Theosophy*[211], *Esoteric Science*[212]. The first details his method for achieving higher cognition — that same clairvoyance that forms the instruments with which his teachings are initially researched. *Theosophy* is an outline of his model of the members of the human being as a spiritual complex and introduces some of the basics underlying his vision of the process of reincarnation. And finally, *Esoteric Science* (also translated as *Occult Science*) elaborates on these other works, but most significantly, provides Steiner's view of cosmic history — the emergence of the earth and humanity out of the womb of the spirit in distinct stages.

These books will appeal to those who like to approach things in a step-by-step way. Others, such as myself, who rather followed their heart into anthroposophy, will sooner or later be resorted to as one wishes to deepen and structure the understanding of the whole of his teachings.

At the same time, just as the word *anthroposophy* is styled by Steiner as "consciousness of being human," and aspires to the realization of the "Universal-human," Steiner, during his active years, spoke on an incredibly wide range of topics: Education — in connection with his founding of the Waldorf Schools; Agriculture — in connection with his founding of Biodynamic agriculture; Medicine, Curative Education, the Arts.

Within the realm of spirituality proper, he spoke to topics from Christianity, Rosicrucianism, Western Mystics, the Bhagavad Gita, Buddhism, Theosophy, the Greek Mysteries, and on and on. In my view — particularly if one is comfortable absorbing ideas in a non-linear fashion — one might do well to find a topic in Steiner that one is already personally enthusiastic about and use that as the "way in" to the broader teachings.

For someone starting their contact with Steiner from the point of view of interest or experience with psychedelic drugs, some of the most relevant aspects of his thought can be found in his teachings on the nature of the human being. This embraces his understanding of the different members of our spiritual being, his teaching on the Guardian or Double, and of the experiences of the threshold generally; his insights into the higher modes of cognition, which he styles *Imagination, Inspiration,* and *Intuition*; and finally, his teachings on reincarnation.

In *Knowledge of Higher Worlds and its Attainment*, in addition to the meditative exercises, self-regulation of the soul and *moral* development are stressed as preconditions for successfully pursuing higher knowledge and entry into the spiritual world. Eating a mushroom or whatever contributes nothing in itself to this process. For me, it is a primal insight in examining one's own worldview to recognize that a view that sees the outer creation as simply a chance process of the evolution of millennia of cosmic particle interactions up through the chance interactions of natural selection offers no basis for any genuine moral perspective. From this materialistic point of view, Steiner sees that the idea of "everyone for themselves" is perfectly rational and that, correspondingly, efforts to establish an ethical standard absent a spiritual perspective are, in the end, empty and without substantial foundation[213]. One must alternatively see in one's self that the *moral* is the essential stuff that non-physical understanding of reality is composed of when the process of soul-formation between life and new birth is understood. Moral action, from this cosmic viewpoint, is what sustains the universe and moves it forward.

It bears repeating here that Rudolf Steiner's method of developing cognition of the spiritual world — or, ultimately, of *living into* the spiritual world, does, of course, not itself involve psychedelic drugs.

Alongside this, Steiner stresses that such acquisition of higher cognition is, meanwhile, not a necessity and that it is possible to develop an understanding of the findings of spiritual research (for instance, into the life between death and a new birth) through the application of unprejudiced reasoning to the teachings of spiritual science.

One can enjoy a meal without knowing the recipe. To the extent that his teaching resonates with our own sense of truth, the proof is in the pudding.

As previously commented, psychedelic drugs were all but unknown of in the European cultural milieu Steiner lived in during his lifetime, and as far as I am aware, he has made no reference to them. In this connection, there are, at the same time, interesting (albeit inconclusive) tidbits scattered here and there.

In *Knowledge of Higher Worlds*, where Steiner prefaces his description of the pivotal idea of the Guardian of the Threshold with a reference to its appearance as an element in the fictional work *Zanoni* mentioned earlier. The protagonist undergoes an initiation process under the tutelage of an "immortal" — a human initiate who has lived continuously through thousands of years of human history — which begins with the drinking of a special draught or potion. This element (consuming a substance) is accepted as a matter of course without comment (from one point of view, it is merely a plot device in a novel). Elsewhere, Steiner talks about how in the past, certain states of spiritual consciousness were entered into by ingesting tinctures of metals, then goes on to state that with our hyper-intellectualistic consciousness of today, this is simply not effective. The experiential data of psychedelics provoke a re-examination of the question of the efficacy of substances.

It is intriguing that in his biography, he recounts how as a young man, he was befriended by a herbalist — who gathered medicinal herbs in the forests and meadows, and of whom he said that he could speak to him as one familiar, as Steiner experienced himself to be, with the spiritual world. It seems a valid thought to consider if this herb knowledge extended to psychoactive plants.

More than a few anthroposophists (certainly, within my own age cohort) have psychedelic experience in their own biographies, and some have half-speculated: could he have experienced psychedelics? This question is really from a place of astonishment at his spiritually perceptive capacity, which is only paralleled, in their experience, by psychedelic drugs. The fact that this is even a question is indicative of the strength of the sensed intersection of knowledge-experiences of psychedelics and the content of Steiner's own perceptions.

My personal view is that Steiner's capacities were, at first, karmic, that is, bestowed upon him at birth as a result of previous strivings in prior lifetimes, and then cultivated through his own efforts to understand his experienced relationship to the spiritual and to the earthly existence. That he met with Goethe's scientific writings in his youth and worked with them intensively allowed his natural vision to be informed by a kind of organic thinking that was both capable of absorbing the full scope of the emerging scientific worldview of the late nineteenth century while at the same time, seeing far beyond it. In his process of maturation, he tells of leaving behind his "given" clairvoyant experience, which can in some ways be considered a dreamy atavistic throwback to an earlier stage, and replacing this with a consciously cultivated instrument of higher cognition, starting in a sense from Goethe's "Exact Percipient Fantasy."[214]

Steiner always stressed that one must keep an open mind. In various works, he would have occasion to describe what he would characterize as the objective results of well-known stimulants and drugs, including coffee, tea, opium, and cocaine. In discussing these effects, he would comment that in some cases, for example, coffee or tea could be useful. Likewise, in his discussion of vegetarianism, which he practiced, he held that it was not necessary for everyone and simply tried to characterize how the soul-physical human organism responded differently in each case. In every case, a given substance must be understood relative to the individual in terms of context, degree, and individual karma or life biography. In the case of vegetarianism, alcohol consumption, and vaccination, for example, despite being a vegetarian and seeing that it supported spiritual perception, and holding that alcohol use (he was known to have indulged himself in alcohol in his youth) was deleterious to the unfolding of the *I* consciousness; and despite having a certain reticence around the practice of vaccination (which reserve diminished over the years), he stressed that all of these matters were individual and that he would not dictate or agitate for any hard and fast viewpoint.

An essential element of Steiner's worldview is its picture of the change in the unfolding of human consciousness throughout human history. He sees humanity — that is, our very souls, incarnating again and again on earth — descending first from a primal spiritual condition, gradually emerging into the physical world and over millennia of pre-history, "awakening" from a kind of dream-consciousness wherein contact with higher beings — "Gods" — was experienced. Spiritual advancement in this context was an accelerated awareness of the reality of and experience of the *I* — as opposed to the earlier "group soul" consciousness — in a wide-awake experience of the increasingly sharply-countered physical, earthly reality. If humanity was seen to have "fallen" from paradise, Steiner's position was to embrace this fall as a gift.

In connection with this process, Steiner relates that the consumption of alcohol, for example, in the Dionysian mystery cults, was a factor appropriate to the times in bringing to humanity intensified or awakened consciousness of the *I* and, simultaneously, suppressing the old dreamy clairvoyance. Consumption of alcohol accelerated the fading of what he called the instinctive clairvoyance associated with the tribal, group-soul consciousness which characterized earlier humanity. This consciousness of existing together with the gods needed to give way to the awakening of the *I*, in order for humanity to develop into freedom. The developing consciousness of the *I* implies that, at some point, the soul will experience a disconnection from the spiritual world of origin. The process of becoming conscious of our "I-hood" through the "god-forsakenness" of modern life, with its alienation and soullessness, its lack of coherence with the spiritual world, is necessary for the development of freedom.

It has been taught by some traditions that the angels do not have free will. If we can imagine the nature of such higher beings, we can see that this lack of freedom is essentially a function of their clear and direct knowledge of the Godhead — wherein the divine will, spiritually omnipresent, is known. The overwhelming *rightness* of what is revealed in their vision and consciousness of the Godhead is infinitely compelling and leaves no room for the pursuit of reasoned objections or alternative impulses of will. Similarly, a dreamy consciousness of being together with the gods but lacking the *I* leaves freedom unrealized.

The evolution of humanity is, in part, to enable a created being to perceive the Godhead and reflect it in freedom. The fact that we have been thrown out of the garden, that we no longer can hear the harmonies of the spheres, that we stand alone and bereft of tribe: these are the same conditions that *dampen* the power and force of the vision of the divine will such that we can *choose* our role in a cosmic game, dance, drama, or enterprise *freely*, as we may understand it. The divine *Lila* is seen as a process of expanding first, freedom, and then, love.

At the same time, this alienation is real and can be soul devastating inwardly. We long for a connection to the livingness of our source, and pursue it outwardly in a million ways.

This process of having been alienated from the connection with the primal gods of ancient humanity is affected nowhere so completely as through the permeation of our modern culture by the thoughts and deeds associated with technology. Through our reduction of the world process to consist only of what can be encompassed as number, weight, and measure, we have apparently conquered nature — and are now in the process of destroying it throughout the earth. From the point of view of the spiritual world, as Steiner would have it, our technologically structured inner and outer worlds are under the influence of the being (or hosts of beings), the Ahrimanic[215], who serve as opposing powers that, from one side, stimulate the development of the human being. And from another side, there is a spiritual force that he characterizes as the Luciferic, which challenges our humanity from another angle — by (for example) tantalizing us with visions of the spiritual world before we are fully prepared. These two will be explored subsequently.

When we cross the threshold of the spiritual world, through death, initiation, or, possibly, through psychedelics, there can exist the longing and temptation to shun earth life, to return to and merge with the spirit.

To do so, according to Steiner, would be to renounce the possibility of all future possibility of development. In his *Knowledge of Higher Worlds,* he describes the stage of the acknowledgment of that which can bar one's entry into the spiritual world. This leads one to commit one's self through internalization of the "mystic vow" to *transform* the karmic deformities of the Double (Guardian).

> ... we can now speak further of what is called the *mystic vow*. Before the spectacle of their own inadequacy, everyone must register the vow that in future they will work at their soul to their utmost capacity in order to make up for past negligence[216].

In my own experience, there was no point in time when this "vow" was articulated as an event: it was rather a process of inner growth, of internalization, of a new orientation. Looking back to my realization of the power to say "yes" to existence when I was at the lake served as the turning point in my own process.

> This vow gives life a new content, in keeping with true and effective self-knowledge; one no longer broods but works actively at their own self. This experience can take a twofold form. As long as we are only aware of it as a mental process, something is still lacking in us, is still fettering us, and there is still reason for cosmic evolution to pass us by. In such a case the experience has been in the astral body only. But if the feelings of thankfulness and duty are experienced over and over again, they

will be transformed ultimately into definite vision which becomes an inner experience, and then a force, a power[217].

In general, soul experiences become embedded in our etheric body as elements of character through repetition and deepening of feeling — in this case, of blissful thankfulness and cosmic responsibility.

An implication of all this would seem to be: the content of spiritual psychedelic experience, in general, is similarly an experience taking place in the *astral* body — that is, consciousness. It is only through our own efforts of will that we can embed the inspiration it may have been possible to receive into a force of life. These efforts must be pursued independently of the occasion of the sojourn in the psychedelic realm if they are to become fully effective in the world. This corresponds essentially with what Steiner says about initiatory experience in general.

A lecture of Steiner's which I found resonated deeply with my own psychedelic experience is titled *The Three Decisions on the Path of Imaginative Cognition: Loneliness, Fear, Dread*[218]. This entire lecture, I think, is worthwhile for anyone entering psychedelic spaces. He describes three stages of the spiritual path as if in sequence, although pointing out that different people may bypass stages or experience them out of order. The first stage, he calls entering the spiritual world through *the Portal of Death*[219], the second through the *Portal of the Elements*, and the third he calls *the Portal of the Sun*.

He describes how, in the first stage:

> At first, when one has passed through the Portal of Death, one is in the spiritual world which *does as it likes with one*.

This certainly can mirror a phase of the psychedelic journey.

Continuing:

> One learns to act for oneself in the spiritual world by *identifying oneself with one's destiny.* This can only be achieved by degrees. Thoughts then acquire being which is identical with our own. The deeds of our being enter the spiritual world. But in order to achieve this in the right way one must pass through the second portal. When, with the power acquired from identifying oneself with destiny, one begins to weave in the thoughts in such a way that they do not carry one along as in a dream-picture but one is able to eliminate a thought and call up another — to manipulate them at will — when this begins one experiences what may be called the "passing through the portal."
>
> And then the power of will we are now using shows itself as a simply fearful monster. This has been known for thousands of years in mysticism as the encounter with the "lion." One must go through this encounter with the lion. In the life of feelings this gives rise to a dreadful fear, a fear of what is taking place in the world of thought, of this living union with it, and this fear must be overcome, just as the loneliness of the Portal of Death must be overcome.

It is not difficult to see an analog with possible phases of the psychedelic experience.

> This fear can in the most manifold ways simulate other feelings that are not fear; but it is, in reality, fear of what one approaches. And what now occurs is that one finds the possibility of mastering this wild beast, this "lion" who meets us. In Imagination it actually appears as if it were opening wide its enormous jaws, wishing to devour us. The power

of will which we want to use in the spiritual world threatens to devour us. One is incessantly overcome by the feeling; "You are obliged to will, but you must do something, you must seize something." Yet concerning all these elements of will which one contains, one has the feeling: "If you seize it, it devours you, eradicates you from the world." This is the experience of being devoured by the lion.

So — and one can speak of this in pictures — rather than surrendering to the fear that the elements of will in the spiritual world will seize, devour, and strangle us, *one must swing oneself to the back of the lion*, grasp these elements of will, and make use of them for action. That is what must be done when this happens.

He then goes on to say: "One must insert oneself into the cosmic harmony."

For me, this final guidance echoes the state I came to after my two high-dose sessions (the cast party and the lake) when, later that summer, I was on the beach and felt myself as if centered underneath the canopy of a starry astral sphere, wherein souls and beings were weaving creatively above me in the vastness. I was no longer resisting the flow of my destiny in the spiritual world, I felt that I had accepted, and was accepted by, the spiritual world and felt as if I had, in some sense, "swung myself to the back of the lion" and "inserted myself into the cosmic harmony."

Elsewhere Steiner speaks of coming to see ourselves as having emerged out of the harmony of the spheres.

If this sense of harmony can be experienced in even a small measure, the desire will arise to cultivate and deepen it, and to make it effective in one's outer life — in a way, of course, that is not solely dependent on the psychedelic agent. Seeing the spiritual world transparently as all-permeated with cosmic being, anthroposophy can provide signposts to deepen one's ability to read the spiritual reality that lies behind the outer life of the senses.

14

Interweaving Destinies

Working through my biography — now moving backward in time from the time of my mushroom dose with my second wife, back to the nineties, I was to experience a series of life challenges in their way as harrowing as the most turbulent psychedelic journeys.

At that time, I was married to my first wife, had three young children, and until things started to unwind, a fulfilling and successful career at Apple Computer, managing a team of product marketing managers for software development tools. We were part of the group that worked with third-party software developers, and it was all a lot of fun. It was an exciting scene in the pre-internet personal computer industry.

In 1989 I developed a set of symptoms that led to the diagnosis that I had a chronic hepatitis C infection. Among all the experimentation with drugs in high school, I had, under the banner of "I'll try anything once," used IV drugs one time with a friend from my immediate circle. I thereby contracted hepatitis C. This infection, of which I had been until then unaware[220], was now twenty-plus years into a slow but inexorable process of progressively damaging my liver.

With a long grinding inevitability, my health began to fail. Work became increasingly difficult. I had moved into a new business unit within Apple (a kind of CD-ROM-based App Store,) which took our team two years to develop. Shortly after launch, it was quickly deemed to be underperforming and therefore folded in the midst of a general downturn at Apple in the years just prior to the return of Steve Jobs. We were given two months to find another position or be laid off. During that time, I was diagnosed with end-stage liver disease. "End stage," meaning fatal.

I took a medical leave of absence just as the window was closing on finding a new position at Apple and was placed on the waiting list for an organ transplant.

This was the start of a period that was to span almost five years, where surviving (and ultimately thriving) was my primary focus in living. I experienced two liver transplants, waiting nine months on the list the first time, and the second I received three years after the first, also with a nine-month wait. The second was extremely successful.

As one might well imagine, the challenges involved with such a life-and-death medical journey are, in their own way, of a similar depth of soul-trial to the kind of psychedelic explorations of my youth — with much more outer consequence.

During the nine-month wait from first listing until my first transplant, I underwent the steady progression of liver failure, which, absent a transplant, is a slow dying.

I won't detail my list of symptoms, but I found myself gazing into a newly-opened window into the story of my friend Milo's own demise.

During our early twenties, after I finished school, Milo, who had been knocking around California, came home to his family suffering from a chronic illness, first diagnosed as hepatitis. It progressed into other symptoms, puzzling doctors at the time. I now saw much more clearly what his own disease progression must have been like, and with it came the painful realization that I had been, to a large extent, blind to the miseries of his own experience. I was naively believing at the time that he would simply get better. I was shocked when after a short hospitalization, he died at age twenty-four.

As I waited for a donor organ to be found, I was riddled with the awareness that in order for me to receive a liver transplant, someone else would have to die. How to reconcile this with my own wish to live? I experienced a sense of what I came to call "anticipatory survivor guilt." Why should I live when another dies? I eventually came to the place, first, of accepting the possibility of not receiving a transplant and, secondly, moving to a place of detachment relative to the possible destiny of whoever my eventual donor may be — detachment in the sense of withholding myself from any possible wish to interfere in another's destiny.

During the wait and progressive awareness of my possible impending death, I reached the point of realization that I would perhaps have to surrender. The most difficult part of this was letting go of my responsibility for the care and upbringing of my children. My core beliefs in the eternal nature of the soul allowed me to start moving into the space of acceptance. Shortly after this point was reached, I received the call that a liver had become available for me.

The surgery lasted 14 hours, and although it did indeed save my life, the transplanted liver was ultimately to prove problematic.

There is one intersect of interest to mention in the post-surgery recovery phase of my first transplant: among the many, many pharmaceutical drugs you are treated with immediately post-surgery, primarily immune suppressants and then secondarily, medications to guard against opportunistic infections, you can wind up in some pretty trippy states. Aside from the morphine and steroids, the primary immune suppression medication I was given, tacrolimus, has a very definite psychedelic effect at the high dosage levels that are often administered post-transplant. I mention all this because I did experience day after day of fairly crazy-making drugs, complete with waking delusional fugues, fear and panic states, speech aphasia, and a background full of gnome-like elemental spirits hammering away constantly. I also experienced moments of profound waves of love and gratitude, of truly cosmic proportions, in the sensed flow of love and support to me from well-wishers. Indeed, I felt that I was suddenly able to see something that, in fact, was always there — love — but only in my extreme state could I perceive and receive it.

I found myself grateful for my earlier psychedelic experiences in that they enabled me to ride out this period. It really seemed like a non-stop low-dose trip that went on for days. Finally, the doctors who said of my psychological symptoms "good, that means it's working," decided I needed a "tacrolimus vacation" and discontinued the medication for a day. A woman I had befriended through the support group, who received her transplant shortly after mine, wound up in a severely persistent psychotic. The doctors had to discontinue tacrolimus, the most effective immune suppressant, and revert to an earlier, somewhat less efficacious one, but also less crazy-making.

I spent a few days in intensive care and altogether two weeks in the hospital. When I had moved out of intensive care, I was able, after a day or two, to get myself out of bed for the first time. I stood and looked in the mirror. I was shirtless, which gave me a clear view of the huge "Mercedes"[221] incision across my abdomen, with dozens of staples holding my skin together — the surgery had completely split me open. The ascites fluid in my belly, along with the many liters of fluid I absorbed intra-operatively, filled my belly, distending it like I had swallowed a basketball. As my new liver was now producing albumin and the leakage of plasma fluid from my veins had stopped (which caused the ascites or accumulation of fluid in the abdomen), my upper body was no longer "puffed up" with fluid as it had been pre-operatively. Above the stapled wound, I was mere flesh and bones, with no fat, no muscle; you could see the outlines of ribs and joints protruding, and my head looked like a skull with flesh painted onto it. And meanwhile, in the mirror, I could see the aura of a semi-crazed, electric glow, both from the drugs and the fact that I was, as it were, still re-entering my bodily form after 14 hours of anesthesia.

It was a fascinating and terrifying sight. I quickly resolved that I didn't want my children to see me like this, and next, found myself in sober contemplation of the being I had become.

I found myself recalling to mind the statement of Steiner's somewhere that the Ahrimanic beings — beings essentially inimical to the progressive spiritual evolution of humanity — seek to bring the technology of the future inappropriately, that is, before their proper time, into the present. This aligns with his general notion that evil has to do with something that would have been right in its own proper time, becoming evil when in the wrong time. Certainly, medical transplant technology in all its facets is, from the point of view going back to Steiner's time at the beginning of the 20th century, "future technology." I asked myself: has this come too soon? I had no answer other than to inwardly *will* the inner time-gradients in *my* life to the point where, *for me*, it was a medical technology "in the right time."

Steiner once gave a lecture[222] where, among other things, he foresaw that in the near future — that is, our times — souls would sacrificially offer the bodies that were karmically meant for their own incarnation to others as an expression of love. Although the context in which he discussed this implied that this was a pre-earthly decision, the parameters of organ donation seemed to me to closely parallel the situation Steiner described. Many things that Steiner similarly envisioned seem to have come to pass, albeit in somewhat transformed actuality. In turn, it seems only natural that vision into the future is somewhat sketchy in that what can be discerned are only the trends while the actual, situational vehicles of realization of those trends are dependent on a complex set of contingent circumstances.

Needless to say, the sense of gratitude and responsibility for such a gift is profound.

Transplantation involves questions of genetic identity at the level of the living physical body. Our normal immune response to foreign tissue is to attack it, leading to the problem of organ rejection. This can be controlled, with various degrees of success, with medication. The liver is fortunately the least likely organ to be rejected. In thinking about this, I would ponder the weaving of the disengaging etheric of the donor and the uptake of the organ in my own etheric structure. Thinking of this in terms of three-dimensional geometry and ponderable matter is not appropriate for the nature of the etheric. Inwardly, I conceptualized my relationship to the two genetic streams I was now dwelling within. From the viewpoint of my *I*, I am not the genetic "self" of my birth body; neither am I my donated liver. I visualized the situation as that of a parent with both a natural and adopted child, and strove to love each "child" equally.

My first transplant survived three years. I was able to eventually return to work, but the problems with the first transplant — scarring of the biliary ducts due to "preservation injury" — became unmanageable, and I was re-listed for a second transplant. In the first six months after my transplant, I was to undergo three more major surgeries trying to fix the problems arising from the scarring — or, in some cases, fix the problems arising from the attempted fixes. Not fun.

One situation developed where after what was supposed to be a low-risk endoscopic procedure, I developed a biliary leak. Bile, which is caustic, leaked into my abdominal space, fairly quickly landing me in intensive care after a few painful hours of increasing distress. I found myself coming to more than a day later, having experienced a complete twenty-four blackout (aided by the amnesiac properties of the drug Versed), during which I had undergone an emergency laparotomy[223] surgery to clean up the bile and repair the leak. I returned to consciousness at first very dimly and experienced myself as if floating outward into the surrounding ether — losing touch with my surroundings and my body. As I expanded outward, I felt a gentle push approach, moving me away from the motion into the periphery — back to my body in the bed. An image arose as if I was experiencing Milo as he swam across the lake; I could feel his smiling face approaching me and feel the waves of his breaststroke pushing through the ether as he approached me. It felt as if he was gently bouncing me back to earth. I began to bestir myself and found my first wife and my parents — my parents had flown 3000 miles from back east during my surgery — at my bedside, starting to explain to me what had happened.

My parents were an unshakable loving support through all this. During my first week out of the hospital from my transplant hospitalization, I was still in a highly dependent state and had the sense of re-experiencing, now in conscious awareness, the same love and care I would have known as an infant.

After two more surgeries and dozens of procedures, I returned for a time to work, but eventually, nine months after my re-listing, I received a second transplant. This happened on Easter Sunday.

The whole process this time was one where, rather than (almost) everything that could go wrong, did so, as the first time, everything went right.

Less than a month before my second transplant, I had lost my friend Henry to brain cancer. I first met Henry in a Steiner study group I joined shortly after moving to California; as it turned out, his wife had a small marketing agency that contracted with Apple, and I was eventually to use that group for some of my department's own needs. Meanwhile, because of our shared interest in anthroposophy, we had grown quite friendly, with comparably aged kids, and became somewhat near neighbors when my family and I moved to the San Lorenzo Valley near Santa Cruz. During my illness, he had included my boys in "dad-like" activities I was unable to perform.

His illness materialized shortly after my first transplant. Although I tried to help and be present as I could, part of me was still "in recovery" from the ordeal of my first transplant. His illness and diagnosis — which was essentially terminal from the get-go — was tragic for a man with a young family in his early forties. Even though my illness had been full-on "life-threatening," there had always been the prospect of a life-saving transplant.

On the night that he passed, I felt his presence wake me, and then shortly thereafter, I received the call from my then wife telling me that Henry had passed; she, along with Henry's wife and other friends, had been making the overnight vigil at the hospital. I had felt of him, as with Milo, that we were dharma brothers connected through lifetimes past.

In the week in the hospital after the second transplant, I found myself strangely possessed of the question: did Henry have to die before I could get my transplant? A similar thought regarding my grandmother, who died shortly before my first transplant, had occurred to my sister. Something in the calculus of the soul and destiny prompts this question; do they put their angelic finger on the scale from the other side? In cold rational thought, it seems an unlikely proposition.

And then, more or less directly after my second transplant, my then-teetering first marriage fell apart, the details of which aren't particularly relevant here. It would be stating the obvious that the whole medical ordeal was a huge strain on the relationship — which, in our case, was already more than a little laden with unresolved issues.

Very blessedly, I came out of my second transplant healthier than I had been in many, many years and full of the "whatever doesn't kill you makes you stronger" strength and energy.

My outward active connection with anthroposophy had naturally receded into the background during my years of illness. As an inner resource, it was very much a source of strength, as part of my own inner resources of faith and strength that emerged from my youth. In connection with the end of my marriage, however, I experienced a vaguely defined kind of reaction against elements of my previous relationship with anthroposophy. The breakdown of my marriage revealed to me that it might, in part, have been the case that I had not been showing up in the right way for that relationship and that, in some way, my perhaps too-heady involvement with anthroposophy had been a distraction inwardly from the development of certain other necessary interpersonal skills. Aspects of inner cognitional development can proceed in certain ways independently of other aspects of personal development. This is something to be aware of — the different developmental tempos of head and heart.

Somewhere in all this, I felt myself inwardly "putting anthroposophy on the shelf for a time" as far as active engagement. With my newfound health, my single status, and my responsibility as a part-time single parent, I was re-engaging at a basic level with my body and the world. At the same time, I felt deeply secure in my sense that anthroposophy's ethos and thought had permeated my soul and my values to the core and that my connection with it was unshakable regardless of how I related to it outwardly.

In the early months after separating from my first wife, I made several trips to Harbin Hot Springs.[224] My various illnesses, open wounds, and biliary fluid drains had exiled me from there for the past five years. I was now doing serious self-care and finding myself restored. It was a four-hour drive from Santa Cruz, and it was a place with its hippie spirituality. I had treasured it as a soul-restoring getaway before I became too ill to visit there.

Harbin is a pretty magical holdover from the sixties: bodywork, large, clothing-optional hot springs, and a human development conference center, sort of like a poor man's Esalen. It attracts new agers of all stripes, some of whom tend to strike this seeker after spiritual rigor (in his own fashion) as maybe a bit wooly. Unfortunately, Harbin was all but destroyed in the Valley Fire in Middletown in 2015. It is being lovingly restored, but much of its hippie-built craftsmanship will be slow to return.

On one of my visits there, I found myself in the large "warm pool," somewhat willy-nilly present for a loose, hippie-paganish, and traditional at Harbin "new-moon ceremony." I had to first dismount from a kind of spiritual high horse that I sometimes found myself riding upon in order for me to open up to it. In the warm pool, I fell into an inner reverie wherein I wrestled a bit with the possibility that my spiritual posture had maybe become too narrow and one-sided. I tried to imagine myself as if I had not encountered anthroposophy when I did and tried to consider how the various other spiritual elements and streams I was already influenced by might have evolved in whatever different direction. As I considered, I found myself affirming to myself that I was already on a good path prior to my contact with anthroposophy and that I needed to allow myself, and of more to the point, others, more latitude. I summarized all this to myself by saying I could give myself permission to "liberate my inner hippie."

In reality, of course, it had not been anthroposophy that had imprisoned my "inner hippie" — the world, the times, becoming an adult, becoming who I essentially was — these had all conspired to drive away the pure idealism and adventure of the "spirit of my youth." My "inner hippie," I knew, wasn't even really a hippie. I was just an affluent kid with long hair that liked rock and roll music and LSD.

There was something effective in this process, however. I let my hair grow long for a number of years following — which I experienced as a Samson-like regeneration of my vital strength after my transplant.

In those first untethered months, I explored various other interests, including a weekend Holotropic Breathwork[225] workshop with Stan Grof. I found him urbane, congenial, and interesting (he gave a talk on Friday night). The workshop itself was interesting but did not become an avenue for further exploration. My biggest takeaway was realizing that if I ever became involved as a facilitator in any similar therapeutic venue, I would need to work on cultivating my patience in order to meet with compassion and care the intensity of issues that some folk showed up with. More than a few people there seemed to have a lot of stuff that was plaguing them.

Six months after the separation from my first wife, I became involved in a love relationship that lasted through the next five years. I resumed my career in tech and focused on being a single half-time parent. I continued my reading of anthroposophy and maintained a modest level of involvement with a local study group and the occasional talk or other events.

Returning to active work again, I would again, on occasion, travel to Europe on business. My older brother was working in Zurich for a couple of years during that time, and I was able to coordinate a visit to him in connection with some other travel. We arranged an overnight "road trip" that started with a train ride to Basel, where we rented a car and then made a short trip to the Goetheanum[226] in Dornach[227]. During the train ride of about an hour, I had the opportunity to familiarize him with some of the basic concepts of anthroposophy, something I had never had the chance to do; he listened with interest, and I imagine he found the visit to the Goetheanum likewise interesting. We continued onward to Colmar to see the Isenheim[228] altarpiece and enjoy a lovely dinner there. The Isenheim altar was a destination for pilgrims suffering from St. Anthony's fire (ergotism) — a hallucinatory and potentially deadly condition induced by consuming the same ergot of rye from which LSD was later to be derived. The next day we drove home to Zurich via Freiburg and the Black Forest.

Three years after my second transplant, through a chain of circumstances, I was able to make direct contact with the family of my liver donor, which was a profound blessing. We were able — in a way, making what I felt was a conscious choice — to relate to each other as family — as you might if you came to meet a second cousin for the first time, who was otherwise a stranger. It made me realize that the ability to relate to others with this degree of regard and care is something that we can choose to do with anyone.

And then the relationship of five years had run its course just before my fiftieth birthday. I attended a workshop at the Esalen Institute the weekend of that birthday and recall, among other things, a conversation with a woman there on the subject of psychedelics. I was exhorted to try Ayahuasca. Although I had certainly heard of it, it moved it onto my radar as "a thing."

Shortly thereafter, I met my present wife. Together we established a family unit of her two girls (much younger) and my (older) two boys (my eldest daughter had since started living on her own).

I found myself reborn yet again.

15

Lucifer and Ahriman

Looking to stitch together the strings of my life, my psychedelic explorations, and Steiner's thought, it will be helpful to come to an understanding of one of the signature ideas in Steiner's worldview: the nature of what he sometimes describes as the "oppositional powers" influencing human life from the spiritual world.

Steiner's cosmos — the spiritual world — is populated with myriads of creative beings; beings who watch over humanity, who help us weave our future destinies together in our lives in the spiritual world between incarnations, and who are themselves involved in their own process of spiritual evolution. These discarnate beings can be generally seen as having evolved spiritually beyond present-day humanity.

Some of these higher beings are variously described as being "adversely commanded," "stragglers," "backward," and so on, and who function out of the spiritual world as influences that appear to work contrary to the goals of the "Good Gods."

Steiner sees *two* categories of these beings, two polarically related primary and distinct personifications of influences that can become stumbling blocks across the path of spiritual growth.

In the last years of his life, Rudolf Steiner labored diligently at a wooden sculpture group, working along with the sculptress Edith Maryon[229] (1872 - 1924). This large sculpture featured three figures — one whom Steiner referred to in this context as the *Representative of Humanity*, about whom he said that it represented the "spiritualized, inwardly deepened humanity." He continued further that "It would be natural for many to connect this picture immediately with the Christ. That would be right, but to brand the work with the name Christ Group would not be good. Let us leave it to everyone to interpret it as he thinks fit."

The other two figures he names more concretely: they are Lucifer and Ahriman. Through as it were a deeper wisdom, these opposing powers are seen as also serving in their way to bring humanity forward, provided the proper balance is achieved — this balance is then seen reflected artistically in the sculpture group as the function performed by the central figure, the "Representative of Humanity."

If one begins to experience or understand life in a spiritual world occupied by countless higher and elemental beings, one might reasonably apprehend that not all of them are, even though fulfilling their own spiritual nature, not necessarily inherently well-disposed to the ultimate best interests of humanity. They may wish to steer or influence individuals, as well as humanity altogether, in directions that may appear to the lights of these beings as ideal but which may not serve what for humanity is its highest possibility in the world of spirit.

The name *Lucifer* echoes the biblical tradition of the fallen angel or, more poetically, of the morning star or light-bringer. The Luciferic tendency would inspire humanity to leave the earthly behind, forsake its cosmic evolutionary tasks entirely, and return to the heavens of our spiritual origins, bypassing the cosmic dance of evolution. Through this influence comes also the source of the artistic, the creative flight of fancy, and the tendency to "space out" or have one's head in the clouds. Thus, it also, in a certain way, illuminates our inner spiritual power of self-development. As such, the Luciferic influence serves a critical role in the life of the individual and humanity, leading them toward awareness of the spiritual and away from the merely earthly.

Ahriman, and the Ahrimanic beings, represent those influences that would have humanity bind itself to the earthly, to live only in the domain of the senses, and to seek the origins of the human in the realm of earthly forces of number, weight, and measure. All technology, machinery, and especially computer technology, would be seen as reflecting or embodying the Ahrimanic. The Ahrimanic influences harden and calcify us in our souls and bodies. Ahriman derives his name from the dark being who opposes Ahura Mazda, the being of light, in ancient Persian Zoroastrianism[230].

Psychedelics can thus generally be seen as partaking foremost in the Luciferic nature. They can, quite literally, loosen our connection with the earthly and bring our consciousness into the realm of the spiritual, into the realms of light. As such, the Luciferic can liberate us from our one-sided, sclerotic thinking and doing. The discovery of LSD and the burgeoning of psychedelic exploration might be seen as a Luciferic counter-influence to the increasingly materialistic, industrialized, hardened element that entered the life of humanity since the scientific and industrial revolutions.

The Luciferic impulse is also understood by Steiner as having particularly brought about an event that occurred in humanity's long-ago emergence from the world of spiritual origin. This Luciferic impulse introduced a kind of imbalance in humanity's reception of its proper form from its cosmic archetype. This occurs in the penultimate stage before the spiritual birth of the *I*.

The nascent human soul was as if pervaded by a too-strong sense of self. The proper development of the true *I* consciousness is a central task in human evolution; in turn, it is this properly developed *I* that, in turn, brings about the transformation of all of the components of the given human structure into their higher divine-spiritual possibilities of being.

This Luciferic impulse and the overweening sense of self it induced had, at the same time, the inestimable benefit of allowing humanity to develop, through (or despite) this imbalance with its countless consequences, *freedom* — freedom, that is, from the compulsion of acting out of the higher cosmic willing, rather than from a purely human and freely-given assent to the highest will.

We meanwhile swing — as humanity and as individuals — between this heavenward-escaping pole and the other, the Ahrimanic pole, which would bind us to an earthly sense-existence. The Ahrimanic beings would, if they could, keep us from the transformative encounter with the spirit that occurs in the life between death and a new birth.

These spiritual forces enter our life and world at every turn, and for Steiner, it is not a question of avoiding or trying to shun their influence but rather to perceive their presence and effects and navigate from a poise or balance relative to them. When either one-sided influence becomes predominant, it invites the other to follow suit in a sort of one-two punch, creating further entanglements.

In my own life, psychedelics would appear to have acted as a primarily Luciferic impulse — opening my soul to a world beyond the earthly. In my own life of contemplation and striving for knowledge, I have wrestled inside of myself with the, to me at times soul-oppressing, weight of scientific materialism as an exclusively valid worldview — with Ahriman.

Growing up through my school years, I had swung between interest in the sciences and interest in the humanities. One would, after a time, seem too soft, then the other, too cold. Emerging into adulthood, I found myself first drawn to a career in book publishing — the literary, artistic, Luciferic side. After five years in publishing in New York, I, in turn, made a shift with the result that I spent the bulk of my career in the computer software industry. My roles were usually as a product marketing manager, working with the engineering teams and developing the specification of market requirements, and then launching products into the world.

Computers are, in some ways, the image *par excellence* of the Ahrimanic nature: they can reflect the cold, calculating, and unfeeling consciousness that Ahriman represents and which he would gladly permeate reality with. Yet, as a medium for the expression of the human soul, computers can reflect — seemingly infinitely — a Luciferic sheen of a certain beauty and artistry. Engagement with a computer can become fascinating and all-absorbing, whether the mode of interaction is gaming, digital media, or programming itself. Although I was not engaged employed as a software developer, I knew and understood the satisfaction, gratifying feedback, and sense of control that comes with mastering a programming challenge as a thought exercise.

There is definitely an intersect between the historical psychedelic counter-culture, the rock and roll tribe of the sixties and seventies, and (particularly) the early personal or microcomputer industry. Steve Jobs, one of the founders of Apple, was almost exactly my age, and as far as I can tell from his biography, he grew up in a high school and college psychedelic scene highly parallel to mine. He even did me one better in actually making the trip to India. In the early days of Apple, Jobs reputedly would ask job candidates if they had tripped or how many times they had tripped. A positive answer was considered part of a good qualification. The personal computer industry had a powerful nexus in northern California, which of course, had many of the people and places of the sixties culture all about. Apple's headquarters is about an hour from San Francisco, ground zero for the hippie acid years.

Part of this affinity can be understood in the sense of personal liberation and empowerment, and also the sense of the magical that the computer can bring. The computer software domain also tends to attract the more cerebral types, with many interested likewise in experiencing the psychological possibilities of psychedelics.

Psychedelics and computers form, in their way, an almost mirror-like picture of the beinghood of Lucifer and Ahriman, as described by Steiner.

Psychedelics can bring the experience of light, the loosening from the grips of the earthly, possibly leading the individual toward the advent of spiritual knowledge. Ahriman on the other hand is the being who chains us to the earthly, who lives in the mechanical, the calculated, and the measured. Confusingly at times, they intertwine and seem to "cooperate" in distracting the soul. Computers, with their ability to simulate alternative realities, generate brilliant media effects, and represent artistic human interfaces, can meanwhile host the Luciferic.

The psychedelic example of this intersect with the Ahrimanic can be seen in the story of my early psychedelic hero, John Lilly, as told in his several autobiographical works (*The Center of the Cyclone, The Scientist, So Far*) where he develops his model of the human biocomputer. From one point of view, this model is in service of his notion of the "self-metaprogrammer" — the higher entity within the self which defines the "metaprograms" or basic assumptions or beliefs that determine our everyday awareness and behavior. But it is explained and pictured through a materialistic, mechanistic concept of the functioning of the human brain as if it were a computer, a kind of machine, which is held to provide the fundamental underlying basis for the operation of the mind. The not-so-subtle implication is that we are simply a by-product of a materialistically conceived world process that is essentially a matter of chance and mechanics.

Under the influence of LSD, this set of Lilly's beliefs and ideas became intensely animated for him as a full-blown reality. The primary reality in the domain of the experienced "self-metaprogrammer" — the experiencing self — Lilly saw existing within the whole universe as if contained inside of a giant computer. Our thoughts, actions, behavior, feelings — all were simply coded instructions embedded of the giant "cosmic computer."

For him, this experience was implied by not only his own theories of the function of the brain, and therefore his way of thinking, of consciousness; but also more generally through his deep buy-in into the current scientific paradigm that has the universe arising from a random big bang, planets, and solar systems forming out of accidental collisions of particles, and life itself arising out of purely random acts of natural selection. In the end, all is seen and experienced as meaningless, as existing simply as a set of programs in a large but unliving computer — that is, the ultimate amplification and extension of the "biocomputer" model. It was like *Tron* meets *The Matrix* meets the White King's dream in *Alice Through The Looking Glass*, and he experienced it as terrifying, meaningless, and punishing. In this domain, he saw himself as being "repaired" by robot intelligences inside of the machine.

In Lilly's experience, as related in *The Center of the Cyclone*, it seemed there was no "way out." Lilly goes on to report that he came out of this experience "cleansed" of the rigid beliefs that underlay this vision. In the Arica work that he goes on to describe, he seems to be moving on to an affirmation of spiritual reality.

In subsequent years of further psychedelic exploration (in particular with Ketamine, as reported in his further autobiography *The Scientist*), Lilly came — in his psychedelic state — to reify, to make into a concrete, existing external entity this "cosmic computer," now styled as "the solid-state entity" and saw it as a really-existing malignant competitor with what he called water-based life forms, like humans. He saw it pervading and infecting, virus-like, all computer networks and systems, comprising a single intelligence. And note rather than talk about humans as having souls, they are simply a competing life form opposed to the "solid-state" — the electronic machine.

This all aligns, more or less precisely, with what Steiner calls the influence of Ahrimanic beings in the cosmos and human consciousness. Within the spiritual world, the Ahrimanic *would* pervade all with its cold intellect — its wish is to become the "cosmic intelligence" ruling and organizing all. Lilly had taken his original experience of the Ahrimanic in the "Cosmic Computer" and externalized it, projecting it as a psychedelically envisioned physical reality. In both cases, there is an image of the permeation of reality by a cold, calculating intelligence. For Steiner this would be the reality in the spiritual world of the Ahrimanic; however, in that vision, this being is balanced by various other spiritual entities — such as Lucifer in one sense and the Christ being in another. Lilly's plunge into his vision of the solid-state entity is an example of how his psychedelic explorations continued to reinforce what can be seen as a one-sidedness in his thinking. Steiner always stressed the necessity of seeing things from as many different viewpoints as possible.

Technology, and in particular, computer technology, including the internet and AI, nowadays permeates every aspect of modern culture on the grid. The Ahrimanic tendency is encapsulated in one of its most extreme forms in the aspirations of some in the so-called transhumanist school. Some aspire to achieve a state of immortality by uploading the "data" believed to reside in the brain and thus held to comprise the whole of human consciousness and personality into some sort of computer. It would then — in this theory — persist with some kind of continuity of consciousness with its human origin.

I expect many readers will simply find this notion absurd. Still, the fact that it is even voiced with any shred of plausibility illustrates the depth to which the mechanical model of reality penetrates our thinking. It parallels the belief that consciousness is simply the by-product of a complex organization of material particles. If this can yield consciousness and soul, why not uploaded binary data?

My involvement with computer technology has instilled in me the understanding that they are, at the end of the day, nothing but elaborate pinball machines that pattern logical operations. The low-level elements that provide the foundation for the layering of what operate and appear *as if* logical operations, and upon this, *as if* numerical operations, and upon this, *as if* other symbolic operations, and so on, are, in fact, simply machines. We *project* concepts and interpretations on the results of the operation of a computer, and in so doing, we lend them life — our life. If the same machine state can now represent a number, now a letter, now a pixel, it is clear that it is the perceptual context and interpretation that we add that makes the operation appear significant. "There is nothing either good or bad, but thinking makes it so."[231] This is true all the way to the "expression" of the most sophisticated AI chat engine.

It is meanwhile, easy to see that psychedelic drugs — or, as the Indian sage Patanjali[232] described in the *Yoga Sutras*, "light-bearing plants" — reflect the Luciferic tendency in creation. Psychedelics can induce an "earth-dissociating" process, an activation and amplification of "inner light." When we become "spaced out," we are moving away from the bounds of the earthly. From the anthroposophical point of view, this would be seen as an "etheric loosening" where the forces that bind us to the connection with, and the growth of, the body tend to drift back into the cosmos. This loosening is a transformation of the integration or adhesion of the etheric forces to the three-dimensional, solid form of the physical body in a manner that can be understood as a partial death process. If this process were to continue, it *would* eventually result in the death of the physical body — the psychedelic state, meanwhile, is maintained only for a definite period of time, and only effecting, primarily, the connection of the etheric part of the nerve-brain system as an intensification of the way in which our awake consciousness acts destructively on the brain.

In the role of light-bringer, Lucifer has a benign aspect that can free us from overweening attachment to the earth and bring us knowledge of the spiritual. It is everywhere a question of balance. The "positive" psychedelic experience should perhaps be understood as a *gift* of Lucifer. Considered as such, its incorporation into one's soul journey ought to be viewed with caution and balance; it is well to look this gift horse in the mouth. Lucifer is a bringer of light but also the source of temptation relative to what anthroposophy understands as the best destiny of humanity: to fulfill the aspirations of the creative gods and realize, across ages of time, the realization of the "ideal human being". For this, we will need to live out our karma in connection with the earth's own evolution, incorporating countless soul lessons meanwhile. Lucifer bids us to enter the spiritual world and to remain there before we have fully developed our own highest potential through the challenges of the earth life.

In my life, I found that the study of anthroposophy serves as a balancing and integrating force, leading away from the possibility that our illuminations are swamped by our lingering, underlying materialistic beliefs and assumptions that have come to us through the advances in natural science, and likewise reminding me that spiritual challenge of our existence as human beings is the completion of the task of self-transformation. It envisions a far-off goal wherein human spiritual freedom and spiritual individuality are achieved in full consciousness, in union with the divine, in the realization of love between fully conscious beings, and not merely as a retreat to our primal spiritual condition.

This requires that we find and acquire our own deep faith in this value, that the trip will have been worth it when, at last, our reunion with our highest spiritual nature is realized, and that we will have thereby created something cosmically new and of eternal value.

16

That Tiny Word

Recalling Stephen Gaskin's use of "ego death" — not a term original to him, but when I first encountered it, it was the first place I could clearly recognize that someone else was talking about a very specific experience that mapped to what I had gone through at the cast party. That is the very distinct (and more or less abrupt) sensation that some sort of outer covering of self had been ripped off, exposing one to an entirely new world of cosmic dimension without, and exposing a feeble and unprepared or undeveloped "real self" within. In this sense, the "ego" here is seen as a mask or shell that covers and "protects" the sensitive core within. It is also implied that what has been removed is the source of negative thoughts and behaviors and as something that has served as a constricting lens through which one's previous experience has been organized.

Unfortunately, the little word ego (Latin for I) gets a lot of use that is highly context-dependent; it is freighted with all kinds of meanings and connotations and value judgments. In Gurdjieff's teaching, he contrasted "real I" with false personality and the "many I's" that masqueraded as the integral entity. In Arica, ego was the thing to reduce or eliminate so that "essence" would emerge.

In the contemporary everyday speech of educated people, the use of the word ego has a pretty close association, first of all with Freud's notion of the ego; and also, more simply, the connotation of egoism or egocentricity, that is, with an overweening evaluation of one's own self. He or she is said to have a "big ego."

In the context of Steiner's thought, the Ego or *I* is primarily understood as the eternal spiritual essence of the human being. It is also the agent of the transformation of the self into higher forms of spiritual existence.

The name I itself is a very special word. No one can use the word I as a subject other than referring to their own self, their own *I* — and that's maybe a clue to something of the mystery of the *I*.

In many contexts, the term ego has an almost totally negative connotation as the source of selfishness, as being preoccupied with its own defense and being "nothing but" a psychological construct. Its non-reality is associated in the prevailing understanding of Buddha's teaching that there is no "self" that passes from incarnation to incarnation.

This kind of terminology ("ego death") is one way of looking at certain kinds of transformative psychedelic experiences. It is alternatively possible to see in some of these experiences the crossing of what Rudolf Steiner would describe as "The Threshold of the Spiritual World." This implies a complete transformation of the experience of self — to a fuller perception of the self as it exists within the spiritual world now known and realized. In terms of a sense of boundaries of self, if one accepts the idea that in crossing the threshold, one enters into a conscious experience of a real, existing supersensible world, then naturally, one's former boundaries and touchstones of reality and reality of self will change. One is experiencing both a new sense of "the world" and also of "the self" out of an entirely different cognitive capacity that is no longer tethered to the world of three dimensions, the qualities of number, weight, and measure as we conceive them in our given everyday consciousness.

Steiner would contend that it is critical that one develop the ability to think about the spiritual world in a way that does not rely directly on concepts derived from the sense world. The fact that this is nevertheless our tendency makes statements as to what is real, what is a construct or illusion, difficult to discuss. The fact that the self and world can be experienced in different modes of consciousness requires that we be vigilant in understanding that our vocabulary of "the self" needs to be understood as operating at different semantic levels.

Insofar as the psychedelic state can fundamentally change the way we are psychically bound or attached to our physical bodies, it follows that to the extent that one (quite naturally to begin with) identifies one's self with the experience of being in incarnation in a physical body, one may correspondingly experience a "loss" of the sense of self to the extent that the physical body is no longer felt as previously. At the cast party, I went through what seemed to be the lack of coherence of my physical body and a sense of impending dissolution. Who then was experiencing this?

The eternal, spiritual *I* that Steiner references is in some senses beyond change: at the same time, obviously, the manifest individual in earth life is subject to growth, change, disease, aging. Steiner asserts that what changes is the body's ability to reflect the nature of the *I*.

From Steiner's viewpoint, the condition of being in a physical body is an important stage in humanity's development of the consciousness of having an *I*. At the same time, he sees our everyday experience of the I as being a kind of reflection of the true spiritual *I*.

This relationship of the spiritual *I* to our earthly *I* is expressed in this verse by Steiner:

> *I gaze into the Darkness.*
> *In it there arises Light —*
> *Living Light!*
> *Who is this Light in the Darkness?*
> *It is I myself in my reality.*
> *This reality of the 'I'*
> *Does not enter into my earthly life.*
> *I am but a picture of it.*

But I shall find it again
When with good will for the Spirit
I shall have passed through the Gate of Death.[233]

The conventional understanding of the teachings of Buddha notwithstanding, in Steiner, it is precisely this true I-being that exists from incarnation to incarnation that is the actual agent of our experience of spiritual reality. As our consciousness extends or evolves into realization of the spiritual world, the overshadowing of this I begins to dawn. The experience of so-called "ego death" in the psychedelic context should not imply that there is no longer any Ego in this spiritual sense — in the sense of the "*I* am" consciousness.

The lower ego, the conditioned ego, built up from our everyday world of experience and corresponding consciousness, is, among other things, liable to the two conditions of "inflation" — being puffed up, having a "swelled head," an overvaluation of one's self — and correspondingly, deflation, an "emptying out," a loss of self-esteem. Neither of these conditions are possibilities of the spiritual *I*.

Looking back to Gurdjieff's method of seeing our everyday selves as composed of "many I's" that usurp the station of "real I" with momentary thoughts, desires, and will-impulses, and then applying self-observation and self-remembering (understood in part as intentional disidentification with these momentary I's) we can see a parallel with ideas found in Steiner. This process, of perceiving the self as composed of countless fragmentary I's, is one that in its way leads to an induced disassociation. The element of stress in intentionally seeing one's self as fragmentary is part of the discipline. Each I has its own set of triggers — thoughts that prompt feelings or actions, gestures or postures that prompt feelings or thoughts, and feelings that, by association, stimulate fixed thoughts or actions.

It is precisely this kind of disassociation that Steiner describes as occurring spontaneously as, in the practice of his method of cultivating Imaginative perception of the spiritual world, one comes to experience the overshadowing of the spiritual I as one crosses the threshold of the spiritual world. At this stage, Steiner describes that thinking, feeling, and willing begin to become seen and felt as operating independently of each other. It is very important to note that there are, unsurprisingly, degrees of this. This variability in the degrees of this kind of disassociation is readily observable in psychedelic experience.

It seems that the loosening of the connection between what Steiner describes as the etheric body — which is also, from one point of view, a "thought body" — from the physical body existing in the world of purely natural laws, is, in some ways a "death process" (in that death occurs when there is complete severance between the etheric and physical body). It also is accompanied by a variety of dissociative effects — our automatic linkages become less active.

The mechanical, associative relationship between our psychological functions of thinking, feeling, and willing, are the forces tending to compel our identification with our "everyday" ego and our identification with our physical body. It is as if we invest something of our sense of self — not of the I itself — into the woven-together complex of associations across the different functions.

In realizing and experiencing this disassociation, one can explore and discover new patterns of being that are more inwardly harmonious, that are psychological positives, when one inevitably returns to the everyday earthly consciousness, wherein we will again, perforce, rely precisely on our habitual associations to various degrees in order simply to function. In the right context of support and intention, it becomes possible to discover what Stan Grof describes as the holotropic possibilities of psychedelics, the tendency to orient and move toward wholeness.

In the life between death and a new birth, the point or center-oriented sense of *I* gives way to holographic unity oriented towards the periphery of existence as we undergo an inner turning "inside out" as we transit from one earth life to the next. Our sense of "*I* am" can transcend the point-oriented perspective associated with incarnation in an individualized bodily form. To grasp this, we must leave behind the conviction that our sense-experience uniquely defines the known and the categories of thought.

In anthroposophy, it is through the awakening to the activity of this spiritual I that the transformation of the "lower" bodies into higher ones can proceed. Initially this work takes the form of mastering the self-seeking, in the lower sense, elements of the astral body. From this point of view, one's notion of the spiritual *I* is to be seen as that which is effective in the transformation of the lower sheaths of the human being.

Steiner describes this:

> Now what is it that originates in earlier lives, works on from life to life, and maintains itself through all its sojourns on earth? It is the Ego, the *I*, designated by the name which a person can bestow on no-one but himself. The human Ego goes from life to life, and in so doing fulfils its evolution.
>
> But how is this evolution brought about? By the Ego working on the three lower members of the human being. We have first the astral body, the vehicle of pleasure and pain, of joy and sorrow, of instinct, desire and passion. Let us look at a person on a low level, whose Ego has done little, as yet, to cleanse his astral body and so is still its slave. In a person who stands higher we find that his Ego has worked upon his astral body in such a way that his lower instincts, desires and passions have been transmuted into moral ideals, ethical judgments. From this contrast we can gain a first impression of how the Ego works upon the astral body.
>
> In every human being it is possible to distinguish the part of the astral body on which the Ego has not yet worked from the part which the Ego has consciously transformed. The transmuted part is called Spirit-Self, or *Manas*.
>
> The Ego may grow stronger and stronger, and will then transmute the etheric body or life-body. Life-spirit is the name we give to the transformed etheric body. Finally, when the Ego acquires such strength that it is able to extend its transforming power into the physical body, we call the transmuted part *Atma*, or the real Spirit-human being.[234]

THAT TINY WORD

Considering all this in light of the traditions of Buddhism, it should be remembered that the Buddha's response to the question of whether or not there was an existing self was to answer that that is not a question that conduces to enlightenment.

Yet here we are, inevitably discussing the very question. Today, however, the evolving spiritual life of mankind would seem to require a more nuanced understanding. There is a pendulum swing between the perception of the "bad ego" and the "healthy ego." There is an extreme of this so-called Buddhist perspective that can yield a condition which the Beatle John Lennon describes in an interview about his LSD use: "I got a message on acid that I should destroy my ego, and I did. ... I was slowly putting meself together round after Maharishi, bit by bit, over a two-year period. And then I destroyed me ego and I didn't believe I could do anything. And I was nothing. I was shit.[235]"

Relative to our earthly ego-bearer — understood not only as the picture of the spiritual I, but as a complex of soul forces that, in a sense, carries or supports the active manifestation of the spiritual I, it is clear to see and understand that it is possible that our egotism be either too strongly developed and expressed, or conversely, too weakly. From a spiritual development point of view, it is the spiritual "*I* am" that journeys from life to life that we must develop a place for in our world conception.

And today, the whole world is essentially under the sway of the industrialized, Europeanized West to one degree or another. In its wake, this brings, among other things, a profound inner "cosmic alienation," a divorce for the earlier forms of tribal consciousness that was more in tune with nature, its rhythms, and its elemental character. This divorcement is necessary for humanity as a whole to go through, in one way or the other, to develop the realization of the independent, potentially spiritually free, eternal "I Am." This alienation, isolation — reinforced as it is by, among other things, our modern scientific materialism — plays a key role in stimulating the awakening to the true *I* — if the soul is not overwhelmed or suffocated by it.

This process of evolution in humanity also brings a history of karmic misdeeds on a global scale, particularly as the aggrandizing spirit of the West, in its realization and development of its effective power, trampled, exploited, and destroyed — intentionally or else as collateral damage — indigenous or aboriginal societies which had remained isolated from the technological development of the European-American dominant culture.

As we come to understand this process, through different phases of consciousness that Steiner describes, we are called to realize that it is we ourselves, as reincarnating *I*'s, who have lived in earlier history and in many cultures and positions of different degrees of relative dominance, privilege, or disadvantage. We will likewise also incarnate again as future humans, in karmically-determined lives we ourselves will select, ultimately, for our own best development and the development of humanity and the earth. With this, we realize the enormous responsibility any degree of fortune, advantage, or privilege confers.

This responsibility will include working toward social justice across all peoples and societies. This will include working to preserve and nurture the social and sacred traditions of peoples of less privilege, struggling to maintain their traditional values in the tidal wave of cultural and economic dominance and residual imperialism, while at the same time helping to form a footing in an ecologically and economically healthy relationship with the global order.

Our sense for justice in this regard should not, however, discourage those of a more privileged position in the dominant culture from embracing the spiritual gifts — comprising a broad spectrum — of the West. The realization of "The Universal Human" across all peoples will require moral artistry of the highest degree. Our challenge is to transform, not deny — not risk throwing the baby out with the bathwater. It is these gifts in their noblest forms that have awakened our noblest humanity.

The making effective of the spiritual "*I* am" in one's self, in one's own journey toward inner freedom, implies the most profound deference to both the spiritual freedom, including freedom in the life of rights, of all others. In the highest level of Steiner's scheme of Imagination, Inspiration, and Intuition, Intuition is the state where love becomes seeing and knowing, and recognizes itself through unity with the spiritual natures of other beings within one's self.

17

Reincarnation, Living Time, and Eternity

My own psychedelic experience was laced with riddles, questions, and visions of time, eternity, and the source and destiny of the soul, with the question of death and rebirth, of ultimate import to my very core.

Through my reading I found myself absorbing an at times confusing array of various doctrines and teachings. At length, as I came to study Steiner's teachings more and more deeply, his understanding of reincarnation became increasingly embedded in my own view and provided the clearest resolution of my most profound experiences while in the psychedelic state. It hangs together with his other teachings concerning our spiritual origin and our individual evolution into freedom.

Nowhere in my own psychedelic explorations did I experience anything on the order of a "past life regression" or what I took as an experience of a previous incarnation. I did, however, clearly experience both a sense of "my life existing in eternity" and a clear realization of having been born out of the spiritual world, that is, out of a pre-incarnation state, and of something living in me that had lived before.

Teachings about reincarnation have existed in the West, but they were largely supplanted by the evolution of orthodox Christian teachings of the eternal salvation (or damnation) of the soul being the outcome of the judgment of a single life. With the advent of

Theosophy in the latter part of the 19th century, H. P. Blavatsky and others re-introduced into the West what had become an essentially Eastern concept.[236] An important text, first published in English in 1925, is the *Tibetan Book of the Dead* (in Tibetan, the *Bardo Thodol*). Walter Evans-Wentz, the editor, was a Theosophist, and his editorial commentary shows that influence. The book was later remarked upon by Carl Jung and then, through Aldous Huxley, became the inspiration for Timothy Leary and Ralph Metzner's *The Psychedelic Experience*. Although the currency of that latter work has faded, it was influential in the early days of broad experimentation with LSD. Some of the attitudes and doctrines it reflects, as well as those of the *Bardo Thodol* itself, still overshadow much of contemporary thought on the subject of reincarnation in relationship to psychedelics. Leary and Metzner's idea was that a high-dosage LSD experience paralleled the transition between lives as in the *Tibetan Book of the Dead*.

This outline of an Eastern notion of reincarnation hovered in the background of my thinking and would have been the first "alternative model" regarding our after-death existence to the conventional teaching of eternal judgment to either heaven or hell as absorbed since childhood.

The Hindu and Buddhist teachings that have since filtered through into the West, starting in the time of Blavatsky, the principal early popularizer of them through her Theosophical Society, can be seen to largely inform the views of many of what may be characterized as "New Age" movements and related psychedelic trends of thought. In this form, it is essentially rooted in the idea that incarnation as such is suffering (*dukkha*) and that the ultimate goal of spiritual effort is a state of enlightenment characterized by total non-attachment and consequent liberation from the "Wheel of Rebirth." One should seek escape from this Wheel. What is lacking in the various expressions of this view is the mindset that sees earth-incarnation as a stage for the development or evolution of the individual soul. Correspondingly, the earth-realm is not seen as possessing any ultimate cosmic significance in its own nature other than as a platform for escape.

I can't specifically recall when I would have first read *The Tibetan Book of the Dead*, but the essentials of the Buddhist concept would have been known to me by the time I first read Hesse's *Siddhartha* at sixteen. In Ram Dass' *Be Here Now*, which I also encountered near that time, I would have come to internalize that within the framework of this reincarnation teaching, the goal was to *avoid* rebirth, to "close the door to the womb."

This implied to me that failure to avoid birth during the traversal of the bardo state, which in my concept seemed to require a superhuman kind of self-denial, would be significantly catastrophic. It would yield another purportedly miserable (*dukha-laden*) incarnation. The wrinkle in all this was that, instead of experiencing life as misery, despite its infinite ups and downs, I experienced life as an essentially good thing and had a powerful desire for experience — including, of course, sexual experience. Of course, the teaching implied that regardless, it was only a matter of time before it *would* be experienced as misery.

As I came to develop my understanding of Steiner's thought regarding reincarnation, particularly as it dovetailed elements of my own psychedelic experience, I began first to grasp his general ideas regarding the evolution of consciousness.

Psychedelic experience having given me the felt and known awareness that there exist very different states of consciousness, which could reveal unknown layers of cosmic reality, made Steiner's essential teachings about the evolution of consciousness make rational sense.

From a purely spiritual origin, man and the "world," as we experience it, have developed through the creative activity of higher beings who sacrificed a part of themselves to provide a platform for the development of the individual spiritual human being through the world-process, across all but measureless time.

Our existence as spirits is seen as a gradual awakening out of a paradisiacal state of blissful union with these higher beings, but wherein we initially lacked clear self-consciousness. Humanity on earth gradually connected with the developing external human forms — physical bodies — out of an earlier life in the purely spiritual world and had only dim awareness of an experienced difference between the incarnate state and the after-death state when the primitive human forms man inhabited underwent physical death.

Early human civilizations, as they emerged, maintained a consciousness that provided a memory, as it were, of its experience in the spiritual world in communion with higher beings — Gods — and this informed much of the content of their culture. I found this idea in my first encounter with Steiner in *Ancient Myths*.

The more humanity became awake to the earth life, however, the more the distinction between birth and death became starker, and the more the discarnate life became darkened and shadowy. It became the retrospective reflection of the separation from the primal spiritual source that is experienced in the increasingly spiritually darkened earth consciousness. This reached a point such that in the times of ancient Greece, Homer has Achilles state: "Better to be a beggar on earth than a king in the realm of the shades."[237] Our spirits could no longer connect clearly with their primal sense of unity with the spiritual world[238].

Some thinkers have tried to relate psychedelic use by earlier cultures to the origin of religion, the development of higher mental capacities, and so on. The viewpoint that humanity's pre-history was one of a fading, originally-given contact with the spiritual world of "gods" or higher beings, suggests that the historical use of psychedelics may perhaps be better understood as the means by which this fading contact was preserved. What this implies for their current and future use remains to be seen.

More and more, in the properly historical times since the time of Christ, humanity has experienced itself as "walled in" between the gates of birth and death, with the consciousness of having existed before birth completely faded and a corresponding fear and uncertainty developed concerning death.

Anthroposophy teaches that we who are alive today have experienced numerous cycles of reincorporation through physical birth, with a shifting and evolving consciousness or awareness of our agency as an *I* and, with that, increasing consciousness of freedom — paid for, initially, at the cost of a cosmic alienation. To the extent that we were dreamily living in the spirit consciousness, we were acting "unfreely" at the prompting of the inspiration of creative spiritual beings rather than out of our own pure "love of the deed."

Steiner, through his clairvoyant perceptions or higher consciousness, details what in Eastern wisdom would be described as the *bardo* state, or as is generally referred to by him, the life between death and a new birth. He describes a metamorphosis of consciousness passing through definite stages in the life between death and new birth.

Steiner, who was greatly inspired by his study of Goethe's scientific works when he was given the commission to serve as the editor of them and worked at the Goethe archive, was animated by the idea of metamorphosis. One of the pivotal ideas exemplifying Goethe's approach to science, which embraced multiple modes of thinking and saw the role of the perceiving thinker as instrumental in the process of knowledge, was his concept of the *urpflanze*, or primal plant.

To Goethe, this was a living concept that reflected the underlying reality of the plant world: he saw all plants as variations of a primal plant. The differentiation into various species was seen as an endless transformation and metamorphosis of the *urpflanze*, which was a spiritual reality. The plant itself he saw as developing in a series of transformations, through processes he referred to as polarity and heightening, applied to the same basic pattern which for him was best represented by the *leaf*[39]. In part, comprehension and vision of the *urpflanze* meant developing the ability to recognize the self-similarity of the parts to the whole. This self-similarity underlies the readiness with which visual simulations of natural forms using fractal functions effectively approximates, for example, the generated image of a forest of similar-but-different trees.

Steiner's vision came to discern likewise, in his clairvoyant penetration into the life between death and new birth, a process of metamorphosis. Many of course would dismiss out of hand the idea that an individual such as Steiner could obtain and relate certain knowledge of life after (or before) death. In my own case, I came to see through my psychedelic experience that it is possible for one to experience higher states of cognition, in vivid reality, that at any rate touch on the edges of birth and death. Meanwhile, traditional spiritual works such as the *Tibetan Book of the Dead* were understood as reflecting knowledge and wisdom derived from yogic practice and experience, that is, from a consciously-cultivated higher knowledge. It then becomes a question of trying to discern within the various teaching streams what is most consonant with the sense of truth, and fits, coherently and resonantly, with the needs and realities of the contemporary world as we find it today.

Present humanity experiences a sharp distinction between the earth life and the life between death and a new birth. Today, as the soul leaves the earth experience behind, it moves through stages of detachment and purification. Free from the etheric-physical body complex, it undergoes what could be described as an inversion process: the outer world experienced in earth life becomes our inner world, and our inner world is expanded and becomes our outer environment. Deeds, thoughts, and tendencies of one life are transformed — in concert with other human and spiritual beings in our individual web of destiny — into capacities and predispositions of the next life. It is a constant, forward-moving weaving from life to life.

The first stage, where the connection between the etheric body and the physical body that pertains during life is fully loosened (that is, severed) brings with it the experience of a "life tableau"

The period immediately following death is experienced as the vision of the etheric body, freed from its connection with the physical body and its role as builder and maintainer of the physical body against the death-dealing forces of nature and earthly matter. After death, the physical body of course returns to its constituent elements. This life tableau corresponds to the classically-described experience of "one's life passing before one's eyes" in the moment of shock in reports of near-death experiences.

During this phase, the vision of the "life-tableau" brings before the soul one's entire life as if experienced "all at once".

An extremely vivid account that corresponds accurately with the phenomenon of the "life tableau" is found in the book *LSD and the Mind of the Universe*[240], by Chris Bache[241]. During one of his high-dosage LSD experiences as part of his disciplined program of exploration, he experiences himself as dwelling within both his past and future life "all at once" as it were, and experiencing in consciousness the stream of life coming to him from the future as well as occupying a complete memory-picture awareness of his life to date.

This is a key linking the psychedelic experience as a temporary "loosening" of the etheric with Steiner's insights into the stages of the life between death and new birth.

Bache describes his experience as follows:

> Today it was as though I was young and old at once.
>
> I was my entire life experience with time collapsed, as though someone had turned my life on end and looked down its length, like looking through a paper towel tube. Seen end to end, time disappeared and my soul appeared — the being beneath the stages of my life. Enduring relationships stood out in bold relief. Bonds with people, with ideas, with life tasks. People I had found and who had found me. Ideas that have circulated round me all my life, returning in different forms again and again.
>
> I was my past present, and future — one — in a way that was certain to me, doubt not being possible.
>
> Even more difficult to convey than the riddle of time is the extreme saturation of detail in this mode of experience, the extraordinary richness of layers upon layers of information. These details coalesced to form a "deep reading" of my life. The authority of this reading was incontestable; its truth was obvious. It was as though all the evidence was present. This way of knowing was unlike anything I have ever experienced before. It was a knowing that was not linear but whole. Not a conclusion but a seeing-things-in-their-entirety. It was a depth of vision so much richer than ordinary vision that to call it a "vision" lies. It was more a "being tuned" than a seeing. It was saturated textures of experience from different periods of my life symphonically orchestrated.
>
> In these experiences, I not only saw and observed my future life, I tasted it experientially...

In Steiner's teaching, the experience of the etheric elements that compose this tableau of the life persists for approximately three days after physical death, and then recedes into the cosmic background, allowing a new phase of soul-consciousness to emerge.

A mirror phenomenon is seen in the process of incarnation. Before birth, the etheric body is woven together from the whole spiritual world, and the pattern of the qualities and experiences of the life to come are foreshadowed as an outline or blueprint. Life itself consists of "filling up" this pattern with actual lived experience. From the timeless perspective — "turned on end and looked down its length" — the life is perceived as a single whole, or as Bache continues to say: "... it was to see your lives [with others] happening and having happened simultaneously."

These points of intersection illuminate how psychedelic insight can align very directly with anthroposophical teachings.

One can see that, in the psychedelic state, this "perspective in time" is subject to alteration and transformation. Navigating this, accepting it, and connecting through the now, are requisite as the soul may partially detach itself from the orderly progression of linear time in the psychedelic state.

Psychedelic agents appear to act in the soul by amplifying aspects of the "death process" in the nervous system (while essentially leaving the rhythmic and metabolic life forces active) in such a way that the part of the etheric body that corresponds to the physical brain is loosened from its connection with the nerve-sense system, and processes that normally "benumb" our full experience of our own thought-life, which, as a spiritual activity, would normally include the elements of consciousness which Steiner describes as corresponding to Imagination, Inspiration, and Intuition.

The fact that we don't normally experience these higher elements present in our sense experience, with its corresponding elemental thought components, allows us to develop our individualities in freedom and develop the perception of our I as a free, independent agent. It is this realized independence which we must bring with us as we move, through death, initiation, or the psychedelic state, toward the spiritually-centered I consciousness.

In the arc of human evolution, as Steiner describes it, we are at a stage where we must begin, in consciousness, to undergo that self-transformation that enables us to regain the experience of coherent alignment with the spiritual world. Our heart's wish is to ultimately regain that lost experience of primal humanity wherein all of creation, including the human being, is experienced as the expression of the cosmic word — and wherein at the same time, our own conscious and independent I has agency. That is, to transform the created physical, etheric, and astral bodies received in the course of evolution into higher manifestations of the ideal human being. These transformed elements Steiner refers to these as the Spirit Self, Life Spirit, and Spirit Human Being (he sometimes uses the eastern terms, Manas, Buddhi, and Atman), the transformed astral, etheric, and physical bodies respectively.

In trying to understand these modifications of the sense of time that psychedelics can induce, of shifts in context relative to the "sense of eternity," one of the more important ideas to feel into, in order to begin to grasp Steiner's view is the idea that, in a certain way, during earth-incarnation, we are actually existing in two different "time currents" — one from the past to the future, the other, from the future to the past. The first is of course what we experience day to day as "passing time". The second is the expression of the idea that, as spiritual beings, we actually exist outside of time, in the eternal spiritual world. As such, we "connect" with our earth life through the etheric body, which in addition to being the bearer of the forces of up-building (as with the plant) in physical life, also can be understood as the "time body" — a "something" which stretches from our entry into physical life at birth and allows us to arrive, moment by moment, at the currently experienced "present moment" in our lives. However, as this "time body" itself also exists within eternity, there is a flow likewise as if from the future in determining its structure and with it, our actual existence as considered in time. Steiner describes how we are directly involved in this stream, albeit unconsciously, at night, when we separate our soul-spiritual being from our physical-etheric, and journey back "in time" to the time of birth, that is, back to the spiritual world. In doing so, we traverse our lives "in reverse" and participate in the path of time from the future.

In my own psychedelic experience, there were several "distortions of time" that I experienced and which, in a sense, were stepping-stones toward the comprehension of Steiner's teachings as I am attempting here to reflect in part.

The first of these is perhaps a common one among psychedelic experiences: at the cast party, I fell into a state where I believed that the sense of soul paralysis and terror that I believed would last forever. I now understand this as a confusion where the "sense or experience of eternity" that occurs when the etheric loosening overshadows a place of psychological impasse, wherein there appears no way forward. In the "now" that we can experience when our brain-bound thinking is suspended, the sense of eternity dawns in some fashion. We need to be able to distill this out of the content, whatever it may be, that makes up the rest of our experience. Individuals "looping" in this state can sometimes be restored to a more grounded sense of time if they have a guide or companion that can re-affirm their safe and whole presence in passing time, and with that, the assurance of the eventual ending of the present psychedelic state.

At the lake, when I was rushing with adrenaline pumping and walking around the shore with Derek, hoping to find Milo safely on the other shore of the lake, I experienced a kind of "bouncing back in time" that at the same time was a "shaking loose" from the physical and produced (in a feebly understood way at the time) an expanded sense of my life existing as an entity as a whole, although bounded on one side by birth and the entry into life from the spiritual world. The event of birth was in a sense a "wall" blocking my perception beyond; indeed, I was in a liminal state wherein I felt challenged to re-cross the "oceanic abyss" of the lake as if (again) at the starting point of life.

Later as I wandered, confused, I came again to an impasse or crossroads where I dithered and vacillated painfully. Outwardly, there was in fact a crossroads of two paths through the woods surrounding the lake; but the confusion as to which I was to choose was experienced as of much greater import than the simple choice of which way to wander through the woods.

It is of course very difficult to remember in true fidelity such an experience years later, having absorbed any number of concepts that might apply to (and thereby color) the experience — I can only reflect here what has resolved itself within me.

RECINCARNATION, LIVING TIME, AND ETERNITY

I see the impasse of having to make a choice, which at the time was anguishing, as founded first in a dawning realization from all the thoughts, images, and intimations I was experiencing, that I had, as a being with an origin in the spiritual world, in fact, taken (again) incarnation. And thereby, left my "home," which I now experienced an intense longing for. The choice I felt compelled to make, at bottom, was either to retreat back to the spiritual world — which it only seemed I coud achieve by choosing death — or go forward and accept the path through and into incarnation. From one angle this could be the choice between seeking death and rebirth, or accepting and affirming the present fact of birth, and all its karmic challenges. Simply at the layer of experience of being a teenager as I was, was naturally fraught with the effort of growing into the everyday world.

This feeling of "the shadow of eternity" fell over the moment, and in seeing myself incarnated (in a sense, in exile from the spiritual world), I vividly in one sense, and dimly and in confusion in another, beheld the existence of previous incarnations — in some "times" — existing in eternity.

It seemed the pathway from eternity to everything in my view and perception was as if an echo of something "already seen;" that everything I could see was in a sense "eternally existing" and at the same time flowing dynamically through time. One interpretation of this sense might be, "Everything has existed before, and has come back into existence in the same form."

In my day-to-day mind at that time, I did not have a particularly settled idea of reincarnation. I was already familiar with the Tibetan and Hindu concepts, in outline anyway, but through my readings of Ouspensky I had come within the sway of his idea of "eternal recurrence". In the view of "eternal recurrence," we live our lives again and again, returning at birth to the same set of conditioning influences and bereft of memory or knowledge of the previous "life" — and therefore, absent some miracle, doomed to relive that life and its — especially poignant, apparently for Ouspensky — mistakes and disappointments. This is, for Ouspensky, *dukkha*.

Ouspensky's picture is, in my view, consequently pretty grim. Nietzsche put forward the idea in one sense to urge us to live so boldly that we would be content to live our lives again and again.

We would embrace our destinies, warts and all. Ouspensky instead saw nothing but the eternal repetition of the countless bad choices that are inevitably made in life, and in that, an expression of the "mechanicalness" or unfreedom of our lives — to only be remedied by a "waking up" experience that allowed one to, finally, choose an alternate path in "the next recurrence"

There are of course any number of logical impossibilities reflected in this idea; a change in one life would inevitably require changes in the supposed deterministic experience of the others on a given time path. It is riddled with science fiction time-travel quandaries. Imagine the complexity of each of us experiencing our own private "Groundhog Day" alongside of everyone else.

Later in my twenties, I read Steiner's autobiography, The Course of My Life, and he devotes several pages to Nietzsche and in particular the development of Nietzsche's idea of recurrence[1][242]. His analysis is quite interesting, which I will try and nutshell here.

Nietzsche's idea of recurrence has a physical-mechanical idea of the universe underlying it, as it posits that eventually all possible mechanical interactions of particles will have been exhausted and the universe will return to its starting point, to repeat itself exactly. (Never mind quantum mechanics and the rest).

Steiner describes discovering a volume in Nietzsche's library by the materialistic scientist Eugen Dühring where he discusses this idea and then dismisses it as an impossibility.

Steiner, meanwhile, was very sensitive to what he saw as the tragedy of Nietzsche. He saw him as a great mind who could not overcome the scientific materialism of the 19th century. Steiner sees Nietzsche as having felt intuitively the idea of repeated earth lives; however, as he could not conceive of the intermediate sojourn in the spiritual world, he was boxed into the only structure of "repeated lives" that he could conceive. Eternity was only endless time, cycling forever.

Ouspensky, whose thinking was also permeated also by then-current popular thoughts of the mathematics of "the Fourth Dimension[243]," bits of (ostensibly rejected) Theosophy and whatnot, along with current scientific ideas of Relativity, and, as voiced in his Strange Life of Ivan Osokin, an uncanny, and morose, sense of the tragic inevitability of ill-fate as the result of unconscious drives and behaviors.

The sense of the eternal existence of the life in time can give rise to hellish experiences if one is in a negative state: one has always been here, and will always be stuck here. This is perhaps suggestive of the origin of the belief in the possible eternal damnation (or salvation) of the soul, understood as infinite continued existence in passing time, in either a hellish or heavenly state.

Indeed, our missteps can create patterns that we will recur to, not in precise repetitions, but instead in recurring patterns and situations that arise continuously to the extent that we do not transform and redeem the lessons imposed on us by the present moment. This kind of psychological recurrence is a well-known commonplace of pop psychology in the 21st century, such as in the context of romantic relationships where a new partner is discovered to possess many of the negative, as well as attractive attributes, of an old, failed-relationship partner. We repeat life's lessons until they are mastered — not, indeed, as exact repetitions, but rather as repeating patterns and dynamics.

The viewpoint of anthroposophy sheds additional light on the experience of having "lived before". Steiner relates how, both in sleep and in the life after death, the soul does indeed re-experience the life (or day) just lived, only in reverse order — like a film being played in reverse — and re-experienced with a profound shift in awareness which embraces the moral significance of our deeds. The soul, in its review or re-experience, judges its deeds in the light of its now vivid experience of how they are experienced by others. One views and experiences one's self in full empathy with the experience of the other. One's consciousness does, in a sense, return to the moment of birth; but not in a mechanical circle of repetition, but more fully, by being experienced as a participating in a parallel counter-current of time within the broader reality of eternity.

This review, which the soul experiences during sleep (without remembering except through the twilight filter of dreams) is in fact an experience of the spiritual (or eternal) component of our existence, which, Steiner asserts, is in fact present while we experience or perform our deeds and experience life's impressions, but which, because of the demands and constraints of earthly consciousness, we do not experience at the moment (indeed, if we did, we would begin to lose our connection to the earth). However, this reality — the moral judgment (not in any sense of conventional morality, but in the sense of our own insight into the consequences of our deeds for the world's sustenance) of our deeds from the viewpoint of the eternal is present in the soul.

The awareness of the reverse flow of time can be experienced in extreme or special states of consciousness. Because we lack the categories of experience to understand and properly interpret such states, the soul can experience itself as if an 'exact repetition' were being experienced — that is if it brings to the experience the categories of materialistic thinking. What is really happening is the aspect of eternity is dawning on the soul: past, present, and future are all intersecting in the present moment. What the critical idea to grasp is, from the viewpoint of human freedom, is that from the timeless vantage of 'eternity', the expression of human will, of choice, can reflect not only the compulsions imposed by the past but the simultaneous determination of what we will meet the present moment out of the stream from the future, where the soul also exists in its ultimate, highest form, just as the past and our spiritual origin is always existent in eternity.

What actually takes place in the present moment in this life is determined out of eternity; the more present we are to the moment itself, to now, the closer we are also to eternity, where all is determined, all exists, and all is possible, and where our most free inner impulses hold sway in shaping our destiny at the moment.

The idea of mechanical recurrence or repetition is, in effect, a shadow of eternity, cast into our earthly lives and minds. Steiner's anthroposophical teachings can clarify our comprehension in this domain so that we do not mistake the shadow for the true form.

In the life between death and a new birth, we, together with figures and companions of our past lives and the guidance and leadership of higher spiritual beings, weave the etheric form of the next life, with its patterns and dynamics embedded such that our life in passing-time can unfold most soul-constructively in terms of lessons yet to be learned. Life will be saturated with detail in the now of the passing time of the next life.

Bache's account, of a lived psychedelic experience within the incarnate life in time, illustrates the intersection of the flows of time across eternity.

In Steiner's concept, with its different orders of time, it is clear that the soul can experience itself as existing in eternity. But if our conception of time is limited to that of passing time, of clock-time, of before and after time — further, if our conception of the world is narrowed by materialism, as it was for Nietzsche — when the deep soul intuition of these realities as described by Steiner flashes before us during a psychedelic session, it may be one can only conceive — and thus, only experience — the connection of eternity, the present moment, and passing-time, by conceiving of eternal repetition or recurrence; or else revert to the escape from the "wheel of life" of eastern thought. The soul must free itself to identify with the eternal, with the timeless, with the unborn. In so doing, it must transform its earthly sense of identity — itself the creation of passing time.

The livingness of each moment in eternity is part of the livingness of the etheric body. Everything good and true that is experienced in life on earth is preserved in the universal ether or akasha. To begin to become conscious of the life existing in eternity is to become free to be ever more living into eternity at all points of the life. To the extent that we are conscious only of passing time, that is doom enough; the danger is not, as Ouspensky describes, that we will be doomed to "repeat" the life; we are already "repeating" it insofar as we are not conscious — if only dimly or abstractly — of being timeless in our true essence, that is, unborn and undying. This unborn and undying part is present in us the more we are fully present to the now, the present moment.

The fact that the soul does indeed repeat successive lives on earth, as understood in the way Steiner describes, can lead to profound feelings of anguish to the extent that incarnation itself is experienced as divorce from the spiritual if one is still unreconciled with the Double. Once awakened to the realization that earthly life is instead the platform for both self-transformation and self-expression and self-revelation, the sense of divorcement will be healed.

As far as "why incarnate" — from Steiner's thought as I understand it, it is twofold — to develop a conscious realization of our essential nature in freedom, as opposed to a paradisiacal unconscious unity with our divine natures (a learning, in one sense) — but also, to participate in the process of transforming the earth collectively which can of course, further to the "learning" process, also require of us a karmic self-redemption process "in the flesh" as opposed to "merely" abstractly. We learn by creating karma.

With the idea of multiply intersecting streams of time, in my understanding, we are always in the present moment experiencing the "results" of our pre-earthly intentions — reflected in the "life blueprint" we have authored into our etheric in concert with the beings of the cosmos — and, to the extent that we may be (to whatever degree) "consciously present" in the here and now, we can also be in coherence with that phase of our being in the spiritual world (eternity) wherein we form our pre-earthly intentions, out of a knowledge of, among other things, our need for x, y, or z karmic resolution. The streams are always shuttling back and forth; and of course, as we move through incarnation, it is our tendency to experience what seems local to 'right now' in the sequence of time. The actuality of our realized experience gets painted into the etheric body as "memory," which we experience as the full-blown accomplished life tableau at death. The paint-by-numbers detail of the etheric template is filled with the actual "as it happened" opportunities wherein the script of our "empty" etheric is populated, improv style. Our possibility of karmic intersections with the freely-determined behavior of others in our world is so rich that "random" situations or individual encounters a, b, or c, provides an opportunity for the local realization of some aspect of the blueprint. Of course, there are all kinds of higher "coincidence control[244]" factors at work as well. And indeed, our inborn tendencies can be felt as having compelled our steps to many a fateful encounter.

Our birth etheric is not simply "potential" but a distinct formative structure woven out of the cosmos that patterns, as it were, astrologically, the way we will form our embodiment. It allows us to meet the experiences of life through a lens or tendency, a predisposition, to act out in a certain way that aligns with our pre-earthly intentions.

This pre-earthly intention may appear as clothed purely in the garb of our earthly conditioning of nationality, family of origin, of experience. While recognizing our predisposition toward certain inevitabilities, we at the same time can learn to be in a dialog with the possibilities coming purely from the future, to alternate pathways through the structure of our own deep pattern: to listen for opportunities to redeem destiny and to act creatively out of the guidance of that which is highest in us and the spiritual world.

The dissolution of the etheric at death allows then the arising in the consciousness of the "life review," which can be seen as a purgatory or *kamaloka* phase, is really an awakening to the realization of what we experienced each night in sleep, which was an unwinding (rewinding) of the previous day's events from the "outside-in" view ("how others see me,") which in its nature prompts the question: have I enhanced or detracted ecologically from my role in the cosmos?

The soul, in the full light of its own eternal divine being, is through this nature possessed of the impulse to make amends and re-balance the harm it may have done to the universe of fellow beings. This can only be concretely achieved by returning to the domain where the karmic imbalance occurred. During the second phase of the life between death and a new birth, the soul is active, with higher beings of the spiritual hierarchies and its own cohort of companion souls, working creatively to weave the possibilities of the future earth life. We leave the crude eye for an eye "justice" of the *lex talionis* and work together with others to optimize the growth of humanity into the spirit.

I envision this as a form of extreme psychedelic ecstasy, working and weaving with the divine natures of millions of souls, working together holographically on the unified ideal human being. Each time we enter a new life, we tear a shard from this all-encompassing structure and form the nucleus of our next life in time. As each part of a hologram can generate a smaller portion of the whole original image, so we can embody the universal human in our particular way. The sliced shard meanwhile has an affinity with the karmic residue we have left behind when detaching from our previous physial existence.

The product of this weaving appears in the etheric body which forms in the process of incarnation and is mirrored in the astrological milieu into which we are each born, as well as the real-world conditions of time, place, family, people, and heredity.

18

Psychedelics and Alchemy

Someone who takes a pill and finds their soul experience and consciousness radically transformed and altered, even if all the while characterizing the experience in some way as "spiritual" — transcending some of the constraints of the normal experience of the physical sense world — will have to sooner or later come to terms with a notion which, subtly or not, can insinuate itself even as we aspire to the spirit. The thought can persist: perhaps human consciousness *is* "nothing but" a side effect of the material world, and the psychedelic agent has brought about a change in the mechanical functioning of the brain, seen as the ultimate material source of consciousness.

Indeed, our thought patterns and everyday assumptions are so ingrained with materialistic ideas and forms of expression that we can find ourselves at times taking a step or two back for every advance we struggle through in our understanding — perhaps even without noticing this. The human being is profoundly complex, and in trying to develop an insight into the permeation of our incarnate existence by the soul-spiritual, one must struggle to find new ways to represent this to ourselves.

It is immediately apparent to the user of psychedelic drugs that they have triggered something that profoundly alters one's inner energetic embodiment, creating a substantial shift in the way one "metabolizes" (or digests) one's self and the world. We now see our reality expand to include an experience that expands to include something beyond the "stuff" of the world perceptible to our senses.

I first encountered the idea of a conscious inner alchemy while I was actively exploring psychedelics in my study of Gurdjieff began when I was sixteen. I encountered in there the idea that the "sly man" simply prepares a "pill"[245] for his (or her) self and easily obtains thereby what they seek by way of inner experience, avoiding the many long labors of the fakir, the monk, or the yogi.

It was part of the method of Gurdjieff to provide allusions, contradictions, and models that required the would-be pupil to always dig deeper. His teaching presented a system, on the surface novel and unique, intended to illuminate the various grades or levels of "matter" in the universe and show how they *alchemically* could be blended and transformed to create the psychic energies that fuel the subtle and intense experience of "higher states of consciousness." Although he was active before the advent of psychedelics in the Western world, these ideas seem to find ready correspondence with the psychedelic experience. He also held that grades of "matter" alternatively can be understood to be various interpenetrating "levels of vibration." One might fall into the misconception that these vibrations were nothing but oscillations in space of "matter" or "energy" after the fashion of electromagnetic energy or vibration, which contemporary science sees as a fundamental aspect of the entire universe.

It is rational to suppose that regarding this "pill," Gurdjieff was speaking metaphorically; the context was part of his characterization of his "Fourth Way." His primary point was that the individual could get what they need — with an intelligent and esoterically informed approach to one's internal alchemy that allowed one to work across one's mental, emotional, and vital-physical natures simultaneously. From one angle, this can be seen to correspond with Steiner's idea of the *Rosicrucian* way insofar as neither requires a withdrawal from the world for their pursuit.

One finds a similar idea in the alchemy of Taoism, where their yogic process — really, a meditative-breathing process — is also sometimes described as the preparation of the *pill of immortality*. The underlying notion here can also parallel the "philosophers' stone" of medieval European alchemy.

Alchemy is sometimes simplistically understood as the misguided attempt, or worse, charlatanry, that would turn lead into gold. Alchemy as a *spiritual* process has always been understood as the transformation of the "base material" of the natural soul into the "gold" of the realization of humanity's divine potential.

Continuing in my study of Gurdjieff, I found his further teachings presented the idea of *sense impressions* forming a kind of "food." This supplemented the food we take in through our mouth and gut, and the "food" of the air that we breathe. These latter two are seen by conventional science as each in their own way, contributing to the energetic, building-up cell metabolism that underlies our physical life. This characterization of sense impressions as *food* is, of course, not so understood.

Traces of this idea can be found here and there: we can find the visionary English romantic poet William Blake says in his *Marriage of Heaven and Hell*:

> "Man has no Body distinct from his soul; for that called Body is a portion of a Soul discerned by the five senses, the chief inlets of Soul in this age."

Reading "inlets" as channels or openings for the assimilation of soul nourishment.

In Search of the Miraculous includes an elaborate scheme of vibrational levels or primary materials referred to as "hydrogens,"[246] illustrated in a "food diagram" which indicates energetic flows within the three "stories" (head, chest, and gut) of the "human factory." It is all part of the complex cosmological scheme of Gurdjieff. In Gurdjieff's cosmos, everything exists as "food" or nourishment for something else, and the "level" of something is in some sense determined by the "level" of the next higher being it can serve to nourish.

Gurdjieff presents a diagram of the "human factory," which aims to show that matter and energy are naturally flowing and transformed in the "human machine" *except* in the head, where the evolution of "finer energies" that would be provided through sense impressions, comes to a halt, lacking a certain impetus.

This further impetus is only provided by the energy of the sense impressions being consciously and correctly integrated with the naturally-evolved energies of the breath and of food. This, in turn, can only be brought about by certain efforts in the sphere of our consciousness in Gurdjieff's method. This links back to Gurdjieff's idea of preparing the "little pill," which provides the "substances" needed by the aspiring soul.

This elaborate scheme is quite suggestive, although generally speaking, as far as my exposure to followers of Gurdjieff is concerned, perhaps not terribly well understood.

In the stream of esoteric Christianity which Gurdjieff indicated his alignment, these higher "substances" are understood as the "daily bread" of the Lord's prayer.

As the breadth of my psychedelic viewpoint was expanding, it seemed here was a key to the process of transformation indicated in the LSD experience.

It was meanwhile clear to me, for many reasons, that a continued diet of psychedelics was not practical, sensible, or necessarily healthful. To further attain to the complete spiritual reality that harbored these experiences, it became clear that an internal and, in some senses, sacrificial, transformation was called for. My journey through psychedelics had given me an appetite, a longing, to move my consciousness again into the places of wonder, of blissful liberation, of seeing and knowing — the edges of which — sometimes terrifyingly, sometimes blissfully — they had opened up for me.

I needed to orient my soul and its efforts in the direction of the eternal, finding in the physical-earthly the platform and fulcrum of such transformation.

My interest in finding this key was reinforced when I read in Lilly's *The Center of the Cyclone* how he finds, through his connection with Oscar Ichazo and his work at Arica in Chile, a way to correlate discrete psychedelic experiences recounted in the earlier chapters of his book with mappings on to the different "vibrational levels" found in Gurdjieff's teaching.

As there was nothing in Gurdjieff's work to indicate that this transformation involved any actual substances such as LSD — his work having transpired well before its discovery — coupled with Lilly's misleading characterization that his blissful realizations, vividly detailed, where the result of the training, and not psychedelics, the seed was planted that these states might be explored and achieved through alternative means than psychedelics.

Gurdjieff had once told Ouspensky, "We are more material than the materialists" — the materialists whose thought was ruling the day intellectually at the beginning of the twentieth century.

In all this, despite its status as an "esoteric teaching," one might again misread that it is merely a matter of the right *physical chemistry* to experience the "higher states."

My own spirit revolted against this idea. No matter how candy-coated with quantum indeterminacy, wonder at the vastness of the galaxy, or other elaborate models, this reading seemed to be seen as a variation of the "nothing but" verdict of reductionist science.

It might be understood that from one angle, Gurdjieff was rather trying to rouse and awaken the many disillusioned Theosophists among his students (starting perhaps with Ouspenky himself), seen as having blithely absorbed the words of Blavatsky and others too dogmatically. By providing a kind of "scientific" intellectual veneer that veiled the mystery while offering more of the "substantiality" of scientific theory (which science Gurdjieff heartily mocked elsewhere), he counters the tendency to substitute fantasy for rigor in spiritual effort and development.

Around the same time, at the beginning of the 20th century, this materialist trend was found, for example, as the "pseudo-spirituality" in the monism[247] of the German popularizer of Darwin's thought, Ernst Haeckel[248].

Steiner was a younger contemporary of Haeckel, and he admired him in certain ways while ultimately denouncing his monistic worldview as philosophically juvenile and in the end, warmed-over materialism. It is interesting to note that some trace the influence of Haeckel's monism as an influence in the development of Jung's concept of the Collective Unconscious, which in its concept of a "racial" or "collective" unconscious tends to lean on the existence of a material substrate for all this. Haeckel's monism would appear to provide an explanatory mechanism for the phenomenon of the hypothesized Collective Unconscious. In Steiner's worldview, one rather recognizes the source of the universal archetypes as arising from a spiritual world proper.[249]

I came to understand Gurdjieff's claim of being "more material than the materialist" rather in the sense of "more *substantial* than the materialists" — the substance itself simply being the substance of God, the Absolute, the *Prakriti* to *Purusha*, pure consciousness. At the soul level, "man does not live by bread alone, but by every word that cometh out of the mouth of God" — the latter perhaps conventionally understood as the "words of scripture," but esoterically, it is the Word — the Logos at the beginning — that creates and sustains human life and consciousness.

These ideas, of the substantial transformation of sense impressions were active in me, although fragmentary (Ouspensky subtitles his work on Gurdjieff as *Fragments of an Unknown Teaching*) on into my Arica experience, still connected with Lilly's psychedelic experiences, and then into my encounter with the work of Rudolf Steiner, where they were to undergo further development in my understanding.

In my non-linear absorption of Steiner's teachings, at length I began to find references here and there that seemed to resonate, at first strangely, with ideas I had encountered in Gurdjieff; ideas which, one way or another, indicate something transformationally significant in the way we process the experience of the senses. I found myself sensitized to these comments, which are not particularly well-structured into a specific doctrine across Steiner's teachings. In his other comments regarding the life of the spirit, various processes and shadings or nuances are indicated here and there, either more or less directly. These are to be considered and understood alongside Steiner's more straightforward indications regarding meditation and the spiritual life.

Near the end of his life, Steiner delivered his agricultural course, which would inaugurate the biodynamic farming movement. Almost buried within it, one finds him concretely describing what he calls "a cosmic nutrition stream" flowing through the senses in contrast to the "earthly nutrition stream" in our normal foodstuffs. He details flows in two directions, of different cosmic-energetic quality, permeating and forming the complex of embodiment — there, as applies to animals, but as could be generalized to human beings. As is very often the case in Steiner's pictures of the operation of spirit in human life and existence, one finds things apparently the opposite from what one might expect: the more *cosmic* elements form the *physical* being and are derived from the cosmic nutrition scheme, through the senses; and the head itself is built up by the energies of the earthly nutrition stream. The energetic metabolism, as observable by science functions as a *stimulus* to the formation of the body from the cosmic nutrition stream. Of course, these ideas can only be at rationally understood and conceived if one sees existence as a process of a supersensible spiritual world and its beings.

To begin to understand all this and to eventually relate it back to the question of psychedelics, there are other elements of Steiner's view of the human being to bear in mind. He sees the incarnate human being as threefold: a nerve-sense head human being, a rhythmic being of heart, lungs, and pulse; and a metabolic-limb being.

In Steiner's worldview, all of creation is the deed of higher beings and, in fact, *held in their consciousness*, to the extent that it is not nested and held in ours. Just as in Steiner, humans have *Imaginative*, *Inspirative*, and *Intuitive* consciousness and knowledge — the stages of higher cognition — so too the higher hierarchical beings experience these consciousness-states, which, in their cosmic scope and activity, effectively *create* thereby everything about our existence both in the life between birth and death, and the life between death and a new birth. For Steiner, "The World-Word is not some combination of syllables gathered from here or there, but the World-Word is the harmony of what sounds forth from countless beings."[250]

If we shift ourselves in thought into this other perspective, Steiner would further have us understand certain foundations underlying our daily existence. One rather difficult for us to accept or grasp is that there is no such *functionally distinct* thing as the so-called "motor nerves." Or rather, that the (obviously really existing and anatomically distinct) nerves do not act as is supposed, that is, our "willing" is not actually effected out of our brain and mediated through these nerves to our muscles. This is despite all superficial appearances, which Steiner explains as indicating how we *sense* the activity of the will in the same manner in which we sense with our eyes and ears. The will, which Steiner sees as a primal cosmic element, arises *directly* in our limbs and metabolic activity itself. In the will element, however, Steiner sees our consciousness as *asleep*.[251] If a nerve is cut, we can't move the corresponding limb because we can no longer *sense*, and thus control, the will potential in the limb itself. "Motor nerves" serve a function alongside the proprioceptive nerves, that is, those nerves that allow us to sense the position of our limbs and skeleton.

While thus asleep in our will and metabolic-limb system, in the rhythmic system of heart, lung, and pulse, where our feelings originate, we are not asleep but rather *dreaming* all the time. Images constantly arise, only partially observed, in all of the activities of the body and feeling life. [252]

It is only in the head, that is, in our thinking and nerve-sense system, that we are fully awake. Across this spectrum of degrees of consciousness within our own being, there is thus a gradient between the forces of death and life: our waking, thinking consciousness is, in a sense, deadly to our organism, and we must have an interval of unconsciousness during which the effects of the disorganizing and deadening influence of consciousness can be restored in sleep. (This corresponds to the image of the eagle — thought — devouring the liver — life — of the mythic Prometheus chained to the rock, which is then restored each day.) The alternation of waking and sleeping brings about a rhythm of "creative destruction" — i.e., of consciousness — and restoration, where the intensified etheric process corresponds to our unconscious phase. On awakening, we are restored to a regenerated brain/nervous system that has meanwhile structured itself to incorporate the learning processes of the previous day.

These degrees of vitality or vivification in the conscious experience of the body correspond to the degree of activity or engagement of the etheric body — the body of formative forces that underly all growth and which we as humans have in common, first of all, with the (profoundly sleeping) world of plants. One can speak in the sense of degrees of loosening of the etheric: the looser the etheric — which, cosmically/spiritually understood, is a body of thought — the closer to death, and the greater the play of consciousness or awakening. The death swoon can be seen as a last effort of the etheric forces to restore the body by completely suppressing the death forces of consciousness.

The elaboration of finer shades of energetic and substantial intensification occurs entirely within the inner soul nature of the human being. These processes can only come into our scope of conscious awareness through the loosening, through whatever means, of the connection between the etheric body and the physical body. In this framework, we might suppose that psychedelic drugs somehow act to further loosen the etheric, particularly, it would seem, the activity of the etheric in the brain.

It is notable that in recent writings, such as Michael Pollan's *How to Change Your Mind,* one finds reference to a conventionally conceived model of the brain and mind that means to show that under the influence of psychedelics, what is explained as the "default network" — the "normal" patterns of connection between different parts of the brain — is disrupted. While obviously the MRI readings and other brain state measurements these theories are based upon are indicative of different functional states, this "network" model would suffer, from the anthroposophical perspective, from the kind of "nerves as telegraph wires" fallacy that Steiner sees in the modern doctrine of the motor nerves[253.]

What we can understand from Steiner, as mentioned previously, is the idea that it is when the true *I* begins to emerge in the process of higher cognition that the activities of thinking, feeling, and willing are no longer as mechanically interdependent. They begin to disassociate and to function increasingly free of one another, that is, an activity in one function no longer merely associatively triggers a corresponding deterministic response in another. The brain, with its billions of interconnections, does perhaps form a system of reflexive *perceptions,* wherein our thinking, feeling, and willing — understood already as a spectrum of different shades of consciousness, wakefulness, and vitality — responds to the organized filtering of these perceptions in determined ways, and conditioning the way in which elements within our awareness are associated. And perhaps our brain overall is thus itself a "self-configuring sensory organ," delivering the final perceived experience of our conscious reality. As Goethe said, "*The eye is formed from the light for the light*"; likewise, the brain is formed from consciousness for consciousness. The transformative work is thus to more consciously organize the sensed reality of our earthly existence. The work includes "seeing through" the web of perceptual automation that form the "narrow chinks" referred to by William Blake.

We can think then of our entire embodied experience as a form of sense impression — a single net percept — and thus "food." We consume this, our lives, digest it, metabolize it — psychologically.

The psychedelic experience perhaps restores the nervous system, temporarily, to something resembling that of the child — that which we must become to "enter the kingdom of heaven." A key difference possible in our adult consciousness as compared with that of childhood is that, if we are so equipped internally, we can retain and maintain our *I* consciousness — providing our ability to recall our soul experiences, whereas our memory of being an *I* does not extend to the earliest years of childhood.

Studying anthroposophy, we can begin to learn that there is a complex of spiritual-physical process involved in our sense experience and daytime consciousness that weaves into the deepest layers of our souls. These processes form a substantial intermediary in the transformation of our consciousness and, indeed, substantial being.

It seems apparent from the phenomenology of psychedelic experience that there is somehow a physical-material aspect to the way in which we modulate the experienced consciousness of our physical embodiment. Expressed alternatively, we can effect the modulation of the degree to which our etheric natures adhere to the physical body, particularly to the instrument of the physical brain. In our day-to-day awareness, this tension between the etheric and physical is maintained such that by default, we experience the relatively bland and hum-drum experience as compared to the "turned on" experience of psychedelics, or, in another mode, certain spiritual experiences of higher cognition. We can, again, readily echo Huxley's invocation of Blake in describing his own psychedelic experience back in the 1950s:

> If the doors of perception were cleansed every thing would appear to man as it is, Infinite. For man

has closed himself up, till he sees all things thro' narrow chinks of his cavern.

The "narrow chinks" are formed by the web of unconscious, habitual associations which enables us to function reliably in the three-dimensional physical world. It may be understood, however, that this "adhesion" of the soul to the body and world of the senses has become excessively unhealthy insofar as it has bound us to the physical earth world as if it were the sole reality.

There is, from the esoteric perspective of Steiner, a hidden depth to these processes, which he touches upon in his lecture cycle, *The Effects of Spiritual Development*, he refers to the human skull as being the "grail castle."

> ... the Legend of the Holy Grail tells us of that miraculous food which is prepared from the finest activities of the sense impressions and the finest activities of the mineral extracts, whose purpose it is to nourish the noblest part of man all through the life he spends on earth; for it would be killed by anything else. This heavenly food is what is contained in the Holy Grail. And that which otherwise takes place, that which presses up from the other kingdoms, we find clearly represented if we go back to the original Grail legend, where a meal is described at which a hind is first set on the table. The penetrating up into the brain where for ever floats the Grail, that is, the vessel for the purest food of the human hero who lies in the castle of the brain, and who is killed by everything else — all this is represented. [254]

This passage has both intriguing echoes of Gurdjieff's so-called "food diagram" and also the thought that psychedelics somehow catalyze processes in the brain. The whole question of how substance, sense, brain, and consciousness intermingle to result in the spectrum of experience possible in earth existence is, obviously, profound, and as stated, there is a broad seam of indications in

Steiner to indicate paths to deeper consideration. I will restate my own conviction that the primacy of the spirit as the source of consciousness is paramount and that however deeply we penetrate into the neural functioning of the brain, this needs to be balanced by a worldview that can see beyond the concept that the merely particulate, the inert, point-centered provides the foundational fabric of life.

Just as countless physical happenings within the body, including even the processes that support consciousness within the nerve-sense system, "chip away" continually at our life forces till, at length, the body succumbs to death, so psychedelic substances create a certain kind of (ideally) "controlled burn" within the brain and cause a *temporary* loosening of the etheric parts of the brain from the physical brain.

It would seem obvious from this concept that a process of recovery, integration, and ultimately, the unconsciousness of sleep is required to restore the brain-body complex to the state of healthy day-to-day function. Indeed, it is one of the most perilous conditions for the individual to be deprived of sleep for any extended period, and in some individuals, an intensive manic state can persist, triggered by the psychedelic episode, preventing sleep and leading toward an uncontrolled disassociation from external, conventional reality.

The question to be addressed elsewhere is, to what extent does this intensified "death process" interact with our ability to perform the long-term transformational work of sculpting the etheric into a more perfect microcosmic reflection of the spiritual world as can be experienced in our episodic detachment of the etheric as with psychedelics.

This mechanism of "etheric detachment in the brain" seems to correspond in some ways with earlier methods of healing and initiation, such as "temple sleep" and total immersion baptism, in their own way acting to loosen the etheric.

The anthroposophical worldview strives to understand the whole of creation as the product of the deeds of spiritual beings, who call into being all that we perceive and experience in the creation as fundamentally the expression of the *Intuition, Inspiration,* and *Imagination* consciousness of spiritual beings, whose reality provides the true substance behind what we experience as "reality" — whether of physical existence or of our own "higher consciousness" in *Imagination, Inspiration,* and *Intuition* as may be realized in our own being.

When speaking to medical doctors, Steiner once explained how during states of fever or delirium, the "hallucinations" experienced are disordered perceptions of our bodily organs. To some anthroposophists, this reference may sanction the dismissal of the "hallucinations" of the psychedelic state as "nothing but" the analog of the delirium of fever; but a broader and deeper reading of Steiner would understand that perception of the *spiritual reality* behind the physical organs is in itself a profoundly significant phase in experiencing the cosmic reality behind earthly existence: their actuality is that of higher cognitive-being states of higher spiritual entities.

Our present-day consciousness is the accumulated result of a process of an inevitably-destined divorcement from the spiritual world, compounded in recent cultural history by an outwardly highly successful intellectual evolution of the scientific method in the nineteenth century, so materially fruitful in many ways. Having all but abandoned the traditional sources of connection with the spiritual world, which, in the West — whose culture has become all but global — we find our souls greatly vitiated and attenuated by the superficially contradictory findings of science and a generally undeveloped spiritual conception. The traditional forms can no longer be squared with the many domains of humanity's modern knowledge of the world. The resulting forces in our head are stale, abstract, and deadening, and unable, without proper leavening, to transform the realm of the senses.

These ideas about sensory impressions and how we "consume" them as playing an alchemical role in the individual's process of spiritual development and evolution are underscored by indications by Steiner elsewhere in his work that there was a change in the essential aura of the earth sphere such that before The Mystery of Golgatha,[255] our primary soul-nourishment was provided through the *breath*, and afterward (and more and more) it is to be provided through the *senses*. At the simplest level, it is, of course, a truism that our destiny and karma are fulfilled through "what we experience" — that is, seasonally — but this indication is to be taken, in my understanding, that it is a matter of our learning to see the spiritual reality *behind* the sense appearance. We can learn to *Imaginatively* read the outer semblance as a revelation, in every detail, of spiritual beings and realities, as a reality of living thought.

The etheric loosening occasioned by the psychedelic state has the possibility of precipitating this domain of perception. The question that immediately attends this statement is — will the individual respond with sufficient discernment to disentangle the concurrent loosening of their own astral (soul) nature and its attendant reality-distorting possibility from the other possibility: a coherent encounter with the spiritual world. The loosening also leads to the transformative inversion the soul experiences.

Individuals striving to see that psychedelics can find their best destiny in modern culture must struggle to come to grips with the implications of the "little pill" of the sly man and discover a means to contextualize it in a modern conception of an evolving world of spirit.

In understanding Steiner's teaching about reincarnation, the cycle of birth and death can be seen as the ultimate transformative process impelling the metamorphosis of our earthly sensory experience into spiritual gold. In our review and beholding of our previous life from the perspective of the spiritual world, we come to see the soul-inward changes we must follow in order to build the forces of the next lifetime. We find inward moral energies activated that, in the end, can be seen as ultimate world-creative forces when we see them from this life and look back at the pre-earthly perspective, the coming into incarnation.

Gurdjieff's model suggests that the stream of sense impressions is to be consciously transformed with an activity in the head in order to bring the potential of the "substantial" energy of the senses to a higher level.

Contrariwise, Steiner's characterization of the "cosmic nutrition stream" is described as if it were something *already effective* in the household of the human being.

Surely, if we are to see the metamorphosis between life and a new birth as the ultimate "alchemist" in the cosmic process, the material of the soul experience of a given earth life must, of course, influence the degree of creative realization in the spiritual world that is possible. What, then, is the role of the aspiring individual consciousness?

Steiner depicts the realm of soul-spiritual that is known in full intensity after the karmic life review as that of the *harmony of the spheres*. In this state, the entire world process is experienced intensively as operating from a unified, all-embracing, all-manifesting, all-expressive *harmony* of beings and actions everywhere. And indeed, in higher states of cognition and being within the earth-life — states which can include the psychedelic in some instances — it is possible to sense and experience a reflection of this harmony and see it effective in the world around us that we perceive through our senses. This may be muted, or perhaps all-absorbing, by degrees as may depend.

Looking at Gurdjieff's food diagram, which he provides as if an indication of the preparation of the "little pill," he indicates the point in the "human factory" where a disjunction occurs. This is explained as taking place where the sense impressions enter into the dynamic process. I came to understand this as simply showing the point at which we must bring our souls into harmony with the harmony of the world-process. This world process is expressed in the experienced world in which our souls, collectively and in concert with the beings of the higher hierarchies, have created as the platform for the fulfillment of our countless individual destinies.

In a passage by Steiner cited earlier, he explains that we must "insert ourselves into the cosmic harmony." I came to this with a sense of "arrival" during my psychedelic experience with Ash on the nighttime walk to the beach in the summer after I finished high school. It is both a cognitional process — to see *Imaginatively*, to experience *Inspiratively*, and to unite with, in spiritual *Intuition* — and a will process, a process of embracing one's destiny, of identifying not with one's "little I" but with the step-by-step unfolding of the path we ourselves architected in the pre-earthly existence, in concert with the highest wisdom. This cognitive-will process is a process that is driven by and assented to by the true spiritual *I*. One finds in Steiner an image of a state of development where thinking becomes enlivened and permeated by will, and the will becomes awakened through living thinking.

The "new energies" of the Gurdjieff model are the *existing* energies of the spiritual world; they do not "accumulate" to our personal account other than by way of momentum and by providing a platform for the transformation of our vehicles of existence from lower created forms, gifted us by the cosmos, to higher spiritual forms, wrought by our own deeds of knowing. What is to be gathered in the alchemical process is the energy of the myriad psychic splinterings that draw our energies into countless different conditioned personas.

The threads, currents, and weavings of our destiny are knit into the outer world we perceive with our senses and with the inmost sinews of our being. If we can learn to perceive the spirit we seek within and beyond the forms and substances of the earth world — and come to see this earth we inhabit together as a new *heaven* in formation, we align ourselves in balance with the progressive trend of spiritual evolution.

It is ultimately a question of assent to the spirit.

19

To Dose or not to Dose

I'm mindful that through this writing, some people will reasonably expect that I make a straightforward, definitive statement about the use of psychedelics, pro or con. This question — to dose or not to dose — was, of course, the one posed by my fifteen-year-old self at the opening of this book.

It should already be obvious that as far as my own biography is concerned, psychedelics have played a significant role, one that I see as a critical part of the arc of my own process of inching toward awakening. By implication, this could apply to countless others.

I find there is no unequivocal answer. I can, however, say that the assurance given by my friend Alan — that one won't see God, in whatever fashion — is one I can't provide. You may find yourself challenged — and perhaps, graced — spiritually.

One of the principal characteristics of psychedelics is they will tend to amplify — to a point — whatever is already present in you. If you are mostly good, happy, and healthy inside, that is good. Most of us are probably neither wholly good nor wholly bad, wholly sane, or wholly imbalanced, and, by and large, we all stand in need of some degree of realignment and awakening. Good or bad, regardless, one may also be carrying an instability, known or unknown, psychological or neurochemical, that complicates the equation. Instabilities also can be amplified — and possibly resolved — or not. As was sometimes the case with my own age group peers, psychedelics were associated with long-term psychiatric consequences.

With a little openness, sincere intention, courage, supporting surroundings (people and places), and some good karma, you may find in psychedelics something that heals or awakens. It is not a path without obstacles.

The categories of "bad" or "good" in describing a trip are perhaps too simplistic and judgmental. But some trips are definitely challenging, possibly very challenging, and some quite possibly disruptive.

If you are drawn to exploring psychedelics, particularly as an avenue of spiritual unfoldment, my advice is first to start at the low end of the dosage spectrum. Even if you feel that you have "got your bearings," these agents demand deep respect. You may or may not wish to explore higher dosage psychedelics, as you find yourself drawn that way or not: but one cannot be too prepared for the intensity with which reality can break in on one.

Having opened the psychedelic box, its proper role in both self-development and spiritual research itself then comes into question.

My own path was only half-consciously approached. I was lucky insofar as there was a lot I had absorbed to structure my experience and its integration, such that in the end, it could have a net favorable outcome for me. There was also definitely the stage of finding I had signed up for a lot more than I had bargained for. In my experience among age-group peers, my impression is that those who actively prepared themselves by learning about the possibilities in some way before their first psychedelic trip tended to have the most favorable outcomes.

Initially, some may wish simply to experience the wonderous and kaleidoscopic re-shuffling of one's experience that low or medium-dosage psychedelics can provide for its own sake. But eventually, one will either quit and say that was fun/interesting/weird — or even bad — or else likely find oneself compelled, sooner or later, to come up with shifts in one's paradigm of reality.

All in all, I would advise the individual to approach these agents with appreciation, in whatever way that is meaningful for one, that they have a sacred character.

When I first conceptualized to myself the idea of working toward and aspiring to a higher level of myself — a spiritual level — it was couched in the idea of the attainment of some state of unity with some ultimate spiritual reality. This idea was styled as the transformation of being along the lines of classical notions of satori, samadhi, and so on that come from Eastern traditions. This was reinforced particularly by Lilly's scheme of levels in *The Center of the Cyclone*. Lilly had also correlated these levels with the various types of samadhi described in the *Yoga Sutras* of the yogic scholar Patanjali (who lived over two thousand years ago).

In Steiner, we find the focus of self-transformation expressed primarily in terms of the development of higher forms of cognition — of *knowing* and *seeing* in the spiritual world. He delineates three levels of higher cognition: *Imagination, Inspiration*, and *Intuition*, and to each of these terms, he gives a very special kind of meaning beyond their usual everyday sense, although they are related.

They do, of course, also correlate with corresponding states of being, and their attainment is predicated on certain changes within one's nature. *Intuition*, in the sense that Steiner uses it, is a state of knowing that is achieved through lovingly merging with the spiritual being of the object of knowledge. It is, in fact, axiomatic for Steiner that "for every single step that you take in seeking knowledge of hidden truths, you must take three steps in perfecting your character towards the good[256]." Again, Steiner is in no sense referring to specific ethical or moral strictures as may be culturally or traditionally defined — although obviously, they bear some relation. He rather refers to the intimate sense of responsibility for one's actions within a spiritual universe. That is, a spiritual universe where everything has a karmic consequence in the sense of leading the individual and the world forward, or else holding it back, across the destined drama of cosmic spiritual evolution toward deeply realized, actualized *love*.

Very often, psychedelic drug use is initially something one does to get high — to experience well-being, ecstasy, release. Yet *passively* getting high as an end in itself is, in the long run, a blind alley. The spiritual world — the ultimate source of true bliss or blessedness — will only invite you fully into its domain if you can bring yourself into alignment with the broader destiny of, to start with, one's fellow humans and with the cosmic relationships this implies.

All manner of content may become active in the psychedelic session and appear visually, aurally, through feelings, intimations, visions, and so on. Again, the nature of psychedelics is to amplify much of whatever exists in one's "container of consciousness" — or, alternatively, astral body. Thus beliefs and assumptions will tend to color one's entire experience, even as new sources of input and experiences begin to impinge. Indeed, one may find one's self confronted, for example, with some form of "ultimate implication" of one's beliefs played out.

How, then, does one come to discern what is actual, assuming one has accepted the idea that there is a spiritual world that lies beyond the physical? In physical reality, we are more or less able to test our assumptions about reality in a way that others will also agree with: "fire burns," "rock is heavy," "the sun shines," and so on. In states of higher cognition, it is entirely different.

The first such stage of *Imaginative* perception, as understood in Steiner, is characterized first and foremost by being composed of *Images*.

The soul is constantly weaving images: images first formed out of our physical vision; thoughts; dreams; and, if we are alert to it, a subtle stream of images emerges as a faint background to our bodily and feeling life.

Imaginative cognition, for Steiner, is the development of the art of reading the meaning behind our soul images. Just as one may "read someone's face like a book" — and grasp what is being expressed outwardly or transpiring inwardly in the facial gestures, the physiognomy of another, so one can learn to "read the book of nature" and understand a non-physical reality lying beyond appearances. This is the sense, for example, that Goethe, in his "Theory of Color," implied when he referred to colors as "the deeds and sufferings of light." For Goethe, light bursts forth upon the world, revealing through its actions (deeds) a part of the color spectrum (the "brightened dark" of the blue colors); and suffers the darkness to modify it (it must "suffer" the darkening in the yellow-orange), revealing another part of the spectrum.

We hold our image of the world together, our picture of it, having since childhood learned to associate certain pictures or occasions with others, other feelings, sensations, and finally, associations with other memories and their pictures.

During the psychedelic experience, what can be understood anthroposophically as an enhanced loosening of the etheric body begins to occur. This loosening is analogous to the ultimate separation of the etheric body from the physical body that occurs at death, but here the loosening is primarily seen as localized to the etheric analog of the brain-nervous system.

There also seems to be what can be understood as a loosening of the astral from the etheric/physical complex in a manner similar to what Steiner describes as occurring in sleep. We get a sense of the first stage of this kind of loosening by considering the in-between state of hypnagogic awareness and the state of dream recollection. One can also observe how drugs that may be anesthetic at high doses can give rise at lower doses to an in-between state of flowing images. Ketamine is an example of this, but it can also be seen in opiates and other hypnotic drugs.

In this motion away from the close association with the body and sense experience, the overshadowing of the *I* can begin to be experienced such that the broadly defined soul functions of thinking, feeling, and willing, active respectively in the nerve-sense, rhythmic, and metabolic-limb systems, shift their habitual modes of interaction among themselves. This can unfold variously depending, among other things, on the classic psychedelic parameters of set, setting, and dosage. Set, however, should be understood not merely as one's psychological mindset or disposition but as the state of one's whole psycho-physical being.

This disassociation of the soul functions, as described by Steiner, is not necessarily a clean, straightforward process but rather surfaces when the various integrations between thinking, feeling, and willing — which we have built up throughout the course of our life — begin to shift and dissociate in various ways. This may be experienced as overwhelming or as liberating. Or — both. One observes that the functions have been bound together in different ways and react upon each other variously with the force of habit and that they can unwind playfully, serendipitously, chaotically, or surprisingly as well. Correspondingly, this plays out in our image consciousness as it likewise becomes unbound and less rigid as all manner of inward boundaries and contours dissolve.

The contents of our astral body flow across the loosened etheric interconnection of the soul functions. One's soul content mingles with the imaginative experience of the "outer" world: physical, elemental, spiritual. The ability to see across different semantic levels of experience, to hold one's soul, not in a point centered on our bodily awareness, but holographically out of our spiritual essence, out of a relation to the spiritual "I am," is what must be cultivated.

We thus move into an entirely different relationship to the "world" around us — a world which, if we so understand it, is purely a world of spirit. We come to see that this includes the so-called physical forms apparent to the everyday consciousness. One can become aware of an elemental-etheric world of forces and beings all around one, and within and alongside of all of this, one's own soul-being can likewise stand revealed as if outside of one. In our everyday consciousness, we are blind to the elemental being of the spiritual. As our eyes are opened, we discover *ourselves* as we exist as spiritual beings.

Across the continuum of intention and attention or focus as expressed in one's own self-conscious thinking — which, as in daily life, can vary in its balance, its focus, its resolve — one can come to see through the psychedelic state that one's thinking and the images, as they appear before one's inner sight, seem to more and more reflect a dynamic world of being and *beings*. One's imaginative view can be re-configured, as it were, as the boundary between one's inner self, the content of one's soul — the entirety of what conventional understanding would call one's unconscious — can transform and migrate into the pictures of what appears as "outer world" or non-self. In a way, this can be seen as a kind of turning inside-out.

This etheric loosening creates, in various degrees, an "unbundling" of one's entire experience of self in the world. As one's etheric ambit seems to expand, one may "feel into" what appears as different levels of reality. The amplified sense of expansion and disassociation from the properties of the "physical world" can give rise, for example, to the confused sense that one can (physically) fly. One must be alert to the danger of confusion of semantic levels in how one's experience of reality is composed.

This type of de-structuring of one's previously tightly-adhering set of associations can, at the extreme, lead to undesirable results such as psychotic states of various degrees of detachment from outer reality and absorption in an inner landscape and its narrative. At extreme, this can occur such that so-called "normal" interlock with outer reality cannot be maintained either at challenging stages of a psychedelic episode or, much more concerning after the primary metabolism of the agent should have completed and a more normative "poise" within the composite self restored.

The perhaps most significant marker that this poise has not been re-established once the drug has been metabolized is if the individual is unable to sleep subsequently and instead is maintained in a high-energy activated state. In my view, individuals in this condition (unable to approximate normal sleep 24-48 hours after dosing) are best served by a medical (pharmaceutical) intervention that can interrupt the activation, which can otherwise become self-propagating and increasingly disturb essential equilibrium. Opinions may vary, but this is my view.

The ability to restore one's default parameters of connection to the outer world is stressed by Steiner as a basic requirement for a healthy relationship with the spiritual world — one has stretched this to an extreme when one commits one's self to the duration of a psychedelic agent's metabolic elimination period.

However, it is possible to bring one's self into a state of poise within this change and to even possess a certain sense of control over where one goes with one's image-world and total sense of context. Indeed, being able to re-orient and discern, for example, different semantic levels of reality emerging, and to become aware of tracks of experience — such as, for example, the disassociation of thinking, feeling, and willing from their more mechanical relationships is itself a form of Imaginative "reading."

In Steiner, we also find that certain canonical "*Imaginations*" are present within and accessible to the spiritual human being, and some of these we could characterize alternatively as "archetypes" more or less after the manner of Jung. However, in Steiner, these "*Imaginations*" are "*realities* to be perceived *Imaginatively*" and are concrete expressions of thoughts and impulses of spiritual beings. Because they are accessed cognitively through the individual's image-forming capacity, they may appear variously and tinged, as it were, with accidents of the individual's soul-formation as determined by their life experience.

Amidst this image-flowing, so greatly amplified under the influence of psychedelics, where then is the touchstone of spiritual reality? In my understanding, it comes on the one hand from a sense of truth that arises with the awakening to the reality of the spiritual *I* that may be found as the self witnesses the decomposition or de-structuring of the accidental, conditioned "self." This sense is then coupled with the recognition and acceptance that, relative to the world of higher spiritual existence, one is, willy-nilly, burdened by one's personal allotment, as it were, of world karma that has, consciously or unconsciously, become one's own possession and responsibility. Plus, of course, one's own karmic catalog. In Steiner, this portion is revealed to one's self through what he describes as the encounter with the Double (*doppelgänger*) or "Guardian of the Threshold."

Any descriptions of spiritual reality, such as that of the Guardian, are limited by the necessity of using everyday language to attempt their description. Although the Double is sometimes characterized as if it appears as a genuine Double — a literal mirror-image of the physical self — its appearance as experienced or sensed will be various. It is the dynamics of the encounter that are what is significant.

Returning for a moment to Jung, the Double, in some ways, can be seen as corresponding with the "shadow" — one's unrecognized and unacknowledged negative features that function nevertheless as an unconscious source of psychic dynamics underlying awareness and behavior.

In Steiner, we have to transform ourselves to recognize in this nature a kind of *actual* spiritual entity (as opposed to a Jungian "psychic complex") which, on the one hand, can be seen and owned as part of one's being and at the same time, held apart. It must be recognized as an independent actor in the spiritual world. Our karmic predispositions, which are sourced in the Double, can and do operate independently of our conscious awareness.

The Double undergoes a process of transformation into a kind of "guardian spirit" as one embodies within one's self the ethic of the "mystic vow" referred to elsewhere. Present as such, it can serve to contextualize the cognitional landscape to allow us to render transparent and thus distinguish the merely personal, our own private Idaho[257], our "reality distortion field[258]," from what one otherwise may know as spiritual reality in the highly dynamic and relativistic imaginative state.

Jung studied the dynamics of what he hypothesized as the "Collective Unconscious" primarily through dreams and what he called "Active Imagination" (very distinct from *Imagination* in Steiner). All of these ideas must be transposed into the domain of actual spiritual reality. Unfortunately, much of psychedelic theoretical work leans too heavily on Jung's notion of the Collective Unconscious and the Archetypes in a way that, in my view, impedes the understanding of the relationship to the spiritual world that can be awakened by, as discussed here, psychedelic consciousness. And it is this actual relationship that humanity so desperately needs if it is to surmount the challenges confronting us on every hand.

The further understanding of what Steiner denotes as *Inspiration* and *Intuition* is perhaps best left to one's own study of anthroposophy. The simplest characterization is that they tend toward a spiritual knowing that is experienced through direct union with spiritual beings, wherein love itself becomes a cognitive force, leading one into the ultimate source of reality. Deeper forms of dialog with the spiritual world imply a degree of poised surrender to a higher level of being.

If we come to the idea that it may be possible to truly discern truths and aspects of higher reality while in the psychedelic state, we are next called to make a distinction between personal self-transformation and what an anthroposophist, at any rate, would call spiritual research proper.

"Spiritual Research" can encompass both the knowledge of the human process of development and also the knowledge of broader spiritual details of humanity and world evolution. In as much that psychedelic exploration is, first, a "research" into one's own self in the process of development and transformation, the idea that these agents may, in some cases, be helpful would seem to imply that they likewise may have a role in this kind of wider "spiritual research." Concerning the second notion, that of usefulness in discovering *new* details of cosmic knowledge, I am a little bit more dubious.

The primary reliance on a chemical agent to provide one with access to one's "research tool" in this second category suggests an unseemly impatience for the pursuit of a discipline that, in essence, requires the precision tuning of the primary instrument — that is, the spiritual organs of the investigator. And if, for continued research, repeated recourse to the agent is seen as a primary part of the means of knowledge, it does not seem hard to make the case that too-frequent (and what this means obviously varies by individual) use of these tools can have an unbalancing effect. A balanced earth-consciousness and power of judgment, as well as modesty, seems an absolute requirement to effectively discern and communicate universally relevant tidings of the spiritual world.

Meanwhile, our understanding of these two categories of knowledge as distinct needs to be balanced with Steiner's repeated view that knowledge of self and world are inextricably intertwined. This is reflected in Steiner's verse at the front of this volume.

In his time, Steiner was a very vocal critic of the trend of spiritualism and mediumship that emerged at the end of the nineteenth century. Seances and mediumistic communications with the dead — insofar as they were not mere charlatanry — were seen by Steiner as an unwholesome path to spirit, in that the medium yielded their own consciousness to the control of other spiritual entities that spoke through the medium, whose consciousness was lowered or effectively obliterated for the duration of the visitation. As I understand Steiner, his concerns were at least twofold: the individual should rather be developing their own spiritual nature, to in effect, "posses" their *own* bodies with their *own* higher selves, in clear consciousness. This latter is necessary, then, to discriminate and evaluate in rational, earth-bound consciousness (a thing, of course, quite distinct from that of the merely materialistic worldview) the messages and influencing of the dwellers of the spiritual world. This is, ideally, pursued most effectively if it is the experience of one's *own* higher self that one is thus soberly reviewing.

Steiner sees our souls, astral natures, as being interpenetrated by countless spiritual beings that influence and affect all manner of our functions and awareness. These are normally held in balance by the instincts and habits of our earthly consciousness; one must do this consciously as one expands one's horizon into the spiritual.

What Steiner refers to as mediumship would be more likely described as channeling today. In general, his concerns would seem to apply to channeling as well. It should be noted that Steiner acknowledges that, in certain cases, valid and valuable information from higher spiritual beings can be voiced in this way. For Steiner, the age of priest-kings, of initiates overshadowed by higher beings, ended at the time of the Mystery of Golgatha, and the earth-sphere is now illuminated by the being Paul encountered directly at the gates of Damascus, the story of which serves to indicate that each individual is able to form their own relationship with the highest aspects of the Godhead, individually and without an intermediary, without priest or guru.

This is not to say there are no beings in the spiritual world trying to break into earthly consciousness with tidings and teachings from the spiritual world. Psychedelics can provide such a window for them; as with channeling, the question rather becomes how to evaluate these once we recognize that there are a host of differing agendas amongst the beings and forces we can encounter as coming to us from the spiritual world.

There is another kind of "mediumship," or rather unconscious influence from spirit entities that are not aligned with what Steiner sees as the best destiny of humanity. This may be seen in the permeation of all aspects of our culture with the presence of digitally mediated data, occupying an ever-increasing portion of our consciousness and, more importantly, pervading our unconscious mind. The flavor or character of this cultural medium is essentially Ahrimanic or technical; just as spiritual beings pervade nature, the technical invites the influence of the Ahrimanic class of beings. Steiner never shied away from accepting the value of technical advances; he only stressed that each step deeper into the culture of technology needs to be balanced by a corresponding advance in our spiritual development.

This Ahrimanic or devilish aspect of technology as such is reflected in images like William Blake's "Satanic Mills" of the industrial revolution, ranging on to the fantasies of the transhumanists (many of whom have a relationship with the technology industry), who wish to create a kind of mechanical immortality. There is a wish, for example, to transpose the human soul (as understood by them) into a virtual reality heaven. The envisioned "extension" of the mind to some kind of "supercharged" state with "all the world's information" at the fingertips is a picture of a soul-stifling reality far more perilous than a mediumistic seance.

Psychedelics, in certain respects, can provide a direct experience by the individual of spiritual realities while preserving the element of individual consciousness. The success of this is, however, conditioned by many factors. In this light, we might see the advent of psychedelics in the culture as a counterweight from the Luciferic pole opposing the arid and mechanical digital onslaught.

However, these two elements can — as always with the Ahrimanic and Luciferic trends as Steiner sees them — intertwine, mingle, and amplify each other if not properly recognized and understood and balanced and held apart. The balance between them is the critical question.

It can, I think, be observed fairly that there may be a point at which individuals who repeatedly and frequently (there is no precise metric here) resort to the psychedelic state without a counterbalancing of integration, reflection, and self-development in the non-psychedelic state can yield a trend of thinking (in particular, regarding their experiences) that, even at the broadest remove from "bourgeois consensus reality," must be considered as dubious.

Gleanings from the stories of others are meaningful — why else might I share my own experience? I see these "travel diaries" as perhaps signposts and models of transformation as well as testaments of inner witnessing and, in some cases, warnings of what to be on the lookout for.

We can see that one of our problems is, starting with our early explorers — clearly, we are at the "early days" stage of understanding psychedelics — that we have lacked adequate concepts and frameworks with which to think about them. Certainly, any number of frameworks have been resorted to.

It may be useful to observe a few of the particular streams of thought that have emerged within the dialog around psychedelics.

The first stream, certainly relative to LSD, is found in psychoanalytic and psychiatric thought — this was the first channel through which the LSD psychedelic journey was promulgated. Timothy Leary *et al.* were originally part of this. We can see that a lot of Carl Jung's thinking on the so-called "Collective Unconscious" and its archetypes is often applied and extended to suit the psychedelic context. Another psychiatric schema found applied is that of Stan Grof and his "Basic Perinatal Matrices," which evolved out of his early psychiatric studies of LSD in what is now the Czech Republic. This traces itself back to the birth trauma thinking of Freud's one-time disciple Otto Rank. This medicalized approach, which may, in the end, yet be instrumental in both facilitating therapeutic approaches and promoting legalization, is burdened by the implied materialistic framework of Western medicine. Western medicine has, nonetheless, countless valuable services to perform.

Next, and perhaps foremost from an avowedly spiritual perspective, is what can be called the Eastern trend of thought as reflected in Hinduism, Buddhism, and Taoism, in particular. These were often resorted to by some of the early popularizers, such as Aldous Huxley, Gerald Heard, and again Timothy Leary (among many others). And, of course, this trend led to the emergence of Richard Alpert as Ram Dass, the perhaps quintessential example of the "straight" psychedelic explorer transforming themself into a profoundly committed spiritual seeker. Anthroposophy itself represents a spiritual stream that can acknowledge and appreciate the Eastern traditions, which it has many points of contact with while providing a reflection of the best in Western spiritual and esoteric traditions. From an anthroposophical viewpoint, this Western stream is perhaps better suited to a global life of humanity, which, for better or worse, has been effectively Westernized in countless dimensions.

Other trends include what might be referred to as variations of neo-shamanism; this is consistent with the fact that psychedelic practices have been preserved by shamans and other keepers of knowledge in parts of the non-Europeanized world, despite colonial efforts at suppression. Peyote, psilocybin, and ayahuasca are native, particularly, to the Americas, and knowledge of their sacramental use has existed through millennia within indigenous American populations. The American mainstream awareness of psychedelics was reinforced in 1955 by Gordon Wasson,[259] who located and then convinced the Mexican curandera María Sabina[260] to introduce him to the magic mushroom (psilocybin) experience. This trend was continued in the late sixties and seventies by the writings (now seen as of dubious authenticity) of Carlos Castaneda.

Another broad stream might be called the rationalistic-scientific (or quasi-scientific), of which John Lilly is an exemplar. This stream is also reflected in the adoption and application of ideas of quantum physics, computer technology, and so on to the understanding of "far-out experiences." Terrance McKenna perhaps can be seen as straddling the neo-shamanistic and rationalistic streams of thought. On the one hand, McKenna seems to romanticize (cf. *Archaic Revival*[261]) a psychedelically inspired cultural past while projecting into his story a view of evolution that is itself the product of the most spiritually bereft phase of consciousness and un-psychedelic rational thinking. I am referring here to, among other things, his "stoned ape" theory. This theory, as I understand it, is more or less something bolted onto a conventionally Darwinian origin story.

Regarding the "stoned ape" and similar "psychedelic backstories," — If psychedelic drugs have a legitimate use in forward-looking humanity, they do not need to be "baked in" to an origin story to somehow increase their validity. Building many of these kinds of stories tends to simply reinforce the scientific materialism of the nineteenth century. Spiritual life can, in the end, only be sustained by a vision of a spiritual origin. But it is understandable how, lacking an origin story that can speak to the modern consciousness, attempts to form bridges such as these are resorted to.

Where, then, does the anthroposophical worldview fit into the discussion?

There is a spectrum of possibilities for people engaged to whatever degree with the work of Rudolf Steiner, regardless of their relationship to psychedelics. One pole might be defined as those on one end who wish to start by studying and absorbing

Steiner's teachings as support and guidance in the understanding of their own process of self-development and also in their participation and creative expression in the life of ideas. Or in developing an understanding relative to the practical results of Steiner's work, such as Waldorf Education, Biodynamic farming, or anthroposophical medicine.

The other pole would comprise those who primarily wish to follow Steiner's indications for developing higher cognition.

In between, there are any number of points along the continuum.

In the context of this discussion, in part because of the — in many ways, traumatizing — extreme stigmatization of psychedelic drugs that our culture has suffered, and in part because their use does not factor into the path Steiner delineated, questions arise.

Steiner was first and foremost the advocate of personal freedom in all areas of life, with spiritual activity uppermost. At the same time, he was candid and direct about, among other things, various well-known substances ranging from tea and coffee to opium, cocaine, and alcohol, among others, in terms of how their effects are perceived and understood from the perspective of the clairvoyant consciousness he claimed.

Alcohol is the case regarding which he perhaps expresses himself most emphatically. He views that its use is diametrically opposed to the becoming development of the *I*, and that it is essentially disqualifying for the pursuit of the path of higher cognitional development that he teaches. At the same time, he recognizes that, as a matter of individual karma, not everyone has the destiny or opportunity to pursue this particular development, and that meanwhile, the study of anthroposophy itself and the incorporation of the spirit of anthroposophy as a force in an individual's life can be pursued independently of his path to the development of higher cognition. It is known that he himself did consume alcohol at early stages of his own biography[262].

He has also remarked, matter of factly and without judgment, that simply through the karma of vocation — in his example, that of a wine merchant — one would be inhibited from pursuing his path of higher cognition — while still participating in the life of anthroposophy.

Repeating a general principle of his about the requirements of safely pursuing conscious experience in the spiritual world, Steiner emphasized that one must retain the freedom and self-control to return to the everyday world of normal waking consciousness *at will*. The nature of psychedelic drugs introduces a question here insofar as the drug effect will persist for as long as it takes for the physical body to metabolize it. And meanwhile, at certain dosage and experience levels, some individuals may largely maintain an ability to relate "normally" to the outer world.

If we allow that psychedelics can unlock a doorway to a radically enlivened experience of the spiritual world, what then are we to make of all this? Recognizing that the times have perhaps unveiled a perhaps challenging, perhaps significant, new doorway, at the very least, it seems appropriate to reflect on the underlying anthroposophical wisdom and attempt to apply it to the psychedelic case as follows: to exercise great caution in striving to utilize psychedelic substances specifically to do what might be called "concrete spiritual investigation" without regular and fully-grounded recourse to the drug-free context of the earthly day consciousness and the kind of integration that is only possible there.

Steiner has commented that in order for the spiritual investigator to discover anything new, they must first establish a deeply grounded relationship with what humanity has already discovered in the spiritual world. There is, of course, such a diversity of viewpoints in these matters that it is perhaps difficult to establish what is and isn't truly known. The suggestion for me is that one must root one's self in a profound study, of some character, of what earlier spiritual explorers have uncovered. This is not "traditionalism."

Consider then the case of John Lilly. With respect for all of his groundbreaking achievements, it seems apparent that he became unreliable as a witness to reality during the peak of his Ketamine involvement. I recall hearing him speak at Wainwright House about how a psychedelic drug (such as LSD) was a "contract" that kept you committed for at least eight hours. It seems that on the one hand, the attraction of the short-term effects of Ketamine gave the semblance of allowing him to avoid the "long-term" contract and to return to the "here and now" of earth reality, but through his repeated "chain-smoking" type usage, wherein he would maintain the psychedelic state for hours (and days), he was bypassing the critical phase of integrating the experience from the earth-grounded consciousness.

This would seem essential not only from the point of view of being able to express and articulate, and test, one's experienced insights from a neutral point of rational judgment but also to integrate the whole individual soul-complex in alignment with the constraints of being an embodied individual. The excesses he so ruthlessly documents in his *The Scientist* should serve as a cautionary tale to the would-be, so-called "psychonaut."[263] One might also observe that his "skeptical scientist" posture, to a large extent, disconnected him from a deepening relationship with any form of traditional spiritual practice. Such linkage with the spiritual aspirations of historical humanity can provide a kind of soul ballast as one explores.

The felt need of some to sever themselves from exoteric (or esoteric, for that matter) traditions that, for them, are understood as stifling, repressive, narrow, etc., can pose for the individual a special challenge in this regard.

Steiner, who was profoundly impressed and influenced by Friedrich Nietzsche (while ultimately seeing him as unable to overcome the materialistic trend of the 19th century), observed candidly that Nietzsche would regularly work intellectually and creatively under the influence of chloral (chloral hydrate), a sedative with potentially soul-stimulating effects. He did not judge but simply characterized that it let his *spirit* act more freely of the body. As mentioned, Steiner viewed that Nietzsche was, in the end, tormented by his inability to reconcile his felt, half-conscious spiritual intuitions with the all-pervading intellectual influence of the so-called "limits of knowledge" and 19th-century scientific materialism.

We come then to the general question, how much psychedelic use is "enough?" I find myself reminded here of the old Ex-Lax commercial about using prunes to relieve constipation: the debate being "Is one enough, is six too many?".

Alan Watts, author of the work *The Joyous Cosmology*, describing an idealized psychedelic trip, is well known for having stated therein: "When you get the message, hang up the phone. For psychedelic drugs are simply instruments, like microscopes, telescopes, and telephones. The biologist does not sit with eye permanently glued to the microscope, he goes away and works on what he has seen."264

And yet one reads about early explorers like Leary and Alpert tripping what seems like countless times; early explorers like Roshi Joan Halifax (ex-wife of LSD researcher Stan Grof) report hundreds of high-dose (600 mcg) sessions, and more recently Terence McKenna, or Chris Bache who likewise reports a very focussed course of over 70 high-dose (600 mcg) experiences. These explorers seem to have pursued these sessions at various levels of discipline and, perhaps, with differing goals.

At the extreme, the attraction of this repeated desire to experience the psychedelic space might possibly seem to correlate in a certain way with a scenario Rudolf Steiner describes taking place near what he calls "The Cosmic Midnight" in the life between death and a new birth.

In Steiner's description, the soul has been living in the spiritual world for some time; it has reviewed its past life and released itself from the attachment to the earth, and dwells as a spirit among spirits. A moment occurs when the harmony of the spiritual world is suddenly sensed as bestirred by a troubling onset of disharmony: it is the dawn of the call to a new earth life. Near this time, the being of Lucifer would tempt the soul with the prospect of remaining in the spiritual world — that is, the world between death and a new birth, despite one's imperfections — which are promised to become, indeed, perfections. However, if the invitation of Lucifer were to be accepted, the human being would forgo their possibility of fulfilling the goal of the "Good Gods" — the creation of the ideal human being, the full realization of the highest spiritual potential. The Good Gods intervene, however, and project the human spirit back into the world of space toward the womb of the next birth265.

The repeated dosing with psychedelics for the sake of the experience perhaps reflects, at bottom, our longing to dwell eternally in the spiritual world as spirits. Of course, in earth life, simply the metabolism of the agent itself leads us back to the earthly consciousness again.

It should be noted at this point how essentially different the thrust of Steiner's vision of the life between death and a new birth — the bardo state — is in certain ways from what you might understand from, for example, the *Tibetan Book of the Dead*. One can see many points of contact, but there the taking-on of a new incarnation being seen as a sort of "temptation" — which one is to resist in order to dwell, not in "heaven" but the nirvana of the clear light. In Steiner, it is instead the light of the spirit as mediated by Lucifer that is to be dimmed to prompt the return of the soul to earth life, where its future destiny may unfold toward the realization of the ideal human being.

And so, in what way are a life path that includes psychedelics and anthroposophy compatible?

I can only speak from my own case. My destiny led me through fairly intense use of LSD before I encountered anthroposophy. I can say that this prior history was absolutely instrumental in guiding me eventually toward it. The richness of that lived psychedelic encounter continues to serve as a prompt in my embrace of anthroposophy.

In my early contact with anthroposophy, there was a period of a year or two where I would study anthroposophy intensively, although still in the process of "working it in" to all else I had absorbed — while continuing to use psychedelics. There are points where I can see my thinking about anthroposophy definitely seemed to influence the content of my acid trips. During this time, I didn't experience any sense of contradiction but rather reinforcement.

When my psychedelic use waned and then essentially stopped, I found my study of anthroposophy integrative relative to my LSD use and that my LSD background meanwhile provided a huge context of data for almost everything I took in as anthroposophy. At length, my absorption of the anthroposophical worldview came equally to contain my insights into my psychedelic experience. I have tried to somewhat indicate this process in these pages.

Having years later dipped into the psychedelic stream with mushrooms on a single occasion, I can acknowledge to myself the possibility that some time or other I would explore that again. Should that transpire, my motivation today would, I think, fall into the category of celebration or the festive. I have the notion that I would find myself observing a certain boundary between the experience and the engagement in the direct study of the works of

Steiner: that is, I would leave Steiner on the bookshelf. I would, of course, very significantly carry within myself all that has been wrought in my soul by their study and related practice. There are a lot of other things I wouldn't do while tripping either! My sense here is that Steiner spoke and wrote for us to digest his material from the platform of our fully-grounded earthly consciousness and reason. This is simply my predisposition.

Psychedelic use and exploration will be a phase of practice and encounter for countless people as we straddle this evolutionary period of transition out of our present cosmic alienation with its hyper-intellectualistic worldview. It will take humanity a long time, I think, to purge itself of the burden of crude materialism and move forward into a more avowedly conscious knowledge of the spiritual world and grow into the love that is to be found there.

20

Therapy and Celebration Container and Intention

Although my narrative begins with psychedelic exploration motivated initially by a purely recreational interest, the focus has been centered on the spiritual aspect, on the role of psychedelics in the individual process of awakening. There is a third type of intention, the explicitly therapeutic one, seeking healing from trauma, unresolved issues, or chronic psychological syndromes such as long-term depression. Healing, of course, in the broadest sense, can be understood as the restoration of wholeness — a need that can be seen as applying to us all.

It is perhaps generally helpful then to discuss three distinct areas of usage: therapeutic, spiritual, and recreational (or, with more dignity, the celebratory).

An organic threefoldness would find each of its constituent elements reflected in the other. That is, the therapeutic perspective would have aspects of the spiritual and the celebratory within it; the spiritual, the therapeutic and the celebratory; and the celebratory, the therapeutic and the spiritual. However, our culture today is fragmented such that there is not a unified worldview that makes integrated understanding and practice within and across these domains fluid and complementary. These categories can instead have a tendency to be treated as if more or less siloed to a certain extent. But the reality of these substances is such that it is impossible to make any such categories water-tight.

This splintering of perspectives reflects a more general aspect of our cultural development. In earlier times, science and religion, therapy and the mysteries were, in various ways, integrated as part of a comprehensive worldview. Healing might take place in the temple, and spiritual mystery teachings were revealed through festivals.

These categories can be thought of as containers — specific "sets and settings," or, alternatively, types of intentions — within which the psychedelic experience is pursued. The therapeutic and spiritual containers are sometimes seen as operating through the sanction of corresponding stewards or authorities who monitor and legitimize their use within that domain. So, the therapeutic container can be seen as the domain of the psychotherapist or psychiatrist, and the spiritual domain is sometimes associated with specific rituals and traditions, as guided, for example, by indigenous elders and shamans (this is particularly the case in the ayahuasca community). Of course, the individual is free (disregarding legal constraints) to pursue spirituality or healing however they may wish. Yet, from some points of view, there is the idea that stewardship, guidance, or elderhood is needed for psychedelic use to be pursued responsibly.

The recreational or celebratory space may however be characterized as the domain more or less defined by the absence of any kind of credentialed steward. Indeed, due to the illegality of most psychedelic substances, this category, in particular, has an "outlaw" quality. That is not to say that individuals in this domain are initiated into psychedelics willy-nilly: in my experience, one always tripped for the first time with someone who was "experienced." The parameters of trust, of appropriateness, of competence, however, are necessarily rather loosely defined. In all categories, the potential for abuse, particularly sexual abuse, exists when one comes under the influence of another in the highly vulnerable psychedelic state. Where to confide one's trust is a critical question.

There are certain types of "containers" within which the "recreational" experience is typically pursued, such as concerts and festivals. The "outlaw" quality however leaves the question of "set and setting" essentially wide open.

Aside from the stewardship of peer companions — friends — a certain form of stewardship initiatives have evolved in the efforts in *harm reduction* through peer support, as best exemplified by the Zendo Project at events such as Burning Man. Zendo organizes both a safe physical space and a cohort of psychedelically experienced peer "sitters" and has evolved a set of principles, ethics, and best practices that comprise the training of volunteer sitters. This is made available to support individuals who find themselves experiencing a challenging psychedelic episode within the essentially celebratory context and container of the Burning Man experience. In this way, there is a community of users proactively supporting responsible use.

In the end, of course, it is a matter for the individual to determine for themselves how these agents may be used most responsibly. It is clear enough that they are powerful and are not to be trifled with or approached frivolously, although the human predisposition to pursue the liberating sensation of intoxication in whatever form can certainly bring that about. My personal observation is the better educated an individual is about the possibilities of the psychedelic experience, the more likely they are to have a net favorable outcome.

These incredibly powerful and transformative agents call to us to work from an image of the human being and of the world that provides a context wherein these domains — as they relate to the psychedelic experience, practice, and understanding — begin to harmonize.

Although one may first approach the psychedelic state with an implicit intention that is limited to either the recreational or the therapeutic, the agents are no respecters of our categories, and in the end, the inherent tendency of these agents towards the spiritual node will eventually assert itself, especially at higher dosages and/or repeated frequency of session.

In the context of therapy, one, of course, hears the word *healing* used in connection with what psychedelics can offer. When one looks at the domain of psychedelic therapy, it becomes clear that there are deep reservoirs of trauma in our world that perpetuate cycles of suffering at many levels.

In my own biography, I have no formal experience with psychedelics in a conventionally therapeutic context. I have probably a somewhat typical familiarity with the contemporary psychotherapeutic process through more conventional modalities of marriage counseling and the like, or friends or family members who have suffered with, for example, depression and had recourse to conventional pharmaceutical therapies.

Neither of these two domains, of therapy and of recreational (or celebratory) use, can be properly (or fully) integrated into our cultural life without the development of a more comprehensive spiritual understanding. It is in the nature of these substances that only in this way will the proper unfoldment into usages and practices emerge that will have a net favorable impact on humanity's forward progress. That is, through the many perils of our time, we can move toward our best destiny within a spiritually understood cosmos.

This is not to say that much good does not already occur in the forward-striving efforts in these separate domains. The step-by-step efforts, for example, of those guiding MDMA through the rigors of safety and efficacy trials with the FDA in the treatment of PTSD[266] will, if we assume success, undoubtedly bring much healing and relief from suffering to countless individuals. Similarly, Ketamine, which can legally be prescribed, is undergoing increasing adoption by the psychiatric community for use in the management of treatment-resistant depression. Its use will expand the understanding of psychedelics in the clinical context greatly.[267]

From every indication, it seems that there are many specific therapeutic uses of psychedelics as part of an integrated course of therapy with a guide or therapist qualified with the requisite skills. What this qualification is, at present, is still in the process of forming.

And similarly, it must be acknowledged that the large scale if ultimately illicit, distribution of psychedelics starting in the sixties has let the psychedelic genie out of the bottle and, despite any number of less desired consequences in individual cases, brought the question of an immediate experience of alternate realities to humanity's doorstep as a challenge that must be answered.

Soul-healing, in the form of psychotherapy and counseling, however, can be seen as having a somewhat dubious relationship with the medical profession. The "medicalization" of psychoanalysis, of psychiatry, goes back before Freud and to the custom of referring disturbed individuals to medical doctors. Today psychiatry, a field that was once the domain of psychoanalysis and the "talk cure," is overshadowed by medication-oriented treatment. Indeed, much of the current enthusiasm for psychedelics such as ketamine or psilocybin reads as if it is a breakthrough pharmaceutical treatment for the miseries of depression, anxiety, and so on, in the form of yet another pill prescription. Within the domain of Ketamine therapy, there are shades of practice and understanding as to whether the therapeutic effect is primarily, or even solely, a mere pharmacological effect or a result of the catalyzing of specific experiences and subsequent integration at the level of cognitive therapy. Excepting, perhaps, the case of micro-dosing, the "purely pharmacological" viewpoint strikes me as a simplistic and disingenuous characterization. When the spiritual perspective is included, it seems self-evident that deep healing is brought about as a result of the content-rich experience the psychedelic session can induce and the corresponding processing and integration — in the psychotherapeutic context, with the involvement of a counselor.

Thinkers such as Thomas Szasz[268] argued against the definition of social or personal problems as medical conditions. The primary point of Szasz's thesis was that by medicalizing certain conditions, society exerts unwarranted control over individual choice and freedom. The issues raised by Szasz are extremely relevant in the context of the societal regulation of psychedelic drugs, and to play the medical psychiatry game at all is to invite social control of the use of psychedelics in general. We have only to look at the Covid vaccine controversy to underscore how fraught medicine, society, and individual freedom can be.

From the spiritual perspective, an underlying concern is the fact that with the conventional medical model, one is largely buying into the model of materialistic science. This model assumes that life, soul, and consciousness are ultimately derived from chance combinations of eternal, anonymous material particles. This image is bereft of spiritual substance and the possibility of acknowledging an eternal dignity and destiny of the individual human soul. Yet it is this very dignity that is the essential source of any true healing, and of course, awakening, in the soul domain.

Progress in the domain of establishment psychotherapy is, of course, fraught due to the legal situation with respect to psychedelics such as psilocybin. As in the case of MDMA, the way forward toward de-scheduling seems to be through demonstration, through measured outcomes, efficacy and safety. One might further suppose that this could result in sufficient cultural acceptance, as has seemed to occur with marijuana, to lead to eventual legalization for recreational use, to becoming essentially unregulated.

I am not in a position to make anything resembling a further proper critique of the state of psychedelic therapy, I can only offer impressions and certain observations.

One sense that I do have is that a deeper understanding of the idea — which will be difficult to import into conventional therapy — of the "etheric loosening," which is an obvious notion in an anthroposophical consideration, and more specifically of the idea of the "imaginative life tableau", will be useful. I get the sense that, for some individuals at any rate, the ability to "view their life in a long shot" — as a whole, all at once, as was so well described by Bache — is in itself essentially therapeutic. In this regard, psychedelics so applied are analogs of the ancient healing art that Steiner refers to as "Temple Sleep," wherein the sufferer of a specific illness was put into a trance state for three days — sojourning meanwhile in experiences of the spiritual world. It is also reminiscent of the earlier tradition of full-immersion baptism, originally not an outer ritual but rather part of an initiatory awakening — as a trigger to the detachment or loosening of the ether body from the physical. How this understanding of psychedelic experience might be developed into therapeutic protocols that can be effective and safe for modern individuals and modern psyches remains a question to be developed[269]. In the domain of spiritual transformation, it is an essential insight into the psychedelic state.

One of the leading psychological thinkers that one encounters in literature today is Stanislav Grof, who has perhaps the most extensive hands-on experience with psychotherapeutic psychedelic session work going back to the sixties.

A great benefit of Grof's writings is that it helps depathologize psychedelic experience and, in so doing, help provide a framework for the deeper understanding of related psychotic conditions — in line with the original psychiatric thinking about psychedelics as "psychotomimetic," that is, modeling in experience the psychotic state. It can be observed that the typical medical "therapeutic" response to individuals presenting with extreme dissociative symptomologies is that their experience is wholly pathologized and discounted. Rather than being met with any degree of sympathetic comprehension of the internal state, individuals are medicated back to a more stable state that disconnects them from the — admittedly disturbing — flow of inner experience. The pharmaceutical disruption of the state may indeed be appropriate to restore the individual to the possibility of a balanced integration of the experience; it is support for this integration that psychology needs to develop models and methods for. The vigorous suppression of the material of the disruptive consciousness may, however, further disrupt the "hydraulics" or dynamics of these soul-stirrings.

Grof is further notable for some key concepts — one is the idea of what he refers to as the *holotropic* nature of altered states; that is, the tendency or instinct to find wholeness when psychedelic or similar (ie, holotropic breathwork)[270] states are induced.

His other primary idea, extensively developed, is that of "Basic Perinatal Matrices," referencing stages of the birth process as providing insight into, among other things, neurotic or other maladaptive psychological effects resulting from (real or imagined) birth trauma. These ideas are interesting in that they provide a fourfold map of the psyche, and further, they direct attention to the time before the soul had memories formed by its conscious *I*.

There have been any number of fourfold psychic maps. These include the classic idea of the four temperaments, the Jungian idea of four psychic functions, and so on. Generally speaking, one can find similarities between different systems simply because of the way they divide the conceptual space.

In the light of the idea that the real soul-spiritual process underlying the psychedelic experience is an actual loosening of the spiritually real body of formative life forces, Grof's theories do not take us far enough. Such a loosening can serve as a step toward developing the consciousness of the soul's pre-earthly existence — which, again, anthroposophically understood, is itself the source of karmic or destiny-laden formations or configurations of the individual psyche. Birth is seen as the doorway from the spiritual world and not the primary root of individual psychic structure.

And frustratingly, for all of his far-reaching readings of the spiritual life of humanity and observations of the way in which material that reflects echoes of this spiritual life can emerge in a psychedelic session, Grof — as Jung in the psychoanalytical context before him — often hews close to the posture of the "legitimate scientific spokesperson" and exhibits a certain reserve or reticence about the reality of spirit[271]. This, again, is part of the shadow of 19th-century materialism that remains part of the foundation of contemporary medical science. Some will see Grof and Jung as brilliant modern-day conceptualists of the spiritual life; considering their work as a whole, however, they at times rather dance or vacillate across the borderline between asserting truths of the spirit and retreating to the pose of the skeptical scientist[272]. That said, it also remains true that we must maintain our ability to examine all things free of prejudice — with the intellectual possibility of skepticism available.

Of course, this reserve is understandable from one perspective, and as the case of the academic reception of Steiner shows, navigating this frontier — affirming spiritual truths while according with the verifiability needs of the scientific approach — will challenge mankind for times to come. There is no disputing that in contemporary civilization, asserting the primacy of the spirit in anything resembling a scientific context is to flirt with discredit. Rudolf Steiner himself is perhaps the best example of why not to do this: despite his more or less impeccable academic credentials, he is readily dismissed or pooh-poohed by many one would think might be best equipped to take him seriously. My hope, however, is that within the psychedelic community writ large, a foundation will be formed to contextualize the activity of integration into a modern, spirit-affirming framework.

But in the domain of psychedelics, to fail to discover and assert the primacy of spirit is to invite a failure to achieve the possibilities of the moment. To serve humanity, it is necessary that we integrate them in such a way that one is able to move forward with the development of a progressive, spirit-informed vision of the future, rather than, for example, simply adopt a backward-looking romanticization of traditions — which, undoubtedly, have much deserving of our respectful interest — preserved by non-European cultures.[273] It is true that the conventional Western exoteric spiritual tradition (as in the form of the churches) is ill-equipped to provide needed guidance in this area. It is the thesis of the present book that anthroposophy is a deep reservoir of wisdom to be plumbed as humanity, including those drawn to psychedelics as a tool for transformation, strives forward.

What then of the category of use that we might dignify as being that of celebration, but which, of course, also includes the idea of recreation — a word which can mean "just for fun" or, more deeply, providing an opportunity to truly re-create our life-affirming soul forces. Of course, "good clean fun" in itself is re-creative.

Students of Rudolf Steiner will know that he was at pains to stress and re-animate the observance of the traditional seasonal festivals — which he often would characterize from the point of view of the traditional Christian calendar: Christmas, Easter, St. John's Tide, and Michaelmas. These reflect his teaching of the cycle of the year reflecting a "breathing process" of the earth — conceived as a spiritual being — and how deepening our consciousness of the passing of the seasons can enhance our meditative relationship to the cosmos. (This is reflected particularly in his weekly meditations, the 52 verses titled *The Calendar of the Soul*.)[274]

Although they are redolent with a certain spiritual element, the typical seasonal festival among anthroposophists are rather tame affairs and don't quite reflect, for me anyway, the spirit or image of a cosmic jubilee. It is perhaps difficult to picture how Steiner might have seen the further resurrection of the festival spirit amongst elements of today's humanity.

Meanwhile, the psychedelic has certainly been active in animating "festivals" from the days of Woodstock (and before) to today, with the most avant-garde of planetary celebrations being, I think unquestionably, Burning Man.[275]

One could, of course, devote several books, at least, to the many facets of Burning Man — a weeklong gathering in the unforgiving heat of the desert playa in the Black Rock Mountains of Nevada.

Considering Burning Man is to observe that there is a deep-seated urge to celebrate, to celebrate communally, and to, in some manner, give oneself over to a context where the strictures of consciousness wherein which we dwell from day to day are somehow relieved. And some will turn to the possibilities for celebration that psychedelics can afford.

Somewhat typically, or, at any rate, as I experienced it, many people will first experience their introduction to psychedelics at a low or moderate dose in what might be considered a recreational context (many others, of course, come to their first experience with a more transformational intent) — this is perhaps also a function of youth versus more mature years.

From there, the experience can range from "didn't like it," "that was interesting," to "that was beautiful," and, of course, much more. For some, it will be simply a brush-up; for others, the start of a deeper exploration. It is my thought that one cannot expect to continually drink from the wellspring of psychedelic joys without, at some point, encountering the threshold and what Steiner refers to as the Double or Guardian — however that may paint itself into one's psychedelic context. This is to simply say again, there is no waterproofing the silos.

Relative to the recreational-celebratory pole, then, we can perhaps see that the therapeutic — that is, the task of untangling one's bedeviling soul-knots — and the spiritual — achieving one's footing on the path of spiritual development — elements will assert themselves as demands of the psychedelic consciousness sooner or later and that the *purely* recreational use, or intention, is likely not a long term option — at least, not at any level of intensity. It is reasonable to suppose that ill-effects of repeated use of psychedelics as experienced in some cases are a function of trying to solely enjoy them in their recreational aspect as an end in itself.

Looking into my own life, I can see that there is, perhaps, a place for therapeutic-integrational work around the accumulated inner-karmic material of a lifetime: after all, my intensive engagement with psychedelics was as a largely inexperienced and, in a certain way, (mostly) innocent youth. At the same time, I feel I meanwhile have access to a broad set of alternative tools to work through ongoing self-development needs without necessarily resorting to the therapeutic psychedelic session.

On the other hand, I can see myself being attracted to the idea of the occasional celebratory use. It was clear to me during the more recent mushroom experience that simply being in the heart-and-soul opening space of me, mushrooms, spirit, and nature was deeply fulfilling. And I felt an inward blessedness at the way spirit had revealed itself to me in my life — through the two facets — anthroposophy and psychedelics — which I try to discuss together here.

As to the spiritual intention proper, my anthroposophically-informed spirituality would certainly flow (as it did) into celebratory use; as far as psychedelics as a primary agent for my own continuing development, I feel that in many ways, I have "got the message" as Alan Watts would say. But life in all its facets is grist for our continual self-transformation.

Considering all of this, where do we want to go in conceiving a more psychedelic-positive future? Marijuana still exists in limbo between state and federal legality. Will psychedelics enter the toolset of establishment psychotherapy? This, to me, implies pharmaceutically manufactured (and sold) agents, and with this form of legalization, strict regulation. Will this be able to (legitimately) support spiritual or recreational use?

Meanwhile, knowledge of psilocybin mushroom cultivation is rapidly becoming deeply socialized, almost certainly in a way that makes its future availability impossible to restrict in our present society, and indeed, at a local and state level, it is on its way to legalization or decriminalization. As such, it will likely be increasingly available for all categories of use for those who seek it out.

There is presently an understandable, from one point of view, hyper-animated enthusiasm for all things psychedelic; the repressed, once released, gushes forth in self-assertion. Somewhere the best spirits within the psychedelic community must find the balance to cultivate and promote the sane and progressive use of these agents in a way that minimizes possible harm. If we see the present shift in expanded interest and acceptance of psychedelics as tokening a renaissance, this early phase is in some ways challenged with the recovery and recapitulation of the psychedelic blossoming of the sixties with a sober appreciation of "lessons learned." As Edward Albee said in his play *The Zoo Story*[276], sometimes it is necessary to go a long distance backwards in order to come a short distance forward correctly.

The best near-term future may be a therapeutic milieu that can accommodate the spiritual perspective while achieving the standard of being pharmaceutically "safe and effective" (in the context of concurrent counseling) — while at the same time, a legally decriminalized domain for, at any rate, psilocybin, wherein a responsible set of norms evolves that further the best use of these powerful agents. Initiatives underway as of this writing in Oregon and Colorado will be most interesting as they develop[277].

The most intense of my own experiences herein include what should be considered results of high-dosage usage, which are bound to bring the individual into the domain wherein the threshold of the spiritual world can be encountered definitively. This type of high-dosage use was perhaps more typical in the days of the ready availability of LSD. To the extent however that the more or less unrestricted availability of psychedelics such as magic mushrooms — which are perhaps, most typically experienced in more moderate doses — will allow some individuals to explore these high-dosage domains, the development of a container of healthy spiritual concepts across the psychedelic community is a critical need especially if high-dosage experiences will be integrated back into society in a constructive manner. It is from the spiritual understanding of these high-dosage states that needed insight into more measured use must come.

21

Closing Thoughts

For those who have come this far, having started the journey with little or no previous familiarity with anthroposophy — I hope I may have motivated your own further interest, independently of the subjective biographical elements to which these ideas are attached here. I'm not going to suggest — as disingenuously, John Lilly did at the end of his *The Center of the Cyclone* with respect to Arica — that anthroposophical study and practice will lead you in a short time to a spiritual experience comparable to the full-on psychedelic state. I will state that Rudolf Steiner's teachings offer a worldview and practice that allows one to pursue earthly destiny with an ever clearer sense of purpose, of meaning, and of coherence with the reality of higher worlds. It can also foster the cultivation of an underlying, readily available mood of harmony with the unfolding of cosmic reality in the multiplicity of earth life. It is a question of pondering and reflecting on how one sees oneself progressing through the world and one's individual destiny.

With the idea that at least some few of my readers are already committed anthroposophists, both with or without psychedelic experience, I want to acknowledge that the path to higher cognition as outlined by Steiner is perhaps the safest and surest in the long haul and that the purpose, meaning, and mood of harmony indicated can unfold without psychedelic drugs.

At the same time, I want to address further comments regarding some of the several instances of individuals who, generally well-grounded in anthroposophical thought, have made various remarks about psychedelic drugs, just as I do here. More often than not, it seems these thoughts expressed are more or less dismissive or outright negative. One finds psychedelic drugs grouped with other drugs which are very well understood to have severe abuse potentials, such as opiates and amphetamines. Recourse to anthroposophical concepts is made in rationalizing these statements.

An example of this can be found in the work of the late William Bento[278] — who contributed much that is praiseworthy in advancing an anthroposophically informed approach to psychotherapy — in his *Lifting the Veil of Mental Illness*[279]. He writes as follows, where psychedelics are included in a more general discussion of addiction. I single this passage out because it is written many years after the initial influx of psychedelic controversy in the sixties and seventies, and perhaps summarizes any number of, in my view, misapprehensions of some in the anthroposophical community.

> When thinking is somehow impaired and is not able to reach out in perception to find a context of meaning in the environment or situations, then there arises the wish to give up the attempt. An interest develops in something otherworldly. This is the addiction towards fantasy. The fantasy is, "I cannot really think my way through the world. I have not the courage to continually meet the fear of not understanding." This leads to a particular kind of addiction to hallucinogenics such as LSD, whereby the sheaths are loosened to such an extent that the ego swims in the world of cosmic ethers. The individual dissolves into a oneness in which everything is active, moving, and dynamic, but there is no center. There is no ego to it, and one becomes everything. The types of people that are more or less addicted to LSD and certain kinds of hallucinogenics find it very difficult to reconcile themselves to the century. And in their own being, an old memory gets distorted — an old memory that I would say belongs to previous incarnations we have all gone through.

> There was a time when it was reasonable to have certain hallucinogenic substances as part of one's introduction to the spiritual world. These were parts of rituals and religious or spiritual paths of initiation. We have here a kind of distortion that becomes evil when attempted in a time when it does not belong. This is the evil by which the ego is being attacked and taken away from its development. It is a retrogressive experience.

It seems that the chain of soul challenges and the presumed logic in his cascade of precipitating events leading an individual to recourse, as he seems to suggest, to psychedelics as some form of self-medication assumes a lot. I believe this characterization would be difficult to substantiate relative to the varied experiences of any number of users of psychedelics.

It reads to me like more than a stretch to assert that individuals brought through curiosity, destiny, or karma, as you will, to explore the possibilities of psychedelic drugs, are, *ipso facto*, sufferers from an "impaired thinking" that "gives up on the attempt" to "find a context of meaning in the environment or situations". As a diagnosis of a psychic condition, it seems more than a little vague. There may of course be some individuals that might fit into the pattern here. As a generality, it does not serve.

Anthroposophically understood we do exist in a continual interchange of forces within the cosmic ethers. The "loosening" of our individualized ether body — as occurs fully at the time of death — can reveal to the individual their inward posture relative to their spiritual Ego. The loosening can be experienced as a liberation from the weight of the physical body, and the soul can give itself up to the awakened bliss nature of the astral body — and it may surrender some of its discriminative powers in the interim. One may also experience the encounter with the Double or Guardian, including awakening to the distortions of the self and higher Ego that one may see reflected in the loosened etheric.

One could go on and on attempting to detail the varieties of experiences possible and the variations in the relationships between the soul members. Dosage, set, setting, biography, and level of experience — all are determinative in the net experience and, in my view, the degree to which the experience can be progressive or retrogressive in the most rigorous anthroposophical sense.

The concluding remark that the ego is "invariably attacked" is too broad a statement for what is a very nuanced situation.

It would be unfortunate if anthroposophical efforts in the realm of psychotherapy can only relate to the psychedelic experience as a species of addiction. The notion indeed of *addiction* is generally held to be essentially non-meaningful in the context of psychedelics, in anything resembling the meaning it has in the domain of opiates, amphetamine, or alcohol. It is certainly possible that within the broad population of psychedelic users, there is a category of individuals that create a lifestyle supportive of regular psychedelic use and apparent disregard for establishing a conventional bourgeois existence. To suggest that this implies a difficulty "to reconcile themselves to the century" seems more than a little narrow. It is of course possible to observe and reflect on a variety of trends of thought within various psychedelic communities.

Leaving my own experiences out of the question for the moment, I remark further that I have known hundreds of individuals with psychedelic drugs in their biographies — disregarding the thousands upon thousands found across all domains of public life — who are now all manner of accomplished people in the world, least of all, a number of anthroposophists. And more than a few whom I consider, in particular, to be spiritually and intellectually rigorous in their thinking as well as moral conduct.

It is of course fair to say that in a way, the appeal of psychedelics *is* to find a form of escape — this is already seen in the earlier discussion of its Luciferic component. However, this "escape" is not necessarily to be understood as the "escape" sought, for example, by a shirker of work. Rather, the spirit of contemporary humanity is, in fact, cramped and imprisoned and often in *need* of an escape from the narrow "chinks" of our cavern, as William Blake observed over 200 years ago. The loosening, of that which variously welds our souls to the external world degree by degree, depending on the individual, can, in my view, unquestionably serve a therapeutic and progressive function in individual instances.

The characterization that the result of the psychedelic experience is that the ego "swims in the cosmic ethers" and that "there is no center" is at best, a vague characterization and a gross generalization. It seems much more precise to observe that in the psychedelic experience, one *may* approach the threshold of the spiritual world, and that all of the considerations that Steiner remarks in terms of dangers, preparation, steadfastness of strength, and inner integrity, unquestionably apply.

This threshold, meanwhile, is not necessarily encountered as a foreground experience in every psychedelic state. At moderate doses — perhaps, typical doses — one experiences what might be called "peri-threshold" experiences.

To speak of the "loss of center" is to misunderstand the nature of Ego experience in the spiritual world. Describing the transition when the ether body begins to fade after death, Steiner describes a "Dionysian dismemberment" [280] where different soul elements as it were migrate to different domains of the "outer world" that we start to experience as a transformation of our earthly inner world. The unifying *I* is experienced as persisting not in the center, but in the infinite periphery; our psychic unity is holographic, not pointwise.

The assertion "There was a time" does, indeed, reflect an awareness, as asserted by Steiner, that methods evolve and change throughout the ages in the development of mankind. At the same time, it must be understood that, relative to the teachings of Rudolf Steiner in his lifetime, it is not possible to make an authoritative statement in this regard because these specific types of agents were essentially unknown in his contemporary situation.

One must consider instead that, anthroposophically understood, the contemporary psychedelic experience is one that is undergone and experienced today by individuals who have, at any rate, been born into the era of the modern consciousness soul[281], and rather than being victims of an "old memory" that "belongs to previous incarnations" (what precisely this memory is, is quite obscure to me in the above quote) they are, in the main, fully endowed (or — cursed or blessed variously) with the individualized — in the sense of, cosmically and tribally *alienated* — souls and Egos of modern humanity. It is certainly true that there is a very broad spectrum of soul configurations that may be more or less suitably disposed to have a favorable or unfavorable response to the psychedelic experience. The presumption that the dissociative effect of the psychedelic agent invariably results in the condition that "there is no center" is again a generalization. Indeed, as suggested earlier herein, as the etheric loosening brings consciousness over the threshold, our reflection of our spiritual *I* relies increasingly on an ability to integrate the experience holographically and more from the viewpoint of "inside-out" or the periphery. The question of "center" becomes nuanced or possibly even, moot.

Again and again it must be broadly understood that "your mileage may vary".

The idea that the Ego — that is, the spiritual *I* — is being "attacked" is to have, apparently, confused the "little I" ego with the spiritual *I*. Indeed, the "little I" is *in some sense* the bearer or supporter of the spiritual I, but the "dissolution into oneness" glides over a complex process of inner reorganization that can occur in psychedelic threshold encounters, which in almost every sense parallels processes occurring through death or initiation, excepting in the variability with which the phenomenon can unfold. The challenge of psychedelic experience can as much be a question of maintaining a connection with one's holographic coherence across, not oneness, but an intensely-experienced dissociative multiplicity. How one weaves a realized sense of *I* within all this is the question.

What I believe can be said from an anthroposophical perspective more definitively regarding psychedelics is that on their own, psychedelics cannot be *relied* upon to make permanent the cognitional possibilities that they can afford. And that, unlike the cognitional path of Rudolf Steiner, their use is fraught with the possibility of peril for *some* individuals — but this much is already generally known. For certain individuals, in certain contexts of usage, it can indeed be retrogressive. But this is by no means necessarily the default scenario.

In this connection, I am somehow reminded of a turn of phrase employed by Steiner on several occasions when he quoted a saying: "If a head and a book are knocked together and a hollow sound is produced, it is not necessarily the fault of the book." Or in this case, the psychedelic agent.

CLOSING THOUGHTS

Psychedelic drugs will be continued to be used increasingly psychotherapeutically, with many instances of favorable effect; spiritually, also with many instances of favorable effect; and recreationally in both the more trivial sense as well as the sense of true festival and celebration, also in many cases, with favorable effect. And for some others, not so much. Social and cultural context can promote or detract from the experienced outcome.

Anthroposophy, as a movement, has a spiritual mission in the world, relative to both the pervasive ills that continue to beset humanity, and to the vision of love that is to become the flowering of the earth period. The ills of today are in no small part due to the evolutionary necessity that mankind passes through a period of one-sided scientific materialism, compounded by a technologically rooted world economy and culture. These ills are, in many ways, a source of the "mind-forged manacles"[282] of William Blake that, appropriately, we would indeed fain escape.

Anthroposophy, as particularly represented by its active individuals, would do well to be equipped to engage in respectful dialog with the many thousands upon thousands of sincere individuals exploring the possibilities these agents afford. For any number of these, anthroposophy may become a source of guidance and a next step in the process of awakening to the spiritual tasks of the present time. It is my further wish that in particular, those representing the thought leadership of the psychedelic renaissance will find the study of anthroposophy a source of insight that can serve the healthful development of psychedelic practice.

Notes

1   Steiner, Rudolf. From *Wahspruchworte* (GA 40), Dornach: Rudolf Steiner Verlag, 2011 (trans. author)

2   The 'Woodstock Music and Arts Fair' was a three day festival in upstate New York which featured many of the notable acts of the sixties music scene; including Richie Havens; Ravi Shankar; Janis Joplin; Sly and the Family Stone; The Grateful Dead; Creedence Clearwater Revival; The Who; Jefferson Airplane; Joe Cocker; The Band; Johnny Winter; Crosby, Stills, Nash & Young; Jimi Hendrix. It was attended by over 400,000 people, was declared a "free festival" after the crowds overwhelmed gate control, and was a major milestone in the counterculture of the late sixties and early seventies. A film, *Woodstock*, was produced and featured many of the notable performances.

3   Wilson, John Rowan. *The Mind*, New York: Time Inc., 1964

4   *Life* Magazine was published weekly for over fifty years until 1972 as a photo news magazine in large format. It covered a range of human interest and news features. The hippie movement, LSD, and the Beatles (among many other topics of the sixties) often received front cover placement.

5   Henry Luce and his wife, Clare Booth Luce, were publishers of the weeklies *TIME* and *Life*. They essentially introduced psychedelics to the American public in 1957 in a photo feature documenting Robert Gordon Wasson's experience in Mexico

with psilocybin mushrooms. Well into the sixties, they published numerous mostly favorable articles on LSD. Clare Luce was a political conservative, writer, and US Ambassador, who used LSD a number of times and was an enthusiast.

6   Albert Hoffman was a chemist for the Swiss drug firm Sandoz (now part of Novartis). While experimenting with derivatives of the rye fungus ergot (which already had medical uses) he synthesized LSD-25 (in German, Lysergsäure-diethylamide). Having noticed unusual psychological effects upon accidentally absorbing it through his skin, he tried what he thought was a mild dose, not realizing its high potency. He then experienced the world's first acid trip.

7   Wilson, John Rowan. op. cit.

8   Timothy Leary, 1920 - 1996, was an American psychologist most notable for his strident advocacy of psychedelics, which he first experienced in Mexico with psilocybin mushrooms. He later found that synthetic psilocybin had been formulated by Albert Hoffman at Sandoz and began to use it experimentally under the auspices of the Harvard psychology department. He shortly progressed to experimentation with LSD. LSD usage soon became somewhat freewheeling and he, along with Richart Alpert, was expelled from Harvard for, among other things, violating department protocols against providing the drug to undergraduates. He went on to become a relentless advocate of LSD, and became involved in its promotion and distribution, which led to his eventual incarceration. He developed a variety of theories around the nature of LSD and the human being.

9   Leary, Timothy, 1920-1996, Ralph, Metzner and Ram Dass. 1992. *The Psychedelic Experience: A Manual Based On the Tibetan Book of the Dead*. New York, NY, Citadel Press/Kensington Publishing.

10   Richard Alpert, 1931 - 2019, subsequently known as Ram Dass, was a colleague of Timothy Leary at the Center for Research in Personality at Harvard University. He was dismissed together with Leary in 1963 due to controversy surrounding psychedelic use with undergraduate students. He worked closely with Timothy Leary for a number of years until, somewhat disaffected with the experienced limitation of repeated psychedelic use, traveled to

India and ultimately was to meet Neem Karoli Baba, who became his guru and he returned from India as Ram Dass.

Until his death in 2019, he was a well known figure in the new age spirituality community and wrote books, gave talks, and was considered by many to be a leading spokesperson of the late twentieth century spiritual self-development community.

11   Ralph Metzner (1936 - 2019) was a colleague of Leary and Alpert at Harvard. Until his death in 2019, he was involved in a wide variety of research and practices in the area of consciousness research, including an ongoing interest in and involvement with psychedelics. He authored a number of books on consciousness studies and was actively involved towards the end of his life in psychedelic studies at the California Institute of Integral Studies.

12   Richard Nixon was the 37th President of the United States, elected to his first term in 1968. He inherited the unpopular Vietnam war and with it the anti-war protest movement. The anti-war movement was instrumental in shifting sentiment away from support of the war, and was largely seen as aligned with the anti-establishment orientation of the counter-culture movement associated with hippies, drugs (particularly LSD) and rock music. This politicized polarity can be seen as underlying the intense clampdown on LSD that occurred as part of the larger "War on Drugs." Nixon became infamous subsequent to his role in the Watergate coverup and was forced from office, becoming the first President in US history to resign from office.

13   In February 1968 the Beatles (John Lennon, Paul McCartney, George Harrison, and Ringo Starr) traveled to India with friends and family to study with the Indian spiritual teacher Maharishi Mahesh Yogi. The trip was highly publicized, and, among other things, yielded a new creative impulse in some of the Beatles music. Relationships between some of the Beatles and the Maharishi soured somewhat towards the end of the visit. The interest in Eastern spirituality, which came on the heels of their introduction to LSD in 1965, was largely a consequence of George Harrison's interest in Indian music, specifically the sitar, which he studied with well-known musician Ravi Shankar.

14   Allen Ginsberg (1926-1997) was an American poet, writer, and political activist, and one of the leading figures of the Beat

Generation, a literary movement that emerged in the 1950s. Ginsberg's most famous work is the poem *Howl*, initially published in 1956. He was known for his radical politics, advocacy for gay rights, and opposition to war and capitalism. He became involved early in Timothy Leary's experiments with psychedelics at Harvard and was an early promoter of psychedelics. He traveled to India in 1962 and returned bringing the influence of the Eastern spirituality into his cultural orbit. He was among the first to introduce the counterculture scene of the West to the practice of chanting *Hare Krishna*.

15   Jack Kerouac (1922-1969) was an American novelist and poet who is best known for his 1957 novel *On the Road*. He was a key figure of the Beat Generation and its associated literary movement as it emerged in the 1950s. His work explored themes including spirituality, jazz music, and the search for meaning in post-World War II society. Kerouac's writing style was characterized by his use of unfiltered spontaneous prose, aiming to capture the immediacy of everyday speech.

16   Ken Kesey (1935-2001) was a counterculture figure and novelist who first came to notice for his novel *One Flew Over the Cuckoo's Nest*. Kesey was a prominent figure in the 1960s counterculture movement and was a "ringleader" for the Merry Pranksters, a group who traveled across the United States in a psychedelic bus. His writing often explored themes of individual freedom, rebellion against authority, and the search for meaning in a changing world. While a student at Stanford University, Kesey participated as a volunteer for LSD studies conducted at the nearby VA Hospital. This exposure (under US Government auspices) proved pivotal in his becoming an advocate for LSD and instrumental through his writing and social circles in helping precipitate the emergence of the psychedelic scene in northern California.

17   Wolfe, Tom. *The Electric Kool-Aid Acid Test*, New York: Farrar, Strauss, Giroux, 1968

18   Located in the heart of New York's East Village, the Fillmore East was a music venue that played an influential role in shaping the counterculture of the time as it unfolded on the East Coast. It was opened in 1968 by concert promoter Bill Graham, who had already gained a reputation organizing rock

concerts at the original Fillmore Auditorium in San Francisco. It was a favorite destination for, among other things, suburban youth such as myself keen to experience the musical scene that had first started in San Francisco. The Fillmore East quickly became the place to be on the East Coast for anyone interested in music and counterculture. It hosted some of the most significant and influential musical acts of the time, including Jimi Hendrix, Janis Joplin, The Who, The Doors, and Led Zeppelin. The venue featured an advanced sound system and light shows which provided a psychedelic backdrop to the music. The smell of marijuana smoke typically hung over the audience. The Fillmore East closed its doors in 1971.

19   On that same visit to the city, as we wandered back uptown, we walked past 211 Madison Avenue. We strolled by the storefront window of what then was the Rudolf Steiner bookstore and branch office (subsequently demolished in 1985). I recall pausing and looking in the window at the display of books and the portrait in the window — of Rudolf Steiner — and being momentarily arrested before walking on. At the time, I had no idea who he was.

The building at 211 was the former carriage house for the J. P. Morgan mansion (now J. P. Morgan Library and Museum) nearby at 36th Street and Madison Avenue.

20   Art Linkletter was a radio and television personality.

21   In 1967, an article in *Science News* claimed that researchers had discovered that LSD use was linked to a higher incidence of "broken" chromosomes. This received a fair amount of press at the time. By 1971, it was generally accepted by the scientific community that there was no evidence to support this.

22   Mescaline is a naturally derived psychedelic substance, found in several species of cactus, most notably the Peyote cactus. Mescaline, in the form of Peyote, has a long history of use in indigenous cultures in Mexico and the Southwestern United States, where it has been used for religious and medicinal purposes for centuries. In the 20th century, mescaline gained popularity among artists and intellectuals as a tool for exploring consciousness and creativity. It was notably used by Aldous Huxley, who wrote about his experiences with the substance in his book *The Doors of Perception*. Peyote has been over harvested since the sixties and is considered

endangered. Its traditional availability to indigenous cultures is at risk.

23 Aldous Huxley (1894 - 1963) was an English writer who developed into a philosophical essayist with a deep interest in mysticism and what he called the Perennial Philosophy. He experimented in the early 1950's with mescaline, and later LSD. His experience reflected his mystical predisposition, and he became an early, and articulate and measured, advocate of psychedelics in several of his later writings, and was influential in the development of early thought around psychedelic use. He died in 1963 on the same day John Kennedy was assassinated, and his death was notable in that he was administered LSD as he transitioned into "active dying".

24 Huxley, Aldous. *The Doors of Perception*, NewYork: Harper & Row, 1954

This references William Blake's verse on the "Doors of Perception" being cleansed (*The Marriage of Heaven and Hell*). The sixties rock group The Doors referenced Blake and Huxley in their name.

25 The phrase "get off" was routinely used to describe the transition between one's "straight head" and tripping. To my thinking, it was a metaphor of altitude — have you achieved lift-off? In the fifty years since, "getting off" has perhaps become more loaded with the notion of experiencing sexual orgasm, possibly through resonance with the phrase "getting one's rocks off." This sense was not current in the psychedelic culture of the time.

26 This would have been *Pete Hamill at Mai Lai* narrated by WNEW-FM disc jockey Rosko.

27 An armillary sphere is an astronomical instrument that consists of a spherical framework of rings, representing the celestial equator, the ecliptic, and other important celestial circles. The rings are connected by an axis, which allows the sphere to be rotated and moved into different positions. The armillary sphere was first developed by ancient Greek astronomers, and it was used to model and study the movement of the stars and planets in the sky.

28 The Firesign Theatre was a comedy group that was active from the late 1960s to the early 2000s. The group was formed by

four friends — Phil Austin, Peter Bergman, David Ossman, and Philip Proctor — who met while studying at the radio station of Los Angeles City College. They first became known on LA radio, and their skits often abound with LA area references. Their unique style of absurdist humor and innovative use of sound effects and music became popular among counter-culture circles. Their early radio plays, including *Waiting for the Electrician or Someone Like Him* and *How Can You Be in Two Places at Once When You're Not Anywhere at All*, were subsequently produced as record albums. Their humor seemed tailor-made for the stoned mind. The group officially disbanded in 2012 following the death of Peter Bergman.

29 The James Gang were a rock band coming out of Ohio, whose period of greatest success was during the tenure of Joe Walsh (of later Eagles fame), who recorded their first four albums (including a live album) with them. In 1970 they had just released their most successful album, *James Gang Rides Again*.

30 Staples High School was fairly unique in managing to host and organize a number of big acts to perform on campus, including the Yardbirds, Cream, and The Doors. These latter three were while I was still in Junior High and still a little too wet behind the ears to get myself organized to get tickets. All through my high school years, there was a steady stream of top-tier acts that were booked in by the very enterprising social committee.

31 I am retired now from thirty-odd years in the tech industry and have served for the past ten years on the core group of the local branch of the Anthroposophical Society, where I live here in Santa Cruz, California. I work with my colleagues to help foster, in our way, the anthroposophical life of fifty-odd active members here.

32 Shakespeare, William. *Hamlet*, 1.5, 167-168

33 Johann Wolfgang von Goethe (1749-1832) was a German poet, statesman, dramatist, and scientist. He is considered one of the greatest literary figures of Western civilization and a key figure in German Romanticism. Goethe's most famous works include the novel *The Sorrows of Young Werther*, considered the leading work of the Sturm und Drang ("Storm and Stress") movement and the epic poem *Faust*, which he revised and worked on for most of his life. He was also a polymath, with interests in natural

science, philosophy, and art. Goethe's scientific work, including his *Farbenlehre* (*Theory of Color*) and his contributions to botany, was highly influential although controversial. He was a close friend of Schiller and a leading figure in Weimar and Jena. Goethe's impact on German literature and culture was enormous, extending far beyond Germany. He was a passionate opponent of Newton's Color Theory and said of himself: "I do not pride myself at all on the things I have done as a poet. There have been excellent poets during my lifetime, still more excellent ones lived before me, and after me there will be others. But I am proud that I am the only one in my century who knows the truth about the difficult science of color." His scientific thinking is notable for its development of the idea of the observer as a participant in the structuring of an experiment.

34   Carl Jung's theory of synchronicity is the idea that events that seem to be coincidental may actually be connected in a meaningful way. These meaningful coincidences are not just the result of chance or probability, but rather an expression of a deeper order in the universe.

Synchronicity may be said to apply when two or more events coincide in a way that cannot be explained by cause and effect but rather by a connection in meaning. These events may be linked by shared symbols, archetypes, or other unconscious patterns. Jung held that synchronicity was meaningful in the psychological process of individuals.

The universal order implicit in the idea of synchronicity can validate the use of oracular methods such as the *I Ching* or Tarot cards: the apparently random result of a given oracular casting is seen as linking the universal ordering inherent in the moment with the individual's psychological state.

35   Op. cit., Wilson, John Rowan, 126-127

36   The April 8, 1966 issue of *TIME* magazine asked the question, "Is God Dead?" in bold red letters on a solid background. It was broadly controversial and inspired over 3,000 letters to the magazine. It was intended as a thought-provoking theological question.

37   I had a fairly normal set of literary interests otherwise ranging from *Dr. Dolittle* through *The Catcher in the Rye*, *1984*, and much else.

38 Dante Alighieri was an Italian poet and was noted primarily as the author of *The Divine Comedy*, which in three volumes describes a putative voyage through hell (*Inferno*), Purgatory (*Purgatorio*), and heaven (*Paradiso*). He is guided through hell and purgatory by the classical Italian poet Virgil, and through heaven by Beatrice, an idealized woman, modeled upon a neighbor, who he fell profoundly in love with upon first sight. He wrote about her also in his *La Vita Nuova*.

39 John Ciardi, 1916 - 1986, was an Italian-American poet and translator, and contributor to the *Saturday Review*. He also taught literature at Harvard.

40 This would have been the A. M. O. R. C. organization, the Ancient and Mystical Order Rosae Crucis, founded in this form by H. Spencer Lewis in 1915.

41 *Zen Buddhism*, Mount Vernon: Peter Pauper Press, 1959

42 The penultimate paragraph of *Siddhartha* reads: "Not knowing any more whether time existed, whether the vision had lasted a second or a hundred years, not knowing any more whether there existed a Siddhartha, a Gotama, a me and a you, feeling in his innermost self as if he had been wounded by a divine arrow, the injury of which tasted sweet, being enchanted and dissolved in his innermost self, Govinda still stood for a little while bent over Siddhartha's quiet face, which he had just kissed, which had just been the scene of all manifestations, all transformations, all existence. The face was unchanged, after under its surface the depth of the thousand-foldness had closed up again, he smiled silently, smiled quietly and softly, perhaps very benevolently, perhaps very mockingly, precisely as he used to smile, the exalted one."

43 Perls, Fritz. *Gestalt Therapy Verbatim*, Lafayette: Real People Press, 1969

44 It seems more than reasonable to me that this kind of dichotomous experience of self in adolescence is a developmentally significant stage provided it doesn't get out of hand.

45 Pyotr Demianovich Ouspenskii (P. D. Ouspensky) (1878-1947) was a Russian journalist and author who wrote on topics of mysticism and new paradigms, with a particular interest in the ideas about the fourth dimension along the lines of Charles

Hinton. He traveled in search of the "Miraculous" and flirted with Theosophy; his meeting with George Gurdjieff in 1915 was to influence his work for the remainder of his life.

46 George Ivanovich Gurdjieff (c. 1866–1877 – 1949) was a spiritual teacher and led various groups of which Ouspensky was a one-time member. He held that the majority of humanity was "asleep" and did not possess a unified consciousness but rather dreamed that they did. He introduced a novel set of cosmological ideas which Ouspensky tried to systematize. He felt his legacy would be his (intentionally) almost indigestible work *Beelzebub's Tales to His Grandson*, in which his ideas are presented in veiled and difficult-to-grasp stories.

47 This break with Gurdjieff was fairly radical. Ouspensky began to believe that Gurdjieff had somehow lost his way. Others believe Ouspensky had failed a test put to him by Gurdjieff. It might also be supposed that Gurdjieff sent him away consciously as a phase of his teaching and to remove him from dependence on him.

48 Friedrich Nietzche (1844 - 1900) Influential 19th century philosopher, admired by Steiner among many others.

49 In Steiner's teaching one finds a certain analog to this idea at its deepest level in his Foundation Stone meditation, exhorting the individual:

> *Practice spirit remembrance*
>
> *Practice spirit contemplation*
>
> *Practice spirit-seeing*

These urgings are found in respective verses related to the threefold human being. cf. Steiner, Rudolf. *The Foundation Stone*, London: Anthroposophical Publishing Company, 1957.

50 The Kabbalah is a teaching of Jewish mysticism that has been influential through the ages of Western esotericism. In addition to providing an esoteric exegesis of the Torah, and various mystical practices, it details a spiritual cosmology of great depth.

51 Roughly stated, this was a principle that saw all interactions in the world process such that events were characterized as proceeding in steps or stages that correspond to notes on the diatonic musical

scale from *do* to *do*. A simplistic application might be as follows:

I think I want to go to the movies — *do*.
I check what is playing — *re*.
I decide if I like anything on offer — *mi*.

And so on, with the final *do* — at the end of the scale, a full octave above the start being the result: I see the movie. At certain intervals (between *mi* and *fa* and *si* and *do*, the place on the piano of the missing semitones or black keys) an outside impetus is required if the intended outcome is to be reached; that is, the series of events was to achieve the sounding of the final note do.

The *mi-fa* point might be — I'm not sure if I like what is on offer, or else maybe I can't decide which of two choices I prefer. Someone else comes along and nudges a choice — this is the outside application of impulse.

Of course, as in the example, it is perhaps a question of intuitively sensing the stages of the scheme, as the assignment of steps and their corresponding notes might otherwise appear to be more or less arbitrary when the flow of events in the world process is considered altogether.

52   Robert Fludd (1574 - 1637) Occult philosopher-Rosicrucian.

53   John Lilly, 1915 - 2001, was a medically trained scientist who was notable for numerous researches in neurophysiology, inter-species (dolphin-human) communication research, and the development of the solitude/isolation tank (popularized today as the "floatation tank"). He conducted a number of experiments on LSD within the sensory deprivation space of the isolation tank. He became involved with the Esalen Institute and the early formation of the Arica Institute.

54   Oscar Ichazo grew up in Bolivia and Peru. As a child, he underwent seizures that were experienced as out-of-body states. As a young man, he encountered a group of seekers which led to him establishing worldwide connections with various esoteric traditions and schools. He began developing his ideas around

human psychology which became the substance of his protoanalysis method that became the center of the Arica Institute.

55 The "food diagram" or "food factory" is a schematic representation of the development of energies or materials referred to in Gurdjieff's system as "Hydrogens" (primal atoms). It is detailed in Ouspensky's In Search of the Miraculous. It is intended to depict the human organism as a three-story "factory" divided into regions of head, chest, and lower parts of the body, including the back. Within this structure, "Hydrogens" evolve through a process of, first, entry into the body as either food, air, or impressions in each of the stories, respectively. Having entered the "factory," they blend with higher elements already present in the body and produce new energies or substances of an intermediate level. The vibrational level of each element is assigned a number, built out of a cosmic scale detailed elsewhere in In Search of the Miraculous, where higher-number elements represent "lower" or grosser elements, and lower-number elements are more refined. The scale of elements in the food diagram is numbered starting at 6 and doubling (12, 24, 48 ...) all the way to 768, which is shown entering the organism as ordinary food; air is hydrogen 192; impressions begin the scale of "psychic hydrogens" at 48. These three streams are shown to interact according to the "law of the octave," where each food, on entering the body, sounds the note *do* of a new octave. This is meant to show that there is a point at which the energy of sense impressions and the octave of breath can fail to develop harmoniously due to the possible "harmonic misalignment" (my term) that occurs at the *mi-fa* interval of the diatonic scale at the point where "sense impressions" should be harmonized. It is essentially a species of "speculative music" that can provide a contemplative indication of how the different energies of the human being relate to the spiritual-cosmic energies as in the classical notion of the "music of the spheres" as found in Pythagoras and throughout the Western esoteric tradition. It is also meant to indicate a possible kind of "alchemy".

56 *Groundhog Day* is a 1993 film that follows its protagonist — who to begin with is depicted as more or less self-centered and nasty, through a magically occurring series of repetitions of Groundhog Day. Day after day he applies knowledge from the previous day to bit by bit, improve the lives of those around him, and, finally, in

perfect Hollywood style, get the girl. It is distinct from Ouspensky's notion of recurrence in that, in the film, memory from day to day is preserved.

57   A simplistic characterization of the akashic chronicle (or akashic record) might be to describe it as a permanent "recording" of everything that ever happens. However, as with the general idea of the etheric, especially as developed in Steiner, is is more complex. Another way in which this could be understood is the idea that the essence of things occurring in time persist within eternity (whence they ultimately originate), rather than a "copy" or "recording" of them. It is understood that what is "persisting" is the experience held in the consciousness of a living being and not the material substratum. When the clairvoyant perceives an event in the chronicle, it is, in a way, as if they were perceiving it as it existed in its own time. Obviously, we experience ourselves as traversing time linearly. As consciousness and higher cognition broaden, it more and more is seen as embracing, ultimately, the whole of time and moving to a viewpoint in some ways outside of time. The etheric body of the individual — which maintains the life and growth of the body in earth life and earth time — also serves, among other things, to mediate between time and the eternity of the spiritual world. The key notion at this point is, Steiner develops a picture of cosmic evolution and of our origins avowedly derived from his direct perception of past events as seen in the Akashic chronicle.

58   Carlos Castaneda (1925 - 1998) was the writer of a series of books about the purported Mexican shaman Don Juan. They describe a shamanistic teaching involving use of (among other things) the psychedelic peyote or *Mescalito*. He avoided the public and shrouded himself in mystery. In later years, the consensus developed that the works were largely fictional.

59   Castaneda, Carlos. *The Teachings of Don Juan*, Berkeley: University of California Press, 1968

Although at the time of publication, it was presented as authentic anthropological fieldwork, it has come to be regarded, along with the series of subsequent books concerning the supposed Yaqui sorcerer Don Juan, as fabrication. In it, Don Juan teaches through the use of various psychedelic substances, notably peyote, which reveals the being "Mescalito".

60   Thompson, Hunter. *Fear and Loathing in Las Vegas*, New York: Random House, 1972

Originally serialized in Rolling Stone magazine in 1971.

61   Alan Watts, 1915 - 1973, was a writer on spiritual themes with what might be called an "East-West" perspective. As a young man, he was a student of Theosophy, which introduced him to Buddhism and Zen in particular, went on to be for a time an Anglican priest, and emerged in the fifties and sixties as a kind of counter-culture philosopher-guru. Regarding psychedelic drugs (of which he was an early experimenter), he is notable in particular for his comment that "If you get the message, hang up the phone" — suggesting that repeated use beyond a certain point is unfruitful. He authored numerous books, including *The Joyous Cosmology*, which described an idealized LSD trip.

62   Watts, Alan. *The Book: on the Taboo Against Knowing Who You Are*, New York: Pantheon Books, 1966

63   Watts, Alan. *The Joyous Cosmology*, New York: Pantheon Books, 1962

64   Esalen Institute is a retreat center devoted to the development of human potential, located near Big Sur, California. It provides various psychological and spiritual workshops, especially as developed out of the so-called Human Potential Movement of the 1960's. A notable feature of the Esalen experience is the hot tubs overlooking the Pacific Ocean. Numerous luminaries of the Human Potential Movement, including not only Alan Watts but Fritz Perls, Alan Maslow, Arnold Mindell, Stan Grof, Joseph Campbell, Ram Dass, John Lilly and numerous others, have been involved with residencies and teaching fellowships.

65   The Temptations were an American vocal group recording on the Motown label, perhaps best known for the song *My Girl*. In 1970 (*Ball of Confusion*) their material was positioned broadly to the psychedelically-inspired rock music of that time.

66   A snippet of lyrics:

Ball of confusion
Oh yeah, that's what the world is today
Woo, hey, hey
The sale of pills are at an all time high
Young folks walking round with their heads in the sky
The cities ablaze in the summer time
And oh, the beat goes on

67   Blake, William. *For Children, The Gates of Paradise*, Plate 15, 1793

68   Lilly, John and Keene, Sam. *From Dolphins to LSD*, Psychology Today, December, 1971

69   Lilly, John. *The Center of the Cyclone* New York: Julian Press, 1972,

70   Arica Institute was established in the United States in 1970, with centers initially in New York, San Francisco, and Los Angeles, to bring the training developed with Oscar Ichazo and around fifty individuals, largely from Esalen Institute.

71   Gurdjieff, George, *Beelzebub's Tales to his Grandson*, New York: Harcourt, 1950

72   Sputnik was the first artificial satellite, launched by the Soviet Union in 1957. It triggered the cold war "space race" that led to the United States putting humans on the moon in 1969. It is a significant milestone of the technological era.

73   Sandoz was a Swiss Pharmaceutical company, since merged into Novartis, which employed Albert Hoffman, the discover of LSD. They were the original manufacturer of LSD and freely distributed it as an experimental drug throughout the 1950's and into the 1960's, prior to its change of legal status. As a pharmaceutically manufactured product, LSD acquired from Sandoz ("pure Sandoz") was desirable for its purity and dosage specificity.

74   See Lilly, John, *Programming and Metaprogramming in the Human Biocomputer*, Miami: Communications Research Institute, 1968.

75   Lilly, John, *The Center of the Cyclone*, page 142

76   J. Geils were a successful rock band of the late sixties and early seventies, led by guitarist John Geils. They toured heavily in the early seventies and had minor hits with songs including *Must of Got Lost* and *First I Look at the Purse*.

77   *The Magician's Nephew* was a children's fairy tale from C. S. Lewis' *The Chronicles of Narnia*. The children protagonists first get involved with the "Magician" by crawling through a shared attic space into the neighboring house.

78   Carl Jung, 1875 - 1961, was a Swiss psychiatrist, early colleague of Sigmund Freud, and subsequently the developer (after a break with Freud) of what came to be known as Depth Psychology. He is noted for the development of the idea of the Collective Unconscious, a shared psychic stratum populated by archetypal figures and complexes, and the idea of synchronicity as an "acausal connecting principal". His ideas have been influential in certain circles of psychedelic thought.

79   Jung, Carl Gustav.   *Psyche and Symbol*, Garden City: Doubleday Anchor Books, 1958

80   Ram Dass (Richard Alpert), *Be Here Now*, San Cristobal: Lama Foundation, 1971

81   *Chonyid Bardo* is the bardo stage of the Vision of the Wrathful Deities.

82   Jung, Carl Gustav. *Psychology and Religion: East and West*, London: Routledge and Kegan Paul, 1958, 520.

83   The Celestial Rose is a rapturous vision of Dante's, described at the end of his *The Divine Comedy: Paradiso*. The rose itself is composed of the heavenly forms of all "whom Christ in his own blood espoused;" the vision continues and Dante sees what appears as a "swarm of bees" in eternal transit between the Rose and God.

84   Jacob Boehme, 1575 - 1624, was a German Christian mystic, notable for his mystical experiences. His writings were a major influence on the development of Western mystical and occult thought.

85   The "Brotherhood of Eternal Love" was an organization of LSD distributors working out of southern California. They were notable for their sense of mission in bringing about a psychedelic revolution,

and the high quality and high dosage of their orange sunshine LSD. This supply ended shortly after my cast party experience.

86   Alan Watts in *The Book on the Taboo Against Knowing Who You Are* says that most people are "aware of themselves as isolated 'egos' inside bags of skin." Page 8.

87   cf. Lewis Carroll's well-known *Through the Looking-Glass*.

88   Steiner, Rudolf, *Knowledge of the Higher Worlds and Its Attainment*, New York: Anthroposphic Press, 1947

89   Projective Geometry is a non-Euclidean geometry that defines certain axioms differently. For example, unlike the notion in Euclidean geometry that parallel lines never intersect; in projective geometry, they are said to intersect at infinity. These and other axioms result in a spatial concept that proves to be well suited to the understanding and conceptualization of etheric-spiritual "spaces" and forces, particularly growth forces as in plants. Projective geometry also conceives a space dual to the space of Euclidean space ("counter space") wherein forms are derived from the "infinite plane at the periphery" rather than pointwise, as in our conception of aggregated atomic particles composing the outer reality. The concept of the dual in projective geometry incorporates the idea that propositions expressed in terms of Euclidean geometry regarding points and lines are equally valid and correspondingly provable in projective space for lines and planes. These concepts have been developed especially in relation to Steiner's thought, notably by George, Adams, Louis Locher-Ernst, Ernst Lehrs, Olive Whicher, and others. See especially, Whicher, Olive. *Projective Geometry*. London: Rudolf Steiner Press, 1971, for a good overview aimed at the interested non-mathematician. The notion of a "loosening" of the etheric body would include the idea of a change in its spatial geometry and tendency to reflect more of the "infinite periphery" rather than the pointwise particle appearance.

90   *Bitch*

I Got the Blues

Sister Morphine

Dead Flowers

Moonlight Mile

NOTES

91   The Cóiste Bodhar, or death coach, is a norther european folk belief; it is the harbinger of death, as it comes to claim a soul to the land of the dead. It is believed in Ireland that once it comes, it can't leave empty.

92   *Incipit Vita Nova,* Thus Begins the New Life.

93   The last verse of *Eskimo Blue Day* reads:

Snow called water going violent

Damn the end of the stream

Too much cold in one place breaks

That's why you might know what I mean

Consider how small you are

Compared to your scream

The human dream

Doesn't mean shit to a tree

94   A "backplane" is a term from computer systems. It describes an element (i.e., electronic circuit board) with a number of connectors with multiple contacts that permit the insertion of special purpose cards into the system and allows them to access the general system "bus" (system of connectors or traces that connect the internal circuits of the system). It is a general purpose design and a variety of cards — memory expansion, secondary processors, graphic or other media interfaces or other device interfaces — to be attached In the context used here, the idea is that individual souls are connected to a larger system.

The usage here is not meant to imply in any sense that reality is somehow of the nature of a computer system.

95   The genderedness of divine beings is, at best, symbolic and traditional. In Steiner's view, we are all both male and female and in fact, tend to alternate between the different sexes from one incarnation to the next. Insofar as the human being is seen as spiritually beyond gender, how much more for the divine.

96   Brahma is primarily viewed as the Hindu supreme God. He is sometimes conceived as the "absolute" impersonal god, at other times, as part of the trinity, Siva - Brahma - Vishnu. Various Hindu sects alternatively see different members of the Trinity as supreme.

97 Zoroastorian God of Light, opposed by Ahriman whose name is used by Steiner to label one of the "opposing" forces.

98 Encounter groups were a popular form of group therapy promoting intensive group process to develop insight through direct verbal and emotional interactions.

99 Odin, the ruler of the Norse gods, looked out into the world, and wanted to know all, to gain wisdom and knowledge of hidden things. He sacrificed his eye in Mimir's well, and in a form of (symbolic) ritual suicide threw himself on his spear. He hung himself upon the tree of life, Yggdrasil, for nine days and night. Through this sacrifice, he gained knowledge of other worlds and understanding of the oracular runes.

100 Stephen Gaskin was an instructor at San Francisco State College at the time of the Hippie flowering. He became a kind of psychedelic guru holding an event known as the Monday Night Class where he taught out of his own psychedelic experience.

101 Gaskin, Stephen. *Monday Night Class*, New York: Random House, 1970.

102 Haight-Ashbury is a San Francisco neighborhood identified by the intersection of the two streets, Haight and Ashbury, that was "ground zero" for the 1960's hippie movement. For a time it was seen as the nexus of a beautiful "flower power" movement, but by the time George Harrison of the Beatles toured it with his wife Pattie Boyd, it had entered a decline and he described it saying "We were expecting Haight-Ashbury to be special, a creative and artistic place, filled with Beautiful People, but it was horrible – full of ghastly drop-outs, bums and spotty youths, all out of their brains."

103 Most notable was her copy of *The Whole Earth Catalog*, which was peppered throughout with reading list material for the well-informed hippie type. reading of hers I recall were *Centering in Poetry, Pottery, and the Person*, by M. C. Richards and *Touch The Earth, A Self Portrait of Indian Existence*, compiled by T. C. McLuhan. M. C. Richards was an anthroposophist, although that work does not reference Steiner explicitly.

104 The Gurdjieff Foundation is a lineage school organized under the auspices of Gurdjieff's pupil Madame Jeanne de Salzmann.

105 Maurice Nicoll, 1884 - 1953, was a follower of Ouspensk and subsequently Gurdjieff's, who led his own teaching groups in England. He was notably an early student of Jung, working closely with him and practicing Depth Psychology out of his Harley Street practice in London until he encountered Ouspensky. He authored an early book on Jung, *Dream Psychology*. He was subsequently to publish a number of books related to the Gurdjieff work.

106 Nicoll, Maurice. *Psychological Commentaries on the teachings of Gurdjieff and Ouspensky*, Volume One, London: Vincent Stuart, 1952

107 Édouard Schuré, 1841- 1929, was a French author, poet, and playwright. He wrote on the esoteric and the occult, influenced by the earlier French occultist Fabre d'Olivet. He came into close contact with Rudolf Steiner and translated some of his works, while Steiner produced some of his plays. During the first world war, Schuré's friendship cooled but was restored after the war. Schuré was also in contact with other notables of German culture such as Richard Wagner and Friedrich Nietzsche.

108 Schuré, Édouard. *The Great Initiates*, New York: Harper Collins, 1980

109 Rodney Collins, 1909 - 1956, was a young pupil of Ouspensky's. His devotion to Ouspensky was nigh-on fanatical. His works including *The Theory of Celestial Influence* and *The Theory of Eternal Life* build upon work ideas especially as enunciated by Ouspensky (include Ouspensky's idea of eternal recurrence) and attempt (with marginal success, in my view) to integrate them into more conventional ideas of modern science. They do illustrate in some ways the "law of correspondence" showing how various levels of the visible universe can be seen as connected. My own view came to be is that they are more or less permeated by an overweening influence of materialistic science. He died in Cusco in Peru, falling from a church bell tower, apparently the victim of a heart attack.

110 Nicoll, Maurice. *Living Time*, London: Stuart & Watkins, 1952

111 Meher Baba, 1894 - 1969, was an Indian spiritual leader who identified himself as an avatar of God. He become well-known internationally in the 1920's. In 1925, he took a vow of silence, which he maintained until the end of his life.

He was an early spiritual influence on some LSD enthusiasts of the sixties. He discouraged the use of LSD but was tolerant to a point. He was particularly well known in the late sixties as the spiritual leader of Pete Townsend, the guitarist for the rock group The Who.

His early impact was at least partly due to having been an "established" guru on the world scene before the flood of "gurus" coming to the West started.

112 The Who were a highly popular rock group of the sixties onward. Pete Townsend, the lead guitarist and principal songwriter, became a disciple of Meher Baba. They are notable for their "rock opera" *Tommy* and albums *Who's Next* and *Quadrophenia*. Some number of lyrics include references to Baba or his teachings. It is meanwhile, very hard-core rock and roll.

113 In his book *The Center of the Cyclone*, Lilly details the levels as follows:

Lilly, after Ichazo, maps them as so:

48 is the neutral, rational state

24, the "professional" state, "in the flow," lost in the activity of the moment

12 is the "blissful sharing body" — a high-energy, blessed, psychedelic state, "the Christ"

6 is "the Buddha," an out-of-body point of light and consciousness

3 is the state of being one of the creators of the universe, in direct sight of God

These can be readily seen to correspond to the various "psychic hydrogens" with similar number values found in Gurdjieff's "food factory".

114 *The Village Voice* was an alternative newspaper published in New York City starting in 1955, growing out of the beat scene and covering primarily the East and West Village cultural and political scene.

115 Paramahansa Yogananda was another mid-century spiritual teacher from India who had a certain established stature as the psychedelically-inspired interest in Eastern spirituality developed, and his *Autobiography of a Yogi* was popularly read. As I note the author's interest in the music of Yes, an example of his influence

is that one of the group's noteworthy double albums, *Tales of Topographic Oceans*, is (very loosely) inspired by a passage from his Autobiography.

116 Old Huckleberry Road in Wilton, Connecticut, leads to Rock Lake, the Lake in this chapter.

117 Tao and Taoism: the Tao is sometimes translated as "The Way" — the eternal spiritual force pervaded the universe as it flows through eternity. Taoism is the Eastern spiritual practice intended to cultivate mindfulness of the Tao.

118 This image referenced here is a sketch for the large cupola of the original Goetheanum (a building since lost to a fire, that housed the original center of the Anthroposophical Society in Dornach, Switzerland). I had the opportunity to see this while visiting the second Goetheanum and a copy of it is included in the book *The Language of Color in the First Goetheanum*, by Hilda Raske. Dornach: Walter Keller Verlag, 1983, page 75, captioned "The circle of Twelve."

119 The reference is to a well-known line from the Pete Townsend song "Baba O'Riley" on the Who's album, *Who's Next*. It includes the lyrics:

Out here in the fields

I farm for my meals

I get my back into my living

I don't need to fight

To prove I'm right

No, I don't need to be forgiven

Yeah, yeah, yeah, yeah, yeah

Don't cry

Don't raise your eye

It's only teenage wasteland

120 *Vagina Dentata* (Latin, toothed vagina) is a complex image found in various folk stories around the world. Simplistically, it can refer to the threat of castration that a male can fantasize is possible through sexual intercourse; it also can be seen as a symbol of the trauma of birth.

Although I personally think too much is made of Grof's Basic Perinatal Matrices, this vision plays well into such an analysis of this trip.

121 *Roundabout* was an FM radio hit for Yes, it is from their album *Fragile*, released in November 1971. Its lyrics include:

> *In and around the lake*
> *Mountains come out of the sky and they stand there*
> *One mile over, we'll be there and we'll see you*
> *Ten true summers, we'll be there and laughing, too*
> *Twenty-four before my love, you'll see I'll be there with you*

> *Along the drifting cloud, the eagle searching down on the land*
> *Catching the swirling wind, the sailor sees the rim of the land*
> *The eagle's dancing wings create as weather spins out of hand*
> *Go closer, hold the land feel partly no more than grains of sand*
> *We stand to lose all time, a thousand answers by in our hand*
> *Next to your deeper fears, we stand surrounded by a million years*
> *I'll be the roundabout, the words will make you out-and-out*
> *I'll be the roundabout, the words will make you out-and-out*

122 This picture (of Yes) in a way echoes the conceit behind the Beatles *Magical Mystery Tour:* "Away in the sky, beyond the clouds, live 4 or 5 Magicians. By casting wonderful spells they turn the Most Ordinary Coach Trip into a Magical Mystery Tour. If you let yourself go, the Magicians will take you away to marvellous

places. Maybe you've been on a Magical Mystery Tour without even realising it."

This picture would have been buried somewhere in my memory.

123 This image strangely parallel's that in one of musician Richard Bruno Heydrich (father of Nazi Reinhold Heydrich) operas: "The world is just a barrel-organ which the Lord God turns Himself. We all have to dance to the tune which is already on the drum."

124 The movie *Being John Malkovich* provides an amusing caricature of this state.

125 *Hold Your Head Up* was a song by the British rock group Argent that was well placed in the charts at the time.

The lead-in lyrics are:

> *And if it's bad*
>
> *Don't let it get you down, you can take it*
>
> *And if it hurts*
>
> *Don't let them see you cry, you can make it*

and it ends with the line "Hold your head up" repeated again and again.

126 In the Hindu worldview, Prakriti is the spiritual-cosmic primal "stuff" of the universe, ever paired with Purusha, the universal conscious spirit.

127 This phenomenon as a factor in everyday psychological life is explored with insight in Arnold Mindell's work. He holds that in addition to our "foreground process" in which we are conscious, there is also a "secondary process" of which we are essentially unaware but which can interact with the foreground or background states of other individuals. He asserts that in our secondary process,we are essentially dreaming, acting out in certain ways the symbolic stories of our individual psychology. His idea that we are essentially dreaming in our secondary process corresponds quite closely with Steiner's idea that in our feeling life, we have only a dream consciousness. Anthroposophically understood, this implies that there we are embodied (or incarnated) in different ways in our different soul functions. The implications of all this for the psychedelic experience are significant.

128 Randy Newman (1943 -) is an American singer-songwriter, pianist, and composer. He has been active since the 1960s and is known for his distinctive voice, satirical lyrics, and eclectic musical style. He has released over a dozen albums, including the hit songs *Short People*, *I Love L.A.*, and *You've Got a Friend in Me* from the *Toy Story* franchise.

129 *Mama Told Me Not Come* was also a minor hit for the popular rock group Three Dog night, and that would have been the initial source of my familiarity with it.

130 Maharaj Ji (Prem Rabat), born in 1957, was an Indian "perfect master" who founded the Divine Light Mission at age 13. He provided a form of initiation which was called "receiving knowledge." This involved receiving specific meditation techniques as well as the establishment of a devotional connection to Maharaj Ji as one's spiritual master. His devotees came to identify him as "The Lord of the Universe". In the early seventies he attracted thousands of youthful followers, including any number of age group peers from my hometown of Westport, Connecticut.

131 Steiner describes a condition where we experience how "When we continue the exercises to strengthen the soul, ... We feel ourselves as particular beings in the supersensible world, who seem to be the rulers, directors, and masters of their elemental bodies, and who by and by awaken these bodies to supersensible consciousness." in *A Road to Self-Knowledge*. London, Rudolf Steiner Press, 1975, page 47.

132 James Joyce, 1882 - 1941 was an Irish novelist and writer. He is noted for his development of the modernist stream of consciousness literary style, notably in *Ulysses* and *Finnegan's Wake*.

133 *Finnegan's Wake*, first published in 1939, is a work by Joyce in an experimental style and in an idiosyncratic language. It portrays among other things the death of its protagonist, a dream, and a history of sleeping humanity inspired in part by the theme of historical cycles of humanity. It is largely viewed as being all but impenetrable.

134 Joseph Campbell, 1904 - 1987, was a scholar and writer in comparative literature and comparative religion, perhaps best know for his work *The Hero With a Thousand Faces*, tracing the

archetypal phases of the hero journey of initiation. His thinking was influenced by Carl Jung and he was a popularizer of his ideas through the television series *Myths to Live By* with Bill Moyers.

135 *A Skeleton Key to Finnegan's Wake* was an early work of Joseph Campbell and coauthor Henry Morton Robinson. It attempts to elucidate the many peculiarities of Joyce's work.

136 Giambattista Vico 1668 - 1774 was an Italian philosopher whose *The New Science (La Scienza Nuova)* outlined the development of the various peoples of the earth through a cycle of development from divine to heroic to human ages.

137 *Reefer Madness* was a 1936 intended as a morality tale warning of drug abuse, but landed more as an exploitation film. With the popularization of wide spread use of marijuana (reefer) in the 60's, it became a cult classic, best seen, of course, under the influence.

138 *Martian Space Party* is a mockumentary spoof of the fictional 1972 National Surrealist Party convention, in support of George Papoon campaign for the presidency. A campaign watchword is "He's not Insane!". A lot to take in on your first gulp, if you are under the influence.

139 Osho, aka Bhagwan Shree Rajneesh, 19331- 1990, was a Hindu spiritual teacher who developed a large following, with a cultish element manifesting at length (1981) in the creation of a large (population 7000) community, Rajneeshpuram, in Oregon. The community developed a fractious relationship with its neighbors. He has followers today and their are numerous published works by him. At the time I first encountered his work, he was known as Bhagwan Shree Rajneesh and was initially more as a scholar of spiritual matters but transitioning to the posture of a guru.

140 *The Nag Hammadi Library* is a collection of thirteen ancient books discovered in upper Egypt in 1945. These works are those of Gnostics writing around the time of the life of Christ and evidence diverse perspectives on, among other things, the mystic nature of Christ. The Gospel of Thomas was one of the earliest texts published in English. The contents of the entire library were published in English translation in 1978. Robinson, James. M. (ed.).*The Nag Hammadi Library*, New York: HarperCollins, 1981.

141 Nicoll, Maurice. *The New Man*, London: Stuart and Richards, 1950. Nicoll examines some of the parables and miracles of Christ and interprets them from a point of view informed by, among other things, his understanding of "the Work" of Ouspensky and Gurdjieff.

142 Nicoll, Maurice. *The Mark*, Longon: Vincent Stuart, 1954. It explains that the word usually translated as "sin" from the New Testament more literally means, missing the mark. He describes the awakening of an inner man that can turn away from being outward-driven, using New Testament ideas. Published posthumously.

143 Martin Buber, 1878 - 1965, was an Austrian (later Israeli) Jewish philosopher noted particularly for his elaboration of the *Ich-Du* (I and Thou) relationship or dialog, as being fundamental to the understanding of human existence.

144 Pierre Teilhard de Chardin, 1881 - 1955, was Jesuit priest and paleontologist. He wrote extensively, although was at times suppressed by or in conflict with the church. He is most known for the development of his concept of the *noosphere*, the thought or idea sphere or environment of the earth.

145 Wilhelm Reich, 1897 - 1957, was an early follower of Freud who broke with him in pursuit of his own theory of sexual energy and its repression in the development of character. He held that individuals were "armored" in their physicality to repress the free flow of universal life energy, or orgone energy, which seeks ultimate expression in humans through the orgasm. It was seen as the universal creative force. He ended up being persecuted for his promotion of "orgone accumulators" as medical devices to increase the flow of orgone energy.

146 Allegro, John. *The Sacred Mushroom and the Cross*, Garden City: Doubleday & Company, Inc. 1970. Using philological methods relating various middle eastern word roots, attempts to create a picture of the religious life of biblical times and suggests that certain elements of Christian iconography may have their origin in practices involving the use of psychedelic plants and mushrooms.

147 Fuller, John Grant. *The Day of St. Anthony's Fire*, New York: Macmillan & Co., 1968. It documents what was believed to be an outbreak of ergot poisoning in a 20th century French village.

148 R. Gordon Wasson. *Soma: Divine Mushroom of Immortality*, Harcourt Brace Jovanovich, 1968. It provides an ethnographic survey of the Fly Agaric (*Amanita Muscaria*) mushroom in history and attempts to identify it as the Soma of the Hindu Vedas.

149 Leary, Timothy. *Jail Notes*, New York: Grove Press, 1972.

150 Naranjo, Charles, and Ornstein, Robert E. *On The Psychology of Meditation*, New York: The Viking Press, 1972.

151 Helena Petrovna Blavatsky (1831-1891) was a Russian philosopher, writer, and founder of the Theosophical Society. As a writer, she is best known for her works *The Secret Doctrine* and *Isis Unveiled*, which helped popularize (in particular, Eastern) esoteric and occultist beliefs in the late 19th century. Blavatsky claimed to have been trained by masters of wisdom, whom she said communicated with her by non-physical means. Her writings explore the nature of reality, spirituality, and the occult, and have had a wide influence across subsequent related movements, including anthroposophy. She is generally recognized as a unique character. Some have accused her of charlatanry.

152 Blavatsky, Helena. *The Secret Doctrine*, London: The Theosophical Publishing Company, Limited, 1888.

153 ISKCON is the International Society for Krishna Consciousness, better known as the Hare Krishnas. Their founder was A. C. Bhaktivedanta Swami Prabhupada. During his lifetime, the tonsured and orange-robed Hare Krishnas were ubiquitous in major cities, recruiting disciples, chanting Hare Krishna, and handing out free copies of Hindu spiritual books such as the Bhagavad Gita, all from a devotional/Bhakti yoga viewpoint. After the founder's death, it broke into competing factions, and there were various cultish bad things that happened. Still extant.

154 Bhakti yoga is devotional or heart-centered yoga, typically expressed as in the Hare Krishna movement through devotion to a godhead figure such as Krishna. One of the three "ways" of which Gurdjieff's "fourth way" is the synthesis. Raja Yoga is the path of the mind, of knowledge; Hatha Yoga as a way is the path of physical mastery.

155 James, Laura DeWitt. *William Blake and the Tree of Life*, Berkeley: Shambala, 1971.

156 *Ida* and *Pingala* are two psychic channels or *nadis* in the body according to yogic tradition, they are most specifically associated with kundalini yoga.. They are said to represent the dual aspects of the human being, such as masculine and feminine, or sun and moon. Ida is the left channel, associated with the moon, the feminine aspect, and the cooling energy. Pingala is the right current, associated with the sun, the masculine aspect, and the heating energy. The yogi aims to balance and activate these channels, which in turn awakens the Kundalini energy, which rises up the central spinal channel or Sushumna. The two channels are often depicted as intertwined serpents similar to the Western image of the caduceus.

157 The *enneagon* is the name Ichazo uses for the figure generally known elsewhere as the enneagram.

158 Wainwright House is a lovely estate in Rye, NY, which among other things hosts workshops. It sees itself as "a sanctuary dedicated to creating a more mindful human existence through meaningful programming."

159 Franklin Merrill-Wolff (1887-1985) was an American philosopher and mystic who explored the nature of consciousness and spirituality. He was born in New York City and studied at Harvard University and the University of California, Berkeley. After experiencing a series of spiritual awakenings, Merrill-Wolff became interested in Eastern philosophy and spent time studying with Hindu and Buddhist teachers. He wrote several philosophically oriented books out of his experienced realization, including *The Philosophy of Consciousness Without an Object* and *Pathways Through to Space*, which explored themes of nondualism and mystical experience. His work was republished in the 1970s thanks primarily to fresh exposure given to his ideas by John Lilly.

160 John Wheeler (1911-2008) was a theoretical physicist. He was involved with the development of the first atomic bomb and also gave currency to the idea of the black hole, which was a principal area of theoretical work for him.

161 The Heisenberg uncertainty principle is a concept developed out of quantum physics that posits the impossibility of simultaneously determining the position and momentum of

an observed particle. It holds that the act of observation itself interferes with the event being observed.

These ideas, at a minimum, indicate that the deterministic universe of Newtonian physics does not exist at the scale of atomic or subatomic particles. There have been many extrapolations of this idea and its relationship to consciousness.

162 I first learned of the concepts of entropy and thermodynamics in another volume of the same *Life Science Library* I first learned about LSD from. It illustrated a troop of soldiers tiring as they marched and one by one, dropping to the ground.

163 Lilly placed four speakers, one in each corner of the large workshop area, creating a quadrophonic sound space.. The trespaso exercise consists of continued energetic staring (or gazing) into one's partner's left eye. After a short time, this can provoke the appearance of patterns in the visual field. The speakers play a recorded track of low, rumbling scratchy sounds that move back and forth across the room. The colored patterns that appeared in connection with the eye-gazing begins to move through the three-dimensional visual field as if impelled by the moving sounds.

164 Karlfried Graf von Durckheim (1896-1988) was a German philosopher, psychotherapist, and Zen teacher. Born in Munich, Durckheim served in the German army during World War I and later studied philosophy and psychology. He became an ardent Nazi. It was subsequently discovered that he is partially of Jewish descent; this became an embarrassment for the Nazis and he was sent to work in Japan, which led to his interest in Zen Buddhism. He spent time in Japan studying with various Zen masters. He was imprisoned after the war, and describes experiencing a "spiritual rebirth. Durckheim's teachings blended Western psychotherapy and mysticism, especially the influence of Meister Eckhart, with Eastern spiritual practices. He wrote several books on the subject, including *Hara: The Vital Center of Man* and *The Way of Transformation*. One of a catalog of so called "traditionalists" of apparent depth who manage to have acquired the taint of association with fascism, which they resolved to various degrees across their biographies.

165 Keen, Sam. *Voices and Visions*, New York: Harper & Row, Publishers, 1974.

166 A work published a few years later that illustrates the kind of thinking going on is: William Irwin Thomson. *Passages About Earth, An Exploration of the New Planetary Culture*, New York: Harper & Row, 1974.

167 As we are mentioning Ichazo's vision for society, which was based idealistically on transformation of society if individuals were transformed, it is worth noting that Steiner had a very well articulated model for society. His vision is referred to as the Threefold Social Order, and posits a separation between the spiritual-cultural, the economic, and the rights sphere. He lectured very actively for this vision in the period immediately following World War I when the social structure of Germany was in chaos.

168 It is perhaps a bit of a stretch, but one might somewhat meaningfully explore resonances between these levels and Steiner's four stages of cognition — physical cognition, *Imagination*, *Inspiration*, and *Intuition*.

169 Ichazo's system posits three core instincts: conservation, relationship, and syntony (variously labeled over the years). Individuals, idiosyncratically through their biographies, develop the experience of "imbalances" which become "fixated" or constellated around nine possible points, which are illustrated as corresponding to the nine points of the so-called enneagram or enneagon. At various times, Ichazo has stressed a distinction be made between the enneagon and the enneagram, as originally introduced by Gurdjieff, in an apparent desire to assert the originality of his system. The distinction centers around the presence or absence (or significance) of the inner figure drawn at the points 142857 — which, as a repeating decimal, corresponds to one divided by seven. It is rather a fine point. My own sense is Ichazo doth protest too much. If one develops an insight into the enneagram, one begins to understand how, as Gurdjieff says, the so-called law of three and law of seven can be seen to interoperate regardless of the scheme one applies. This however is all rather too far afield to survey further here.

170 Ouroboros is the snake eating its own tail, a classic image in Western Esotericism.

171 Wilhelm, Richard. (Baynes, Cary, trans.) *The Secret of the Golden Flower*, London: Lund Humphries, 1931.

172 Luk, Charles. *Taoist Yoga Alchemy and Immortality*, New York: Samuel Weiser, 1970.

173 Titus Burkhardt (1908-1984) was a Swiss traditionalist author, scholar, and Sufi. He was born in Florence, Italy, and spent his life traveling and studying the world's religions and spiritual practices. He was a follower of René Guénon, and was influenced by Guénon's ideas on the metaphysical principles underlying all religious traditions. His most well known books include *Alchemy*, *Sacred Art in East and West*, and *The Foundations of Oriental Art and Symbolism*. He emphasized the importance of traditional knowledge and the need to preserve the wisdom of the past in the face of modernity. He believed that the traditional arts and sciences held a key to understanding the spiritual dimension of life.

174 Burkhardt, Titus. *Alchemy, Science of the Cosmos, Science of the Soul*, London: Vincent Stuart and John M Watkins, 1967.

175 Like James Clerk Maxwell in seeking to understand Faraday's electrical field findings, I wanted (among other things) to know "the go of it".

176 I was to take an interest in statistical analysis for sales forecasting when I found it useful for my publishing job years later, and implemented linear regression and similar techniques on my (early days) desktop computer.

177 The Rider (or Waites-Rider) desk is one of the most well-known Tarot decks currently available.

178 Patrick Watson (1936-1992) was an English Tai Chi instructor who founded the School of Tai Chi Chuan in London in the early 1970s. He was a pioneer of Tai Chi in England, and his school played a significant role in popularizing the practice in the UK. He was a participant in the original Ichazo training in Arica, Chile.

179 Lilly, John. *Farther On*, Los Angeles: Jeremy F. Tarcher, 1990.

180 In its way, one can see some congruency in what Ichazo articulates here with Steiner's notion of the presence of the real Ego existing "outside" of us.

181 In later years, Oscar has taken to describing the framework of Arica as Integral Philosophy. I think however that Ken Wilber with his Integral Spirituality has a slight branding jump on him here.

182 Sri Chinmoy was a spiritual leader (or "guru") and meditation teacher. Born in 1931 in what is now Bangladesh, he moved to New York City in 1964 and established the Sri Chinmoy Centre. He became known for his teachings on inner peace and harmony, and for a time attracted notables such as musicians John McLoughlin and Carlos Santana, who would later fall out with him. He became increasingly preoccupied with demonstrating his athletic prowess, such as lifting heavy weights with one arm and running long distances, and also with composing thousands of songs and poems, painting over 140,000 paintings. Sri Chinmoy passed away in 2007 at the age of 76. Despite advocating celibacy in the spiritual life, as with many in positions of spiritual leadership, he was the subject of multiple complaints of sexual abuse.

183 Yogi Bhajan, came to the West and became a spiritual teacher and leader and popularizer of Kundalini Yoga. Born in India in 1929, he moved to Canada in 1968 and later settled in the United States. Yogi Bhajan founded the 3HO Foundation (Healthy, Happy, Holy Organization), which promotes Kundalini Yoga, meditation, and healthy living. He also founded the Yogi Tea Company, which thrives as a health-oriented brand. He was known for his charismatic personality and trained thousands of students and disciples, many of whom continue to spread his teachings today. Yogi Bhajan passed away in 2004 at the age of 75. He likewise has been accused by former female disciples of sexual impropriety.

184 Pir Vilayat Inayat Khan was a spiritual teacher and successor of his father, Hazrat Inayat Khan, who was instrumental in bringing Sufism to the West. He was born in Switzerland in 1916, he was trained in Sufi philosophy and meditation from a young age. He passed away in 2004 at the age of 87, His sister, Noor Inayat Khan, was an Allied secret agent in occupied France. She was killed by the Nazis in World War II.

185 Edgar Cayce was an American psychic, mystic, and healer who lived from 1877 to 1945. He is regarded as one of the most prominent psychics of the 20th century. Cayce would enter into a trance-like state and access and apparently access information about a person's health, past lives, and spiritual path. During his life, he gave over 14,000 readings to people seeking his guidance and healing. His readings covered a wide range of topics, including mi, Atlantis, the nature of the soul, and the mysteries of the universe.

NOTES

186 Owen Barfield was a British philosopher, writer, and critic born in London in 1898 and passed away in 1997. He worked professionally as a solicitor. He was a close friend and colleague of C.S. Lewis and J.R.R. Tolkien, and together with them, was a member of the Inklings literary group at Oxford. Barfield is known for his contributions to anthroposophy and the evolution of human consciousness, particularly his theory of "original participation," which suggests that in the earliest stages of human consciousness, there was a lesser separation between the subject and the object. Barfield wrote extensively on the works of William Shakespeare and Samuel Taylor Coleridge. Throughout his life, he authored many books, including *Saving the Appearances* and *Poetic Diction*.

187 Edward Bulwer Lytton (1803 - 1873) was an English politician and popular writer. Several of his novels were the subject of spiritualist, occult, or Rosicrucian themes, including, in addition to *Zanoni*, the novel *A Strange Story*. Many of his works were based on historical topics, such as *The Last Days of Pompeii*.

188 The Roosevelt Raceway event featured Crosby, Stills, Nash, and Young as the headline act of the "New York Summersault '74", a concert that was held on a racetrack located in the town of Westbury, New York, and gathered a crowd of around 75,000. Jesse Colin Young opened the event followed by The Beach Boys and Joni Mitchell who also sang with CSNY in several of their songs. A rumble went up over the crowd when the PA announced that President Gerald Ford had just pardoned the disgraced Richard Nixon, who had resigned a month earlier.

189 David Hume (1711-1776) was a Scottish philosopher, economist, and historian, best known for his influential contributions to empiricism, skepticism, and naturalism. Hume's philosophy is characterized by the rejection of traditional metaphysical concepts such as substance, causation, and the self. He argued these could not be justified by empirical evidence. He believed that knowledge comes exclusively from sensory experience and that reason alone cannot provide certainty about the world. Hume also argued that moral principles are based on sentiment and feeling rather than reason.

190 Epistemology is essentially the attempt to understand how we know what we believe we know. It is the theory of knowledge.

191 Barfield, Owen. *Romanticism Comes of Age*, Middletown, Wesleyan University Press, 1967.

192 This would have been Fred Paddock. He served as the head librarian of the Rudolf Steiner Library, most recently in Ghent, New York. He was born in 1941 and passed away on July 25, 2013. Paddock's tenure at the Rudolf Steiner Library began at the former library location at 211 Madison Avenue in New York. Under his leadership, the library's collection grew significantly and became a valuable resource for scholars and researchers interested in anthroposophy and related fields.

193 I first learned of Dr. Bronner's soap when I went to school at Emerson and was chided by Hank and Edie for my ignorance of it. The original label included among other things the following:

> When we teach the Moral ABC all mankind is united brave-strong-just-free!
>
> For the future will be better when we are better; times will change when we change; conditions will improve when
>
> we improve if you & I cooperate by full truth to accomplish them!
>
> We're all sisters & brothers!
>
> You & I, Here & Now, Today! Not them nor they! You & I Today!
>
> 1st: If I'm not for me, who am I? Nobody!
>
> 2nd: Yet if I'm only for me, what am I? Nothing!
>
> 3rd: If not now, when???!!!
>
> Unite we must!

... and so forth!

Interestingly, the son of the founder and current CEO (Cosmic Engagement Officer) David Bronner is a big supporter of the psychedelic renaissance.

194 This would be the *second* "First Annual Picnic."

195 The Anthroposophical Society thrives today world-wide, is headquartered in Dornach, Switzerland, the location of the second Goetheanum as designed by Rudolf Steiner. Branches and national societies exist worldwide.

196 Terence McKenna (1946 - 2000) was an American author, philosopher, and ethnobotanist who is best known for his work on the intersection of psychedelics, shamanism, and human consciousness. He was born in Colorado and grew up in California, where he developed a lifelong interest in plant-based shamanism and the use of entheogens in religious and spiritual contexts. McKenna's writing and lectures on psychedelics and spirituality were highly influential in the psychedelic community towards the end of the twentieth century. He and his brother Dennis were instrumental in popularizing the cultivation of psilocybin mushrooms. He was a prominent voice in the field of psychedelic studies until his death in 2000. He authored several books, including *Food of the Gods*, *The Archaic Revival*, and *True Hallucinations*. He was a popular speaker at events and conferences around the world. He introduced a number of novel perspectives into the psychedelic dialog.

197 Daniel Pinchbeck is an American author and journalist, whose work focuses on the domains of spirituality, ecology, and psychedelic experience. He was born in 1966 in New York City and attended Wesleyan University, where he studied literature and philosophy. Pinchbeck has authored several books, including *Breaking Open the Head: A Psychedelic Journey into the Heart of Contemporary Shamanism, 2012: The Return of Quetzalcoatl,* He has also contributed to a number of publications, including *The New York Times*, *Rolling Stone*, and *Esquire*. He is a notable voice in the contemporary psychedelic scene. He has been criticized for what some have deemed inappropriate sexual advances, which he has spoken about forthrightly, and claims to have addressed. Of interest, he has included references to Rudolf Steiner's work in several of his works. See http://www.pinchbeck.io.

198 Their song, well known in the sixties, *Legend of a Mind*, includes the lyric:

> *Timothy Leary's dead.*
> *No, no, no, no,*
> *He's outside looking in*
> *Timothy Leary's dead.*
> *No, no, no, no,*
> *He's outside looking in.*
> *He'll fly his astral plane,*
> *Takes you trips around the bay,*
> *Brings you back the same day,*
> *Timothy Leary.*

199 Long time director of the FBI

200 "Lion of the Senate" — brother of John and Robert Kennedy, and part of the Senate panel interviewing (along with others) Timothy Leary.

Kennedy was sympathetically disposed, in that his wife had benefited from LSD psychotherapy, although LSD was clearly becoming a political hot potato. Leary's performance is pricelessly high. The outcome was that LSD was moved to Schedule I status.

201 Hey, it's Santa Cruz.

202 The concept of eternal recurrence is a philosophical idea that suggests that everything that has happened, is happening, and will happen in the universe will recur again and again infinitely. According to Friedrich Nietzche, this theory was first introduced by the pre-Socratic philosopher Heraclitus, and was later developed by Nietzsche in his book *Thus Spoke Zarathustra*. Nietzsche believed that the idea of eternal recurrence could serve as a test of one's will to power, and as a way to overcome the limitations of traditional morality and embrace the cyclical nature of life, to live life as if one would be content to live it again and again.

NOTES

203 Dionysius the Areopagite, also known as Pseudo-Dionysius, was a Christian theologian and mystic who lived in the late 5th to early 6th century AD. He is traditionally identified with the Dionysius mentioned in the Acts of the Apostles (17:34), who was converted to Christianity by St. Paul in Athens. The written works of Pseudo-Dionysius can be considered a pious fraud by an inheritor of the oral teachings of the biblical Dionysius. He is best known for his writings on Christian mysticism, including *The Divine Names*, *The Mystical Theology*, and *The Celestial Hierarchy*. These works explore the nature of God, the hierarchy of angels and divine beings, and the mystical union of the soul with God. Dionysius's ideas had a significant influence on later Christian mystics, including Thomas Aquinas, Meister Eckhart, and John of the Cross.

204 Carl Jung's concept of the Collective Unconscious is the idea that there is a deeper layer of the human psyche that is inherited and shared by all humans, regardless of cultural or historical differences. It is composed of universal archetypes, which are primal and symbolic images that represent fundamental human experiences and behaviors. These archetypes, such as the mother, the hero, and the shadow, are expressed in myths, religions, and dreams across cultures and time periods. The Collective Unconscious is believed to be the source of creativity, spirituality, and the unconscious psychological processes that influence human behavior. According to Jung, becoming aware of and integrating the Collective Unconscious can lead to greater psychological wholeness and self-realization. While a significant transitional concept, from the viewpoint of a spiritual understanding, the phenomenology of the Collective Unconscious can be more profoundly understood as relating to an existing spiritual world. The intellectual apparatus around Jung's concept is ultimately rooted in, or at any rate, attached to, the materialistic science of the 19th century. As such, it can form a conceptual impediment to the formation of a modern concept of the reality of the spiritual world.

205 Arnold Mindell is an American author and psychotherapist. He was born in 1940 in New York and received his PhD in psychology from the University of Michigan. Mindell's work, which he characterizes as Process Psychology, integrates Jungian psychology, Taoism, quantum physics, as well as ideas from

shamanism to develop a holistic approach that emphasizes the interconnections between individual and collective experiences. Through his "process work," individuals can explore and integrate their unconscious experiences and develop a greater awareness of their physical and emotional states. Mindell has written numerous books on psychology, including *The Dreambody in Relationships* and *Quantum Mind*.

206 Immanuel Kant (1724 - 1804) has cast his shadow across alll philosophical thinking since his day. His writings (notably *The Critique of Pure Reason*) have undergird the widely held belief that the essence of "things in themself" is unknowable, and that there are definite "limits to knowledge" that it is not possible to transcend. Steiner first read Kant in his youth and contested, philosophically, many of Kant's conclusions.

207 Steiner, Rudolf. *The Philosophy of Spiritual Activity*, West Nyack: Rudolf Steiner Publications, 1963. (Also published as The *Philosophy of Freedom* and as *Intuitive Thinking As A Spiritual Path*). This is one of Steiner's seminal philosophical works, wherein he develops the concept of the primacy of thinking in the act of knowing and further develops the foundation for the understanding of human freedom, and the possibility to act without compulsion, but rather the "pure of love of the deed."

208 *Inherit the Wind* was an American play (and subsequent film) by Jerome Lawrence and Robert E. Lee, which was first staged in 1955. The story fictionalizes the 1925 Scopes "Monkey" Trial and was intended to provide context to the contemporary McCarthy hearings.

209 An excellent work for spiritually oriented individuals who are also scientifically educated or curious is *Man or Matter* by anthroposophist Ernst Lehrs. It takes Rudolf Steiner's view of the evolution of consciousness from a state of "original participation" through a gradual awakening to the physical world, across the history of the development of scientific ideas. He traces how at each step of the process, a corresponding grasp or understanding of the spiritual world fell away. He points to the development of a science after the method of Goethe as the key to a truly holistic world-conception.

Lehrs, Erst. *Man or Matter*, 3rd Edition, London: Rudolf Steiner Press, 2014. An earlier version can be found online on the Project Gutenberg web site.

210 *The Metamorphosis of Plants* is, along with his *Theory of Colors*, one of his principal scientific works, developing the concept of the "Primal Plant" or *Urpflanze*, the ideal form which all plant types descend. He holds that the various forms of the plant are essential transformations of the form of the leaf. On a deeper level, he is articulating the idea that the whole is represented everywhere in the parts.

211 Steiner, Rudolf: *Theosophy*, Hudson: Anthroposophic Press, 1994.

212 Steiner, Rudolf. *An Outline of Esoteric Science*, Hudson: Anthroposophic Press, 1997. Also published as *An Outline of Occult Science*

213 This is expressed clearly in Steiner's view regarding the contemporary initiative of The Society for Ethical Culture — of which Steiner remarked "I notice right from the start that there are men among the founders of the society who I esteem. The founding itself, however, arises from a backward conception of life." October 29, 1892.

214 Alternatively, exact sensory imagination, "exakte sinnliche Phantasie." Goethe, Johann Wolfgang Von and Miller, Douglas, trans., Ernst Sliedenroth: *A Psychology in Clarification of Phenomena from the Soul, Goethe, Scientific Studies*, New York: Suhrkamp Publishers, 1988, Page 46.

215 In Zoroastrianism, Ahriman is a malevolent spirit, representing the principle of evil and darkness. He is the opposed by Ahura Mazda, the creator and source of all goodness. In the Zoroastrian belief, the struggle between Ahriman and Ahura Mazda will continue until the end of time. Ahura Mazda will ultimately triumph over evil. Ahriman is identified in Steiner's worldview as the being that would tie man to the earthly. He is one of two "opposing powers," the other being Lucifer.

216 Steiner, Rudolf. *Macrocosm and Microcosm*, London: Rudolf Steiner Press, 1968 Page 76.

217 Ibid. Page 76.

218 Steiner, Rudolf. *Esoteric Development*, Ghent: Anthroposophic Press, 1987.

219 Ibid. Page 170.

220 Hepatitis C only became a distinct disease entity in 1989, with the isolation of the hepatitis C virus. My condition would have previously been labeled "non-A non-B hepatitis."

221 The "Mercedes Incision" is so called because its three cuts result in a scar figure reminiscent of the hood ornament of a Mercedes automobile.

222 Steiner, Rudolf, *Man's Life on Earth and in the Spiritual Worlds*. London: Anthroposophical Publishing Company, 1952, page 114.

223 Laparotomy is a general surgical term for procedures that involve the opening of the abdomen — in my case, to cleanse the highly caustic leaked bile and suture the leak.

224 Harbin Hot Springs is a hot spring retreat located in Middletown, California; it is owned and operated by the non-profit Heart Consciousness Church. It is an inheritor of the sixties hippie vibe, evidenced by, among other things, clothing being optional in the pools. Bodywork — massage and Watsu, a form of aquatic bodywork developed there — is also offered.

225 Holotropic Breathwork is a method developed by psychedelic pioneer Stanislav Grof to allow the therapeutic utilization of the holotropic ("wholeness tending") qualities of altered states of consciousness, as he originally explored with LSD psychotherapy, to be pursued in the absence of the legal availability of a psychedelic agent. The altered state is induced via breath work that includes hyperventilation.

226 The Goetheanum — named in honor of Johannn Wolfgang von Goethe — is the building that serves as the worldwide center of the Anthroposophical Society. It has a unique sculpturally inspired architecture. It consists primarily of a large performance hall, where, among other things, Rudolf Steiner's mystery dramas are performed. The hall is decorated with colored windows, carved to indicate initiation scenes, and a painted ceiling depicting the evolution of humanity out of the spiritual world. The original Goetheanum was a wooden structure with intersecting double

cupolas. It burned in a fire of suspicious origin on New Year's Eve, 2022. The current concrete structure was designed by Rudolf Steiner and completed a few years after Steiner's death in 1925.

227 Dornach is the location of the Goetheanum, it is a short tram ride from Basel, Switzerland — coincidentally, the location of the Sandoz Pharmaceutical company where Albert Hoffman first synthesized LSD.

228 The Isenheim Altarpiece is a multi-paneled altarpiece, by the 16th century German artist Matthias Grünewald. It is located in the Musée d'Unterlinden in Colmar, France. The altarpiece depicts various scenes from the life of Christ, as well as scenes from the life of St. Anthony. The central panel features a gruesome and realistic portrayal of the crucifixion of Christ. Its most notable panel is a depiction of the Resurrection. The altarpiece was created for the monastic hospital of Saint Anthony in Isenheim. It has been suggested that the representations of the sufferings of Christ were intended to reflect the sufferings of victims of St. Anthony's Fire, that is, of ergot poisoning, which was common in the middle ages. (Ergot is the precursor to LSD.)

229 Edith Maryon (1872 - 1924) was an English sculptor and anthroposophist. She studied under Auguste Rodin and later became a founding member of the Anthroposophical Society. Maryon worked directly with Rudolf Steiner in creating the sculptural group which was to have been the centerpiece of the original Goetheanum. She resided at the Goetheanum in Switzerland at the time of her death from tuberculosis.

230 Zoroastrianism is an ancient religion that originated in Persia (modern-day Iran) over 3,000 years ago. It was founded by the prophet Zoroaster (also known as Zarathustra) and is one of the world's oldest monotheistic religions. Zoroastrians believe in the worship of one God, Ahura Mazda, and his principles of good thoughts, good words, and good deeds. Fire is considered a symbol of purity and is an important part of Zoroastrian rituals. In Rudolf Steiner's teaching about the evolution of world culture, the historical Persian culture and figure of Zarathustra is a latter-day reflection of an earlier developmental phase of humanity wherein, among other things, the dual nature of cosmic reality was

experienced intensely and the awakening to the earth realm as a proper domain of human action was experienced.

231 Shakespeare, William, *Hamlet*, 2.2,247-248

232 The *Yoga Sutras* of Patañjali is a classical text on yoga philosophy and practice, believed to have been written by the Indian sage Patañjali around 200 BCE. The text consists of 196 sutras (sayings) organized into four chapters, outlining a systematic and comprehensive approach to yoga. The *Yoga Sutras* cover a wide range of topics, including the nature of the mind, obstacles to spiritual practice, the eight limbs (methods) of yoga (including asana, pranayama, and meditation), and the attainment of samadhi or enlightenment through spiritual absorption in unity. It is a standard in the field of yoga philosophy.

233 Rudolf Steiner, *Verses and Meditations*. London: Rudolf Steiner Press, 1979, page 197.

234 Steiner, Rudolf. *Metamorphoses of the Soul*, Volume I (GA 58), London: Rudolf Steiner Press, 1983.

235 Wenner, Jann S. (ed.) *Lennon Remembers*, London: Verso, 2000, pages 53-54.

236 Steiner would sometimes refer to the philosopher Gotthold Ephraim Lessing's (1729 - 1781) *The Education of the Human Race* which he concludes saying "... Happy is it for me that I do forget. The recollection of my former condition would permit me to make only a bad use of the present. And that which even I must forget now, is that necessarily forgotten for ever? Or is it a reason against the hypothesis that so much time would have been lost to me? Lost — And how much then should I miss? — Is not a whole Eternity mine?"

The implication in Steiner is that Lessing is an example of the belief in a Western tradition of reincarnation.

237 This is a paraphrase from the Odyssey, wherein Odysseus travels to the underworld and is told by Achilles:

> I'd rather slave on earth for another man –
>
> some dirt-poor tenant farmer who scrapes to keep alive –

NOTES

than rule down here over all the breathless dead.

Homer, Odyssey, Book 11

238 The idea of the fall of man, the cycle of ages, *The Origin of Consciousness in the Breakdown of the Bicameral Mind* of Julian Jaynes, *The Ever Present Origin* of Jean Gebser, Barfield's original participation, and so on, are all variations of this idea which is developed in particular detail by Steiner. Steiner's teaching of phases of the development of consciousness can be seen as refinements of earlier theosophical teachings.

239 There have been extensions of this idea toward, for example, seeing the principle component as the shoot and the leaf as an incomplete shoot (Agnes Arber).

240 Bache, Chris. *LSD and the Mind of the Universe*, Rochester: Park Street Press, 2019. Published by Inner Traditions International and Bear & Company, ©2019. All rights reserved.

http://www.Innertraditions.com Reprinted with permission of publisher.

241 Christopher Bache is professor emeritus in the department of Philosophy and Religious Studies at Youngstown State University, adjunct faculty at the California Institute of Integral Studies, Emeritus Fellow at the Institute of Noetic Sciences, and on the Advisory Council of Grof Legacy Training. (see chrisbache.com).

242 Steiner was for a short time the leading candidate to head up the establishment of Nietzsche archive, along the lines of the Goethe archive in which Steiner had served editing the scientific writings of Goethe.

243 Ideas about the fourth dimension were topical both in physics and theosophy during Ouspensky's time. A popular work of note was Charles Hintion's *The Fourth Dimension* in 1880. Steiner's works include a volume of various lectures (also titled, *The Fourth Dimension*).

244 "Cosmic Coincidence Control" is a (fanciful) term coined by John Lilly and light-heartedly applied here. It implies that significant coincidences, what Carl Jung would call synchronicities, are under the control of higher intelligences.

245 Timothy Leary referenced Gurdjieff's "little pill" in his book *High Priest*, New York: New American Library, 1968.

246 The chemical element hydrogen is the simplest from the point of view of modern chemistry; I read this as an analogy to imply "primary substance". Within the details of his scheme, the terms, Carbon, Oxygen, and Nitrogen are used to indicate Active, Passive, and Neutral forces respectively. Acting together, they form a "Hydrogen" of a given level. Aside from its function as an abstraction, it is interesting to note that these four chemical elements are the principal components (along with sulfur) of protein, which reinforces their status as primal elements in this scheme. Oscar Ichazo somewhat similarly employs the notion of an active force, passive force, and function to yield a result or MMP (material manifestation point) or "level". In Steiner, these same chemical elements are also understood as representing cosmic forces or functions. cf., Hauschka, Rudolf, and Richards, Mary *The Nature of Substance: Spirit and Matter*. United Kingdom, Sophia Books, 2002 and also in Steiner, Rudolf. *The World of the Senses and the World of the Spirit*. United Kingdom, Rudolf Steiner Press, 2014.

247 Ernst Haeckel's Monism is a philosophical and scientific worldview, holding that there is a single fundamental substance or energy that makes up the universe. For Haeckel, this substance was matter as conventionally understood. This orientation should make it understood that it is quite distinct from philosophical or religious non-dualism. He believed that all phenomena, including life, consciousness, and mind, could be explained in terms of physical processes. Haeckel saw Monism as a way to reconcile science and spirituality, and he believed that it could promote social progress by fostering a greater understanding of the natural world.

248 Ernst Haeckel (1834 - 1919) was a German biologist, philosopher, and artist who coined the term "ecology" (*oekologie*) and popularized the theory of evolution. He was a prominent figure in the scientific community, known for his work in marine biology and his contributions to the development of Darwinian evolutionary theory. Haeckel was also a controversial figure due to his advocacy for Monism. Haeckel's work had a significant impact on the development of modern biology and ecology. His naturalist drawings are considered highly artistic. He is notable for his

still debated idea that "ontogeny recapitulates phylogeny" — the evolution of the individual recapitulates the development of the species. This and similar ideas of recapitulation are prominent in Steiner's view of cosmic and world history. He was a proponent of a "race science" which has to be understood as fundamentally racist.

249 The whole subject of psychoanalysis as understood today was in the process of evolving from Freud's thinking. Steiner described Jung as "one of the better psychotherapists" and also commented "In his subconsciousness man is connected with an entirely different world, of which Jung says: the soul has need of it because it is related to it, but he also says that it is foolish to inquire about its real existence. Well, it is this way: as soon as the threshold of consciousness is crossed, man and his soul are no longer in merely material surroundings or relations, but in a realm where thoughts rule". Jung was dismissive of Steiner as representing a scientifically unverifiable worldview, saying in his *Letters* (Volume 1, page 203-204) "But I shall guard against adding to the number of those who use unproven assertions to erect a world system no stone of which rests on the surface of this earth." Whatever the precise meaning of having "no stone ... on the surface of this earth" is, it suggests that a spiritual worldview must somehow be based upon the scientifically provable — that is, in materialism. The psychedelic and spiritual seeker both must come to understand that it is the possibility of evidence of non-sensuous experience that must be grasped.

250 Steiner, Rudolf. *Man as Symphony of the Creative Word*, London: Rudolf Steiner Press, 1970

251 There is a kind of parallel here with Gurdjieff's idea of contemporary humans as being "asleep" — acting purely mechanically.

252 This always-flowing "waking dreaming" is developed and amplified as a therapeutic technique in Arnold Mindell's process psychology.

253 This is the kind of thinking can tend toward the "human biocomputer" of Lilly, which ultimately tends toward transhumanism (the ahrimanic as anthroposophically understood). In other words, the observable change in neural connections is, seen anthroposophically, a secondary phenomenon to the primary

phenomenon of the loosening of the etheric forces that maintain the living brain.

254 Steiner, Rudolf. *The Effects of Spiritual Development*, London: Rudolf Steiner Press, 1978

255 This is how Steiner refers to the mystery associated with Christ's crucifixion. He sees this as a turning point of time in the spiritual evolution of the earth, and associates fundamental changes in humanity's possible relation to the spirit with Christ's deed.

256 Steiner, Rudolf. *How To Know Higher Worlds*, Great Barrington: Anthroposophic Press, 1994. Page 62

257 *Private Idaho* was a song by the B-52s, and also subsequently found as a film title (*My Own Private Idaho*), suggesting (among other things) a narcissistic self-absorption.

258 "Reality Distortion Field" was applied to describe the effect of Steve Jobs' charismatic influence on people's minds and perceptions.

259 Gordon Wasson (1898 - 1986) was an amateur mycologist and executive at J. P. Morgan & Co. He became one of the first Westerners to participate in a psilocbyin mushroom ritual through contact with *curandera* (healer, shaman) María Sabina in Oaxaca Mexico. Although he was thus initiated on a promise of secrecy, he disregarded this commitment and was largely responsible to disclosing the particulars of the psychedelic psilocybin mushroom to the American public. This was a key catalyst in the future popularization of psychedelics.

260 María Sabina (1894 - 1985) came to regret her involvement with Gordon Wasson, as the publicity surrounding it led to an influx of psychedelic-seeking American hippies and tourists in her rural community. She was ostracised as a result, and her house was burned down after she was briefly jailed, and her son murdered. She eventually died in poverty.

261 McKenna, Terrance. *The Archaic Revival*, New York: HarperCollins, 1991.

262 Among his other human characteristics, he regularly used snuff.

263 Psychonaut is a rather vague word that would seem to imply, at any rate, a degree of training and discipline, as one might expect

of an astronaut. It seems rather broadly applied to a range of those who one way or other explore psychedelics. I see on the one hand, how it reflects a spirit of adventure; at the same time I think its casual application can trivialize the challenge that deep pursuit of psychedelics can involve.

264 Watts, Alan. *The Joyous Cosmology*, page 26

The quote is new to the 1965/1970 edition, and not contained in the original 1962 edition of the book.

265 Steiner, Rudolf. *The Inner Nature of Man and the Life Between Death and a New Birth*, London: Anthroposophical Publishing Company, 1959.

266 MAPS is the Multidisciplinary Association for Psychedelic Studies founded by Rick Doblin, PhD. As of this writing, it is making substantial progress toward the approval by the FDA of the use of MDMA as a therapeutic treatment for post-traumatic stress syndrome. This would represent a significant de-scheduling of a psychedelic drug.

267 Ketamine is a dissociative anesthetic that is used and noted for its psychedelic effects, although its chemical structure and mode of action are less closely related to the other well-known psychedelics such as LSD and psilocybin. It was initially used most commonly as a veterinary anesthetic but is also used with humans, particularly in situations where it is desirable to avoid the suppression of respiration. Because of these medical applications, it can be legally prescribed.

John Lilly was an early user and advocate for it as a psychedelic. It has become used on a continuing, broadening basis as a therapy in treatment-resistant depression.

It is also popular in some demographics as a recreational drug. In this area, it seems to have more abuse potential and the possibility of negative physical side effects relative to other psychedelic drugs.

268 Thomas Szasz (1920 - 2012) was a Hungarian-American psychiatrist. He is notable for his influential and controversial views on mental illness and the medicalization of psychiatry. He held that mental illness was a myth and that psychiatric diagnoses were labels used to control and stigmatize individuals with unconventional beliefs or behaviors.

Szasz challenged the traditional medical model of psychiatry and advocated for individual rights and personal responsibility. He wrote extensively on the topics of mental illness, addiction, and the legal and ethical implications of psychiatry. Among his best-known works are *The Myth of Mental Illness* and *The Manufacture of Madness*.

These considerations enter into the question of the possible decriminalization of psychedelics and plant medicines relative to the possibility that their legal use may restricted to the licensed medical-psychotherapeutic community.

269 This notion is not unrelated to what Timothy Leary *et al* were trying to express in *The Psychedelic Experience*. By modeling the changed sense of self upon the *Tibetan Book of the Dead*, Leary saw the psychedelic experience as an opportunity to "re-incarnate" as a more authentic human being. His mantra of "Tune In, Turn On, Drop Out" was rooted in a view that most of society was wrapped up in playing a game (of various sorts) and that one could "drop out" of the game and come back from the psychedelic experience as a more authentic human being.

270 Holotropic breathwork is a set of practices developed by Stanislav Grof that are intended to access the "holotropic" (wholeness-tending) aspects of altered states of consciousness such as the psychedelic state, without requiring the availability of the legally-restricted psychedelic elements. A principal aspect of it is the use by the subject of hyperventilation (short rapid breaths) to bring about a shift in conscious experience.

271 Grof speaks candidly about his own early spiritual awakening with LSD in Roberts, Thomas (ed.) *Spiritual Growth With Entheogens*, Rochester: Park Street Press, 2012, pages 31-56.

272 Not to make too fine a point of all this, but it is striking to me that in Grof's compilation, *Spiritual Emergency*, for example, one finds him citing the disciplines of "clinical and experimental psychology, psychiatry, modern consciousness research, experiential psychotherapies, anthropological field studies, parapsychology, thanatology, comparative religion, and mythology" as the disciplines concerned. From top to bottom, the list reads to me as from cold to maybe lukewarm spiritually.

In fairness, he continues: "More and more people seem to be realizing that true spirituality is based on personal experience and is an extremely important vital dimension to life."

273 Romantic fetishization of "the noble savage" goes back in the West at least to the time of Jean-Jacques Rousseau and the Enlightenment period which developed alongside of the European discovery of America. At the same time, there is a sense of responsibility within the psychedelic community that there be forms of reciprocity developed with indigenous people particularly when it comes to the adoption of usages and traditional wisdom.

The legacy of colonization of peoples of the global south is of course a much bigger issue. At the same time, within the context of world-wide exploration of psychedelic usage, traditional practices (or practices represented as traditional) are not necessarily more or less valid spiritually or appropriately adapted to those acculturated in the Western milieu: it a matter of freedom of the individual how one wishes to relate to these plant medicines, particularly from a spiritual perspective.

274 Steiner, Rudolf, *The Calendar of the Soul*, Chestnut Ridge: Mercury Press, 1999. A compendium of some of the many English translations of Steiner's *Seelenkalendar*.

275 The hard-core Burning Man community repeatedly asserts that "it is not a festival," but this should be understood as meaning it is not a music festival or an experience to be passively consumed.

276 Albee, Edward. *The Zoo Story*, 1959.

277 The Oregon Psychedelic Initiative is a new law passed in the state of Oregon, legalizing the use of psilocybin, the psychoactive compound found in certain mushrooms, for therapeutic and other purposes. It provides for the creation of a state-licensed program for psilocybin use by individuals, with trained facilitators providing guidance to users. The law establishes a two-year development period for the program, during which time rules and regulations will be established to ensure safe and effective use of the drug. Colorado has a similar approach in development.

278 William Bento, Ph.D., (? - 2015) was an author in what he styled as psychosophy (soul wisdom) and astrosophy (star wisdom), and worked extensively as a speaker, teacher, and consultant. He

was the Associate Dean of Academic Affairs at Rudolf Steiner College in Fair Oaks, California. He also worked as a transpersonal clinical psychologist at the Center for Living Health in Gold River, California.

279 Bento, William. *Lifting the Veil of Mental Illness*, Great Barrington: Steinerbooks, 2004, page 50.

It has been remarked to me personally by several of his former associates that Bento was in a continuous process of development of his thinking, and they believed this early formulation as likely to have matured into a more sophisticated view had he lived longer.

280 Steiner, Rudolf. *Man's Being, His Destiny, and World-Evolution*, Spring Valley: Anthroposophical Press, 1966

281 The term *consciousness soul* is a technical term in anthroposophy that points to a further, more nuanced concept of the members of the human being. It refers precisely to the dawning of spiritual knowledge within the context of the awakening of the *I* in the midst of the cosmic alienation that begins to arise at the time of the scientific revolution.

282 Blake, William, in his poem, *London*, describing the suffering of fallen humanity, as below:

I wander thro' each charter'd street,

Near where the charter'd Thames does flow,

And mark in every face I meet

Marks of weakness, marks of woe.

In every cry of every man,

In every Infant's cry of fear,

In every voice, in every ban,

The mind-forg'd manacles I hear.

How the Chimney-sweeper's cry
Every blackning Church appalls;
And the hapless Soldier's sigh
Runs in blood down Palace walls.

But most thro' midnight streets I hear
How the youthful Harlot's curse
Blasts the new-born Infant's tear,
And blights with plagues the Marriage hearse.

www.ingramcontent.com/pod-product-compliance
Lightning Source LLC
Chambersburg PA
CBHW070126080526
44586CB00015B/1570